Beyond Behavior Modification

A Cognitive-Behavioral Approach
to Behavior Management in the School

Second Edition

Joseph S. Kaplan

with *Barbara Drainville*

Illustrated by Nancy Cross

pro·ed

8700 Shoal Creek Boulevard
Austin, Texas 78758

Printed in the United States of America

Library of Congress Cataloging-in-Publication Data

Kaplan, Joseph S.
    Beyond behavior modification : a cognitive-behavioral approach to
behavior management in the school / Joseph S. Kaplan with Barbara
Drainville ; illustrated by Nancy Cross.
      p.   cm.
    Includes bibliographical references.
    ISBN 0-89079-224-0
    1. Classroom management. 2. Behavior modification. 3. Cognitive
therapy.   I. Drainville, Barbara. II. Title.
LB3013.K33 1990
371.1′024—dc20
                                        89-77154
                                          CIP

pro·ed

8700 Shoal Creek Boulevard
Austin, Texas 78758

10 9 8 7 6 5 4 3 2 1   90 91 92 93 94 95

Dedication

*To all the children and adults I have taught
over the years. I hope they have learned as much
from me as I have from them.*

Table of Contents

Preface

When I first wrote this book a number of years ago, I didn't think I might be writing a second edition. Actually, I was surprised that I was even writing a first edition. There were (and still are) so many good textbooks on the subject, and I've often said that the world doesn't really need another one. Over the years I've done a lot of thinking about the first book, and I don't mind saying I was a little embarrassed about my use of the subtitle, *A Cognitive-Behavioral Approach to Behavior Management in the School*. Those of you who are familiar with the first book know that it said very little about cognitive behavior modification: exactly 1 chapter out of 10. I've tried to change all that with this second edition. True, there is still only one chapter with "Cognitive Behavior Management" in the title, but it is an expanded chapter and the cognitive behavior modification strategies in it are covered in far more depth and detail than in the first book. In addition, I have added a separate chapter on stress management that also covers some cognitive behavior modification strategies. I am now less sensitive about the book's title than I was before.

Other new material in this edition includes chapters on ecological assessment and intervention, self-management, and social skills training. I have also revised a number of chapters from the first edition based on the constructive suggestions of the many students in my behavior management course who have used this text over the years.

The changes in the text were not solely the result of my concern about the congruence between title and content. They also reflect the current trends in behavior management. The first trend is a move toward a more proactive (rather than reactive) approach. Teachers, at least in special education classrooms, are no longer waiting for crises. They are beginning to teach students personal and social competence skills from day one. Another trend is a move toward modifying students' cognitions and feelings in addition to their behavior. Problem-solving and stress management skills are becoming more widely used. A third trend in behavior management is a move toward teaching students self-reliance. Teachers are now holding students responsible for their own interventions. This is a good idea, since we aren't always going to be around for them to rely on. Finally, there is the move toward ecological behavior management. More and more, teachers are including themselves, the peer group, the physical setting, and the curriculum (e.g., methods, materials, and schedules) as part of the problem as well as the solution, and their interventions reflect this.

I believe that all of these trends are significant. Unlike so many of the fads in education, they will be around for a while. More important, they are good for children and they work. In my opinion, they represent the most progressive and the most promising of the behavior management approaches available to us today. That is the reason I have included them in this second edition.

I'd like to take this opportunity to thank all of the graduate students who have used the first edition over the years and who candidly shared their constructive criticisms and suggestions with me. They helped to make this second edition a better book than the first. I would also like to thank my wife, Betsy, for her thoughtful and careful editing of this book. Unlike my students, she's not really interested in the subject matter, and she didn't have to read it for a grade. I'm sure it was tedious at times, but she stayed with it and her contributions helped me to say what I needed to say in a way that allowed me to be understood.

Part I
Introduction

chapter 1

Behavior Modification

Upon successful completion of this chapter, the learner should be able to:

1. Explain each of the myths (i.e., misconceptions) regarding behavior modification
2. Explain the difference between behavior modification and behavior influence
3. Correctly identify examples of positive and negative reinforcement, punishment, and extinction
4. Correctly list examples of operants and respondents, learned and unlearned reinforcers, and punishers
5. Correctly describe examples of reciprocal relationships

Behavior modification is ignoring the bad and praising the good.

Misconceptions

Behavior modification is probably one of the most misunderstood concepts in education today. It never ceases to amaze me that so many people can have such strong feelings concerning a topic about which they know so little. At the beginning of each class I teach in behavior modification I ask my students to complete the following sentence: "Behavior modification is . . ." Based primarily on this material, here are the most common misconceptions regarding behavior modification.

1. *Behavior modification is ignoring students' misbehavior and only rewarding their good behavior.* This is nonsense. Who would suggest that a teacher ignore a student who is hitting another student or disrupting the learning environment? Behavior modification teaches that the only time a teacher should ignore a student's misbehavior is when that behavior is reinforced by the teacher's attention.

2. *Behavior modification is using aversive controls such as nausea-inducing drugs and cattle prods.* I can't really blame people for believing this, considering the popularity of novels and films such as *Brave New World, The Manchurian Candidate,* and *A Clockwork Orange.* It is also true that behavior therapy, a form of behavior modification, does employ aversives in the control of certain behaviors, but I hasten to add that aversive controls have been used in such cases only at the request of the client receiving the treatment. Behavior modifica-

tion, as it is (and should be) used in the schools, has nothing to do with brainwashing, posthypnotic suggestion, electroconvulsive (shock) therapy, or the application of physically painful aversives.

Behavior modification is using aversive controls.

1

3. *Behavior modification is giving token reinforcement.* I wish I had an M&M for every graduate student who requested a waiver of my behavior management course on the basis of "already being competent" in behavior modification. As it usually turned out, these students' idea of being competent was using a token economy in their class of mildly handicapped learners. As if behavior modification were nothing more than token reinforcement! Did they collect data on student behavior? No. They didn't have the time, and even if they did, they didn't know how, nor did they see any value in monitoring student behavior. Had they ever used other behavior modification techniques such as shaping, chaining, or fading? They had never heard of them. Did they reinforce on a schedule of reinforcement? No. They reinforced whenever they remembered to. These individuals were not competent in behavior modification because behavior modification is much more than token reinforcement.

**Behavior modification is providing
token reinforcement.**

4. *Behavior modification is giving students M&M's (or Big Macs or Twinkies).* Given the average American's addiction to junk food, I can understand the origin of this myth. In the first place, primary (food) reinforcers do not always have to be used in a behavior modification program. Their use is usually the exception rather than the rule in programs for mildly to moderately handicapped learners. It is often more appropriate to use token reinforcers, activity reinforcers, or social reinforcers. Second, if it is necessary to use primary reinforcers with a particular student, there are plenty of nutritious substitutes for junk food. Raisins, yogurt, and fresh fruit are all superior to dangerous sweets; junk food often works against a behavioral program by pro-

ducing mood swings in children that ultimately may lead to more undesirable behavior.

5. *Behavior modification is for animals such as rats, pigeons, monkeys, or seals or for "subhumans" such as the institutionalized retarded or mentally ill.* The truth is that behavior modification has demonstrated its effectiveness in ameliorating a myriad of dysfunctions across a wide range of subjects. One need only peruse the literature to recognize the many applications and documented successes of behavior modification.

Behavior modification is for animals.

6. *Behavior modification is a philosophy (or a religion or a way of life).* While it is true that a knowledge of behavior modification can help explain a great deal of student behavior, it cannot explain all human behavior. The professional educator who is sincerely committed to helping children would do well to include Piaget and Maslow in his or her readings (in addition to Skinner). I become very suspicious when I hear a so-called "expert" describing his or her system as the "only way." Behavior modification is simply one of many tools that can help children learn. It is not a religion and using it does not make you a behaviorist.

Behavior Influence

Behavior modification is all around us. Anybody who watches television or goes shopping has been exposed to it. Behavior modification is a form of *behavior influence*, which occurs when one person attempts to exert a degree of control over another. Society attempts to influence the behavior of its citizens by requiring them

Behavior modification is a way of life.

to attend schools and study a curriculum that largely reflects the values of that society. Parents use behavior influence on their children. Businesses try to influence the purchasing behavior of people through commercials and advertisements. Politicians attempt to influence the voting behavior of their constituents. What we think, how we dress, what we eat, and much of what we say are all products of behavior influence. It begins the minute we are born and does not stop until the day we die.

While behavior influence has been around since there were at least two humans on this planet, behavior modification is relatively new. It is largely a product of 20th-century thinking and has only come to the attention of the general public during the last 25 to 30 years. Behavior modification is a separate and distinct form of behavior influence.

Operant Conditioning

Behavior modification involves the systematic application of rules or principles of a form of learning called *operant conditioning* by the psychologist B. F. Skinner. Skinner's operant conditioning should not be confused with Pavlov's *respondent conditioning*. Respondent behaviors are controlled by the autonomic nervous system and the involuntary muscles. Examples of respondent behaviors are the eye-blink reflex, the knee-jerk reflex, accelerated heartbeat, salivation, and many other physiological and somatic responses of the body that characterize emotional states such as anger, anxiety, and the like. Respondent behaviors are elicited by

a stimulus. An example of this is the salivation of the dog in Pavlov's classical conditioning experiments (Pavlov, 1897). Meat powder was the stimulus that elicited the response. This sequence may be seen in Figure 1.1.

Operants are controlled by the central nervous system and the voluntary muscles. Operants are usually emitted first and are modified (i.e., changed) or maintained (i.e., kept the same) by a stimulus presented after they occur. Since this stimulus occurs after the operant, it is often referred to as a *consequent stimulus event* (CSE). The term *operant* means to operate and *operate* means to produce an effect. Hence, operant behavior got its name because it is behavior that produces an effect on the environment. This effect will cause the operant to change in some way, or, conversely, it will keep the operant from changing. This sequence is illustrated in Figure 1.2.

Examples of operants are walking, talking, writing, hitting, hugging, and reading. Behaviors such as talking or hitting produce an effect on the environment that will either change or maintain that behavior. When you talk to someone, the effect of your talking is that the person listens to you. Having a person listen to you while you talk will probably strengthen, or at least maintain, your talking behavior. If you hit someone, the effect might be that the other person hits back, harder. Having someone hit you back after being hit will probably weaken your hitting behavior. Notice that I used the word *probably* in each example. Human beings are more complex organisms than rats or pigeons. They have cognitions (e.g., beliefs, expectations, and perceptions) and emotions (e.g., anger and fear) that can influence their operant behavior every bit as much as CSEs. See Figure 1.3.

Operants can also be influenced by environmental events that precede them. In other words, something in the environment can stimulate or elicit an operant. An event that elicits an operant is usually referred to as an *antecedent stimulus event* (ASE). Operant behavior such as talking is often elicited by another person asking us a question. In this instance, the ASE is being asked a question, the operant is answering the question, and the CSE is having the person listen to the answer. This sequence may be seen in Figure 1.4.

Positive Reinforcement

There are two kinds of CSEs: those that strengthen operants and those that weaken them. CSEs that strengthen the operants they follow are called *reinforcers*. Reinforcement is the strengthening of an operant. There are two kinds of reinforcement: positive and negative. *Positive reinforcement* (R+) is the

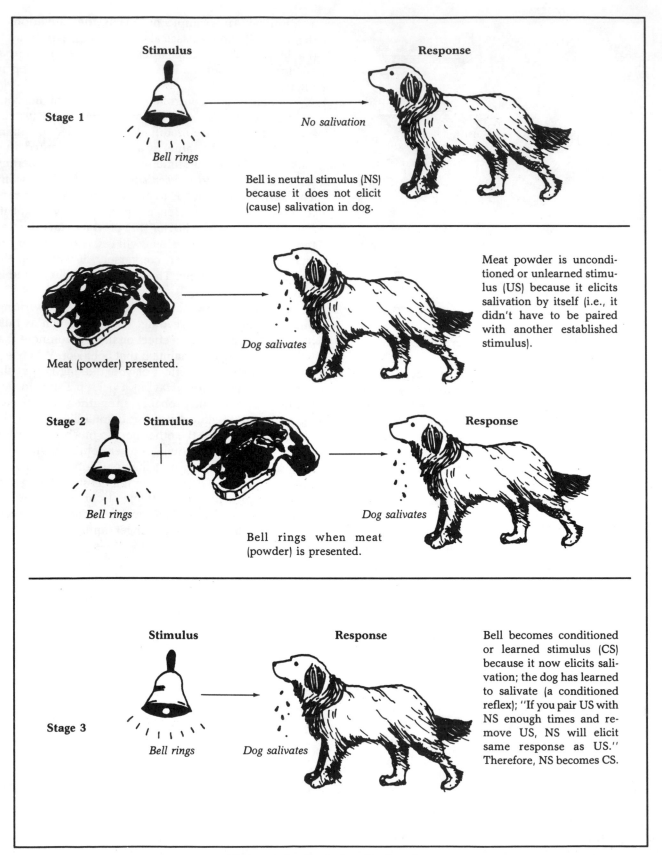

Stimulus   **Response**

Stage 1   *No salivation*

Bell rings

Bell is neutral stimulus (NS) because it does not elicit (cause) salivation in dog.

Meat (powder) presented.   *Dog salivates*

Meat powder is unconditioned or unlearned stimulus (US) because it elicits salivation by itself (i.e., it didn't have to be paired with another established stimulus).

Stage 2   **Stimulus**   **Response**

Bell rings   *Dog salivates*

Bell rings when meat (powder) is presented.

Stimulus   **Response**

Bell becomes conditioned or learned stimulus (CS) because it now elicits salivation; the dog has learned to salivate (a conditioned reflex); "If you pair US with NS enough times and remove US, NS will elicit same response as US." Therefore, NS becomes CS.

Stage 3   *Bell rings*   *Dog salivates*

Figure 1.1. Pavlov's salivating dog.

Operant   **Consequence (CSE)**   **Effect**

Figure 1.2. Operant conditioning sequence.

Operant   **Consequence (CSE)**   **Cognitions Emotions**   **Effect**

Figure 1.3. Sequence expanded to include thoughts and feelings.

strengthening of an operant by immediately following it with a reward or the presentation of something a person likes. An everyday example of this may be seen in the work world. A person works hard (i.e., behaves or emits certain desirable operants); this work is followed by the presentation of something the person likes—her paycheck. The result is that the person continues to work hard. We may then say that hard-working behavior was positively reinforced because (1) it was followed by a reward or the presentation of something the worker liked (money) and (2) hard-working behavior continued in the future. Other examples of R+ may be seen in Figure 1.5.

Negative Reinforcement

Negative reinforcement (R−) is the strengthening of an operant by immediately following it with the removal or avoidance of something the person doesn't like. An example of this is commonly seen in the classroom. A student who refuses to do his work is told that he will have to do it after school if he doesn't finish it by dismissal. The idea of detention is aversive enough to the student to motivate him to start working. He finishes before dismissal and is allowed to leave. We may say that the student's working behavior was negatively reinforced because it was followed by the removal or

Antecedent (ASE)   Operant   Consequence (CSE)

Figure 1.4. Operant sequence beginning with stimulus.

Contingency	Operant	CSE	Effect
Students who raise their hand without calling out will be called on by the teacher.	Jerry raises his hand and waits to be called on.	Teacher calls on Jerry.	Jerry continues to raise his hand and wait to be called on.
Only students who are in their seats will get finger paints.	Mary Beth stays in her seat.	Teacher gives finger paints to Mary Beth.	Mary Beth continues to stay in her seat.
Students will only be allowed to use power tools if they wear safety goggles.	Bart puts on safety goggles when he uses power tools.	Teacher continues to let Bart use power tools.	Bart continues to put on safety goggles when he uses power tools.
Students who ask good questions in class will be told so.	Mr. G. asks a good question in class.	Professor X. says, ''That's a good question, Mr. G.''	Mr. G. continues to ask good questions in class.
People who write to me will receive an answering letter within two weeks of the receipt of their letter.	Aunt Eleanor writes me a letter.	I send an answering letter to Aunt Eleanor within 2 weeks of receiving hers.	Aunt Eleanor continues to send me letters.

Figure 1.5. Examples of positive reinforcement (R +).

avoidance of something aversive to him (detention) and working behavior was strengthened. Figure 1.6 provides more examples of R –.

Negative reinforcement is sometimes confused with positive reinforcement. Let's compare them. How are they alike? Both R+ and R – serve to strengthen a behavior. How are they different? In R +, the behavior strengthened is one resulting from the presentation of a pleasing CSE. On the other hand, in R –, the behavior strengthened is one resulting from the removal or avoidance of an aversive CSE. For example, if you like someone, you want her to pay attention to you. Therefore, whenever you see this person, you will want to greet her. If your greeting results in the presentation of a pleasing CSE (i.e., she greets you in return), the chances are that in the future you will continue to greet your

Contingency	Operant	CSE	Effect
Students who finish their work will not have to stay in after school.	Ken finishes his work.	Ken is dismissed when the bell rings.	Ken continues to finish his work to avoid detention.
Drivers who obey the speed laws will not lose their licenses.	Mrs. Y. obeys the speed laws (i.e., does not exceed posted limits).	Mrs. Y. does not get a speeding ticket.	Mrs. Y. continues to obey the speed laws to avoid getting a ticket and losing her license.
Charlene will not have to go out with Gomer if she makes excuses.	Charlene tells Gomer she has leprosy whenever he calls her for a date.	Gomer says, "Gee, Charlene. I sure hope you get better soon. I'll call again next week."	Charlene continues to lie about her health whenever Gomer calls.
Bobby's pain will go away if he puts ice on a bad bump.	Bobby puts ice on his forehead after he bangs it.	The pain goes away.	Bobby continues to put ice on bad bumps.
Students who study for tests will not fail them.	Sissy studies for her test in English.	Sissy passes her English test.	Sissy continues to study for her tests.

Figure 1.6. Examples of negative reinforcement (R −).

friend when you see her. We may say that the operant greeting has been strengthened because it resulted in the presentation of a pleasing CSE (being attended to by someone we like). On the other hand, if you don't like someone, you don't want him to pay attention to you. We try to avoid people we don't like. Therefore, whenever you see a person you don't like, you might avoid making eye contact with him, turn away, walk away from him, or even try not to let him see you. If these avoidance behaviors work, the chances are that in the future you will continue to use them to avoid the attention of a person you do not wish to see. We may say that the operants looking away, turning away, walking away, or hiding have been strengthened because they resulted in the removal or avoidance of an aversive CSE (being attended to by someone we don't like). In addition to the technical differences between R + and R −, there are also philosophical differences, which are discussed at length in chapter 6.

Extinction

Since reinforcers are CSEs that strengthen operants, it becomes possible to weaken an operant by withholding a known positive reinforcer. This procedure is referred to as *extinction*. Let's go back to the example of the worker being reinforced for her working behavior. Suppose that instead of paying her at the end of five days,

the worker's boss tells her that because business has been bad lately, she won't be paid until the following week. However, after five more days of working, the worker gets no pay and the same excuse. How long do you think her hard-working behavior will last? If there are no other rewards being presented for hard-working behavior that are as desirable as money, her behavior will weaken and eventually become extinguished. Remember that extinction has not occurred unless withholding the known positive reinforcer results in the weakening and subsequent elimination of the operant. If the worker continues to work hard even though she is not being paid, we cannot say that extinction has occurred. We can only assume that another positive reinforcer is present, such as pleasure derived from doing the job or from interacting with her co-workers. Although the worker's boss did not want to weaken her working behavior, there are times when extinction is deliberately used to eliminate an undesirable behavior.

For example, let's say that whenever Aaron wants his parents' attention, he whines. The consequence of his whining is that he is picked up and held by one of his parents. We may say that Aaron's whining behavior has been positively reinforced by his parents' attending behavior. However, as Aaron gets older and continues this behavior, the parents become embarrassed by it and decide to ignore him when he whines for attention. Does Aaron stop whining? Probably not right away. Don't forget, this behavior has been reinforced for a long time. In fact, the whining will probably get worse before it gets any better. One reason for this is that Aaron will probably become frustrated and angry over the removal of the reinforcer and this may result in more intense whining. Second, depending upon how intelligent Aaron is, he may conclude that more intense whining is necessary to get the old response from his parents, and therefore he may escalate his whining behavior. Third, Aaron's whining may simply be perceived by his parents as worse because they have never let it last this long and they are having to deal with their frustration, guilt, anxiety, and anger. Eventually, however, once Aaron learns that his whining won't produce the old CSE no matter how intense it gets or how long it lasts, the whining will stop. Once he stops whining for parental attention, we may say that extinction has occurred as a result of removing the known positive reinforcer (being picked up). Other examples of extinction may be seen in Figure 1.7.

Punishment

CSEs that serve to weaken behavior are called *punishers*. Punishment is the weakening of an operant by following it with an aversive CSE. For example, let's say that

Sandy curses in front of her mother and gets her mouth washed out with soap. If the consequence is aversive enough, it will weaken Sandy's cursing behavior (at least in front of her mother). If, however, Sandy continues to curse in front of her mother, we cannot say that her mother has punished her swearing behavior. She has merely presented a CSE that wasn't aversive enough to Sandy to weaken cursing. A CSE is not a punisher unless it is aversive enough to weaken the behavior it follows. Teachers often use CSEs that they believe are aversive to their students, such as detention, notes home, or being sent to the office, simply because they would have been aversive to most teachers when they were students. Therefore, it warrants repeating that you have not punished a student's behavior unless the CSE weakens it. The same may be said of reinforcement. Don't think that you are going to positively reinforce a student's behavior with a CSE that is pleasing to you. What may be pleasing to you might be aversive to the student. In this case, you might actually be punishing the student's behavior instead of reinforcing it. Figure 1.8 shows how punishment works.

People often confuse punishment with R−. Remember, *to reinforce* means to strengthen. Since *to punish* means to weaken, it should be easy to see the difference between the two. Punishment is the *weaken-*

Contingency	Operant	CSE	Effect
Babies who cry for their parents' attention after they are put to bed will be ignored.	Baby Ruth cries when she is put to bed.	Baby Ruth's mother and father ignore her.	Baby Ruth stops crying and after a few more days, Baby Ruth does not cry when she is put to bed.
Students who call out in class without raising their hands will be ignored.	Todd calls out in class without raising his hand.	Todd's teacher ignores him whenever he calls out in class without raising his hand.	Todd stops calling out in class without raising his hand.
Children who swear in order to get the attention of adults will be ignored.	Sandy swears in front of her mother while her relatives are visiting.	Sandy's mother and her relatives all ignore Sandy when she swears.	Sandy stops swearing in the presence of adults.
Customers who want soda and put money into a vending machine will get nothing.	Kim puts a quarter into a vending machine.	The quarter drops down to the coin return slot and no soda appears.	After two or three more tries, Kim stops putting coins into the machine.
A person who works for pay will not receive any checks.	Mitchell comes to work and does his assigned tasks.	Mitchell receives no paychecks.	Mitchell stops coming to work.

Figure 1.7. Examples of extinction.

Contingency	Operant	CSE	Effect
Children who touch a flame will be burned.	Baby Ruth touches a lit match in her father's hand while his attention is elsewhere.	Baby Ruth burns her finger.	Baby Ruth never touches a lit match again.
People who walk down dark streets in rough neighborhoods will be mugged.	Joey walks through a rough neighborhood one night.	Joey is mugged.	Joey never walks through a rough neighborhood at night again.
Children who say curse words will have their mouths washed out with soap.	Garbage-Mouth curses in front of an adult.	The adult washes his mouth out with soap.	Garbage-Mouth never curses in front of an adult again.
Unpopular people who call Charlene for a date will be refused in a nasty manner.	Gomer calls Charlene for a date.	Charlene tells Gomer, "Bug off, you creep!" and hangs up.	Gomer never calls Charlene for a date again.
Students who ask "dumb" questions in class will be made fun of.	Mr. G. asks a question in class.	Professor X. laughs at Mr. G.'s question and so does the rest of the class.	Mr. G. never asks a question in class again.

Figure 1.8. Examples of punishment.

ing of behavior by *presenting* an aversive CSE after the behavior occurs. R− is the *strengthening* of behavior by *removing* an aversive CSE after the behavior occurs. Here's an example: Let's say that you have a student who is off task by talking to his peers instead of doing his work. If you wanted to weaken talking to peers, you might scold him (e.g., "Stop your talking!") every time you caught him off task. Assuming that he stops talking, we may say that you punished his talking by presenting an aversive CSE (scolding) immediately following the behavior (talking). Unfortunately, the effects of punishment typically do not last long and you have a student who is not talking now but who will probably start talking again the minute your back is turned. Perhaps you will have better luck if you can redirect him from talking to working. This time, you tell him that he will have to complete all of his work before dismissal if he wants to go home on the school bus. Otherwise, he will have to call his parents to pick him up after he has completed his work during detention. The prospect of detention and calling his parents for a ride is aversive to the student. However, since he can avoid this CSE by doing his work, he gets back on task, completes all of his work before dismissal, and is able to ride the bus home with his peers. You may now say that you reinforced the student's on-task behavior by removing an aversive CSE (detention). Other comparisons among punishment, extinction, and R+ and R− may be seen in Figure 1.9.

Reciprocal Relationships

Another important concept to learn is the reciprocal relationship in operant conditioning. When you attempt to condition another person's behavior through R+, R−, punishment, or extinction, the result of that attempt may serve to condition *your* behavior as well. Let's go back to the example of Aaron, who whined for attention. What did Aaron learn when his parents attended to him when he whined? He learned that if he wanted his parents' attention, he should whine. Therefore, we may say that Aaron's whining behavior was positively reinforced by parent attention. Now let's look at the parents' behavior. Aaron's whining was aversive to them, and when they picked him up, he stopped whining. What did Aaron's parents learn? If they wanted to stop his whining, all they had to do was pick him up. Therefore, we may say that the parents' attending behavior was negatively reinforced by removing the aversive whining. This is an example of the reciprocal relationship in operant conditioning. We teach our

Technique \ Comparison	Means	Ends
Positive reinforcement	Follow behavior with presentation of pleasing CSE (e.g., praise)	Strengthens behavior
Negative reinforcement	Follow behavior with removal of aversive CSE (e.g., stop nagging or let student leave detention)	Strengthens behavior
Punishment	Follow behavior with presentation of aversive CSE (e.g., nagging or detention)	Weakens behavior
Extinction	Follow behavior with removal of known reinforcer (e.g., attention)	Weakens behavior

Figure 1.9.   Comparing means and ends of positive and negative reinforcement, punishment, and extinction.

children and they, in turn, teach us. See Figure 1.10 for other examples of reciprocal relationships.

Reinforcers and Punishers

There are two classes each of reinforcers and punishers: *unlearned* (*primary* or *unconditioned*) and *learned* (*secondary* or *conditioned*). Unlearned reinforcers and unlearned punishers do not have to be paired with other reinforcers or punishers for learning to take place. Examples are food (unlearned reinforcer) and physical pain (unlearned punisher). Learned reinforcers and learned punishers usually must be paired with an unlearned reinforcer or punisher in order to become effective. In other words, a smile (learned reinforcer) must first be paired with the food a mother gives her baby when she is hungry. As the child grows and experiences the pairing of the smile with her food, she will learn that "good" things are usually associated with smiles and eventually smiles will have their own reinforcing properties. This sequence may be seen in Figure 1.11. Conversely, a frown (learned punisher) must first be paired with the spanking (i.e., physical pain) the mother gives her infant when he misbehaves. As the infant grows and experiences the pairing of the frown with physical pain, he will learn that "bad" things are usually associated with frowns. Eventually frowns will have their own power to punish behavior in the child. Figure 1.12 shows how the transfer of power occurs.

The Changing Scene

In this section, we take a look at still another facet of behavior modification: its past, present, and future.

Operant 1: Mary gets out of her seat without permission.
   CSE: Mary's teacher yells at her to sit down.
  Effect: Mary sits down.

Operant 2: Mary's teacher yells at her when she is out of her seat without permission.
   CSE: Mary sits down.
  Effect: Mary's teacher continues to yell at her whenever she is out of her seat without permission.

We may say that Mary's out-of-seat behavior (operant 1) has been punished by her teacher's yelling. We may also say that the teacher's yelling has been negatively reinforced by Mary's sitting down.

Operant 3: Gilbert's teacher calls on him to answer a question.
   CSE: Gilbert answers the teacher's questions correctly.
  Effect: Gilbert's teacher continues to call on him to answer questions in class.

Operant 4: Gilbert attempts to answer a question in class.
   CSE: Gilbert's teacher calls on him.
  Effect: Gilbert continues to attempt to answer questions in class.

We may say that Gilbert's teacher will continue to call on him as long as he continues to answer questions correctly and that Gilbert will continue to answer questions as long as the teacher continues to call on him. Both behaviors have been positively reinforced.

Figure 1.10.   Examples of reciprocal relationships in operant conditioning.

Early Years

Pavlov writes a book entitled *Lectures on the Work of the Principal Digestive Glands* (1897) in which he

Stimulus	Response

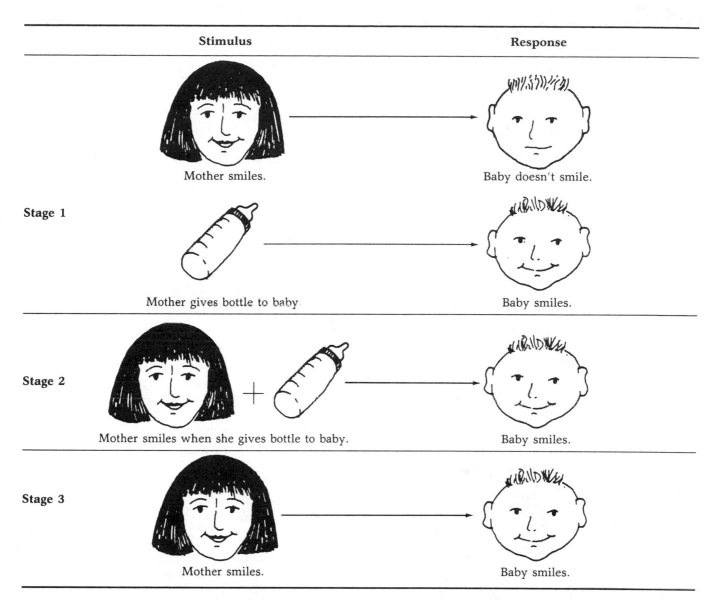

Figure 1.11. How secondary reinforcers are made.

describes his famous classical conditioning experiments, which serve as an impetus for future research. American psychologist John Watson publishes his treatise entitled *Psychology as a Behaviorist Views It* (1913).

Watson and Raynor (1920) publish their famous "Albert and the White Rat" study in which they pair a loud noise with a white rat to condition fear of the rat in an 11-month-old boy who previously had no fear of the animal.

While a doctoral student at Teachers College, Columbia University, Thorndike (1921) conducts his famous puzzle box research and "discovers" the law of effect: When a behavior is followed by a satisfying (rewarding) consequence, it is likely to be learned; when it is followed by punishment or failure, it is less likely

to occur. When he places a cat inside of a box, Thorndike discovers that it is able to escape from the box much faster on successive trials, indicating that learning has taken place. The cat learned the escape behavior because the behavior was followed by a reward (escape). It did not continue to emit any "escape" behavior that was not successful.

Jones (1924) conducts the equally famous "Peter and the White Rabbit" study using behavioral techniques such as counterconditioning, extinction, and shaping to eliminate a 3-year-old's fear of a white rabbit.

Mowrer and Mowrer (1938) use an apparatus of their design to eliminate enuresis in young children. A liquid-sensitive pad on the child's bed has a buzzer that is activated when the child begins to urinate. Awakened

Stimulus	Response

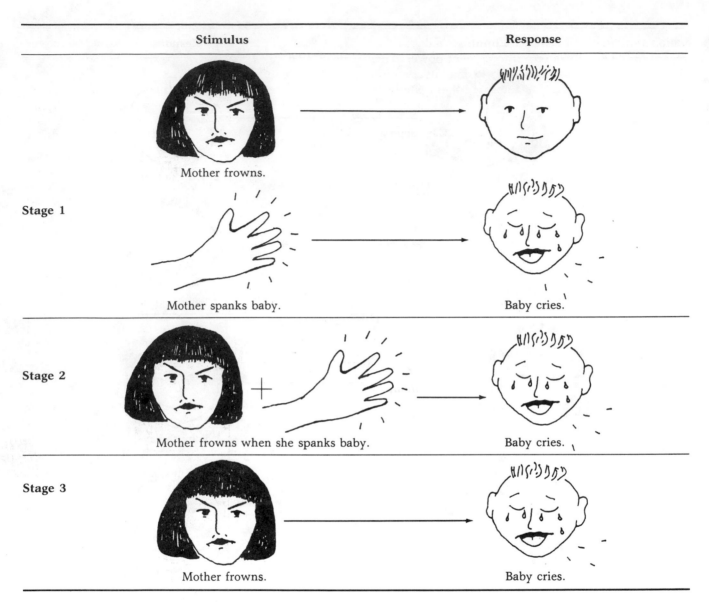

Stage 1

Mother frowns.

Mother spanks baby.

Baby cries.

Stage 2

Mother frowns when she spanks baby.

Baby cries.

Stage 3

Mother frowns.

Baby cries.

Figure 1.12. How secondary punishers are made.

by the buzzer, the child's parents immediately take him to the toilet. In the original study, all 30 subjects treated reached the criterion of 14 consecutive dry nights within 2 months.

B. F. Skinner (1938) writes *The Behavior of Organisms* in which he introduces operant conditioning and the law of reinforcement: ". . . if an operant behavior occurs, and is followed by a reward, its probability of occurring again increases."

Middle Years

Dunlap (1942) uses the behavioral technique of negative practice to eliminate stammering and tic behavior in athetoid cerebral palsied youngsters. By purposely practicing the grimacing and blinking behavior over and over again, they eventually bring it under their control and eliminate it.

Fuller (1949) shapes the arm-raising behavior of an institutionalized profoundly retarded 18-year-old who had not learned anything prior to this. Using a syringe filled with a sugar and milk solution for reinforcement, Fuller shapes behavior never before emitted by the subject.

Sheehan (1951) applies behavioral techniques with stutterers and decreases disfluent speech.

Azrin and Lindsley (1956) teach cooperative behavior to children 7 to 12 years old using principles of operant conditioning.

Gewirtz and Baer (1958) study the effects of deprivation and satiation of adult attention on children with regard to the adult's later reinforcement power. They find that when children are deprived of adult attention, it is easier for that adult to reinforce them later.

Premack (1959) discovers what becomes known as the *Premack Principle:* "If a high frequency behavior is made contingent upon a low frequency behavior, the low frequency behavior will increase in frequency." This is also known as "Grandma's Rule": "You can't have your dessert until you eat all your vegetables" (Grandma Kaplan, personal communication, circa 1945).

Williams (1959) demonstrates that the tantrums of a 21-month-old infant can be eliminated by withholding attention when they occur.

Lazarus (1959) eliminates car phobia in a child by reinforcing him with candy, first whenever he mentions cars, later when he sits in cars, and finally when he rides in them.

Staats et al. (1962) use M&M's with children in a tutorial program at Arizona State University; they find that the children tire of the M&M's (satiation) but do not tire of tokens.

Bandura et al. (1963) conduct a series of studies on modeling and demonstrate that watching aggressive acts in cartoons, peers, and adults makes children more aggressive. Modeling becomes a powerful behavioral technique.

Schwitzgebel (1964) significantly changes frequency of arrests and incarcerations of juvenile delinquents in Boston. By paying them $1 an hour simply to tape-record their delinquent experiences, he manages a 50% reduction in arrests and incarcerations among the experimental group which maintains after a 3-year followup.

Birnbrauer and Lawler (1964) make the first attempt to apply a token reinforcement system in a classroom for retarded children in Ranier, Washington. They are successful in getting students to work for tokens, delaying the need for primary reinforcers. The token system improves the studying behavior of children previously thought to be uneducable.

Hewett (1964) at UCLA uses operant principles to teach reading to a 13-year-old autistic boy who literally has no speech. Cards and pictures are used.

Lindsley (1964) develops a precision teaching model for use in monitoring behaviors and predicting behavior change.

Lovaas et al. (1965) use behavior modification techniques to eliminate self-injurious behavior in autistic children in addition to developing speech, self-help, and academic skills.

Patterson (1965) demonstrates that behavior modification can successfully control the hyperactive behavior of a 9-year-old diagnosed with minimal brain dysfunction (i.e., brain damage). Out-of-seat behavior is brought under control by a box on the student's desk that lights at varying intervals when he is in his seat and produces candy that he may share with his peers. The results suggest that organically induced hyperactivity may be brought under control without medication.

Ulrich demonstrates that an entire school can run on principles of behavior modification. His Learning Village in western Michigan is a 75-student private school where infants through upper-elementary-age students attend school on a year-round basis (Hren et al., 1974).

Ayllon and Azrin (1968) publish *The Token Economy,* based on their experiences in designing and running a token economy with psychotic adults in a state hospital in Illinois.

Hall, at Kansas, develops in-service teacher training programs designed to change the behavior of teachers. Professionals begin to recognize the need for changes in the behavior of adults who are in the child's environment as well as in the behavior of the child (Hall et al., 1968).

Homme et al. (1969) apply the Premack Principle to children in the classroom, calling it "contingency contracting."

Patterson (1969), at Oregon Research Institute in Eugene, trains observers to monitor the behavior of high-risk antisocial adolescents and their parents. Again, the need to modify the environment the child comes from (as well as the child) is recognized.

Later Years

Becker et al. (1971) develop DISTAR learning programs for use with disadvantaged children. Their materials are based on operant principles of learning. Follow-through program research indicates that children on DISTAR increased reading levels by 4.1 grades in 3 years where the typical gain was 0.6 of a grade per year (Becker & Engelmann, 1973).

Wolf, at Kansas, starts Achievement Place with eight delinquent boys and two teaching surrogate parents. This successful program leads to other in-service training programs (Phillips et al., 1971).

Cohen's CASE Project at the National Training School for Boys in Washington, D.C., is described in his book, *A New Learning Environment.* A token economy is used with delinquent adolescents in a detention setting. Cohen finds that his students make academic gains that are three times greater than the standard gains expected of public school children (Cohen & Filipczak, 1971).

Meichenbaum and Goodman (1971) use a form of cognitive behavior modification called *self-instruction training* to prove that hyperactive-impulsive children can be taught to think before they act.

Goldfried (1973) uses cognitive behavior modification to reduce anxiety in adults.

Gottman et al. (1974) successfully use cognitive behavior modification strategies to treat socially withdrawn third graders.

Others apply similar cognitive behavioral techniques to effectively treat speech anxiety (Meichenbaum et al., 1971); test anxiety (Sarason, 1973); anger (Novaco, 1975); social incompetence (Christensen, 1974; Glass, 1974; Kazdin, 1973; Shmurak, 1974); and asthma in children (Renne & Creer, 1976). Cognitive behavior modification strategies (e.g., cognitive restructuring, problem solving, self-instruction, and verbal mediation) as well as other interventions incorporating cognitive or behavioral strategies (e.g., social skills training, stress management, and self-management) are used to successfully treat a wide range of problem behaviors, including poor hygiene and grooming habits (Miller et al., 1987); off-task behavior (Argulewicz et al., 1982; Miller et al., 1987); phobias (Bornstein & Knapp, 1981); impulsivity (Schlesser & Thackwray, 1984; Zakay et al., 1984); aggression (Camp, 1980; Kennedy, 1982; Kettlewell & Kausch, 1983; Schlichter & Horan, 1981; Wilson, 1984); anger (Feindler & Fremouw, 1983; Fleming, 1983; Garrison & Stolberg, 1983; Hinshaw, 1984); disruptive behavior (Allen, 1980); poor motivation (Pearl, 1985); depression (Maag, 1988); poor academics (Bowers et al., 1985; Leon & Pepe, 1983; Wong, 1985); and poor social skills (Gresham, 1981; 1985).

The preceding material represents some of the more significant accomplishments and events in the history of behavior modification. It is not necessary to commit them to memory. My purpose in listing them in chronological order is to give you an idea of how behavior modification has changed over the years. In the beginning, it was limited to animals. Then it moved into institutions, where it was applied to problems of the severely and profoundly handicapped. Eventually, it crept into the public schools and was used with mildly to moderately handicapped learners. The wave of the future seems to be cognitive behavior modification, social skills training, and self-management. Behaviorists have always been concerned about the difficulty in getting newly learned behaviors to generalize across settings and maintain over time. Training in cognitive behavior modification, social skills, and self-management attempts to improve generalization and maintenance.

Chapter One Self-Assessment

See Appendix A for acceptable responses.

1. Read each of the hypothetical cases and decide whether it describes positive or negative reinforcement, punishment, or extinction. Underline the correct label inside the parentheses.

   Benny doesn't like to do homework but he does like to eat pizza. His parents promise to take him for pizza on the weekend if he does all of his homework for the week. Benny finishes all of his homework for the week and gets to go out for pizza on the weekend.

   a. We may say that Benny's behavior of doing homework was strengthened by (positive reinforcement, negative reinforcement, extinction, punishment).

   Most drivers will tell you that they stop at stop signs because they don't want to get into an accident or get a ticket.

   b. We may say that their behavior of stopping at stop signs has been strengthened by (positive reinforcement, negative reinforcement, extinction, punishment).

   Margaret likes to have a soft drink during her break at work. She goes to the soda machine on her office floor, puts in the correct change, and makes her choice. Nothing happens. She hits the coin return button and gets her money back. She tries once more, and again nothing happens. She gets her money back and tries once more. No drink. Margaret stops putting money in the soda machine.

   c. We may say that Margaret's behavior of trying to get a drink from the soda machine has been weakened by (positive reinforcement, negative reinforcement, extinction, punishment).

   Margaret tries to get a drink from the soda machine on the next floor. She puts in the correct change and makes her choice. Nothing happens. She hits the coin return button but only gets a nickel and a dime back. She tries once more. This time the soda splashes out without a cup and she gets some on her new dress. Margaret stops putting money in the soda machine.

   d. We may say that Margaret's behavior of trying to get a drink from the soda machine has been weakened by (positive reinforcement, negative reinforcement, extinction, punishment).

   Jim is taking a graduate course in education. Each time he tries to ask a question during the first night of class, the instructor ignores him. This happens again during the second and third class sessions. Finally, Jim gives up and doesn't ask any questions for the remainder of the term.

   e. We may say that Jim's question-asking behavior has been weakened by (positive reinforcement, negative reinforcement, extinction, punishment).

   Darlene is taking a different course from Jim's. Every time she tries to ask a question in class, the instructor not only answers it but often compliments her on her question. Darlene continues to ask questions in class for the rest of the term.

   f. We may say that Darlene's question-asking behavior has been strengthened by (positive reinforcement, negative reinforcement, extinction, punishment).

continued next page

Reggie is taking a different course from Jim's or Darlene's. Every time he tries to ask a question, his instructor makes a sarcastic remark such as: "Oh, you can't be serious." Reggie decides not to risk embarrassment again and stops asking questions in class.

g. We may say that Reggie's question-asking behavior has been weakened by (positive reinforcement, negative reinforcement, extinction, punishment).

When her teacher asks Beth if she made the mess in the girl's lavatory, Beth lies and says she didn't. She gets away with it. The next time her teacher asks her if she did something wrong, Beth lies again. And again she gets away with it. Beth continues to lie to avoid punishment.

h. We may say that Beth's lying behavior has been strengthened by (positive reinforcement, negative reinforcement, extinction, punishment).

Perry engages in self-injurious behavior. He punches himself in the face when he gets upset. Whenever Perry does this, his teachers grab his hands and shout "No!" in his face. Perry hates being grabbed and yelled at. After a while, he stops punching himself.

i. We may say that Perry's face-punching behavior has been weakened by (positive reinforcement, negative reinforcement, extinction, punishment).

When Benita is standing on line in the cafeteria, an older girl cuts in front of her. Benita tells her teacher and the older girl is told to go to the end of the line. Later that day in the school yard, the girl pushes Benita down and kicks her. The next time someone cuts in front of Benita she doesn't do anything about it.

j. We may say that Benita's assertive behavior has been weakened by (positive reinforcement, negative reinforcement, extinction, punishment).

Jerzy doesn't care if he gets into trouble and has to stay after school. However, none of Jerzy's classmates share his fondness for detention. When Jerzy tries to make his peers laugh by making rude noises and silly faces during a quiet study period, his teacher starts to write the names of those students who are laughing and encouraging Jerzy on the blackboard under the word "detention." Jerzy's peers quickly stop attending to him and get back on task. After several futile attempts to get their attention, Jerzy gives up, puts his head down on the desk, and goes to sleep.

k. We may say that Jerzy's disruptive behavior has been weakened by (positive reinforcement, negative reinforcement, extinction, punishment).

l. We may also say that his peers' on-task behavior has been strengthened by (positive reinforcement, negative reinforcement, extinction, punishment).

When Michelle answers questions in class, her classmates often laugh at her speech impediment. When this happens, Michelle usually puts her head down and sobs, to the delight of her peers. After a while, Michelle stops speaking altogether.

m. We may say that Michelle's peers' teasing behavior has been strengthened by (positive reinforcement, negative reinforcement, extinction, punishment).

n. We may also say that Michelle's speaking behavior has been weakened by (positive reinforcement, negative reinforcement, extinction, punishment).

continued next page

The only time Mary gets any attention from her teacher is when she is scolded for doing something the teacher doesn't like. Each time Mary calls out in class or gets out of her seat without permission, her teacher scolds her (e.g., "Mary, how many times have I told you not to do that?"). The immediate effect is that Mary stops doing whatever it is her teacher doesn't like, but this doesn't last for long. Eventually, she calls out or gets out of her seat again. Mary's teacher continues to scold her.

o. We may say that Mary's calling-out and out-of-seat behaviors have been strengthened by (positive reinforcement, negative reinforcement, extinction, punishment).

p. We may also say that her teacher's scolding behavior has been strengthened by (positive reinforcement, negative reinforcement, extinction, punishment).

After taking an in-service workshop on behavior modification, Mary's teacher decides to ignore Mary's calling-out and out-of-seat behaviors and attend to her when she raises her hand or is in her seat. Eventually, Mary stops calling out and begins raising her hand and staying in her seat more often.

q. We may say that Mary's calling-out and out-of-seat behaviors have been weakened by (positive reinforcement, negative reinforcement, extinction, punishment).

r. We may also say that Mary's hand-raising and in-seat behaviors have been strengthened by (positive reinforcement, negative reinforcement, extinction, punishment).

Leon is at a party where everyone is smoking grass. Leon doesn't like to smoke grass but he is afraid he won't be accepted by his peers if he refuses to join in. When someone passes a joint to him, he takes a hit and passes it on. He does this several times during the evening until he gets stoned and passes out. Leon gets so sick from this experience that he never smokes grass again.

s. We may say that before he got sick, Leon's grass-smoking behavior was strengthened by (positive reinforcement, negative reinforcement, extinction, punishment).

t. We may also say that after he got sick, Leon's grass-smoking behavior was weakened by (positive reinforcement, negative reinforcement, extinction, punishment).

2. List as many examples of operants as you can in 1 minute. Then see how many respondents you can list in 30 seconds.

a. Operants (60 seconds):

b. Respondents (30 seconds):

continued next page

3. List as many examples of learned and unlearned reinforcers and punishers as you can, taking no more than 1 minute for each.

    a.   Learned reinforcers (60 seconds):

    b.   Unlearned reinforcers (60 seconds):

    c.   Learned punishers (60 seconds):

    d.   Unlearned punishers (60 seconds):

4. Describe in detail two examples that illustrate the reciprocal relationship in operant conditioning.

Upon successful completion of this chapter, the learner should be able to:

1. State what symptom substitution is
2. List three reasons why many people believe in symptom substitution
3. Explain how to ensure the maintenance and generalization of new behaviors
4. Describe the basic difference between positive reinforcement and bribery
5. Differentiate between the humanist and behaviorist philosophy of control
6. Make a list of target behaviors that should be reinforced by teachers
7. Describe the implications that current legal decisions may have on behavior modification programs
8. Write rebuttals to typical arguments against the use of behavior modification

---

The rationale for including the material in this unit in a practical "how-to-do-it" book on behavior management is quite simple. Behavior modification is hard work. It takes resolve on your part. There can be no doubts in your mind about whether or not you should be doing it. This is not to say that you must become a total convert to behavior modification or a fanatic. One of the messages you will hear throughout this text is to put the best interests of the student first, above your own. To become an unquestioning believer in and user of behavior modification is not in the best interests of your students. However, once you have determined that a behavior modification program is in the best interests of your students, you must not equivocate. Do what you have to do and stick with it. You will not see changes overnight. There is no such thing as an instant cure. It will take time and you will be tested. Parents and professionals alike may try to deter you from using many of the methods discussed in this book. While they mean well, they may not be as well informed as you. By acquainting yourself with the material in this chapter you should be better able to handle their criticisms and concerns. More important, you will be better able to handle your own.

Most of the criticisms and concerns regarding behavior modification can be grouped into four basic issues: (1) efficacy, (2) morality, (3) legality, and (4) feasibility; each issue has generated one or more specific questions that you will have to answer, at least to your own satisfaction. These issues and questions are addressed here. They are in no particular order; however, we might address the issue of efficacy first, since I believe it is immoral (if not illegal) to use an instructional strategy that does not work.

Efficacy

There is an overwhelming amount of research documenting the efficacy of behavior modification. One need only look at the literature cited at the end of chapter 1 to see that behavior modification works. What do I mean by "works"? I mean that if you use behavior modification techniques appropriately you will be able to change (i.e., strengthen or weaken) most behaviors in most people. At this point you may be wondering why, if behavior modification works so well, anyone would question or criticize a teacher for using it. Simple. No method is perfect. Behavior modification has been justifiably criticized in the past with regard to such issues as (1) symptom substitution, (2) maintenance, and (3) generalization of newly learned behaviors. Let's take a look at each.

Symptom Substitution

Critics charge that behavior modification doesn't really work because it only treats (changes) the symptoms of a behavior problem and ignores the underlying cause. As a result, the individual's behaviors (symptoms) change, but his or her attitudes and feelings remain disturbed and, in time, will produce new symptoms. Consider the following analogue. Let's suppose that you have a leak in the radiator of your car. You can have the leak plugged. However, if the leak is the result of pressure building up in the radiator due to a faulty thermostat, another leak will probably occur at a different weak spot in the radiator and you will have to bring your car back to the radiator shop. The problem in this example is that the symptoms (the leaks) are being treated, while the cause of the leaks (the faulty thermostat) is not.

I'M SO PROUD OF MYSELF. I FINALLY GOT LITTLE ALPHONSO TO STOP BITING THE OTHER CHILDREN.

Symptom substitution.

The preceding example is analogous to the student who physically attacks his peers without provocation. If the hitting is a manifestation of anger, he should not be considered "fixed" (i.e., cured) until this anger has been eliminated. He should not be considered cured if behavior modification simply eliminates his hitting. Like pressure inside the radiator seeking another weak point, anger inside of the student will find another outlet. Instead of hitting, the student may start squeezing or pinching his peers or he may turn his anger inward and engage in self-injurious behavior.

Whenever one behavioral symptom replaces another, behavior modification's critics shout, "Symptom substitution!" How justified is such criticism? The best way to prove that anything exists is to provide physical (i.e., empirical) evidence of it. Up to now, investigators have found little empirical evidence of symptom substitution. Estimates of new maladaptive behaviors (i.e., new symptoms) observed following direct, behavioral treatment have been reported to range from 0 to 5% of the subjects studied (Rachman, 1963). Reese (1966) reported no instances of symptom substitution in any of the cases she reviewed in the literature; Ulmann and Krasner stated that "symptom substitution is the exception and not the rule" (1969, p. 158) and that "considering the significant role [symptom substitution] has played in clinical psychology, experimental

demonstration of its existence is singularly lacking" (1969, p. 157).

If there is little or no empirical evidence supporting symptom substitution, why are so many people still convinced that the phenomenon exists? Behaviorists claim that what people think is symptom substitution may actually be something that might be mistaken for it. Ulmann and Krasner (1969) report on several examples of situations that might be confused with symptom substitution. The first is labeled *resensitization*. A child may develop a phobia of dogs after being bitten at an early age. Following behavior modification, the phobia is eliminated and the child, who formerly ran in terror from dogs, now tries to pet every dog she meets on the street. One day, she tries to pet the wrong dog and is bitten again. The result of this new biting incident is the return of her dog phobia. Ulmann and Krasner argue that this is not symptom substitution, but the return of the previously eliminated symptoms as a direct result of a new trauma.

In a second example, it is suggested that the maladaptive behavior originally treated may have been one of a number of maladaptive behaviors in a pattern of responses. For example, a child may have a tantrum to get what he wants. His tantrum behaviors include lying on the floor, kicking his feet, crying, and shouting obscenities as he pulls at his hair. The change agent may use behavior modification to eliminate his crying and shouting of obscenities. According to Ulmann and Krasner, the fact that the child still lies on the floor, kicking his feet and pulling at his hair, is not a case of symptom substitution. It is simply evidence that the change agent focused on only some of the tantrum behaviors instead of on all of them.

A third situation which may be mistaken for symptom substitution occurs when maladaptive behavior that has been eliminated through behavior modification reappears because correct behavioral procedures were not used to ensure generalization. For example, a student who bites her nails when she is bored may stop nail biting for several weeks after behavior modification and think she is cured of this behavior. However, when she's asked to give an oral book report in front of the class, she starts biting her nails again. Why? Ulmann and Krasner suggest that the student hasn't practiced the elimination of nail biting in stressful situations, only in boring situations. This isn't symptom substitution, they argue, but a case of not extending behavior modification procedures across situations and settings.

Fourth, change in people often creates change in the environment, which can produce maladaptive behavior that didn't exist before. Suppose that a student is passive and unassertive to the point where his peers take advantage of him. After a successful program of assertiveness training, the student's newly found assertiveness produces some aggressive responses from his peers. As a result, the student begins to feign illness to avoid going to school. Ulmann and Krasner point out that the successful change in the student's behavior created a negative change in the environment, which ultimately produced new maladaptive behavior in the student.

Is it justified to criticize the efficacy of behavior modification because of symptom substitution? First, let's go back to the earlier example of the angry student who physically attacked his peers. It seems inappropriate to me to focus treatment exclusively on this student's behavior without also attempting to treat the underlying anger that produced it. Powerful emotional states such as anger or extreme anxiety initially produce physiological changes in the organism, such as increased heartbeat, perspiration, dry mouth, shaking, and muscular tension. These physiological changes are highly aversive to most people. Through prior conditioning they have learned to rid themselves of these aversive states by using *escape mechanisms* such as physical or verbal attack (fight) or running away (flight). I believe that two things must happen: first, the maladaptive behavior must be weakened by strengthening an incompatible behavior to take its place (e.g., assertiveness instead of aggression); and second, the student must be helped to reduce the aversive physiological state he or she is experiencing (through such respondent procedures as deep muscle relaxation). If these steps are not taken, you can probably expect one of two consequences: either no change in the student's behavior at all or a reduction in one maladaptive behavior with a concomitant increase in another (different) one. If you wish to call the latter effect "symptom substitution," you would not be wrong.

While I do believe that symptom substitution exists, I do not believe that it is inevitable in every behavior modification program. With careful planning, it can be avoided. If you are criticized for using a behavior modification program on the basis of symptom substitution, you should be prepared to use any or all of the arguments that have been stated here. Naturally, you should program against the possibility of symptom substitution and carefully monitor student behavior just in case your programming doesn't work.

Maintenance

It's one thing to change a child's behavior and another to make that change last more than a class period, a week, or a month. Unfortunately, the research regarding the maintenance of newly learned behaviors in behavior modification programs suggests that most programs do not automatically produce lasting effects (Marholin & Steinman, 1977; O'Leary et al., 1969; Walker & Buckley, 1972). Notice that I used the word *automatically*. Just as you can program against symptom substitution, it is possible to program for maintenance. This can be accomplished in a number of ways.

Schedules of Reinforcement. It is a common misconception that reinforcers in behavior modification programs must be used continuously until the child emits the desired response and then should be discarded. Students of behavior modification know that the use of reinforcement must follow a systematic schedule. In the beginning, reinforcement must be given on a continuous schedule, every time the behavior is emitted, since the student is not producing the desired responses very often. When the desired responses become more frequent, they may be reinforced on a fixed schedule—for example, at every second, third, or fourth response. This procedure serves to wean the student from the reinforcer. Eventually, she will be placed on a maintenance or variable schedule of reinforcement where desired responses are reinforced intermittently, perhaps on the average of every second or third response. Once she is on the variable schedule, the student will no longer be able to predict when reinforcement is coming. If she wants reinforcement, she will have to respond appropriately all the time. Proper use of schedules of reinforcement will go a long way toward enhancing the maintenance of newly learned behaviors.

Self-Management. A relatively new and promising way to increase the maintenance of newly learned behaviors is to teach students self-management skills. Teaching students how to assess, consequate, and monitor their own behaviors enables them to become independent of the environment for control. The more the student is able to exercise control from within, the longer the newly learned behaviors can maintain. The longer they maintain, the more likely they are to become an integral part of the student's behavioral repertoire (refer to chapter 8 for a discussion of self-management skills).

Internalization. Getting a student to internalize a behavior (i.e., to engage in a behavior without necessarily receiving any extrinsic reward) should be the goal of every behavior modification program. While it is not always an easy goal to reach, there are some rules of thumb that will help the process along.

First, you must remember to attach greater importance to the student's attainment of the target behavior than to the attainment of the extrinsic reinforcer. The following is an example of what *not* to do. A number of years ago, I visited a class for emotionally handicapped students in western Oregon that operated on a token economy. For improvements in academic and social behavior, students were given tokens that were eventually turned in for backup reinforcers, such as food, comics, crayons, models, and other favored items. During my visit, a young student finished reading his first book from cover to cover. Consider the significance of this event. This boy had been a virtual nonreader when he had entered the program in the fall, and in a matter of months he had finished reading an entire book! What was the teacher's response? She gave him his points without cracking a smile and, in a flat monotone, said, "Good job, Joey. Now you have enough points for that model airplane you wanted." And what did Joey say? "Oh, boy! Now I don't have to do any more reading!" You can hardly blame him for losing sight of his accomplishment. Nobody had bothered to point it out to him. It's precisely this kind of teaching that perpetuates a student's need for extrinsic reinforcement. If Joey's teacher had only shown a little more enthusiasm (even if she had to fake it) and impressed upon him how significant his accomplishment was, he might have attached more importance to his reading than to the plastic model he got for a prize. The real prize in this case was that Joey learned how to read.

Another way to program for internalization is to use the student's natural need to succeed. It has been said that nothing succeeds like success. Skinner contends that being effective (i.e., successful) at whatever one does is the greatest reinforcer one may experience (in Evans, 1968). Some go so far as to claim that it is an instinctive need. For example, White (1975) points to the typical 1-year-old who tries to spoon-feed himself even though he would gain greater oral satisfaction if he let his mother feed him. White contends that the child is concerned with achieving mastery over his environment, with the payoff being a feeling or sense of competence. At this point you may ask why Joey wouldn't be as naturally motivated to master reading as the typical 1-year-old is to master self-feeding. Consider Thorndike's law of effect: Behavior that is rewarded is likely to be repeated, but behavior that is punished or meets with failure (i.e., the withholding of a reward) is not likely to be repeated (Thorndike, 1921). Joey's earlier attempts at learning to read had met with failure. He had become so failure oriented that he probably didn't realize the significance of his accomplishment. He needed someone in the environment to remind him that it was still possible for him to achieve mastery over a portion of his world. Once he was reminded, the natural or intrinsic rewards would take over, eliminating the need for extrinsic motivators. The point is that many children come to school naturally motivated, needing little external encouragement to learn. However, once they experience failure at learning, they lose much of this natural motivation and come to rely more heavily on their environment to motivate them. A need that is perpetuated by the environment will always be there, and changes in behavior will last only as long as the environment continues to pay. If, on the other hand, a concerted effort is made to change the student's motivation to natural or intrinsic rewards, newly learned behaviors will last as long as the student wishes, since he or she will no longer look to the environment for motivation.

Is the lack of maintenance of newly learned behaviors a valid criticism of behavior modification? Yes, I think so. However, as I have stated, there are ways of programming maintenance; these methods should be considered before dismissing behavior modification as a viable treatment approach.

Generalization

A common complaint overheard in faculty rooms is: "I don't care how good she is in your class. In my room she's a pain in the neck!" What makes a student behave like Jekyll and Hyde in different situations? Most often, the explanation lies in differences in the interactions between the student and her teachers or peers in each class. For example, teacher A may give the student more positive feedback regarding her performance than teacher B does in his class. Since behavior that is rewarded becomes stronger, and since positive behavior is incompatible with negative behavior, we should expect the student to engage in more appropriate behavior in teacher A's class. If, on the other hand, teacher B ignores her when she's "good," the student will be less likely to engage in good behavior. She will probably misbehave more often—the same student but with different personal interactions. If teacher B consequated behavior the way teacher A did, teacher B would be likely to get the same response from the student. All of this points to the need for internalization so that a student can use self-reinforcement for appropriate behavior and not have to depend upon powerful others in the environment.

Short of internalization, there are some rules of thumb to follow if you want to make sure that generalization occurs. First, try to teach behaviors that are likely to be reinforced in a variety of settings. Compliance is a good example. Everybody wants the child to do what he or she is told. Eye contact, on the other hand, while it may be reinforced in one environment, may not be considered important enough to be reinforced in another environment.

Second, try to expose the student to more than one preceding stimulus or cue. If he learns to respond to the same cue all the time, he will be less likely to respond appropriately to a different cue in another environment. For example, one teacher might place her index finger next to her lips as a cue for her students to stop talking and listen. Another might raise his hand in the air or simply say, "Attention!" It is easier to teach the student to respond to as many different attention cues as possible than it is to try to get all teachers to use the same cue.

Third, enlist the support and cooperation of as many potential behavior modifiers in the student's total environment as possible. This includes other teachers, parents, peers, and siblings. You cannot expect to have everyone's cooperation, but it is worth the effort to get as many to cooperate as you can.

Fourth, before sending the student to another environment (e.g., another class), find out what behaviors she'll need in order to receive positive reinforcement in that environment. Emotionally handicapped youngsters sometimes fail to succeed in the regular classroom after making it in special education. One of the reasons for this is that they are mainstreamed with new, improved social behaviors, but their academic performance is still much lower than that of their mainstream peers. Because they have less opportunity to receive positive reinforcement in the regular classroom, they revert to their old (pre–special education) behavior.

Fifth, use the technique of *fading* (see chapter 6) to ensure generalization of the learned response. This is particularly important when you want the student to emit the response in a particular setting or situation.

Finally, teach your students self-management skills. A student who knows how to manage his own behavior won't have to count on a different change agent from each and every environment he's in to appropriately consequate his behavior. He can do it himself.

Remember, generalization will occur only if (1) the student has internalized the newly learned behaviors enough to engage in the behavior without extrinsic consequences, or (2) the teacher has programmed specifically for generalization to take place.

Morality

While all of the issues discussed in this unit are controversial, none of them come close to morality in stimulating controversy. This is no wonder when one considers what has been presented to the public in the guise of behavior modification. Consider, for example, the government-sponsored program in a Florida school for troubled youth where undesirable behavior was consequated with injections of urine into the blood, shackling residents with leg irons, using electric dog-training collars, and forcing residents to spend the night

in graves they had dug for themselves. Consider also the countless institutions for the mentally ill and the retarded that have used token reinforcement programs to motivate their patients to perform maintenance work so that the institution could save money. Instead of receiving the minimum wage for work on the grounds, in the kitchen, and in the laundry, residents earn tokens that are used to obtain certain privileges, such as a privacy screen or television, or entitlements, such as food, clothing, and a mattress or blankets. All of these programs are real and have attempted to legitimize their inhumane treatment by claiming to have scientific credibility. This is done by calling such treatment "behavior modification." Whenever people object, they are shown the vast amount of supportive empirical data on behavior modification and are told, "This is behavior modification and the research shows that it works. How can you argue against success?" Is it any wonder that the morality of behavior modification is questioned?

These programs are abuses of behavior modification. To appreciate this, you must first understand that behavior modification is simply a tool; as such, it has no morality. In the hands of moral people, it is moral, and when it is abused as in the programs cited here, it becomes immoral. Keep this in mind as you read the following sections.

Bribery

Parents and professionals alike have criticized behavior modification because they consider positive reinforcement of desirable student behavior to be nothing more than bribery. "Why can't she learn for learning's sake?" "Nobody had to give me any prizes to do my math." Webster's definition of bribery is "anything, especially money, given or promised to induce a person to do something illegal or wrong" and "anything given or promised to induce a person to do something against his wishes" (1958, p. 181). While it is true that most failure-oriented students don't like schoolwork, it doesn't mean that they wouldn't like doing it if they were successful at it. Most of the critics who attack behavior modification as being bribery had relatively successful experiences in school when they were growing up. Nobody had to give them any prizes to do reading or math because they were successful enough at these endeavors to provide their own intrinsic rewards. It therefore becomes difficult for them to have any empathy for a student who fails. It is ludicrous to expect a child who has had difficulty learning to continue to want to learn for the sake of learning!

Let's go back to the dictionary's definition of bribery. Are completing assignments; learning to read, write, and compute; and getting along with one's peers examples of things that are "illegal" or "wrong"? These are what teachers "induce" children to do every day. The inducement is a grade (which is a form of token reinforcement). Is it bribery when I tell my college students that if they do a good job on an assignment I will give them a passing grade? For that matter, is it bribery when a worker gets paid for doing his or her job? Why should there be a double standard, which says that a student must learn for the sake of learning (an intrinsic reward) while adults don't have to work unless they get the extrinsic reward of money? What do you say to the parents of a failure-oriented student who refuses to do any schoolwork and is achieving 3 years below grade level? "I'm sorry. I know the research shows that behavior modification is effective in getting students like your Joey to comply, while traditional school payoffs have failed to motivate him, but behavior modification is considered bribery." These parents may not understand why we require our children to work for the love of learning, while our adult athletes and entertainers (with whom our children so closely identify) do not work purely for the love of sport or the spotlight. Even our adult teachers don't (and shouldn't have to) work only for the love of teaching. Money is token reinforcement, a form of behavior modification. It's all right to use behavior modification with adults; we make the rules. With children, it's considered bribery.

Don't misunderstand. There are instances in which an individual may think he or she is using behavior modification when, in fact, it is bribery. A handy rule of thumb to follow is this: If, by rewarding student behavior, you are acting solely in your own best interest without regard for the student's best interest, you are probably engaging in bribery. For example, if you don't like to have your authority questioned and you reinforce students for following your directives without question, your actions are probably self-serving and a case could be made for bribery. However, if, by rewarding student behavior, you are acting in the student's best interest, you are probably not engaging in bribery. An example of this would be rewarding any behavior that contributes to the student's academic achievement, emotional or social development, or physical well-being, such as completing assignments, acting assertively with peers and adults, and accepting valid criticism from others.

Control

Humanists such as Carl Rogers (1969) and A. S. Neill (1960, 1966) contend that children can't learn to be responsible unless they're allowed freedom of choice. They criticize behavior modification on the grounds that it denies children freedom of choice: The change agent manipulates the environment in order to force the student's choice. The teacher decides how the child should behave and, by systematically applying aversives or rewards, manipulates him into behaving this way. Rogers and Neill are not necessarily suggesting there is anything wrong with the responses the teacher wants from the student. They do, however, feel that the chances of the student's internalizing this behavior are greater if he "discovers" it on his own. For example, suppose that a student decides that she wants to read comics in school instead of literature or history. According to Rogers and Neill, if the teacher takes her comics away every time she brings them out to read and gives her a gold star whenever she reads from her literature or history book, the teacher is denying the student's freedom of choice. In this case, the student is being denied the freedom to choose between a passing grade and a failing grade; between learning the material in the literature and history texts and not learning it; and, on a larger scale, between getting an education and not getting one. Humanists argue that by forcing a particular concept of what is "right" or "good" on the student, the teacher is turning her away from education. Instead, they suggest that students be allowed to choose what they want to learn and when. Only then will they be so interested in what they are doing that real learning will take place. When this happens, there won't be any need for behavior modification; students will be so busy learning that they won't have time to misbehave.

This argument, while noble, is also naïve. In the first place, not all learners are created equal. I would argue that the freedom of choice Rogers and Neill want for children would, in many instances, ultimately limit their freedom as adults. Before elaborating, let's make sure we all agree on what we mean by *freedom*. Webster (1958) defines it as "exemption or liberation from the control of some other person or some arbitrary power" (p. 577). Rogers perceives freedom as a "fulfillment by the person of the ordered sequence of his life" (1969, p. 269). Skinner, on the other hand, views freedom as "an illusion that man invented because of his need to be given credit for his 'good' behavior and achievements" (1971). My definition of freedom coincides with Reese's, who wrote:

> A man who has a limited behavioral repertoire and whose behavior produces a limited variety of reinforcers may be considered a man with very little freedom. On the other hand, a man who can read and write and speak effectively—who has, perhaps, artistic or athletic or mechanical skills—such a man has far more freedom. He has many more responses available and the opportunity to obtain the variety of intrinsic and extrinsic reinforcers contingent upon them. (1966, p. 62)

In other words, the more skills an individual possesses, the greater the number of responses he or she can make in a given situation. An adult with few skills is likely to be restricted in terms of where he works and lives, what friends he has, and what his vocational interests are. An individual with the equivalent of a sixth-grade education is likely to have fewer choices in these areas than someone who graduated from high school, and fewer choices ultimately result in less freedom.

Let us return to the original argument that freedom of choice for students may limit their freedom as adults. I believe that many students require the structure of a behavior modification program in which the behavior modifier will make many of their choices. Further, I believe that without such a program it is doubtful that such students will ever achieve up to their full potential. By limiting their freedom of choice and guiding their choices as students, it therefore becomes possible to expand their freedom as adults. Conversely, by giving them freedom of choice as students, we may actually limit their freedom as adults! Essentially, freedom may be correlated with achievement (both academic and social); if controls are necessary in order for a student to achieve, they will indirectly lead to more freedom in the student's future.

The second fallacy in the humanists' argument is the notion that students will have freedom of choice if teachers do not attempt to manipulate their environment. This is nonsense! Even the students in Neill's school, Summerhill, were not completely free. No one is. Unfortunately, it is the nature of human beings to want to control their environment and to have others do what they want. There will always be someone in the student's environment, if not a teacher, perhaps another student, who will try to manipulate his or her behavior. As Skinner said, "To refuse to control is to leave control not to the person himself, but to other parts of the social and non-social environments" (1971, p. 84). Bandura expresses the same sentiment when he argues that the "basic moral question is not whether man's behavior will be controlled, but rather by whom, by what means, and for what ends" (1969, p. 85).

One last word on the morality issue. It has been said that ignoring behavior modification is like ignoring the law of gravity. It is there and we can't change it. Neither can we change the need to control. Therefore, in order for us to remain as relatively free as possible, it is imperative that we learn all we can about methods of control. As Ulrich so aptly stated,

> The control of human behavior is a fact. Pretending that it does not exist will not make it go away. Individuals concerned with personal freedom should at least consider that perhaps the only meaningful form of behavioral freedom must be based on a knowledge of the factors which, indeed, control us. As man comes to know more and more about causative factors, he acquires a new type

of freedom which makes self-control truly possible. So long as man is not aware of the factors which determine his behavior, his ignorance places him in the position of being easily subjected to the control of other people, or of other environmental circumstances. (1967, p. 233)

Legality

No one as yet has said that it is illegal to practice behavior modification. However, there have been a number of recent court decisions that will ultimately make it more difficult to do.

For example, in *Clonce v. Richardson* (1974) and *Wyatt v. Stickney* (1972), the courts found that inmates at a federal prison psychiatric facility in Missouri and residents in institutions for the mentally ill and retarded in Alabama had the rights to basic needs, such as clothing, food, comfortable beds, and privacy. Furthermore, these rights were guaranteed by the Constitution and must be provided. The individual cannot be forced to earn them. The impact of these legal decisions will be felt in token reinforcement programs where entitlements rather than privileges are used as reinforcers. Most token economies allow individuals to earn privileges for appropriate behavior. For example, the student can earn tokens for successfully completing academic assignments and eventually can turn these in for privileges, such as candy, models, or comic books. These are considered to be privileges because the average student wouldn't normally have access to them in school. Needless to say, the use of privileges often makes it difficult to wean students from a token system. On the other hand, it is relatively easy to wean a student from a token system that requires students to earn entitlements. Entitlements are all of the things the average student would normally receive whether or not he or she was on the token system. Students who engage in maladaptive behavior are required to earn benefits they consider they are entitled to. Meanwhile, well-behaved students get these entitlements for "free." Examples of entitlements are taking recess, eating lunch with peers, attending assemblies, watching films in class, and attending school sporting or social events. Given the current mood of the courts, I would not be surprised if the Clonce and Wyatt decisions were used as precedents in a suit brought by a student or his or her family charging that by having to earn access to entitlements, such as assemblies, recess, cafeteria, and the like, the student was being denied his or her constitutional rights.

I was involved in a case a number of years ago that could possibly have led to such a confrontation. Acting as a behavioral consultant to a school for the physically handicapped in Portland, Oregon, I was asked to write

I'm sorry, Louis, but you can't have your OXYGEN until you do your MATH

Entitlements vs. privileges.

a behavioral program for S., a 12-year-old boy with spina bifida. The problem was that S. was not attending to his personal hygiene as he was supposed to and the area around the opening at the base of his spine was becoming infected. S. was given ample lavatory time each morning and afternoon, but instead of completing his toileting in what should have taken him no more than 15 minutes, he dawdled for over an hour. It was decided that S. would earn tokens contingent upon his completing his toileting in the required 15 minutes. Without these tokens, he could not get the same hot lunch as his peers. Instead, everything would be put into a food blender and he would be served a hot liquid lunch. After a few days, his behavior in the bathroom changed dramatically and maintained for the rest of the school year. In relating this case from time to time, I have received some hard looks from individuals who feel that the program was a bit harsh. I doubt, however, that these people would be as upset if they had had the opportunity to sit in on S.'s physical exam before the behavioral program, had seen the condition of his lower back and rectal area, and had heard the doctor's report to the staff. Drastic cases sometimes call for drastic measures. Nobody tried to starve the boy. His lunch had essentially the same nutritional value as the school lunch his peers ate; it just wasn't as appetizing as theirs.

For this reason, S. decided not to eat lunch for the first few days of the program. What if he hadn't given in and had continued his lunch fast? Would he or his family (who originally had consented to the program) have had legal recourse? Could they have sued me and the school for denying a basic right? I would certainly think twice about implementing such a program today.

Besides the issue of basic rights, there is the issue of "equal protection." The 14th Amendment to the Constitution states, in part, "No state shall . . . deny to any person within its jurisdiction the equal protection of the laws." In other words, one group may not be treated substantially differently from another group entitled to the same treatment. According to Martin (1975), "if a school behavior modification project seeking to deal with disruptive students only treats blacks, or boys, or a certain socioeconomic class, then it may well be denying the equal protection of the law" (p. 3). Don't think that this won't create problems for some behavior modification programs.

Another legal development that is sure to create problems in the future is "due process." Both the 5th and 14th Amendments guarantee this right to all Americans. However, it wasn't until *Goss v. Lopez* (1975) that individuals denied due process had any substantial legal precedent to support them. The effect of Goss is that students assigned to behavior modification programs must first be given notice and provided with a hearing. Quoting Martin again: "Even if a student in a regular classroom is treated differently than other students (e.g., given tokens or put into time-out) thus altering the way others view him, it might be sufficient deprivation of liberty to raise the due process issue. Thus, in any separate treatment or classification, there should first be notice and a hearing to discuss the approach with the student and his parents" (1975, p. 171). If you are beginning to feel confused about what you can and cannot legally do to modify the behavior of your students, you may wish to use the checklist in Appendix B to make sure that you are in compliance with the law before implementing a behavior modification program.

There is some irony in all of these developments. For years, severely handicapped individuals were denied education on the basis that such training would be a waste of the taxpayer's money. These individuals were considered uneducable. It wasn't until the courts were shown the results of behavior modification that they moved to mandate education for the severely handicapped. For example, the severely handicapped in the state of Pennsylvania received no education or training until the Pennsylvania Association for Retarded Children won a case against the state. The federal court found that all children, no matter how retarded, can benefit from a program of education and training.

Therefore, the state could no longer deny them access to a free public education (*Pennyslvania Association for Retarded Children v. Commonwealth of Pennsylvania*, 1971). To a large extent, this decision was based on behavior modification research and training manuals presented as evidence in court. In this way, behavior modification made it possible for the severely handicapped to gain legal access to free and appropriate instruction. However, because of the many legal restrictions being placed on behavior modifiers due to the Clonce, Wyatt, and Goss decisions and others, it may be difficult for them to treat the severely handicapped individual in the training program. If this does turn out to be the case, the very individuals who were supposed to profit from these programs will not be able to do so. In other words, while they have been pushed forward by the laws granting them free access to an education, they also have been pushed backward by the laws restricting the behavior modifiers attempting to teach them.

Another bit of irony is that the new lawsuits that ultimately restrict behavior modifiers are being brought by civil libertarians wanting to free their clients from the restraints of behavior modification programs. The behavior modifiers, on the other hand, argue that they want to free their clients from the restraints of their mental retardation or mental illness (Martin, 1975). This touches on the old problem of trying to define freedom, which we discussed briefly in the section on morality. Civil libertarian groups such as the American Civil Liberties Union (ACLU) see freedom and restraint in a different way than behavior modifiers do. Behavior modifiers feel that an individual who lacks academic, social, or vocational skills and who may have an emotional problem as well is operating under some rather heavy restraints. They have demonstrated that they can remove these restraints (and thereby increase an individual's freedom) through the application of behavior modification. Civil libertarians, on the other hand, have a different interpretation of restraint. They feel that the handicapped individual is being restrained if he or she is required to undergo any behavioral modification without informed consent. The behavior modifiers argue that this individual is not always capable of giving such consent and that the next of kin is not always willing to do so. Perhaps a real-life example will put this dilemma into proper focus.

Several years ago, I served as a behavioral consultant to an institution in western Oregon. My job was to design a behavior modification program for a 10-year-old deaf-blind boy who engaged in severe physically aggressive behavior. T. would scratch, kick, bite, and hit or head-butt any children or adults careless enough to get within range. At one point, he sent the teacher

to the hospital with a split lip incurred while she was attempting to restrain him from behind. The reality of the situation was that T. could not live at home, since his mother could not adequately care for him, and if he could not be trained at this school, he would probably wind up in the state training school for the retarded, requiring custodial care for the remainder of his life. After collecting baseline data and discussing the case with T.'s teacher, a behavior modification program was written. It had many components, including a special program to help T. communicate his needs to others; increased monitoring of medication by the physician treating him for his glaucoma; a self-help program to make him less dependent on others; a special sensory program to teach him "gentle" touching; and a compliance program to get him to cooperate and follow directions. The most important part of the program consisted of the aversive consequences the adults had to use with T. to consequate his physically aggressive behavior. It was decided that T.'s hand would be slapped when he scratched an adult, and he would be restrained in a prone position on the floor with the teacher astride him for other physically aggressive behaviors. Drastic cases sometimes call for drastic measures.

The problem arose when we tried to get T.'s mother to give her consent for the program to be implemented. It wasn't so much that she objected to the use of aversives, but she had recently found religion. She said that her son's behavior was in the hands of God, and if God wanted T. to stop hurting people, He would stop him. Instead of using behavior modification, T.'s mother actually wanted us to anoint his head with oil! At the present time, I do not know where T. is or if his behavior is any different. By the time we had convinced T.'s mother that the program was in his best interest, the school year had ended!

I would argue that in this particular case, neither the client (T.) nor his mother knew what was best for him. I believe that here, the legal requirement of consent, which was intended to keep the individual free from restraint, actually had the opposite effect of keeping him restrained. As long as T. engages in his physically aggressive behavior, it will be next to impossible for anyone to teach him anything. Education and training freed Helen Keller from the restraints of her handicap. Unfortunately, T. may never enjoy such freedom.

Feasibility

One thing the reader must remember is that the arguments over the efficacy, morality, and legality of behavior modification all become academic if it isn't feasible to carry out such a program. Webster (1958) defines *feasible* as "capable of being done or carried out; practicable; possible" (p. 531). Behavior modification is carried out by people. If people don't think it is possible to use behavior modification, it doesn't make any difference how effective or moral or legal it is. It just won't happen. This section deals with the controversy over the feasibility of behavior modification. Can it be done? Can it be carried out? Is it possible?

I could simply point to the many behavior modification studies conducted over the years as evidence of its feasibility in many settings and situations. However, I would be remiss if I did not also point out that most of these studies were conducted under rigorous conditions not normally present in the average classroom. These studies were conducted by investigators who had the time, the expertise, the money, the equipment, and the people to control all the independent variables that might influence the outcome of their research. The average classroom teacher is not in this enviable position. Therefore, he or she will not always be able to replicate these studies in the classroom. However, this doesn't mean that it can't be done. More and more articles are appearing in the literature written by teachers themselves about behavior modification programs they have implemented on their own.

While many teachers are taking the plunge into behavior modification, there are still a great many others holding back, not out of concern over efficacy, morality, or legality, but out of concern over feasibility. While some of these concerns are genuine, others are merely excuses to avoid a commitment to action. I like to refer to these excuses as "Yeah, buts." The remainder of this unit is devoted to some of the "Yeah, buts" I have heard over the years, with a rejoinder to each.

1. *"I tried it and it didn't work."* This teacher usually doesn't know the first thing about behavior modification but thinks he's an expert. The first question I ask is, "What exactly did you do?" Inevitably, there is some flaw in his behavior modification program. One common error is using the wrong reinforcement schedule or no schedule at all. Other errors are using the wrong reinforcers (teachers commonly use what is convenient or reinforcing to them instead of to the student) or the wrong contingencies (they are usually too difficult for the student). Another common problem relates to the quality and quantity of the reinforcers, especially when social praise is used. Some teachers overdo it to the point where it actually becomes aversive to the student. While many teachers use social praise in a noncontingent fashion (i.e., they give it away for nothing), others reinforce the wrong behaviors. Some teachers convey so little enthusiasm that their praise means

nothing to the student. Still others forget to praise when they should. Nobody said that behavior modification was easy. There is, however, ample evidence that it works when it is used properly. Therefore, teachers who complain that it doesn't work should seriously question their application of the method rather than the method itself.

2. *"I don't need it. When I tell my kids to do something, they do it or else!"* This teacher is probably half correct; her students do what she tells them to do. However, there may also be a lot of escape-avoidance behavior in this classroom, such as lying, stealing, cheating, sneaking, and tattling. For some reason, teachers who run their classrooms on fear tactics are perceived as strong disciplinarians by their administrators and colleagues. Many parents often request such teachers for their children. Unfortunately, these people have lost sight of the difference between discipline and punishment. Children who experience drill instructors for teachers often wind up hating school, teachers, and sometimes themselves.

But do they like school?

3. *"It's just too hard to keep track of. I can't be bothered collecting data. Who has the time?"* On a number of occasions I have sat in on the classes of these teachers and monitored the amount of time they spend disciplining students. By starting and stopping a stopwatch at the beginning and end of each incidence of "discipline" (for example, a teacher telling a student to do something or not to do something the student should have known on her own), I was able to get a cumulative number of

minutes devoted to discipline. At the end of the school day, I shared this information with the teachers. They were always amazed at the amount of time involved. For some, it's as much as 30 minutes! This is time they could have used instructing the children or relaxing while their class worked independently. Thirty minutes a day times 5 days a week times 40 weeks in a school year equals 100 wasted hours a year! This is probably a conservative estimate since some teachers (especially in the inner-city schools) claim that they spend most of their school day disciplining students. If these same teachers took the time to implement behavior modification programs in their classrooms, the result would probably be less disruptive behavior in their students. This would mean that the teachers wouldn't have to spend as much time disciplining them and would have more time for instruction. There are also very specific practical measures teachers can use to simplify the implementation of a behavior modification program. These will be covered in later chapters.

4. *"I can't afford to use it."* This teacher equates behavior modification with expensive token economies that use only tangibles such as food, toys, and crafts as backup reinforcers. It is not necessary for the teacher to bankrupt himself at the end of every month purchasing special treats for his students. If you must use such incentives in a token program, there's no reason why your students' parents or the school district can't provide the money. There is absolutely no reason why teachers, who are underpaid as it is, should have to fund these programs, especially when there are a number of activity reinforcers available in every school building. Probably the cheapest and one of the most effective reinforcers available to teachers is verbal praise and attention. It doesn't cost a thing to sit with a student for a few minutes as a consequence of good behavior.

5. *"It's only good for changing social behaviors, and I don't have any discipline problems."* Behavior modification is just as effective with academic behaviors as it is with social behaviors. Behavioral techniques including R+, chaining, shaping, modeling, prompting, and fading have all been used effectively to increase students' learning and boost academic achievement. The DISTAR (Engelmann & Brunner, 1973) and Morphographic Spelling (Dixon & Engelmann, 1979) programs are excellent examples of commercially available behavior modification programs that have successfully modified academic behaviors in culturally different students. Lindsley's precision teaching is a formative evaluation system based upon the principles of behavior modification that has also been used effectively to modify academic behaviors (Kunzelmann et al., 1970).

6. *"If we had fewer students, we wouldn't need behavior modification."* There is no reason to believe that a teacher who can't control a class of 30 will be any better at controlling 20. The research regarding class size is not necessarily supportive of the notion that smaller is better. True, with fewer students, the potential number of discipline problems is reduced. But while smaller class size might be advantageous, it still is no substitute for behavior modification.

7. *"It's the kid's home environment that needs changing; go tell his parents about behavior modification."* Realistically, schools have very little control over what happens in a child's home. Schools can, however, control what happens in school. Even if the student stays out and runs around the streets all night, the school cannot excuse misbehavior between 8:00 A.M. and 3:00 P.M. on the grounds that the student's parents didn't do an adequate job of raising him. You have to do what's necessary at school. If the parents cooperate, fine. If not, you still have a responsibility to attempt modification of the student's behavior by the most effective means available to you.

8. *"Won't the other kids get jealous?"* If the other students are working for smiling faces or letter grades while the class clown receives candy and comics for doing the same work, it's obvious that jealousy will become a problem. Who can blame them if they go on

Equal opportunity?

strike for the same privileges? You might even wind up with a whole class of clowns. The key phrase to remember is *equal opportunity*. If one student gets candy and comics for working, all students should get them. If this creates a problem for the teacher (and it should), she should use reinforcers that are more readily available—for example, praise, teacher attention, or favored activities. In fact, the teacher should provide these readily available reinforcers for all the children in the class in addition to the smiling faces and the letter grades. If you have one or two troublemakers, have them earn what the other students normally receive. Turn the jealousy issue around. Try to make the troublemakers jealous of their well-behaved peers. I found that it helps to tell a jealous student, ''If there's a behavior you would like to change, just let me know and I'll be glad to help you set up a program.'' At this point, the student either ''puts up or shuts up.''

One final, albeit critical, notion I must share with you is the idea that you don't have to use behavior modification if you don't need to. Over the years I have met, taught, and observed some marvelous teachers who had what I like to call the ''knack.'' They could handle the most difficult behavior problems without benefit of behavior management skills. They seemed to know intuitively exactly what would work with each student. Many of them also had a certain persona (or even charisma) that allowed them to relate to the most trying students. In short, these lucky souls have made behavior management appear more art than science.

Lord knows I'm not one of them. For those of you like me, who need the science of behavior management, read on. You artists out there might want to pass this book on to a colleague.

Saints don't need behavior modification.

Chapter Two Self-Assessment

See Appendix A for acceptable responses.

1. What is symptom substitution?

2. Name three situations that might be mistaken for symptom substitution.

3. State the author's position on symptom substitution.

4. Explain how you might attempt to improve the maintenance of newly learned behaviors.

5. Explain how you might attempt to improve the generalization of newly learned behaviors.

6. Describe the basic difference between positive reinforcement and bribery.

7. How does the humanist philosophy of control differ from that of the behaviorist?

8. With what does the author equate "freedom"?

continued next page

9.   Describe the implications that current legal decisions may have on behavior modification programs.

10. Write a rebuttal for each of the following "Yeah, buts":

    a.   "I tried it (behavior modification) and it didn't work."

    b.   "I don't need it. When I tell my kids to do something, they do it or else!"

    c.   "It's just too hard to keep track of."

    d.   "I can't afford to use it."

    e.   "It's only good for changing social behaviors, and I don't have any discipline problems."

    f.   "If we had fewer students, we wouldn't need behavior modification."

    g.   "It's the kid's home environment that needs changing; go tell his parents about behavior modification."

    h.   "Won't the other kids get jealous?"

Part II
Deciding What To Change

chapter 3

Identifying and Specifying Behaviors

Upon successful completion of this chapter, the learner should be able to:

1. Produce maladaptive and target (fair-pair) pinpoints that pass both the "So what?" and stranger tests
2. Produce acceptable performance objectives for social behaviors
3. Explain what the "So what?" test is and how to apply it to maladaptive and target behaviors

Specifying Behaviors

Why bother?

Many years ago, while attending a graduate-level course in special education, I had a startling experience. One evening, about 15 minutes into the class, a student named Jack entered the room during the instructor's lecture and noisily walked to his seat. He then took out a newspaper and began to read it out loud. Needless to say, this behavior created much consternation among his peers and, eventually, the instructor stopped lecturing. After being asked to put away the newspaper, Jack began a long harangue about "student rights" and "boring lectures"; then, directing an obscene gesture at the instructor, he walked out of the room, slamming the door behind him. After a brief period of stunned silence, the instructor asked each of us to write a short statement describing the incident, since he intended to report Jack's behavior to the dean of the graduate school. We were told to write down "what had happened" and turn this report in to the instructor without signing our names. After collecting all the statements, the instructor glanced briefly at each of them. Eventually, he put the statements down, and, opening the door of the classroom, he said, "You can come in now." At this point, our old friend Jack walked back into the room and quietly took his seat. While the rest of us sat with open mouths, the instructor proceeded to read aloud excerpts from some of the statements we had written. There were very few objective accounts of what had happened. While a few students had stated what they had seen and heard, most of us had resorted to making value judgments. Jack's behavior had been labeled as "menacing," "awful," "dumb," and "disgraceful," while Jack had been called "drunk," "a jerk," and "inconsiderate." As I recall, one person suggested that Jack might be a "Commie pervert" while others described him as a "psycho."

After reading these excerpts while we squirmed in our seats, the instructor tossed them all into the wastebasket. He then explained that he had asked Jack to behave that way on purpose because he wanted to see how objective we could be in reporting the incident. He had hypothesized that very few of us would be objective and, as it turned out, he was correct. Naturally, many students were angry and embarrassed, and told him what they thought of his "cheap trick." He replied by asking them if Jack also had a right to be angry or embarrassed by their comments. Although some students felt that Jack had relinquished any rights he had as a student because of his behavior, eventually most of us agreed that we hadn't exactly been fair to him in our statements. The instructor then read aloud several statements about student behavior written by teachers, which he had collected over the years. Terms such as "brain damaged," "hostile," "mean," "bad," "lazy," and "no good" were used, among others, to describe student behavior. There were few, if any, verbs or verb phrases used, such as "hits," "reads," "looks out of window," "is out of seat," "makes funny faces," "starts fights," "refuses to work," "cries," or "calls out." The instructor asked how we would feel if, as parents of these students, we had heard or read these statements about our children. By the end of the evening, most of us were convinced that we needed to be more objective in describing the behavior of others.

I share this little story with you because it illustrates so well the tendency we all have to describe behavior in nonbehavioral terms. If you really want to become an effective change agent, you must train yourself to avoid using constructs and instead must learn to describe your students' actions objectively in behavioral terms. A person might argue that it is easier to use one construct to describe another person's behavior than several words or a whole sentence. It is much faster to

Deviancy is in the eyes of the beholder.

describe someone as "responsible" than it is to say that he or she "carries out errands to teacher satisfaction." Unfortunately, while it might be faster to use constructs, they are often open to interpretation; one person's idea of responsibility might be slightly or significantly different from someone else's. Even our own concept of responsibility can change over time. Therefore, while it initially is faster to describe someone as "responsible," it is not very economical in the long run, since we may have to define what we mean by the term at a later date. It may take a few seconds longer to say exactly what you mean now, but it will probably save you time in the future. One reason, then, to train yourself to describe actions objectively in behavioral terms, instead of using constructs, is that it is more economical in terms of communication. By being precise, you avoid confusion and save time in the future.

Another reason why you should avoid using constructs to describe behavior is that a construct often changes the focus from the student's behavior to the student. If you describe a student's behavior by saying that "on the average, she completes fewer than 25% of her assignments," you are talking about what the student does and not what she is or why she exhibits this behavior. On the other hand, if you use a construct such as "lazy" to describe her behavior, you are not really talking about what she does. You are talking about (or at the very least implying) why she does this and what she is. What does the student do? She completes fewer than 25% of her assignments. Why? Because she is lazy. What is the student? She is a lazy person. But how do you know that laziness is the cause of a 25% completion rate? Couldn't there be more than one reason why she completes so little work? Perhaps she doesn't see any value in school or schoolwork but attends for the

social benefits. Or perhaps she doesn't have the prerequisite knowledge or skills to successfully complete her work and finds it too aversive to try to do something she isn't good at. The point is that whenever you use constructs like "lazy," "crazy," or "stupid" to describe a student's behavior, you may be jumping to the wrong conclusion. Even worse, over time you will extend your judgment of the student's behavior and begin to think of the student in those terms. It is likely that you will communicate this to the student and set in motion a chain of events that could make it virtually impossible for you to ever change her behavior.

Students often have labels (constructs) hung on them that stick and ultimately lead to a self-fulfilling prophecy. The student is labeled "lazy," believes she is lazy, and acts accordingly; the individual who hung the label on her in the first place says ever so smugly, "I told you so." If the teacher in this case had used behavioral terms ("completes an average of fewer than 25% of her assignments") instead of using the construct "lazy" simply because it's easier to say, the student's behavior would have been labeled instead of the student and she might have been more motivated to improve her performance. Constructs often become labels that can, over time, inhibit growth in the student.

Perhaps the most important reason for describing student behavior objectively in behavioral terms is that the change agent will be able to detect easily any change in the student's behavior. If you describe the student's behavior as "lazy," how will you be able to tell whether or not her behavior is improving, staying the same, or getting worse? If, on the other hand, you described her behavior as "completes fewer than 25% of her assignments," you can always use the amount of assigned work completed to determine if change has occurred. If she completes 25% of her work during the first few days of your intervention and more than 25% after the first week, you will know that the behavior is changing for the better. Simply describing her behavior as "lazy" will not help you detect change.

Pinpointing

Now that I've demonstrated the importance of describing student behavior objectively, I'll show you how you can do it. The task itself may be referred to as *pinpointing* and, as you might have guessed, the end result is a pinpoint. I have included a number of instances of pinpoints for both maladaptive and target (adaptive) behaviors in Figure 3.1 along with "not-instances" (i.e., poor examples). Notice that verbs are always used in pinpoints. Words such as "hits," "smiles," "cries," and "talks" are less open to interpretation than are "rough," "happy," "sad," or "motormouth." Please notice that nonspecific adverbs (e.g., "talks a lot," "hits hard," "smiles inappropriately," and "laughs loudly") are not used, since they are open to interpretation. What is "hard" to one person may be "light," "moderate," or "soft" to another.

The Stranger Test.   Because change agents may interpret a given construct differently, it is necessary to describe student behavior in terms that would pass what I call the "stranger test." This means that anyone not familiar with the student could read the description of the student's behavior and understand it. For example, if a stranger walked into a teacher's room and was asked to monitor (i.e., observe and record) a student's "hostility," the data collected by the stranger could differ significantly from the data collected by the teacher. The stranger might interpret "hostility" as "hits," "bites," "shoves," and "kicks," while the teacher might have meant "uses provocative language" (e.g., verbal threats or profanity directed at peers). On the other hand, the

stranger might interpret "hostility" as any instance of hitting, whether or not it was provoked, while the teacher might have meant only unprovoked hits. If the teacher had defined "hostility" for the stranger as "each instance of an unprovoked hit," where "unprovoked" means that it was not in retaliation for a physical or verbal attack from a peer, both the stranger and the teacher would be likely to obtain the same results, since they would both be looking for the same thing.

Maladaptive Behaviors

The "So what?" Test
Once you pinpoint the student's behavior, you need to ask yourself, "So what?" Is it really necessary for the student to change this behavior? I believe that before any change agent arbitrarily decides to change a student's behavior, he or she should apply the "So what?"

Maladaptive Pinpoints

Instances

1. Calls out without raising hand
2. Does not complete assignments
3. Is not in seat when late bell rings
4. Hits peers without physical provocation
5. Makes incorrect verbal responses to questions asked
6. Repeats questions he has already asked
7. Says, "I don't have to" or "I don't want to" when given a directive
8. Has no part of anatomy touching seat
9. Cries when teacher takes away recess
10. Plays with younger children during recess

Not-Instances

1. Is aggressive (construct)
2. Is lazy (construct)
3. Is immature (construct)
4. Calls out inappropriately ("inappropriately" is open to interpretation)
5. Is anxious (construct)
6. Cannot accept criticism (open to interpretation)
7. Is out of seat (open to interpretation)
8. Uses back talk (open to interpretation)
9. Is tardy (what is "tardy"?)
10. Is dirty (by whose standards?)

Target Pinpoints

Instances

1. Is in seat before late bell rings
2. Finishes work without being told
3. Raises hand and waits to be called
4. Speaks in a voice audible in all parts of the room
5. Keeps head directed toward book
6. Plays with children her own age during recess
7. Complies with directive first time given, every time given
8. Does not cry when recess is taken away
9. Completes 100% of work assigned
10. Sits next to peers without hitting them

Not-Instances

1. Is mature (construct)
2. Appropriately requests permission to speak (what does "appropriately" mean?)
3. Accepts punishment (open to interpretation)
4. Is considerate of others (what does "considerate" mean?)
5. Does a good turn daily (open to interpretation)
6. Knows how to share (open to interpretation)
7. Is on task (open to interpretation)
8. Speaks in an audible voice (audible from what distance?)
9. Exercises self-control (open to interpretation)
10. Is on time (open to interpretation)

Figure 3.1.   Instances and not-instances of maladaptive and target pinpoints.

test. This simply consists of asking yourself if there is any evidence that the student's behavior is presently or potentially harmful to his or another individual's social, physical, emotional, or academic well-being. Any behavior that is presently or potentially harmful to a student's or his peers' social, physical, emotional, or academic well-being should be considered maladaptive. Once you have defined a behavior as maladaptive, you can say that it passes the "So what?" test and that it should be changed. For example, noncompliance (i.e., refusing to comply with a teacher's directive) is maladaptive because it is harmful to a student's academic well-being. If a student refuses to do any work, the chances are that he or she won't learn very much. Fighting with peers is another example of a maladaptive behavior. Fighting with peers can be harmful to a student's physical and social well-being because (1) he is in danger of being hurt and (2) he is probably going to suffer socially if he tries to hurt someone else. In addition, this behavior may be indirectly harmful to his academic well-being if he loses class instruction time because of suspension or time spent in time out or the principal's office.

Even if the student engages in fighting behavior that is not harmful to his own social, physical, or academic well-being, his behavior may have to be considered maladaptive if it is harmful to others. For example, the student may be achieving academically despite his frequent fighting, he may have many friends because his fighting gives him status among his peers, and he may be so good at fighting that he never gets hurt. However, the social, physical, or academic harm he does to the students with whom he fights should not be overlooked. His fighting may be so disruptive that the class, as a whole, receives less instruction time than they normally might. This would obviously have an effect on the academic well-being of his peers, which qualifies the student's fighting behavior as maladaptive.

The teacher may also judge that a student's behavior, although it is not maladaptive now, is potentially harmful. For example, behavior in one environment, such as a self-contained class for emotionally handicapped students, may not be considered maladaptive because there is no evidence in that environment that it is harmful to the well-being of the student, the teacher, or peers. However, the same behavior might be considered maladaptive in another environment, such as the playground or cafeteria, or in a regular classroom when it's time for the student to be mainstreamed. If the teacher has any reason to suspect that a student's behavior might be maladaptive at a future time (e.g., in a new environment), she or he should make an attempt to intervene now. Figure 3.2 includes a number of student behaviors that may be considered

---

The following behaviors will be harmful to the *social* well-being of most students most of the time:

1. Verbal aggression (e.g., threats, cursing, mocking, teasing, "put-downs")
2. Physical aggression (e.g., hitting, kicking, shoving, pinching, throwing objects, spitting)
3. Stealing
4. Lying
5. Hyperactivity
6. Impulsivity (i.e., acting before thinking of consequences)
7. Thumb sucking
8. Nose picking
9. Disfluent speech
10. Inaudible speech
11. Masturbation (public)
12. Tattling or "squealing"

The following behaviors will be harmful to the *physical* well-being of most students most of the time:

1. Physical aggression (e.g., hitting, kicking, shoving, pinching, throwing objects, spitting)
2. Self-injurious behavior (e.g., head butting, punching self, biting self)

The following behaviors will be harmful to the *academic* well-being of most student most of the time:

1. Noncompliance (i.e., not following a direction the first time given)
2. Being off task (i.e., not paying attention)
3. Disruptive behavior
4. Tardiness
5. Truancy
6. Late assignments
7. Unfinished assignments
8. Lack of preparedness for class

Figure 3.2. Maladaptive behaviors.

harmful to the student's social, physical, or academic well-being or to the well-being of individuals in his or her environment.

Target Behaviors

In a thought-provoking article entitled "Current Behavior Modification in the Classroom: Be Still, Be Quiet, Be Docile," Winett and Winkler (1972) attack behavior modification on the grounds that it is creating legions of passive, conforming automatons willing to obediently follow any new demagogue that comes along. They reviewed behavior modification studies published in the *Journal of Applied Behavior Analysis* (*JABA*) between 1968 and 1970, focusing on the target behaviors of each. They found that the most prevalent maladaptive behaviors were being out of seat and talking to peers. Thus, they concluded that teachers want students to be seen but not heard. The model student, they contend, stays in his or her seat all day, has continuous eye contact with the teacher, attends to the teacher, is on task, doesn't talk to or look at peers, doesn't laugh or sing at inappropriate times, and passes silently in the halls. They accuse behavior modifiers of being instruments of the status quo, who help to maintain law and order at all costs. They suggest that the behaviors that should be reinforced in the schools (and that are currently neglected) are working independently, initiating conversations with others, helping others, and talking and playing with peers.

In a rejoinder to Winett and Winkler, O'Leary (1972) cited a number of research articles appearing in *JABA* that he claims Winett and Winkler ignored. The target behaviors of these studies were increases in (1) academic response rates (Lovitt & Curtiss, 1969), (2) talking (Reynolds & Risley, 1968), (3) use of descriptive adjectives in spontaneous speech (Hart & Risley, 1968), (4) instruction following (Zimmerman et al., 1969), (5) prosocial interactions (O'Connor, 1969), and (6) attendance and achievement test scores (O'Leary et al., 1969). O'Leary goes on to list numerous other studies which had as their objective behavior modification that resulted in making the subjects less dependent instead of more dependent on their environment. He also defends the necessity of training students to attend, since poor concentration, talking, and being out of seat have been shown to impede academic progress.

While the major portion of O'Leary's article is a rebuttal of the Winett and Winkler article, he does admit that their general message should be taken seriously, "viz., if the behavior modifier is to have maximal impact in institutional settings such as schools and hospitals, he must seriously question whether the behavior he is being asked to help change should really be changed" (p. 509). Before implementing a behavior modification program in the classroom, the teacher should ask herself whose interests are best served by the change in behavior, hers or the student's.

Teachers are easily threatened by students who question their authority by asking "Why?" whenever they are told to do something. They are also threatened by noise and movement in their classrooms that they consider excessive, or that was not initiated by them. Students who question authority, or who are noisy or active, probably elicit anxiety in a teacher because their behavior suggests to the teacher that he is not in control of his class. Losing control of one's class is probably the most frightening prospect a teacher can contemplate. We have been conditioned over the years to

Traditional target behaviors.

believe that noise, movement, and the questioning of authority are the three warning signs of an impending revolt in the classroom. Conversely, when students comply without question, sit still, and stay quiet, teachers perceive themselves as being in control. Perhaps this is why we are so quick to punish noncompliance or any questioning of our authority. Unfortunately, punishing such behavior in our students can create a class of passive conformists who are afraid to assert themselves with any adults or authority figures. This is hardly the kind of citizen we are supposed to be grooming to meet the challenges of the real world. Teachers must recognize that schools are primarily for the children, not for adults. This means that in any behavior management situation, the child is the individual of primary concern; "any appropriate target behavior must be one which is justifiable in terms of the demonstrable long-term well-being of the target child or population" (Harris & Kapche, 1978, p. 27).

Instead of only reinforcing behaviors such as staying in one's seat, raising one's hand, and being quiet, teachers should strengthen behaviors such as making positive comments to peers, engaging in assertive behavior with peers and adults (when appropriate), and using spontaneous audible language in group discussions. Again, many teachers are going to be threatened by these behaviors in their students. I recall an incident I observed a number of years ago which is a perfect example of a teacher who obviously felt threatened by spontaneous loud verbal exchanges in her students, even though this behavior was actually positive and represented no threat to the teacher's control.

A colleague and I were teaching gymnastics to a class of behavior-disordered children. On this particular occasion, we were teaching some basic vaults on a piece of apparatus called the "buck," which is a smaller version of the pommel horse without the pommels. The teacher of the class, a devout follower of behavior modification, was watching the lesson in the gym. She had earlier warned the class (without our knowledge) that talking out would not be allowed during the gymnastics lesson. If the students had something to say, they had to raise their hands. As the lesson wore on in silence, all of the students were experiencing success except for one overweight youngster we'll call Ralph, who continuously had difficulty getting over the buck. Each attempt would end in frustration and Ralph would walk dejectedly back to the end of the line of students. However, near the end of the period, Ralph finally succeeded in getting his bulk over the apparatus. This precipitated a number of excited congratulatory comments from his peers (e.g., "Atta way, Ralph!"). There was also applause and much cheering. In the next instant, the teacher was telling all the students who called out that they were losing 10 points for each of their talk-outs. We couldn't believe it! Ralph had hardly ever done anything in his life that resulted in cheers from his peer group. His peers, who usually heaped verbal abuse on him, seldom, if ever, made positive comments to anyone. Their talk-outs, in this instance, should have been rewarded, not punished. This is an example of a teacher acting in her own best interest instead of her students'. Talk-outs in the classroom may have been maladaptive in that they disrupted the learning environment and lowered academic achievement. However, talk-outs in the gym were not maladaptive. On the contrary, in this case they were more likely to be representative of adaptive behavior. If this teacher had taken the time to ask herself in whose interests she was acting, she might have acted differently.

The Fair Pair

Teachers spend an inordinate amount of time focusing on the negative. We tend to "catch kids being bad" and ignore them when they're being "good" (i.e., doing what we want them to). At an education conference a number of years ago, teachers were asked to list behaviors they wanted to work on with their students. The teachers as a group listed twice as many "bad" behaviors as "good" ones. Teachers frequently ask me for advice on how to change a negative behavior. "How can I stop him from hitting?" "What should I do about her calling out in class?" The focus always seems to be on getting the student to stop doing something "bad." The problem with always focusing on negative behaviors is that once you get rid of them, the student is left with nothing in its place. A student might enter your class with 30 social behaviors in her repertoire. Let's say that of the 30, 25 are positive behaviors she can use in school, such as asking permission to leave the room, raising her hand for help, following directives, and being on time to class. The remaining 5 are negative behaviors she should not use in school, such as hitting peers when provoked, talking with peers during study hall, swearing, stealing, and cheating on tests. If her teachers focus only on the negative and eliminate these 5 behaviors without replacing them with 5 positive behaviors, the student may leave the class at the end of the school year with fewer social behaviors than when she entered (25 instead of 30). Our objective as teachers is to have our students leave our classrooms with more behaviors than they had when they entered.

You might argue that the student who enters with 25 good behaviors and 5 bad behaviors and leaves at the end of the year without the 5 bad behaviors is actually better off than she was when she started. Theoretically speaking, she might be. Unfortunately, what usually happens in real life is that eliminating a negative behavior without replacing it with an incompatible positive behavior usually results in the return of the negative behavior. If you punish a student every time he hits a peer when he is provoked, you will eventually weaken his hitting behavior. However, if you don't teach him how to handle provocations in a positive manner, assuming that the provocations continue, you will find that he may do one of three things. He may return to his hitting behavior since he has nothing else to use in its place; he may resort to less physical forms of retaliation, such as threats or name calling; or he may try to hit without getting caught. If, instead of punishing the student every time he engages in provoked hitting, the teacher teaches him a positive response to provocation such as ignoring or being verbally assertive, the chances are that he will not go back to his old behavior or substitute any new negative responses. Not only will the maladaptive behaviors be extinguished, but the student will have replaced them with adaptive behaviors he didn't have in his repertoire at the beginning of the year.

All of this brings us to the concept of the *fair pair*. The term *pair* is obvious; we are talking about two things, in this case, two behaviors. The term *fair* refers to the notion that it is only fair to weaken a student's maladaptive behavior if you strengthen in its place an adaptive target behavior. Thus the term *fair pair* refers to a maladaptive behavior you intend to weaken and an incompatible or competing target behavior you intend to strengthen in its place. Some examples of fair pairs may be seen in Figure 3.3.

The Dead Man's Test

If you have trouble coming up with a fair-pair target behavior, you might use a little test affectionately known as the "dead man's test." The question posed by the dead man's test is this: Can a dead man do it? If the answer is yes, it doesn't pass the dead man's test and it isn't a fair pair; if the answer is no, you have a fair pair. For example, suppose that you wanted a fair-pair target behavior for "swears at peers." Let's say that you came up with the target behavior "does not swear at peers." Does this pass the dead man's test? No. A dead man could refrain from swearing at peers. What would be better? How about "speaks to peers without swearing"? This passes the dead man's test because a dead man does not have the power to speak.

There are two criteria for choosing a target pinpoint that passes the "So what?" test: (1) the behavior should be in the student's (and not just the teacher's) best interest, and (2) it should be a fair pair. It may be considered a fair pair if strengthening it will directly lead to weakening the maladaptive behavior and if it passes the dead man's test.

Performance Objectives

Once you have a fair-pair target pinpoint, you are ready to write it as a performance objective. The reason for doing this is so that you will know when the student's behavior has changed sufficiently to allow you to terminate instruction. As Mager says, "if you're not sure where you're going, you're liable to end up someplace else, and not even know it" (1962, p. vii). Teachers often assume that they know exactly what they want from students in terms of target behavior. For example, they want their students to "do their work," "look at me when I talk to them," "come to class prepared," "obey the rules," and "be on time." How much work must a student do, and under what conditions must this work be done, before the teacher may say that the target behavior has been reached? Must the student always look at the teacher when the teacher is talking? Is eye contact really a valid measure of attentiveness in the first place? What does "come to class prepared" actually mean? Does it mean remembering to bring the textbook, pencils, and paper, or a willingness to work

Is out of seat/is in seat

Eats with fingers/eats with fork and spoon

Bites fingernails/makes fist (when has urge to bite nails)

Teases or makes fun of peers/compliments peers

Steals (i.e., takes property of others without permission)/ requests permission to use others' property

Lies/tells truth

Cries when criticized/when criticized, will ask what he can do to improve

Does not complete assignments/completes assignments

Does not follow directions first time given/follows directions first time given

Is off task (i.e., eyes away from work)/is on task (i.e., eyes on work)

Calls out to get attention/raises hand to get attention

Hits peers when provoked/acts assertively (e.g., says "Stop it" or "I don't like it") when provoked

Punches own face when upset/tells others she is upset

Makes bowel movements in pants/uses toilet to make bowel movements

Picks nose/blows nose

Cheats (e.g., turns in work of others)/does own work

Disrupts learning environment (e.g., makes noises while others are trying to work)/occupies time quietly (e.g., reading) while others are trying to work

Destroys property of others/uses property of others without destroying it

Figure 3.3. Examples of fair-pair behaviors.

and a "sunny disposition"? What rules must be followed? How often and under what conditions? Until all of these questions are answered, the teacher may still not know where he's going. Without this knowledge, he might stop his behavior modification program too soon or continue using it too long. Neither situation benefits the student. Stopping a program before the target behavior is reached may result in an unsuccessful intervention program that turns off both the student and the teacher. Continuing a program after the target behavior has been reached wastes time and may inhibit internalization by making the student overly dependent upon extrinsic reinforcement.

Teachers write performance objectives for academic behaviors such as reading and math. It is every bit as important for them to write objectives for social behaviors as well. Up until now, many teachers have avoided writing objectives for social behaviors because they weren't included in formal instruction. This has changed dramatically with the growth of social skills training programs in special education classrooms. Students are now receiving formal instruction in social behaviors and it is important to determine how well they have learned their lessons. According to Mager, "if you are teaching skills which cannot be evaluated you are in the awkward position of being unable to demonstrate that you are teaching anything at all" (1962, p. 47). Unless target behaviors—academic or social—are written as performance objectives, they cannot be evaluated, and if they cannot be evaluated, you will never know if you have reached them.

Make sure you know how to write performance objectives before you tackle objectives for behaviors from the affective domain. If you have had little experience writing objectives or are considering the need of a refresher course, look at Mager (1962) or Howell et al. (1979), or simply use the objectives provided in Figure 3.4. Notice that the behavior is always stated as a verb in the objective and, if necessary, is described, defined, or amended with an example. This leaves little to the imagination. The conditions are important, too. It's not enough to say that a student will do something. You must say that she will do it "the first time asked" or "without being asked" or "without being reminded" or "without extrinsic consequences." Any of these conditions can make a big difference to the performance of the objectives.

In writing objectives, it is also important to establish criteria for acceptable performance (CAP). It's not enough to say that the student will "stay in his seat." How long must he stay in it? One minute? Ten minutes? One hour? Ten percent of the time observed? How do you decide which of these CAP is the most appropriate for a given student? How do you decide how long a student should stay on task or what is an adequate rate of spontaneous speech from a student who never speaks unless she is spoken to? One method is essentially the same as choosing CAP for an academic objective. You simply find a student or group of students who are already engaging in the target behavior and measure their performance in order to obtain a minimum standard to use with the target child. Instead of using a normative approach by choosing students at random, use the criterion-referenced approach of monitoring a small sample of those students who regularly engage in the target behavior. The specific methods used to monitor such behavior are discussed in detail in chapter 14. Another way of determining appropriate CAP is to base them on the individual student's needs. For example, if you wanted to determine how long the student should stay in his seat, you could simply ask yourself, "How long does he need to stay in his seat?" If his longest in-seat assignment takes him 15 minutes to complete, he needs to stay in his seat for a minimum of 15 minutes at a time.

Many teachers would argue that it's unnecessary to go to such lengths to determine appropriate CAP. They contend that a teacher should be able to arbitrarily determine the CAP for certain target behaviors. In some instances, I would agree. For example, no one would argue that the CAP for self-injurious behavior should be zero. The same can be said of unprovoked physically or verbally aggressive behavior if it appears to be maladaptive. Any teacher who has to deal with these behaviors doesn't need to conduct an ecological baseline to determine CAP. However, there are other behaviors for which teachers have, in the past, arbitrarily determined CAP that are questionable. For example, most teachers want 100% compliance. They want a student to comply with a request every time he or she is asked. They also tend to want students to be in their seats (when it's appropriate) 100% of the time observed. And they usually want students' talk-outs (i.e., calling out without raising their hands) to occur at a rate of zero per minute. Are these CAP realistic? More important, are they in the students' best interests? Do we really want a room full of robots who move and speak only when we push a button? Do we want to stifle the spontaneous reaction of a student who experiences success for the first time? Do we want to inhibit students from encouraging each other? Is it always necessary for a student to raise her hand, wait to be called on, and then ask for permission to give encouragement or praise a peer? Do we want to curb a student's assertiveness with peers or adults? Should students believe everything we tell them or can we be secure enough in ourselves to let them question us openly without fear of anarchy? There are enough sheep in the world. What we need are more leaders or, at the very least, more citizens who are not afraid to question the wisdom of those who lead. All potential change agents must consider these questions before they arbitrarily decide how "well" a child should behave.

In case I've lost you along the way, the following is a list of steps to follow when identifying and specifying behaviors for a behavior change project.

1. Pinpoint the maladaptive behavior.
   (Q) Does it pass the stranger test?
   (A) If yes, go on.
       If no, rewrite.

2. Evaluate the maladaptive pinpoint.
   (Q) Does it pass the "So what?" test? (i.e., does it fit the definition of *maladaptive?*)
   (A) If yes, go on.
       If no, stop and reevaluate the problem.

3. Pinpoint the target behavior.
   (Q) Does it pass the stranger test?
   (A) If yes, go on.
       If no, rewrite.

Maladaptive Behavior	Target Behavior	Objective
Calls out without raising hand	Raises hand and waits to be called on	Given a situation where the student wishes to communicate with the teacher in the classroom (e.g., answer a question asked of the class, ask a question of the teacher, or respond in a group discussion), he will raise his hand and wait to be called on before speaking. He will not make any noise, verbally or otherwise, to draw attention to himself while waiting. He will engage in this behavior 80% of the time observed over a 3-day period.
Noncompliance	Complies with directives	Given a directive by the teacher, the student will comply without having to be told a second time and within a time limit deemed acceptable by the teacher. She will engage in this behavior 100% of the time over a 5-day period with a weekend in between.
Physical aggression	Absence of physical aggression	Given a situation where the student is spending time among one or more of his peers in or out of the classroom, he will not engage in any physically aggressive behavior (e.g., hitting, kicking, pushing, biting). CAP – a rate of zero hits, kicks, pushes, or bites per minute for 2 weeks.
Verbal aggression	Absence of verbal aggression	Given a situation where the student is spending time among one or more of her peers in or out of the classroom, she will not engage in any verbally aggressive behavior (e.g., making threats or derogatory comments or raising her voice). CAP – a rate of zero threats or derogatory comments per minute and an average intensity level of 1 for loudness of voice over a 1-week period.
Swearing	Absence of swearing	Given any situation in school where the teacher is present, the student will not engage in any swearing behavior. CAP = a rate of zero curse words spoken per minute over a 5-day period.
Out of seat	Stays in seat	Given a situation in the classroom when it is appropriate for the student to stay in his seat, he will not leave his seat without permission from the teacher. He will engage in this behavior 90% of the time observed over a 3-day period.
Doesn't do work	Completes assignments	Given work assignments that the student is currently able to do, she will successfully complete all assignments and turn them in on time without being reminded by the teacher. CAP = 70% of assignments given during a 4-day period.
Acts impulsively	Reflects before acting	Given directions by the teacher to perform a task, the student will wait until all of the directions have been given before beginning the task. CAP = 100% of the directions given over a 1-day period.
Loses temper when angry	Displays anger without losing temper	Given a situation where the student is feeling anger, he will display his anger in a socially acceptable manner (i.e., directly at the source of his anger and verbally without using profanity or threatening gestures or language, or raising his voice). He will engage in this behavior 100% of the time observed over a 3-week period.

Figure 3.4. Examples of performance objectives. *Note.* CAP = criteria for acceptable performance.

Maladaptive Behavior	Target Behavior	Objective
Destroys property	Takes care of property	Given materials or equipment by the school (e.g., books, pencils, paper, desk, chair, crayons), the student will use them appropriately (i.e., as they were meant to be used) without deliberate destructiveness (e.g., writing or carving on desks or chairs, writing or marking on or in textbooks, breaking crayons, chewing erasers, tearing pages from books). She will engage in this behavior 100% of the time observed over a 1-month period.
Steals	Acquires things by asking for them	Given that the student wishes to acquire an article or object belonging to the teacher, the school, or a peer, he will ask for it appropriately (i.e., without using threatening language or gestures, profanity, or a raised voice). He will engage in this behavior 100% of the time observed over a 1-month period.
Lies	Tells the truth	Given a query from the teacher or a peer, the student will answer in a truthful manner. CAP = 100% of the time during a 2-week period.
Doesn't pay attention	Pays attention	Given a situation where another person is speaking to a group which includes the student, she will attend by looking at the speaker and be able to paraphrase or at least repeat what the speaker said when asked to do so. CAP = 100% of the time over a 1-week period.
Allows self to be pushed around	Asserts self	Given a situation requiring assertiveness on the part of the student, he will assert himself without becoming aggressive (i.e., by making his feelings known to the other party without raising his voice or using profanity or threatening language or gestures). CAP = 70% of the time over a 1-month period.
Disruptive in a group	Works cooperatively in a group	Given that the student is part of a group working toward a common goal (e.g., winning a game, painting a mural, completing a project, or solving a common problem), she will not engage in any behavior that would delay or hamper the attainment of that goal (e.g., not performing her appointed task or keeping others from performing theirs). CAP = 90% of the time over a 3-week period.

Figure 3.4. *Continued*

4. Evaluate the target pinpoint.
   (Q) Does it pass the "So what?" test? (i.e., is it a fair pair? is it in the student's best interest? does it pass the dead man's test?)
   (A) If yes, go on.
       If no, select and rewrite a new target pinpoint.

Chapter Three Self-Assessment

See Appendix A for acceptable responses.

1. Write a pinpoint that passes the stranger test for each of the following behaviors:

    a. Is off task:

    b. Is punctual:

    c. Talks out:

    d. Uses leisure time wisely:

    e. Is considerate of others:

    f. Lies:

    g. Steals:

    h. Talks loudly:

    i. Comes to class prepared:

    j. Is out of seat:

    k. Laughs inappropriately:

    l. Is responsible:

    m. Accepts criticism:

    n. Is clean:

    o. Acts mature:

    p. Is withdrawn:

    q. Has tantrums:

    r. Does good work:

    s. Has poor self-image:

    t. Is hostile:

continued next page

2. Write a fair-pair pinpoint for each of the following behaviors:

    a.   Is out of seat (e.g., bottom on chair with body facing front):

    b.   Does not complete assignments:

    c.   Calls out without raising hand:

    d.   Is late to class:

    e.   Hits peers when provoked:

    f.   Makes disparaging remarks to peers (e.g., "You're stupid."):

    g.   Gives up (e.g., stops working) when frustrated:

    h.   Directs attention away from task:

    i.   Does not speak unless spoken to:

    j.   Has tantrums (e.g., screams, cries) when request is denied:

    k.   Does not follow directives given:

    l.   Destroys property of others:

    m.   Is truant:

    n.   Acts passive when teased by peers (e.g., becomes anxious, looks to others for help):

    o.   Gives incorrect responses to questions:

    p.   Acts impulsively (e.g., starts responding before teacher has given all directions):

    q.   Eats food with hands:

    r.   Makes bowel movements in pants:

    s.   Bangs head when upset:

    t.   Picks nose:

continued next page

3. Write a performance objective for each of the following behaviors. Make up your own CAP.

   a.   Shares belongings with peers:

   b.   Raises hand without calling out:

   c.   Asserts self with peers:

   d.   Is on time to class:

   e.   Tells the truth:

   f.   Accepts criticism:

   g.   Gets along with peers:

   h.   Uses socially appropriate language:

   i.   Stays in seat:

   j.   Finishes work:

4. Explain what the "So what?" test is and how you would apply it to maladaptive and target behaviors.

chapter 4

Assessing Individuals

Upon successful completion of this chapter, the learner should be able to:

1. Write a task analysis for behaviors from the affective domain
2. Design valid methods and materials to conduct an informal assessment of behaviors from the affective domain
3. Describe in writing the task analytical model for assessing problem behaviors

Assessing Problem Behaviors

Assessment has traditionally played a minor role in the behavioral model. Even today it usually consists of nothing more than a simple analysis of baseline data. The prevalent attitude seems to be, "If you want to find out why a student misbehaves, simply watch what happens before and after the behavior occurs." The underlying assumption is that all student misbehavior is the result of inappropriate antecedent or consequent events in the student's environment. By identifying these events and changing them to more appropriate ones, the teacher is said to be able to modify the student's behavior. I wish all student misbehavior could be explained so easily. In my opinion, students misbehave for a variety of reasons, some of which have nothing to do with antecedent or consequent events. I offer the following hypothetical situation to illustrate my position.

Suppose that a teacher has 10 students in his class who seldom, if ever, turn in any completed homework. Suppose also that, unlike the teacher, we know the real reasons for this. The *first* student doesn't do his homework because he doesn't know how to do it. It's too hard for him. The *second* student, who is able to do the work, refuses to do it because she doesn't see any intrinsic value in doing it; she passes all of the tests at school without doing homework. The *third* student comes from a home environment where caring for six younger siblings while his mother is at work is con-

sidered more important than homework. Consequently, he never has the time to do it. The *fourth* student hates school and all of her teachers. She also believes that they hate her (some actually do) and that homework is their way of making her life miserable; therefore, she refuses to do any. The *fifth* student simply can't remember to do it. This fellow sometimes has trouble remembering where his classroom is. Despite having the ability, the *sixth* student doesn't expect to succeed at the tasks she's given for homework. Since she also believes that it's awful when you don't succeed, she tends to give up easily and consequently completes few homework assignments. The *seventh* student is so disorganized that he often loses his homework assignments, while the *eighth* student spends so much of the time daydreaming in school that she doesn't even know she's supposed to do any homework. Since the *ninth* student considers doing homework more aversive than the consequences of not doing it, he never does any. Finally, the *tenth* student is such a perfectionist that she does her homework assignments over and over until she gets so frustrated and confused that she quits in disgust. Consequently, she turns in assignments late or unfinished, or doesn't do any at all.

While all 10 of these students engage in the same behavior, they each have a different reason for doing so. Let's suppose, however, that their teacher doesn't know this; following the prevalent behaviorist attitude about diagnosis, he simply looks at the antecedent and consequent events surrounding the homework assignments. *What happens before each assignment?* The teacher writes the assignment on the board and tells the students to copy it down. Included in the assignment is what to do and when to turn it in. *What happens after each assignment is turned in?* The teacher makes a check mark next to the name of each student in the class who turns in an assignment and a zero next to the names of those who do not. Following the behaviorist assumption that all misbehavior is the result of inappropriate antecedent or consequent events, the teacher decides to make some changes. First, he decides to modify the directions given before each homework assignment by giving each student a written set of directions telling the student exactly what to do and when to turn the work in. He reads these directions out loud in class and asks if anyone has any questions about the homework assignment. Second, he puts his entire class on a token economy in which students earn points for homework completed. The points are then turned in at the end of the day for a backup reinforcer of the student's choice.

Since this case is hypothetical, I can make it come out any way I want. However, I do feel safe in predicting that if this were a real-life situation, the changes in antecedent and consequent events would not have produced any significant changes in the number of homework assignments completed by the "derelict" group. For example, all the tokens in the world wouldn't help the *first* student get his homework done as long as he doesn't know how to do it. The *second* student might be willing to do her homework for extrinsic rewards even though she doesn't see any intrinsic value in doing it. She would have nothing to lose and something to gain. However, nothing would help student number *three* as long as he doesn't have the time to do his work at home. The *fourth* student, although admittedly tempted by tokens, is so paranoid about teachers and school that she would probably view the token economy as a conspiracy to get her to do something against her wishes and would continue to refuse. The tokens might help student number *five* but only if his memory problem was caused by lack of motivation. Since nobody bothered to check this out, we can't be sure that the tokens would be effective. Something would have to be done about the *sixth* student's expectations before the token economy would work. We know that one's expectations are reinforced as well as one's behavior. Since this student doesn't expect to be reinforced, her behavior probably won't change regardless of how much she might want the tokens. What her teacher doesn't know is that she has an external locus of control. In other words, she tends to perceive the events in her life as being under the control of fate or chance. Because she does not believe that she has any control over what happens to her, she does not expect her behavior to bring her any rewards. Because of this she would probably continue to refuse to do any homework. The *seventh* student would be better off if he learned how to be more organized. As much as he wants to earn those tokens, he will probably continue to be derelict in doing his homework as long as he keeps misplacing his assignments. Student number *eight* first needs to be reinforced for on-task behavior in school. The tokens aren't going to help her if they are given for work done at home. The *ninth* student might still consider the homework too aversive to change his behavior. Nobody has ever bothered to determine why it's so aversive for him. Until they do, and something is done about this, it would be unrealistic to expect him to work for the

tokens. The *tenth* student doesn't need a token economy to motivate her. Her problem is definitely not a lack of motivation. Instead, she must learn how to recognize when a task is successfully completed and must stop telling herself that it's awful if things don't turn out exactly the way she wants. Without these changes, the tokens would probably not be effective.

The point of this hypothetical situation is to show that teachers should never implement an intervention unless they are reasonably certain why students misbehave. If they took the time to diagnose a student's behavior problem rather than simply assuming that they were using the wrong cue (antecedent) or reinforcer (consequence), they would greatly increase the chances of successful intervention. For those of you who are concerned about the time and effort this would involve, I can only quote a line from a television commercial for automobile parts: "You can pay me now or pay me later." In other words, if you don't take the time to diagnose more of the prerequisites necessary for the target behavior, your intervention is not likely to succeed. All that time and energy you put into the intervention will have been for nothing. You will either have to (1) admit defeat and refer the student to special education or, if you teach special education, refer the student to an agency outside of the school district; (2) try another intervention which probably will not succeed either; or (3) diagnose the student's behavior problem as you should have done in the first place. As I said, you either pay now or pay later!

For those of you who absolutely do not have the time to diagnose the behavior problems of each and every one of your students, let me make the following plea. If you intervene in your students' behavior problems successfully, that's great! However, if you should encounter one or two students who do not respond to your interventions, do not give up on them. Special education classes and state institutions are full of young people whose teachers gave up on them. If your intervention doesn't succeed in changing a student's maladaptive behavior, take the time to do an assessment. Surely you will agree that it's worth finding the time to do one or two assessments if it means the difference between a student's (and your) success or failure.

When I urge teachers to take the time to assess a student's behavior problem, I mean just that. *Teachers should do the assessment*—not the school psychologist or a medical doctor such as a psychiatrist or pediatrician. Most of the time, student misbehavior does not require the services of an MD or a PhD. The assessment I'm talking about is much simpler, but just as reliable, if not more so. It can be accomplished by the average classroom teacher with a modicum of training. This assessment procedure is based on the *task analytical* (TA) model (Howell et al., 1979), the underlying assumption of which is that students do not behave in the way we expect because they are lacking a prerequisite skill, knowledge, belief, expectation, perception, or value necessary for them to engage in the target behavior. Most teachers would not expect their students to successfully compute long division without first mastering their multiplication, subtraction, and division facts, or without knowing the steps in the operation. Neither would they expect their students to skip if they had not first mastered standing or hopping on alternate feet. Students are not expected to sound out words unless they have first mastered the sounds in isolation, know left-right progression, have auditory-sequential memory, can isolate (focus on) the symbols one at a time, and can blend all of the phonemes into words. Why then should teachers expect their students to be on time to class if they can't tell time, can't estimate how long it takes to get there, do not value punctuality, or do not consider the class a rewarding experience? Without all of the necessary prerequisites, token reinforcement won't be very effective.

The Task Analytical Model

The flow chart in Figure 4.1 shows each step in the TA process. The first step is to identify and specify the maladaptive behavior so that it passes both the stranger and "So what?" tests, described in chapter 3.

The second step is to decide what you want the student to do. In other words, specify the target behavior. It must also pass the stranger and "So what?" tests.

Once you have decided what behavior you want the student to engage in, you are ready for the third step, task analyzing the target behavior. If you have never done task analysis before, read chapter 7 in *Evaluating Exceptional Children: A Task Analysis Approach* (Howell et al., 1979). If you have written task analyses before, you should have little difficulty applying this technique to social behaviors. Simply list all of the essential skills, knowledge, beliefs, perceptions, expectations, and values the student should have to successfully engage in the target behavior. I have given you a head start by listing in Figure 4.2 many of the prerequisites that are common to most target behaviors. Once you have specified your target behavior, it becomes a simple matter of looking at Figure 4.2 and determining whether or not each of the prerequisites listed there is an essential prerequisite for your target behavior. Remember, I have not listed all of the possible prerequisites for all of the possible target behaviors. Figure 4.2 is only meant to get you started. There may be other prerequisites common only to your particular target behavior that do not appear in Figure 4.2.

Once you have completed the third step, you are ready to evaluate the current status of each prerequisite. Simply ask yourself whether or not the student currently has the prerequisite. This determination may be based upon your judgment (assuming that you know the student well enough); when in doubt, you may wish to conduct an informal assessment. Figure 4.2 also provides a number of examples of informal assessment methods you might wish to use. If an assessment is necessary, be sure to include some criteria for acceptable performance (CAP). These may be determined arbitrarily or by standardizing the assessment on a few of your students who have the prerequisite being measured. If your student passes the assessment, you may assume that he or she also has the prerequisite; if not, you may assume that the prerequisite is lacking.

The last step in the TA model is to write a performance objective for each of the prerequisites the student is lacking. You will need to remediate these deficits before you can work on the target behavior. If you determine that the student has all of the prerequisites necessary to engage in the target behavior, you may then work directly toward modification of the target behavior.

Prerequisites

Before I demonstrate how the model might work in a hypothetical case, I would like to explain the rationale behind each of the prerequisites listed in Figure 4.2. Again, let me say that they are common to most target behaviors expected of students in school, although you may very well find other prerequisites that are specific to a particular target behavior. This is an important topic because it will help you to appreciate the need for assessment through an awareness of the complexity of student behavior. Keep in mind that the prerequisites in Figure 4.2 are not listed in any particular order. My advice is to consider the essential prerequisites in doing your task analysis and then look at the desirable prerequisites if time permits. Lack of a desirable prerequisite will probably prevent a student from internalizing a target behavior. However, not having an essential prerequisite will make it virtually impossible for the student to engage in the target behavior under any set of circumstances.

1. *The student knows and understands what behavior is expected of him.* The first prerequisite listed in Figure 4.2 is certainly common to all social behaviors. Teachers often say, "Oh, he knows what he's supposed to do. He's just being difficult." Sometimes they are right but quite often the student doesn't know or understand how he's supposed to act. Teachers are not always consistent when it comes to rules. Some teachers have differ-

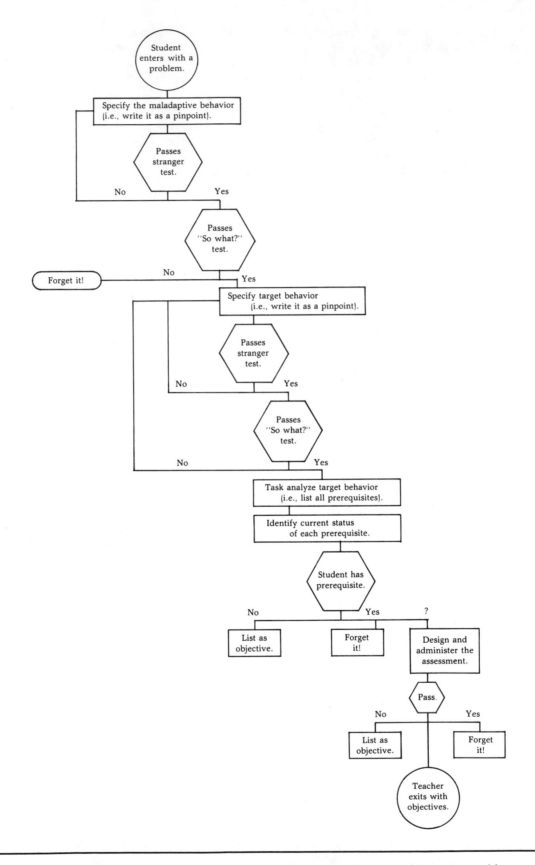

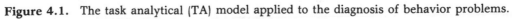

Figure 4.1. The task analytical (TA) model applied to the diagnosis of behavior problems.

Prerequisite	Assessment
1. Student must know and understand what behavior is expected of him. *Essential*	a. Ask the student to repeat the rules to you. He should be able to do so without any prompting from you. If the student is unable to produce the desired response, give him some choices and ask him to identify the correct one. For example, "Should you be in your seat during math or is it all right for you to be out of it?" He should respond correctly 100% of the time he is asked. b. Ask him to tell you the rules in his own words. By paraphrasing the rules he will demonstrate an understanding that may not be present when he simply repeats them. c. If he has difficulty expressing himself verbally, ask him to name the students in the class who are and are not following the rules. If he doesn't know their names, point to a student and say, "Is she following the rule?" He can simply answer yes or no or nod his head. Do this without alerting the students in your classroom so that you have examples of some who are following the rules and some who are not. When necessary, use pictures of instances and not-instances of children following rules, especially with younger students or those with expressive language problems.
2. The student should know and understand why you want her to engage in the target behavior. *Desirable*	a. Ask her, "Why is it important for you to stay in your seat during math period?" She should be able to answer to your satisfaction. Again, if the student is very young or has an expressive language problem, give her some choices and ask her to identify the correct one. For example, "Is it important for you to be in your seat during math period because you would disturb the other students who are working?" (Yes) "Is it important for you to be in your seat during math period because I won't know who sits at your desk if you're not in your seat?" (No) b. If possible, have her explain in her own words the reasons for the rule. This is a better test of comprehension than if she simply repeats a reason she was told.
3. The student should value the target behavior as much as the teacher does or at least should not hold any conflicting values. *Desirable*	a. Give the student a list of behaviors (including the target behavior) and have him rate them according to their importance to him. Do the same thing yourself and compare ratings. You should both place the same value on the target behavior. b. Give the student a number of hypothetical descriptions of students and ask him which of the hypothetical students he identifies with or would most like to be. Do this exercise yourself and compare your responses with the student's responses. They should be compatible.
4. The student must be aware of her behavior (both maladaptive and target). She must know when she is engaging in each. *Essential*	a. Ask the student either during or immediately after the maladaptive or target behavior has occurred what she is doing or what she has done. The student should be able to verbally or otherwise communicate accurately what behavior she was engaged in. The obvious problem here is that the student may be aware of her maladaptive behavior but may lie about it in order to avoid punishment. During this assessment period you must reassure the student that you will not punish her as long as she tells the truth. b. Instead of (a) or in addition to it, have the student monitor her own behavior during a given amount of time when she is likely to engage in the maladaptive or target behavior. Monitor her behavior also and compare it with her records. They should be virtually the same. A modification of this approach would be to ask her at the end of the day or the end of a given period of time (e.g., 15, 30, or 60 minutes) how many times she engaged in the maladaptive and target behaviors. You also monitor her behavior and compare your data with hers. They should agree.

Figure 4.2. Common prerequisites and assessments for target behaviors.

Prerequisite	Assessment
5. The student must be capable of controlling his own behavior. There should be no internal or external variables beyond the student's control that influence his behavior (e.g., a metabolic disorder or food allergy; seizure activity or other neurological involvement; environmental discomfort, such as extreme cold or heat, new prescription glasses, ill-fitting clothes, uncomfortable furniture, medicinal side effects, or physical illness; or extreme anger or anxiety that can only be relieved at the present time through emitting the maladaptive behavior). *Essential*	a. Consult with the student's parents, the school nurse, or the family physician. b. Examine the student's cumulative record folder or health history. c. Examine the environment. Is there enough light? Is the room too hot or too cold? Is the student's desk or chair too small or too large? Does he have adequate room in which to work? Is the noise or movement level in the room too distracting? Does he have adequate materials with which to work? d. Keep a daily record of foods eaten at school—when, how much, and what was eaten. e. Observe the student for signs of extreme emotional lability (i.e., mood swings) or of emotions that are consistently the same (e.g., depressive states).
6. The student must know the consequences for engaging in the target behavior and consider them rewarding. *Essential*	a. Ask her, "What happens when you turn your work in on time?" She should respond to your satisfaction. If the student is unable to produce the desired response, give her some choices and ask her to identify the correct one. For example, "When you turn your work in on time, do you get a chance to correct your mistakes?" (Yes) "When you turn your work in on time, do you get a passing grade?" (No) b. Ask the student to list things she considers rewarding in school. If she has trouble writing, have her dictate them to you. If she has difficulty doing this, give her a list of rewards. The latter should include all of the rewards a student conceivably receives in a school setting. They should be appropriate for her age. Have her check those she considers rewarding. She should include all those rewards you have used with her in the past.
7. The student must know the consequences for engaging in the maladaptive behavior and consider them aversive. *Essential*	a. Ask him, "What happens when you fight here in school?" He should respond to your satisfaction. If the student is unable to produce the desired response, give him some choices and ask him to identify the correct one. For example, "When you fight here at school, do you get sent to the office?" (Yes) "When you fight here at school, do we call your parents?" (Yes) b. Ask him to list things he considers aversive. If he has trouble writing, have him dictate them to you. If you find that this inhibits him from responding, give him a list of aversive consequences. This should include all of the "punishers" a student could conceivably receive in a school setting. They should be appropriate for his age. Have him check those he considers aversive. He should include all those punishers you have used with him in the past.

Figure 4.2. *Continued*

Prerequisite	Assessment
8. The student must not consider the target behavior more aversive than engaging in the maladaptive behavior. Conversely, the maladaptive behavior must not be considered more rewarding than the target behavior. *Essential*	a. Give the student a list of behaviors including the target and maladaptive behaviors and ask her to rate them according to preference of performance with the least preferred behavior rated last. The target behavior should not be rated lower than the maladaptive behavior. b. Give the student a number of pairs of options and have her choose the option from each pair that she prefers. Make sure that the target behavior is listed as an option in several of the pairs. For example, "Which would you prefer to do: try to do some work that you know is difficult, or not do the work and accept the failing grade?"
9. The student must know how to engage in the target behavior. *Essential*	Task analyze the work assigned or the directive given. List all of the prerequisite skills or knowledge the student will need. Through formal or informal assessment, determine whether or not he has all of the necessary prerequisites.
10. The student should not hold any belief that is incompatible with or contrary to the target behavior. *Desirable*	a. Prepare a list of beliefs commonly held by students. Have the student indicate her degree of agreement or disagreement with these beliefs, using statements such as, "No matter how hard I try, I can't change the way I am," and "You shouldn't let people who do things you don't like get away with it." Statements should be followed with labels such as "Strongly Agree," "Agree," "Disagree," and "Strongly Disagree." Be sure that you include a number of statements (i.e., beliefs) that are incompatible with or contrary to the target behavior but not so many that the student will readily determine the true intent of your testing and give you the responses she thinks you want to hear. b. Ask her, "Why do you feel that you have to hit another student who calls you a name?" She may be candid with you and reply honestly. If she won't cooperate, try a third-person approach. Discuss a "hypothetical" student who engages in similar behavior and ask the student to tell you why she believes the hypothetical student behaves the way she or he does. For example, "Jesse calls Raul a 'punk.' Raul socks Jesse even though he knows he'll get into trouble for it. Why do you think Raul socked Jesse even though he knew he'd get into trouble?" Possible responses (with leading questions you ask): "Because Jesse called him a punk." ("What's so bad about that?") "If a kid calls you a punk you can't let him get away with it!" ("Why not?") "People will think you're chicken." ("What difference does it make what people think?") "A lot!"
11. The student must perceive the target behavior as a viable option (i.e, a solution) when he is confronted with a problem. *Essential*	a. State a problem in the third person. For example, "A student is being teased by his classmates. Tell me as many different things that he could do to solve his problem as you can." The student should include the target behavior as one possible solution. b. Be more direct and ask him what he could have done to solve his problem. For example, "Instead of running out of the room like that, what could you have done?" The student should include the target behavior as one possible solution.
12. The student must be able to remember to engage in the target behavior. *Essential*	Periodically quiz the student during the day about the target behavior. For example, "What are you supposed to bring with you to class?" or "What is it you need to do if you want help?" The student should always answer correctly without hesitation.

Figure 4.2. *Continued*

ent rules for different students. This double standard often leads to confusion. Why is it acceptable for one student to leave his seat during a class period and not acceptable for another student to do so? I'm not suggesting that it isn't sometimes necessary to vary the rules. I'm merely suggesting that we don't always communicate this to the concerned parties. "How come you don't yell at him when he gets out of his seat but you always yell at me?" "Why can't I talk? You didn't tell them to be quiet." I don't know about you but I'm the type of person who needs a lot of structure. I always feel more secure when I know what behavior is acceptable and unacceptable in different situations and settings. At various times in our lives we have literally been told how to behave. On other occasions we have simply copied our peers' behavior. However, there are many students who, for one reason or another, don't learn as easily from their peer group or don't even know which peers to emulate. These students may need to be told which behaviors are appropriate and which are not.

In addition to telling the student what you want her to do (or not do), it is necessary to make sure that she understands what you have told her. Again, not all of our students were created equal when it comes to intelligence and receptive language. While some of them are smart enough and are able to process language adequately, they don't always listen (i.e., attend) to us. The student who is told what to do may not have listened to the teacher or she may have listened but not understood the complexity or abstract quality of the directions. Therefore, it is imperative that before you consider a "misbehaving" student incorrigible, you first determine whether or not she knows and understands what behavior you expect from her.

2. The student understands why you want her to engage in the target behavior. While it is not essential that the student know and understand the reasons or rationale for your rules or directives, it certainly would help if she did. "Why do I have to stay in my seat during study hall? That's dumb!" "He called me a name. Why can't I hit him?" Students are always asking us "Why?" As a parent, I'm constantly being asked questions such as "Why can't I stay up to watch that movie?" I have to be prepared to answer these questions or my children may think I'm simply being mean or arbitrary or just exercising my power as a parent. What's worse, they'll never appreciate the fact that I have their best interests at heart. "You can't sleep over at Shelly's because you've already slept out twice this month and you haven't been getting enough sleep lately. You're just getting over a virus which made you miss three days of school this week. You're behind in your schoolwork and we both decided in September that if your schoolwork suffered, you would cut back on your social activities."

Does the student know and understand the rules?

My daughter will still protest that she didn't understand but I know from experience that this usually means that she understood what I've said but didn't like it. I can accept the fact that she doesn't always agree with me; what's important is that she knows and understands my reasons. Not all students will be capable of comprehending your reasons for wanting them to do or not do certain things. However, I do believe that for those students who can comprehend, giving them reasons can often mean the difference between compliance and noncompliance. Put yourself in your students' place. How would you feel if your boss told you, "Never mind why. Just do it!"?

3. The student values the target behavior as much as the teacher does or at least does not hold any conflicting values that would inhibit him from engaging in the target behavior. This is desirable, although not essential. Consider the following example. Joey's teacher wants him to be quiet during study hall. He knows what behavior is expected of him and he also knows why he's supposed to behave that way. If you ask Joey what he's supposed to do during study hall and why, he'll say in his own words something about being quiet so that he and the other students can get their work done. Unfortunately, while Joey knows what to do and why he should do it, he doesn't value achievement as much as his peers or his teacher and consequently doesn't care whether or not he or they get their work done. Joey is a failure-oriented student. Because of a learning problem experienced early in his schooling, he has had very little opportunity to achieve and therefore has received very little payoff for getting his work done. It is true that you may be able to get Joey to be quiet during study hall by using the right punisher or reinforcer but if you want him to internalize this behavior so that it will maintain and generalize to other settings, it would help if he valued this behavior as much as you do.

"What do you mean you think school is dumb? When I was your age, I was a straight "A" student.

Does the student value the target behavior?

4. *The student is aware of her maladaptive or target behavior.* Suppose that you want a student who frequently uses profanity to eliminate swear words from her conversation and use a more appropriate and socially acceptable vocabulary. Won't the student have to be aware of her swearing before she can change it? I've worked with students from home environments where swearing is as commonplace as eating and sleeping. It is so commonplace, in fact, that neither the student nor the family members are aware of their swearing when they do it! Five minutes after you reprimand this student for using profanity she does it again. You look at her in disbelief. Is she crazy? retarded? obstinate? It's quite possible that she isn't aware she's doing it. Or she may not understand the distinction between swearing and other expressions—that is, what words we consider to be swearing.

On the other side of the coin, it is important for the student to be aware of the target behavior when she's engaging in it. For example, if you wanted a student who yells a lot to use a more moderate voice in the classroom, it would be helpful if she knew when she was yelling and when she was using the "right voice."

It would also be helpful if a student knew when she was "accepting criticism," "getting along with her peers," and "being assertive," among other things.

5. *The student is able to bring his own behavior under control.* There must be nothing beyond his control that keeps him from engaging in the target behavior, assuming that he wants to. For example, a student who does not get enough sleep may find it difficult to attend to a task even though he wishes to do it. Another student may find it difficult "getting along with" his peers because of the frequent and extreme mood swings he experiences as a result of poor eating habits. He may indulge in too much junk food, have a food allergy, or suffer from a metabolic condition that produces erratic behavior. I have observed this situation first-hand since my son has diabetes. There has been a marked improvement in his behavior since he limited his intake of sugar. While still a sensitive young man, he is now less likely to overreact to life's "bad tricks" than he was in the past. Some people attribute this to maturity but I believe that much of it has resulted from his improved eating habits. Don't misunderstand. I'm not suggesting that we have no expectations for these children. I once had a student in a class of what was then termed "neurologically impaired" students tell me that I shouldn't expect him to stay in his seat because he had a "little bump" on his brain. I didn't think then and I don't think now that a bump on the brain, a food allergy, or lack of sleep should preclude a student from engaging in appropriate school behavior. I merely make the point that all too often when our students misbehave we make the assumption that they are being rotten kids and we punish them; however, it is quite possible that something beyond their control is causing or contributing to the misbehavior. Once you find the cause, it is often quite possible to do something about it. In addition to neurological or physiological problems that might keep a student from engaging in the target behavior, emotional problems often make it difficult for students to bring their behavior under control. An enraged student who physically attacks his peers when he's teased is going to have difficulty being verbally assertive (i.e., telling them to stop) or ignoring them. Similarly, an overly anxious student who is withdrawn in the presence of her peers is going to have difficulty engaging in spontaneous speaking. A frustrated student who impulsively tears up his paper after making a mistake is going to have difficulty asking for help. In short, it is unrealistic to expect a student who can't control his or her emotions to be able to control his or her behavior.

6. *The student knows the consequences of engaging in the target behavior and considers them rewarding.* Some students engage in the target behavior so seldom (if ever) that they are virtually unaware of the positive consequences of their actions. Others might have engaged in

the target behavior on occasion but received inconsistent rewards from their teachers, parents, or peer group when they did. For this reason they may be unsure of the consequences of engaging in the target behavior. In other cases, the student may know what happens when he engages in the target behavior but he doesn't consider the consequences particularly rewarding. What is rewarding to his teachers, parents, or peer group may not always be rewarding to him. For example, gushing praise on an adolescent student may actually be aversive. The opportunity to go out to recess after work completion may not be rewarding to a student who is uncomfortable with her peers. If the student doesn't know the consequences of engaging in the target behavior or doesn't consider them rewarding, he may see no reason to behave as expected.

7. *The student knows the consequences of engaging in the maladaptive behavior and considers them aversive.* Teachers are sometimes inconsistent in consequating misbehavior. If the student doesn't know what happens when she misbehaves, how can these consequences have any effect on her behavior? Also, a particular student may be functioning at too low a developmental level to make the connection between what she does and what happens to her. Another problem is that what is aversive to the teacher may not be aversive to the student; while the student may know the consequences of her misbehavior, she may not consider them aversive enough to stop.

8. *The student does not consider the target behavior more aversive than the maladaptive behavior.* If you want the student to engage in the target behavior, he should not consider it aversive to do so. At least he should not consider the target behavior more aversive than engaging in the maladaptive behavior. For example, a student may be "punished" with a failing grade for not turning in his work assignments. However, because these assignments are too difficult for the student, he experiences a great deal of frustration in doing them. Each time he tries one, he gives up, thinking he's stupid. After a while, he simply stops doing them altogether. In this instance, the failing grade is not as aversive to the student as doing the work. Because the failing grade is considered an aversive stimulus by the teacher, the teacher thinks that the student is either lazy, crazy, or stupid when the grade has no effect. The teacher doesn't realize that there may be something more aversive to the student than the failing grade. There is also the possibility that the student might find the maladaptive behavior more rewarding than the target behavior. I can empathize with the student who feels like this. I'm usually rewarded (at least intrinsically) for controlling my temper but there are many times when it feels so good to let go that I find it irresistible.

9. *The student knows how to engage in the target behavior.* If the target behavior is completing work assignments, the student must know how to do the work. If it is being assertive with his peers, he must know what to say. If it is asking for help instead of giving up or having a tantrum when she becomes frustrated, she must know how to ask. The student must know how to do whatever it is you want him or her to do. Don't be too quick to say, "Oh, he knows how." If he has been engaging in the maladaptive behavior for years, he hasn't had much practice using the target behavior. Students come from different environments with different skills. Teachers cannot make the assumption that all of them know how to engage in the same wide variety of behaviors. If they don't do what you want them to, they may not know how.

10. *The student does not hold any belief incompatible with the target behavior.* If you want the student to internalize the target behavior so that someone doesn't always have to be around to reward her, she must not hold any belief that is incompatible with the target behavior. For example, if you want the student to complete her work assignments and to persist in the face of adversity instead of giving up, she must believe that there is a relationship between her behavior and what happens to her. If, instead, she believes that what happens to her is controlled by fate or chance, she may simply consider herself unlucky and give up. The degree to which an individual believes that he or she is able to influence the outcome of situations is referred to by social learning theorists as *locus of control* (Rotter, 1966). Students who believe that they have little or no influence over the outcome of the situations in their lives are referred to as *externals*. These youngsters believe that if something good happens to them they are lucky and if something bad happens, it's the teacher's fault. "I don't do too good in her class 'cause she don't like me." Students who have external locus of control may not only fail to internalize target behaviors; in addition, they may not even respond to extrinsic consequences since they are convinced that they have little control over the rewards and punishments they receive.

Locus of control is not the only belief that can influence target behavior. Students who believe "it's terrible if things don't go my way" may never learn to accept criticism. Others who think "schoolwork is dumb" or "school is dumb" may continue to be truant or tardy, come to class unprepared, or fail to do their work. The student who believes "it's terrible when I fail" may not do his work either, and the one who thinks "it's terrible if everybody doesn't like me" may continue to be the class clown and find it difficult to refrain from calling out or making faces during a group discussion. The student who believes: "If people do things to me that I don't like, they must be bad people" will have a hard time learning how to get along with her peers without acting physically or verbally aggressive toward them. Likewise, if a student believes: "It's not macho to walk away from a fight" or "It's cool to beat up on guys," he will have trouble staying out of fights. All of these students will have difficulty engaging in the target behavior because they hold a belief that is incompatible with it, a belief that either encourages them to engage in the maladaptive behavior or prevents them from engaging in the target behavior.

11. *The student must perceive the response to be a viable behavioral option.* Many target behaviors are student responses to problem situations. In order for any student to respond appropriately in a problem situation, he or she must perceive the response to be a viable behavioral option (i.e., a possible solution). For example, a student faced with the frustrating problem of what to do when confronted with a difficult school assignment may not perceive that asking for help is a viable option. Another student faced with the problem of peers who tease him may not see assertiveness or ignoring the behavior as viable options. A psychological construct called the *availability heuristic* occurs when people select the behavioral options that are the easiest for them to recall (Tuersky & Kahneman, 1973). Selection is thought to be a function of past experience. In other words, students who come from environments where giving up or having tantrums have been modeled for them are most likely to perceive giving up or having tantrums as the only viable options when they are confronted with a frustrating event such as a difficult work assignment. They don't perceive other options such as asking for help, being persistent, or taking a work break because these options haven't been consistently or dramatically modeled for them in the past. The same may be said for students who come from environments where verbal or physical aggression is consistently used to "solve" an interpersonal conflict. When these students find themselves in such situations they tend to perceive abusive and provocative language or physical attack as the only solutions to the problem. Telling a student how to behave in a given situation is not enough. The student should be able to perceive as many possible solutions by himself when the need arises.

12. *The student must remember to engage in the target behavior.* Those of you who had a course in learning theory may recall the story of the child who always dropped her coat on the floor after she entered her house. Her mother, annoyed at this behavior, scolded her often and made her go back and pick up her coat. However, this practice was not effective and the coat-

dropping behavior continued. Finally, the mother discovered that if she made the girl put on her coat, go back outside, reenter the house, take off her coat, and hang it up properly, she would eventually remember to do so on her own. This story illustrates the power of conditioning in the learning chain. The old behavioral chain was: enter house → drop coat → see mother → mother says, "Pick up coat" → pick up coat → hang up coat. This chain had been repeated so many times in the past that the child was virtually "locked into" her behavior (pun intended). The only way she could remember to hang up her coat was for her mother to break the old chain and replace it with a new one: enter house → keep coat on → approach closet → hang up coat. When students continue to call out instead of raising their hands, leave their work areas in a mess, or come to class unprepared, we often assume that they don't care about the way they behave. Why else wouldn't they do what we want? Although some students don't care, there are many who do; however, like the girl in the story, they may be so locked into an old behavior chain that they find it difficult (if not impossible) to remember to engage in the target behavior unless we are there to remind them. Often, because the reminders are perceived (sometimes rightly) as a form of nagging, the student may become so angry at the teacher that he or she eventually does stop caring and we have a case of self-fulfilling prophecy.

A Case Study: Rosario

Before I describe how the TA model might work in a hypothetical case study, let me say that there are scores of case studies depicting the actual use of the model. This is not theoretical. The model works! It has been applied by many teachers on their students and by my graduate students on their friends and relatives. A number of these real-life case studies appear in Appendix C. I am using a hypothetical case study in this chapter because it makes it easier to illustrate how the model works.

Rosario was a 13-year-old male student in a self-contained class for the emotionally handicapped where he physically attacked his peers an average of three times per day. Subsequent teacher observation indicated that Rosario's fighting was usually in response to peer teasing. At first, the teacher wanted to modify the peer teasing instead of Rosario's fighting because the teasing precipitated the fighting. However, she eventually decided that this would not be in Rosario's best interests because wherever he went he could conceivably be teased by his peers; the teacher would not always be around to modify the behavior of all the people with whom he would come in contact. Therefore, a more permanent solution would be to change Rosario's physically aggressive response. However, before this could be done, the teacher had to find out why Rosario responded to peer teasing with a physical attack. She could simply have said that he behaved the way he did because he was emotionally disturbed. After all, that's why he was put in her class in the first place! However, this knowledge didn't help her plan an intervention program for Rosario. How does one begin to change emotional disturbance? Instead, she was looking for something more specific—a behavior (or lack of behavior), an attitude, or a belief that she could measure. If she couldn't measure a behavior, she wouldn't know whether she had changed it. And if she couldn't tell whether she had changed it, why bother to attempt a change in the first place? Rosario's teacher could have rationalized that his behavior was caused by his emotional disturbance and that time spent with a psychiatrist or psychologist would eventually render him free of the emotional handicap. However, Rosario was a student in her class and she was responsible for teaching him to his full potential. She also was responsible for teaching his peers, and there was no doubt that Rosario's physically aggressive behavior in response to peer teasing made it more difficult and sometimes impossible for her to carry out this responsibility. With all this in mind, Rosario's teacher set out to assess his problem using the TA model. Her goal was to identify what prerequisite skills, knowledge, beliefs, values, expectations, and perceptions Rosario might be lacking that inhibited his adaptive behavior.

After writing a target behavior for Rosario the teacher task analyzed it by listing all of the prerequisites he needed in order to successfully engage in it. These prerequisites were listed on a worksheet similar to the one shown in Figure 4.3.

The next step was to determine the current status of each prerequisite. In other words, did Rosario have the prerequisite or not? The teacher went through the list and wrote "yes," "no," or "?" next to each prerequisite in the column marked "Current Status." This may be seen in Figure 4.4. Notice that she defended each "yes" or "no" with a brief supportive comment. You might say that she was only thinking out loud, but she felt that this was a good way to ensure her objectivity. In other words, she wanted to make sure there was actual evidence that Rosario did or did not have the prerequisite in question. As you can see from Figure 4.4 Rosario had prerequisites 1, 5, 6, and 14 but was lacking prerequisites 8 and 9. His teacher was in doubt about prerequisites 2, 3, 4, 7, 10, 11, 12, and 13. This brought her to the hardest part of the operation, the informal assessment.

Rosario's teacher now had to find out whether or not he had all of the prerequisites about which she was in doubt. Since there weren't any standardized commercially available assessment tools she could use, she had to design her own. Her methods and her materials are described in Figures 4.5 through 4.8. The assessment tools used in this diagnosis were not standardized on a large population of randomly selected students. In fact, they weren't standardized at all. Therefore, there were no norms or data regarding validity or reliability. How, then, could the teacher be certain that the results of her diagnosis were valid? First, she administered several of the instruments that dealt with values, perceptions, expectations, or beliefs. She realized that such affective variables would be subject to change over time and that they were sensitive to the mood Rosario was in. Therefore, she administered these instruments more than once over a period of time and, ostensibly, across moods, allowing her to evaluate their test-retest reliability. When Rosario's responses to the items on her assessment instruments changed from one time to the next, she knew that the results were not reliable. Without reliability, there could be no validity.

Second, Rosario's teacher evaluated the validity of his performance on these instruments by matching each response against what she had observed about him in the past. She purposely included "reality checks" as items in each assessment. These were items to which she already knew the answers. If Rosario gave an "incorrect" answer to reality-check items, the teacher could assume that his responses on the test in general were not a true reflection of his values or beliefs. In other words, the test results would be invalid. By taking these precautions, Rosario's teacher was able to ensure that her assessment yielded valid results. If you're still not convinced, contrast this procedure with the traditional diagnostic practice of administering personality measures, such as projectives, that have little evidence of validity (or even reliability) and that are given by a stranger in an alien setting on one occasion.

After Rosario's teacher finished conducting her informal assessment, she entered the results on the worksheet (see Figure 4.9). Notice that Rosario passed the assessments for prerequisites 2, 4, 7, and 11 but did not pass for prerequisites 3, 10, 12, and 13. What does all of this mean? First, Rosario holds conflicting values that inhibit him from engaging in the target behavior. He considers it more important to fight with students who tease him than to ignore them or tell them to stop teasing him. He also feels that it is more important for people to be afraid of him than to be nice to him and he cares that people should not think he's a punk. He considers it more important to be macho, believing that it's better to fight with another student than to stay out

Student ___ROSARIO___ Evaluator ___MS. MILLER___ Date ___NOV., '89___

Target Pinpoint ___WHEN R. IS TEASED (I.E., CALLED NAMES) BY HIS PEERS, HE WILL IGNORE OR ASSERT HIMSELF (I.E., TELL THEM TO STOP W/O USING PROVOCATIVE LANGUAGE) AND W/O PHYSICAL ATTACKS 100% OF THE TIME.___

Prerequisites	Current Status	Assessments	Results
① R. KNOWS & UNDERSTANDS THE SCHOOL RULE RE FIGHTING.			
② R. KNOWS & UNDERSTANDS THE REASON FOR THE RULE.			
③ R. VALUES TARGET BEHAVIOR AS MUCH AS I DO (OR AT LEAST DOES NOT HOLD ANY CONFLICTING VALUES THAT WOULD INHIBIT HIM FROM ENGAGING IN THE TARGET BEHAVIOR).			
④ R. IS AWARE OF HIS BEHAVIOR (I.E., HE KNOWS WHEN HE'S FIGHTING, IGNORING, OR BEING ASSERTIVE).			
⑤ R. IS CAPABLE OF CONTROLLING HIS FIGHTING BEHAVIOR (I.E., HE CAN STOP HIMSELF W/O BEING RESTRAINED).			
⑥ R. KNOWS THE CONSEQUENCES OF FIGHTING W. PEERS.			
⑦ R. CONSIDERS THEM AVERSIVE.			
⑧ R. KNOWS THE CONSEQUENCES OF IGNORING AND/OR BEING ASSERTIVE WHEN PEERS TEASE.			
⑨ R. CONSIDERS THEM REWARDING.			
⑩ R. DOES NOT CONSIDER FIGHTING W/PEERS REWARDING OR LESS AVERSIVE THAN TARGET BEHAVIOR.			
⑪ R. IS ABLE TO PERCEIVE ALTERNATIVE SOLUTIONS TO TEASING PROBLEM (OTHER THAN FIGHTING).			
⑫ R. EXPECTS IGNORING AND/OR BEING ASSERTIVE TO BE REWARDING (I.E., TO STOP TEASING).			
⑬ R. DOES NOT HOLD AN INCOMPATIBLE BELIEF (E.G., IT'S MACHO TO FIGHT OR SISSIES IGNORE TEASING).			
⑭ R. HAS THE NECESSARY SKILLS & KNOWLEDGE TO BE ASSERTIVE OR TO IGNORE TEASING.			

Figure 4.3. Listing Rosario's prerequisites.

Student _ROSARIO_   **Evaluator** _MS. MILLER_   **Date** _NOV., '89_

Target Pinpoint _WHEN R. IS TEASED (I.E., CALLED NAMES) BY HIS PEERS, HE WILL IGNORE OR ASSERT HIMSELF (I.E., TELL THEM TO STOP W/O USING PROVOCATIVE LANGUAGE) AND W/O PHYSICAL ATTACKS 100% OF THE TIME._

Prerequisites	Current Status	Assessments	Results
① R. KNOWS & UNDERSTANDS THE SCHOOL RULE RE FIGHTING.	YES, HE CAN EXPLAIN IN HIS OWN WORDS.		
② R. KNOWS & UNDERSTANDS THE REASON FOR THE RULE.	?		
③ R. VALUES TARGET BEHAVIOR AS MUCH AS I DO (OR AT LEAST DOES NOT HOLD ANY CONFLICTING VALUES THAT WOULD INHIBIT HIM FROM ENGAGING IN THE TARGET BEHAVIOR).	?		
④ R. IS AWARE OF HIS BEHAVIOR (I.E., HE KNOWS WHEN HE'S FIGHTING, IGNORING, OR BEING 'ASSERTIVE).	?		
⑤ R. IS CAPABLE OF CONTROLLING HIS FIGHTING BEHAVIOR (I.E., HE CAN STOP HIMSELF W/O BEING RESTRAINED).	YES— I'VE SEEN HIM CONTROL HIMSELF WHEN HE KNOWS I'M WATCHING.		
⑥ R. KNOWS THE CONSEQUENCES OF FIGHTING W. PEERS.	YES— I'VE ASKED HIM "WHAT HAPPENS WHEN YOU FIGHT?"— ABLE TO ANSWER CORRECTLY.		
⑦ R. CONSIDERS THEM AVERSIVE.	?		
⑧ R. KNOWS THE CONSEQUENCES OF IGNORING AND/OR BEING ASSERTIVE WHEN PEERS TEASE.	NOT LIKELY— HE'S NEVER TRIED THIS. (NO)		
⑨ R. CONSIDERS THEM REWARDING.	SAME AS ABOVE. (NO)		
⑩ R. DOES NOT CONSIDER FIGHTING W/ PEERS REWARDING OR LESS AVERSIVE THAN TARGET BEHAVIOR.	?		
⑪ R. IS ABLE TO PERCEIVE ALTERNATIVE SOLUTIONS TO TEASING PROBLEM (OTHER THAN FIGHTING).	?		
⑫ R. EXPECTS IGNORING AND/OR BEING ASSERTIVE TO BE REWARDING (I.E., TO STOP TEASING).	?		
⑬ R. DOES NOT HOLD AN INCOMPATIBLE BELIEF (E.G., IT'S MACHO TO FIGHT OR SISSIES IGNORE TEASING).	?		
⑭ R. HAS THE NECESSARY SKILLS & KNOWLEDGE TO BE ASSERTIVE OR TO IGNORE TEASING.	YES— I'VE SEEN HIM IGNORE OTHER THINGS & ASSERT HIMSELF VERBALLY.		

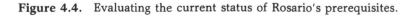

Figure 4.4. Evaluating the current status of Rosario's prerequisites.

Student __ROSARIO__   Evaluator __MS. MILLER__   Date __NOV., '89__

Target Pinpoint _WHEN R. IS TEASED (I.E., CALLED NAMES) BY HIS PEERS, HE WILL IGNORE OR ASSERT HIMSELF (I.E., TELL THEM TO STOP W/O USING PROVOCATIVE LANGUAGE) AND W/O PHYSICAL ATTACKS 100% OF THE TIME._

Prerequisites	Current Status	Assessments	Results
① R. KNOWS & UNDERSTANDS THE SCHOOL RULE RE FIGHTING.	YES, HE CAN EXPLAIN IN HIS OWN WORDS.		
② R. KNOWS & UNDERSTANDS THE REASON FOR THE RULE.	?	R. WILL EXPLAIN TO ME IN HIS OWN WORDS WHY STUDENTS AREN'T ALLOWED TO FIGHT IN SCHOOL. HIS ANSWERS SHOULD INCLUDE AT LEAST 2 OF THE FOLLOWING IDEAS: A. SOMEONE COULD GET HURT. B. FIGHTING INTERFERES WITH LEARNING (DISRUPTS CLASS). C. FIGHTING INTERFERES WITH SOCIAL DEVELOPMENT.	
③ R. VALUES TARGET BEHAVIOR AS MUCH AS I DO (OR AT LEAST DOES NOT HOLD ANY CONFLICTING VALUES THAT WOULD INHIBIT HIM FROM ENGAGING IN THE TARGET BEHAVIOR).	?	GIVEN PENCIL & PAPER TEST ON WHAT'S IMPORTANT TO HIM, R'S RESPONSES WILL SUGGEST VALUES SIMILAR TO MINE OR THAT THERE ARE NO CONFLICTING VALUES.	
④ R. IS AWARE OF HIS BEHAVIOR (I.E., HE KNOWS WHEN HE'S FIGHTING, IGNORING, OR BEING ASSERTIVE).	?	R. WILL KEEP A WRITTEN RECORD OF HIS RESPONSES TO TEASING FOR 3 DAYS, I WILL DO THE SAME. THERE SHOULD BE AT LEAST 80% AGREEMENT.	
⑤ R. IS CAPABLE OF CONTROLLING HIS FIGHTING BEHAVIOR (I.E., HE CAN STOP HIMSELF W/O BEING RESTRAINED).	YES — I'VE SEEN HIM CONTROL HIMSELF WHEN HE KNOWS I'M WATCHING		
⑥ R. KNOWS THE CONSEQUENCES OF FIGHTING W. PEERS.	YES — I'VE ASKED HIM "WHAT HAPPENS WHEN YOU FIGHT?" — ABLE TO ANSWER CORRECTLY.		
⑦ R. CONSIDERS THEM AVERSIVE.	?	R. WILL NAME ALL OF THE THINGS HE DOES NOT LIKE AT SCHOOL. HE WILL INCLUDE CONSEQUENCES OF FIGHTING.	
⑧ R. KNOWS THE CONSEQUENCES OF IGNORING AND/OR BEING ASSERTIVE WHEN PEERS TEASE.	NOT LIKELY — HE'S NEVER TRIED THIS. (NO)		
⑨ R. CONSIDERS THEM REWARDING.	SAME AS ABOVE. (NO)		
⑩ R. DOES NOT CONSIDER FIGHTING W/ PEERS REWARDING OR LESS AVERSIVE THAN TARGET BEHAVIOR.	?	ASK HIM, "DO YOU LIKE TO FIGHT?" HE SHOULD ANSWER IN THE NEGATIVE. ASK HIM WHICH IS WORSE — TO FIGHT SOMEONE WHO BUGS YOU OR TO IGNORE THEM OR TELL THEM TO STOP. HE SHOULD ANSWER, "TO FIGHT THEM."	
⑪ R. IS ABLE TO PERCEIVE ALTERNATIVE SOLUTIONS TO TEASING PROBLEM (OTHER THAN FIGHTING).	?	R. WILL STATE AS MANY DIFFERENT SOLUTIONS TO HYPOTHETICAL PROBLEMS AS POSSIBLE. HE SHOULD STATE AT LEAST 2 SOCIALLY ACCEPTABLE SOLUTIONS TO THE TEASING PROBLEM.	
⑫ R. EXPECTS IGNORING AND/OR BEING ASSERTIVE TO BE REWARDING (I.E., TO STOP TEASING).	?	R. WILL STATE WHAT HE THINKS WOULD HAPPEN IF HE IGNORED THE TEASING OR WAS ASSERTIVE. HIS ANSWERS SHOULD INDICATE THAT HE EXPECTS IGNORING OR BEING ASSERTIVE TO BE EFFECTIVE (I.E., TO STOP PEER TEASING).	
⑬ R. DOES NOT HOLD AN INCOMPATIBLE BELIEF (E.G., IT'S MACHO TO FIGHT OR SISSIES IGNORE TEASING).	?	R. WILL ANSWER QUESTIONS ABOUT HIS BELIEFS. HE WILL NOT HAVE ANY BELIEFS THAT ARE INCOMPATIBLE.	
⑭ R. HAS THE NECESSARY SKILLS & KNOWLEDGE TO BE ASSERTIVE OR TO IGNORE TEASING.	YES — I'VE SEEN HIM IGNORE OTHER THINGS & ASSERT HIMSELF VERBALLY.		

Figure 4.5. Assessments used to evaluate doubtful status of prerequisites.

WHAT'S MORE IMPORTANT TO ME?

Name _____ROSARIO_____ Date _____11-89_____

Directions: What things are more important to you? Choose one of the sentences below in each pair (either a or b) that tells which of the two is more important to you. *Be honest.* You are not going to be graded on this. Don't answer the way you think your teacher might want you to. Answer the way you *really* feel. Circle letter a or b for each of the following:

1. **It's more important:**
   a. that I take a bath or shower every day
   (b.) that I brush my teeth every day

2. **It's more important:**
   (a.) that I change my socks every day
   b. that I change my pants (jeans) every day

3. **It's more important:**
   (a.) that I watch TV when I get home from school
   b. that I do my chores and/or homework when I get home from school

4. **It's more important:**
   (a.) that I stay up late to watch a TV show
   b. that I get to bed on time

5. **It's more important:**
   a. that I ignore students who tease me
   (b.) that I fight with students who tease me

6. **It's more important:**
   a. that I do what I want at school
   (b.) that I follow the rules at school

7. **It's more important:**
   a. that I tell students to stop teasing me
   (b.) that I fight with students who tease me

8. **It's more important:**
   (a.) that people don't think I'm a punk
   b. that people don't think I'm a dope

9. **It's more important:**
   (a.) to be macho
   b. to be smart

10. **It's more important:**
    a. for people to be nice to me
    (b.) for people to be afraid of me

11. **It's more important:**
    (a.) what other people think about me
    b. what I think about myself

12. **It's more important:**
    (a.) to fight with a student even if I get into trouble
    b. to stay out of trouble even if it means not fighting

Comments:

WHEN ASKED WHY IT WAS MORE IMPORTANT TO FIGHT WITH A STUDENT EVEN IF IT MEANT GETTING INTO TROUBLE, R. TOLD ME IT WAS WORTH IT BECAUSE ONCE YOU GET THE REPUTATION OF BEING A PUNK, THE OTHER STUDENTS CAN MAKE YOUR LIFE MORE MISERABLE THAN ANYTHING THE SCHOOL CAN DO TO YOU.

WHEN ASKED IF HE FELT THE FIGHTING STOPPED THE TEASING, HE SAID, "NOT REALLY, BUT IT WOULD BE WORSE IF I DIDN'T FIGHT THEM."

Figure 4.6. Assessment of Rosario's values.

Name ___ROSARIO___ Date ___11-89___

Directions: Read this material to the student and have the student tell you the answers. "I'm going to tell you about a problem and I want you to tell me as many things as you can that you might do to solve this problem. Remember to tell me *as many things as you can.*"

1. Suppose you were locked out of your house late at night. Tell me as many different things as you can that you might do to solve this problem.
   a. *RING THE DOORBELL*
   b. *BANG ON THE DOOR*
   c. *CLIMB IN A WINDOW*
   d. *THROW A ROCK IN THE WINDOW*
   e. *SLEEP AT A FRIEND'S HOUSE*

2. Suppose you lose your money on your way to the store to buy something. Tell me as many different things as you can that you might do to solve this problem.
   a. *LOOK FOR THE $*
   b. *GO BACK HOME AND GET MORE $*
   c. *NOT GO TO THE STORE*
   d. *ASK THE PEOPLE AT THE STORE TO TRUST YOU*
   e.

3. Suppose some students at school keep calling you names you don't like. Tell me as many different things as you can that you might do to solve this problem.
   a. *PUNCH THEM OUT*
   b. *CALL THEM WHAT THEY CALLED YOU*
   c. *FORGET ABOUT IT (IGNORE THEM)*
   d. *TELL THE TEACHER*
   e. *TELL THEM TO STOP IT*

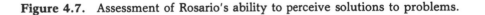

Figure 4.7. Assessment of Rosario's ability to perceive solutions to problems.

of a fight even if it means getting into trouble at school. These values (i.e., what's important to Rosario) will make it extremely difficult for him to ignore students or be assertive with them when they tease him.

Second, Rosario doesn't know the consequences of being assertive with or ignoring peers when they tease him, probably because he has never tried to be assertive or ignore their teasing. As he doesn't know what would happen if he acted assertively with his peers or ignored them when they teased him, it is not surprising that he wouldn't consider these consequences rewarding. How can he consider them rewarding if he hasn't experienced them, and how can he experience them if he's never tried being assertive or ignoring peer teasing before? When asked what he would expect to happen if he was assertive or ignored peer teasing, Rosario's response suggested that he did not have much faith in the effectiveness of such behavior. Certainly, if he doesn't expect the target behavior to effectively weaken peer teasing, we may understand better why he has chosen not to engage in it.

Third, Rosario considers the target behavior more aversive than fighting. In his words, "once you get the reputation of being a punk, the other students can make your life more miserable than anything the school can do to you."

Name ___ROSARIO___   Date ___11-89___

Directions: Read each of the sentences below and decide whether or not you agree with them. It's not necessary to think about each one for very long. Mark your answer quickly and go on to the next sentence. *Be honest.* You are not going to be graded on this. Don't answer the way you think your teacher might want you to. Answer the way you *really* feel. Circle the letter A if you agree with the sentence and D if you disagree with it.

Agree   **Disagree**

Ⓐ   D   1. School is fun.

A   Ⓓ   2. Everyone must like me and it's awful if they don't.

A   Ⓓ   3. It's terrible when people make fun of me.

Ⓐ   D   4. Anybody who lets people make fun of him is a punk.

A   Ⓓ   5. Anyone who calls you names is really rotten.

Ⓐ   D   6. People who try to hurt me should be punished.

A   Ⓓ   7. If somebody doesn't like me, that's his problem, not mine.

Ⓐ   D   8. It's all right to fight with other kids if they start it.

A   Ⓓ   9. When somebody bugs you, the best thing to do is walk away.

Ⓐ   D   10. If you ignore somebody when he bugs you, he'll think you're a punk.

Ⓐ   D   11. Not fighting is a sign of weakness.

A   Ⓓ   12. It's cool to fight.

A   Ⓓ   13. People who do things I don't like are bad.

A   Ⓓ   14. Telling someone to leave you alone when they are bugging you is better than fighting with them.

A   Ⓓ   15. I hate school.

A   Ⓓ   16. I don't have any friends.

A   Ⓓ   17. Nobody likes me.

Ⓐ   D   18. The worst thing you can do is to let people push you around.

Ⓐ   D   19. Lots of people like me.

Ⓐ   D   20. I like myself even though some others don't like me.

A   Ⓓ   21. It's terrible when someone you like doesn't like you.

Ⓐ   D   22. When someone bugs you, the best thing to do is fight them.

Ⓐ   D   23. It's worse to let someone get away with bugging you than it is to get punished by the teacher.

A   Ⓓ   24. I never get into trouble at school.

Ⓐ   D   25. There are worse things people can do to you than tease you or make fun of you.

Underline the word or words that best describes how you *really* feel.

Fighting makes me feel (scared, <u>excited</u>, happy, good, <u>bad</u>, sad, <u>angry</u>).

Figure 4.8.   Assessment of Rosario's beliefs.

Student ___ROSARIO___ Evaluator ___MS. MILLER___ Date ___NOV., '89___

Target Pinpoint _WHEN R. IS TEASED (I.E., CALLED NAMES) BY HIS PEERS, HE WILL IGNORE OR ASSERT HIMSELF (I.E., TELL THEM TO STOP W/O USING PROVOCATIVE LANGUAGE) AND W/O PHYSICAL ATTACKS 100% OF THE TIME._

Prerequisites	Current Status	Assessments	Results
① R. KNOWS & UNDERSTANDS THE SCHOOL RULE RE FIGHTING.	YES, HE CAN EXPLAIN IN HIS OWN WORDS.		
② R. KNOWS & UNDERSTANDS THE REASON FOR THE RULE.	✗ YES	R. WILL EXPLAIN TO ME IN HIS OWN WORDS WHY STUDENTS AREN'T ALLOWED TO FIGHT IN SCHOOL. HIS ANSWERS SHOULD INCLUDE AT LEAST 2 OF THE FOLLOWING IDEAS: A. SOMEONE COULD GET HURT. B. FIGHTING INTERFERES WITH LEARNING (DISRUPTS CLASS). C. FIGHTING INTERFERES WITH SOCIAL DEVELOPMENT.	R. SAID: "A KID COULD GET HURT FIGHTING" AND "YOU WON'T HAVE NO FRIENDS IF YOU FIGHT A LOT." [PASS]
③ R. VALUES TARGET BEHAVIOR AS MUCH AS I DO (OR AT LEAST DOES NOT HOLD ANY CONFLICTING VALUES THAT WOULD INHIBIT HIM FROM ENGAGING IN THE TARGET BEHAVIOR).	✗ NO	GIVEN PENCIL & PAPER TEST ON WHAT'S IMPORTANT TO HIM, R'S RESPONSES WILL SUGGEST VALUES SIMILAR TO MINE OR THAT THERE ARE NO CONFLICTING VALUES.	EVIDENCE OF CONFLICTING VALUES (E.G., MORE IMPORTANT TO FIGHT THAN TO BE CONSIDERED A "PUNK" BY PEERS REGARDLESS OF CONSEQUENCES) [NO PASS]
④ R. IS AWARE OF HIS BEHAVIOR (I.E., HE KNOWS WHEN HE'S FIGHTING, IGNORING, OR BEING ASSERTIVE).	✗ YES	R. WILL KEEP A WRITTEN RECORD OF HIS RESPONSES TO TEASING FOR 3 DAYS. I WILL DO THE SAME. THERE SHOULD BE AT LEAST 80% AGREEMENT.	90% AGREEMENT [PASS]
⑤ R. IS CAPABLE OF CONTROLLING HIS FIGHTING BEHAVIOR (I.E., HE CAN STOP HIMSELF W/O BEING RESTRAINED).	YES— I'VE SEEN HIM CONTROL HIMSELF WHEN HE KNOWS I'M WATCHING.		
⑥ R. KNOWS THE CONSEQUENCES OF FIGHTING W. PEERS.	YES— I'VE ASKED HIM "WHAT HAPPENS WHEN YOU FIGHT?"— ABLE TO ANSWER CORRECTLY.		
⑦ R. CONSIDERS THEM AVERSIVE.	✗ YES	R. WILL NAME ALL OF THE THINGS HE DOES NOT LIKE AT SCHOOL. HE WILL INCLUDE CONSEQUENCES OF FIGHTING.	HE NAMED DETENTION, TIME OUT, BEING SENT TO THE OFFICE, TEACHERS YELLING AT HIM. [PASS]
⑧ R. KNOWS THE CONSEQUENCES OF IGNORING AND/OR BEING ASSERTIVE WHEN PEERS TEASE.	NOT LIKELY— HE'S NEVER TRIED THIS. (NO)		
⑨ R. CONSIDERS THEM REWARDING.	SAME AS ABOVE. (NO)		
⑩ R. DOES NOT CONSIDER FIGHTING W/ PEERS REWARDING OR LESS AVERSIVE THAN TARGET BEHAVIOR.	✗ NO	ASK HIM, "DO YOU LIKE TO FIGHT?" HE SHOULD ANSWER IN THE NEGATIVE. ASK HIM WHICH IS WORSE— TO FIGHT SOMEONE WHO BUGS YOU OR TO IGNORE THEM OR TELL THEM TO STOP. HE SHOULD ANSWER, "TO FIGHT THEM."	R. SAID, "NO, I DON'T LIKE TO FIGHT BUT I GOT TO OR THOSE GUYS WILL BUG ME TWICE AS MUCH AS THEY DO NOW. IT'S DEFINITELY WORSE TO IGNORE THEM OR TELL THEM TO STOP THEY'D THINK I WAS SCARED OF THEM." [NO PASS]
⑪ R. IS ABLE TO PERCEIVE ALTERNATIVE SOLUTIONS TO TEASING PROBLEM (OTHER THAN FIGHTING).	✗ YES	R. WILL STATE AS MANY DIFFERENT SOLUTIONS TO HYPOTHETICAL PROBLEMS AS POSSIBLE. HE SHOULD STATE AT LEAST 2 SOCIALLY ACCEPTABLE SOLUTIONS TO THE TEASING PROBLEM.	STATED 5, INCLUDING: "TELL THEM TO STOP" AND "FORGET ABOUT IT" (IGNORE THEM). [PASS]
⑫ R. EXPECTS IGNORING AND/OR BEING ASSERTIVE TO BE REWARDING (I.E., TO STOP TEASING).	✗ NO	R. WILL STATE WHAT HE THINKS WOULD HAPPEN IF HE IGNORED THE TEASING OR WAS ASSERTIVE. HIS ANSWERS SHOULD INDICATE THAT HE EXPECTS IGNORING OR BEING ASSERTIVE TO BE EFFECTIVE (I.E., TO STOP PEER TEASING).	(M) "WHAT DO YOU THINK WOULD HAPPEN IF YOU IGNORED THE GUYS WHEN THEY TEASE YOU?" (R) "THEY'D THINK I WAS SCARED OF THEM & KEEP DOING IT." (M) "DOING WHAT?" (R) "TEASING!" (M) "WHAT WOULD HAPPEN IF YOU TOLD THEM TO STOP?" (R) "THEY WOULDN'T LISTEN TO ME. YOU CAN'T TALK TO THEM ABOUT IT." [NO PASS]
⑬ R. DOES NOT HOLD AN INCOMPATIBLE BELIEF (E.G., IT'S MACHO TO FIGHT OR SISSIES IGNORE TEASING).	✗ NO	R. WILL ANSWER QUESTIONS ABOUT HIS BELIEFS. HE WILL NOT HAVE ANY BELIEFS THAT ARE INCOMPATIBLE.	R. BELIEVES THAT ANYBODY WHO LETS PEOPLE CALL HIM NAMES IS A PUNK. BEST TO FIGHT SOMEBODY WHEN THEY BUG YOU. ONLY SISSIES WALK AWAY FROM A FIGHT. IT'S WORSE TO LET SOMEONE GET AWAY WITH BUGGING THAN IT IS TO GET PUNISHED BY THE TEACHER. IT'S OK TO FIGHT IF OTHERS START IT. IF YOU IGNORE THEM THEY'LL THINK YOU'RE SCARED. [NO PASS]
⑭ R. HAS THE NECESSARY SKILLS & KNOWLEDGE TO BE ASSERTIVE OR TO IGNORE TEASING.	YES— I'VE SEEN HIM IGNORE OTHER THINGS & ASSERT HIMSELF VERBALLY.		

Figure 4.9. Results of assessments.

Finally, Rosario holds beliefs that are incompatible with the target behavior. He believes that anyone who lets people make fun of him is a punk; that people who try to hurt him should be punished; that if you ignore somebody who is teasing you, he'll think you're a punk; that not fighting is a sign of weakness; that the worst thing you can do is let people push you around; that the best thing to do when someone bugs you is fight him; and that it's worse to let someone get away with bugging you than it is to get punished by the teacher. All of these beliefs made it extremely difficult for the teacher to get Rosario to engage in the target behavior.

Before attempting any intervention, Rosario's teacher wrote a performance objective for each of the missing prerequisites. At a conference with Rosario's parents, the following objectives were added to his individualized education program (IEP):

1. When given a pencil-and-paper test on what is important to him, Rosario will express values similar to the teacher's or at least suggest no conflicting values that would inhibit him from engaging in the target behavior.
2. When asked by the teacher what the consequences of the target behavior might be, Rosario will answer that although it will probably take a while, his peers will eventually stop teasing him, and that the immediate result will be that he won't get into any more trouble at school.
3. When asked how he might feel about his peers not teasing him and his not getting into trouble at school, Rosario will indicate by his answer that he would be pleased.
4. When asked which is worse, fighting in response to peer teasing or being assertive or ignoring peer teasing, Rosario will indicate by his answer that fighting is worse than engaging in the target behavior.
5. When asked what he thinks would happen if he ignores his peers' teasing or asserts himself, Rosario will indicate by his answer that the teasing will stop eventually.
6. When given a pencil-and-paper beliefs inventory, Rosario will indicate that he does not hold any beliefs that might be considered incompatible with the target behavior.

Notice that in no way do these objectives suggest *how* the teacher intends to change Rosario's behavior. They simply describe what behaviors (and thoughts and feelings) need to be changed and when the teacher will know that the change has occurred. It should also be noted that the teacher recognizes that these are intermediate or en route objectives. Even when he has met them all, it is still quite possible that Rosario will engage in the maladaptive behavior. At that point, the teacher may have to implement an intervention designed exclusively to modify the maladaptive behavior. The chances of such an intervention being successful are improved by a factor of 6 simply because the teacher has taken the time and trouble to make sure that Rosario has the six missing prerequisites. My experience with this model has led me to believe that supplying the missing prerequisites is often all that is necessary to produce changes in a student's maladaptive behavior without requiring any special intervention for the target behavior.

Interpretation and Intervention

If, after completing your diagnosis, you find that the student appears to have all of the prerequisites necessary to engage in the target behavior, you should follow these steps. First, ask yourself if, in task analyzing the target behavior, you have listed all of the prerequisites. Go through the task analysis phase once more and see whether there are any prerequisites you might have missed.

Assuming that you have listed all of the prerequisites, check to see if you might have been wrong about their status. It may be that the student does not have all of the prerequisites you think she does. Go back through the status evaluation phase once more and ask yourself these questions:

1. Does she really have all of the prerequisites I said she did? What evidence is there to support this? Is there any evidence to dispute this?
2. When I was in doubt about the status of a prerequisite, did I use a valid assessment to evaluate it? If the assessment was valid, were the criteria for passing the assessment stringent enough? Did the student really pass the test?

Assuming that you have listed all of the prerequisites and the student actually does have all of them, there is only one thing left for you to do: intervene on the target behavior. If the diagnosis suggests that the student has all of the prerequisites to engage in the target behavior, there is no reason why he or she can't be taught how to perform it. Exactly how you should teach the student is not the issue here. However, if the student does not have a particular prerequisite, I will offer some general suggestions regarding interventions you might use. Keep in mind that this is not a chapter on interventions. For more specific information, refer to chapters 6 through 11.

If the student *doesn't know or understand what behavior is expected of him,* you will have to teach him.

Post the rules regarding appropriate behavior in the classroom or on his desk. Remind him daily, before he gets into trouble. Have him paraphrase the rules to you at the beginning of the day.

If the student *doesn't know or understand why you want her to engage in the target behavior,* explain your reasons to her. Don't be pedantic. Use language that she understands. Don't sermonize or lecture her. Above all, try to communicate to her that the rules regarding her behavior are in her best interests and those of her peers. Stories about other children and puppetry are especially effective with younger children.

If the student *doesn't value the target behavior as much as you do* or he *holds conflicting values,* use the techniques described in earlier chapters to facilitate internalization of the target behavior. Also, refer to the text *Values Clarification* (Simon et al., 1972) for activities in this area.

If the student *is not aware of her behavior,* teach her how to monitor (i.e., observe and record) her own behavior. Have her collect daily data. You do the same and compare results. Record the student's behavior on audiotape or videotape and have her listen to it or view it. You and her peers might also remind her when she's engaging in the maladaptive or target behavior.

If the student *is not capable of controlling his own behavior* because of hyperactivity-impulsivity, extreme anxiety, or anger, use the interventions discussed in chapters 9 and 11 to help him bring these counterproductive internal states under control. If there is a physical condition that prohibits him from controlling his own behavior, such as a metabolic disorder, food allergy, seizure activity, medicinal side effects, or other health problem, work closely with the home and family doctor to eliminate it. Collect daily data regarding his behavior, antecedents (e.g., whether or not he was wearing his glasses, was on medication, or ate lunch), and consequent events.

If the student *does not know the consequences of engaging in the target behavior,* you must tell her what to expect. Be consistent. Don't change the consequences from time to time. Ask her periodically, "What happens when you . . . ?" Use if-then statements such as: "If you raise your hand without calling out, then I will call on you." Use a modeling technique by reinforcing the student's peers when they engage in the target behavior. Try to use the same reinforcers with them whenever it's appropriate to do so.

If the student *doesn't consider the consequences of the target behavior rewarding,* collect data to find out what he does consider rewarding. Use one of the techniques described in chapter 6. If the student doesn't know the consequences of engaging in the maladaptive behavior, follow the procedure suggested here for the target behavior. The same applies if the student doesn't consider the consequences of engaging in the maladaptive behavior to be aversive.

If the student *considers the target behavior aversive or the maladaptive behavior rewarding,* try to find out why. Why is it aversive for her to engage in the target behavior? Why is it rewarding for her to engage in the maladaptive behavior? Asking the student or monitoring her behavior over a period of time will usually provide you with some answers. Usually, these answers are more obvious than you might suppose. For example, if a student would rather be talking to peers than doing schoolwork, find out if the schoolwork is too difficult for her. Giving her assignments she can be successful at and rewarding working behavior with time to talk to her peers should prove effective.

If the student *does not know how to engage in the target behavior,* train him. If he doesn't know how to be assertive with his peers, put him through an assertiveness training program. If he doesn't know how to express his anger in a socially acceptable manner, show him how.

If the student *holds a belief that is incompatible with the target behavior,* use the techniques described in chapter 9 to help her dispute the belief and substitute a more rational one. If the student *does not perceive the target behavior as a viable option (i.e., a possible solution) to his problem,* train him in problem solving. Again, use the techniques described in chapter 9. Finally, if the student *is not able to remember to engage in the target behavior,* try the chaining technique described in chapter 6.

A Final Word

The major criticism of this system is its reliance upon the cooperation of the student during the assessment phase. If the student doesn't cooperate, you obtain either invalid data or no data at all. Is it realistic to expect students to take these assessments even once, let alone several times, to ensure their reliability? Furthermore, even if they do consent to take them, is it realistic to expect every student to respond truthfully? Some students may refuse to take any assessments, some may take them only once, while others may take them more than once but fake their responses. At the present time, I cannot predict how many students you can expect to cooperate during the assessment phase (i.e., truthfully respond to the assessments more than once). However, my experience with the system leads me to believe that for every student who doesn't cooperate, there will probably be two who will. Even if a student does not cooperate, all is not lost. Whenever you encounter a student who refuses to respond or who you believe hasn't responded truthfully, simply throw out the assessment and operate under the assumption that he or she does not have the prerequisites you wanted to assess.

If this assumption is true, you will find out soon enough when you implement the interventions later on. If the student does have the prerequisites, this too will become evident during intervention. If you assume instead that the student does have the prerequisites, you will probably not intervene in this area. If you are right, fine. However, if you are wrong, you will have set up both yourself and your student for failure.

This is far from a perfect system. But how many perfect systems are there? It does have some advantages that the more traditional systems don't have. First, it doesn't rely on strangers such as psychiatrists and psychologists to make the diagnosis. Instead, the diagnosis is made by the one person who knows the student better than anyone else—the student's teacher. Most teachers know more about why a student misbehaves at school than any psychiatrist, psychologist, or even the student's parents. The advantage of having the teacher conduct the diagnosis is that it will probably be more valid; in addition, it will be completed sooner, and the person ultimately responsible for the intervention will have ready access to the data.

The second advantage of the TA model is that it focuses directly on student behavior. This is important because the parties involved (the student and the teacher) do not lose sight of the original problem. Too often, when a student's maladaptive behavior problem is assessed through one of the traditional systems, there is a tendency for everyone concerned to forget about the specific behaviors that precipitated the assessment in the first place. Labels and technical terms may be used by students as excuses for their behavior ("I act that way on account of my nervous disorder") and by teachers as excuses for not modifying those behaviors ("My God, how do you expect me to deal with a kid who manifests schizoid tendencies?"). By focusing the assessment on the student's behavior instead of on the student, both the teacher and the student remain mindful of the central issue, which is what the student does, not what the student is. This makes possible a much more optimistic and positive intervention program.

Probably the most significant advantage of this system is that it helps teachers realize that there are more reasons for a student's misbehavior than emotional disturbance, bad genes, faulty parenting, or a rotten disposition. After conducting a TA assessment, the teacher often views the student in a new light. He or she is no longer viewed as "nuts," or "spoiled," or "bad," but rather as a person with certain deficiencies that the teacher can help to remedy.

Incidentally, for those of you who see merit in this model of assessment but who have neither the time nor the energy to apply it "from scratch," a computerized version of the TA model exists that has been applied to 10 common and difficult maladaptive behaviors. All the work has been done for you. Simply enter some relevant data and the software does the rest. This program will provide you with all of the deficit prerequisites as well as IEP-ready performance objectives for each. It is called *PRE-MOD II* (Kaplan & Kent, 1986) and may be purchased from PRO-ED, the publisher of this text.

Chapter Four Self-Assessment

See Appendix A for acceptable responses.

1. State all of the essential and desirable prerequisites for each of the following target behaviors.

   a. Complies with all requests first time given:

   b. Stays on task (i.e., completes assignments on time):

2. Write a performance objective that describes a valid assessment for each of the following prerequisites. Be sure to include the subject's behavior, the conditions under which the behavior should occur, and the CAP.

   a. Understands that he is supposed to raise his hand and wait to be called on before speaking:

   b. Is aware of when she is raising her hand and waiting to be called on and when she is speaking out without being acknowledged:

   c. Knows how to raise his hand and wait to be called on:

   d. Is able to control her impulsivity to the extent that she can raise her hand and wait to be called on:

   e. Knows the consequences of raising his hand and waiting to be called on and the consequences of speaking out without being acknowledged:

   f. Considers the consequences of raising her hand and waiting to be called on to be more rewarding than the consequences of speaking out without being acknowledged:

   g. Only endorses beliefs that are compatible with raising his hand and waiting to be called on and does not endorse beliefs that are incompatible with this behavior:

3. Describe the steps in the TA model for assessing problem behaviors.

chapter 5

Assessing Environments
by Barbara L. Drainville

Upon successful completion of this chapter, the learner will be able to:

1. Write a definition of ecobehavioral analysis
2. Describe in writing the differences between the ecobehavioral model, the psychodynamic model, and the medical model of interventions for maladaptive behaviors
3. List the factors that affect the ecology of behavior
4. Match definitions of *behavioral setting, ecosystem, ecological niche, behavioral "fit,"* and the three levels of behavior settings
5. List the types of assessment useful in analyzing the environmental factors of behavior
6. List five critical elements from each case history

Assessment of the environment is the critical element of ecobehavioral analysis, a technique that can be used to change maladaptive behaviors in the classroom. It is crucial to understand what ecobehavioral analysis can and cannot do in order to make effective use of this method. Essentially, ecobehavioral analysis is the application of the principles of behavior analysis to the environment surrounding the behavior. It focuses on the "poor fit" between the child and his or her environment as the cause of the problem behavior. For example, a high-powered, overachieving teacher is going to create a classroom environment that is difficult for the slow learners, who may act out to get relief from expectations they can't handle. The teacher with a laissez-faire attitude is likely to create an environment that will evoke testing behaviors in students who require a high degree of structure in their learning environment. These teachers may wonder why they often get students with a particular type of maladaptive behavior. The students are giving us clues in their behavioral response to the classroom environment, which has caused their maladaptive behavior. If a teacher has a high number of

talk-outs, for example, the classroom environment and the teacher are probably reinforcing this behavior.

The environment, by definition, is the complex matrix of the physical, social, and cultural conditions that affect the growth and development of an organism. Another term used to describe this matrix is *ecosystem.* The focus of this chapter will be the classroom environment or behavior setting. Other environmental influences also shape a student's behavior; we will examine these influences in light of their impact on the student's behavior in the classroom and the school environment.

Ecobehavioral analysis is a fairly recent application of the principles of behaviorism; it analyzes the environment, or ecology, that evokes and maintains disturbing behavior. It is a natural outgrowth of the task analysis approach to behavior management, sometimes called *behavior modification.* Ecobehavioral analysis owes a debt to the fields of sociology, anthropology, and ecological psychology, as well as to the "hard" sciences like biology and zoology. These disciplines, through observation, have enabled researchers to hypothesize about human behavior.

For example, one of the most notable biologists to affect the field of early education was Jean Piaget. His minute observations of his two sons during their earliest years led him to propose a theory of the developmental stages of learning. He believed that learning occurs through interaction with the environment, and that the critical stages of development progress from the sensory-motor stage of infancy to the formal operations of adulthood. This theory has had a profound impact on the developmental expectations of professionals, as well as on curriculum development, particularly for young children.

Studies from many other disciplines have alluded to the impact of environmental factors on human deviance (Holman, 1977; Rhodes & Paul, 1978). The field of ecological psychology has provided significant observations on human behavior in a variety of settings. However, there is one crucial difference between ecobehavioral analysis and these other disciplines: The

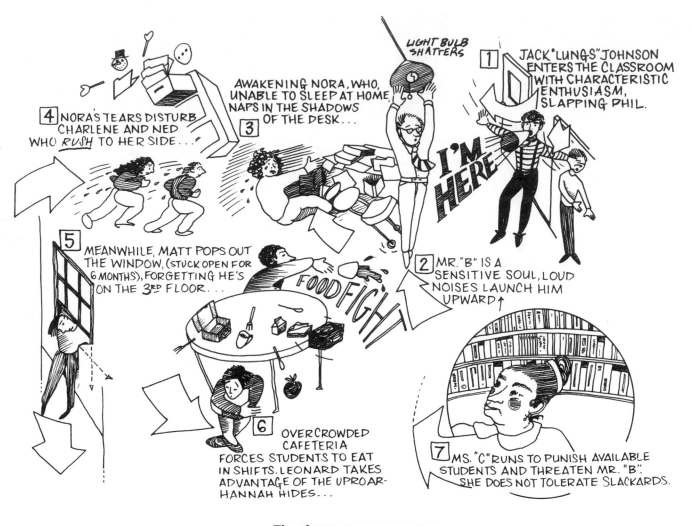

The classroom as ecosystem.

purpose of ecobehavioral analysis is not only to observe but also to change the environment. To change the ecology of maladaptive behavior, we must know exactly what the disturbing behavior is and understand all the environmental factors that affect this behavior. Ecobehavioral analysis focuses on intervention, rather than just observation.

The basic underlying principles that define ecobehavioral analysis also distinguish it from other models of intervention. There are significant differences between the assumptions underlying an ecological model of behavior analysis and intervention and those underlying both the medical model and the psychodynamic model of intervention.

What Is Ecobehavioral Analysis?

The primary assumption of ecobehavioral analysis is that behavioral deviance is the result of a poor fit in the interactions between the child and the environment in which the behavior occurs. The child is not seen as the sole source of the problem, but as part of a dysfunctional interaction between a particular behavioral setting and the child's behavior.

In contrast, both the medical model and the psychodynamic model of intervention identify the child as the source of the problem. The medical model defines the etiology of the problem as organic: a chemical, metabolic, or physiological dysfunction within the child. This model may offer an intervention such as medication for deviant behavior. The psychodynamic perspective is one of social maladjustment on the part of the child; it may focus on internal conflicts caused by dysfunctional relationships with significant others such as parents. This model offers interventions such as psychotherapy to reduce the internal conflicts the child may feel. With these models, the environment, when it is taken into account at all, is viewed as less significant than the child's physical or emotional state.

In contrast, the ecological model identifies the fit between the environment and the child as the problem. The child's physical and emotional state, the physical setting, the child's activities, social and cultural expectations, and other persons in the setting are considered part of the ecology of the behavior. This doesn't rule out the use of medical or psychodynamic interventions. In fact, it encompasses all of the discernable factors of the ecology that evoke or maintain the deviant behavior. It assumes the following:

1. It is the interactions between the child and his or her ecological behavioral settings that are disturbed, rather than the child.
2. The behavioral interventions must modify the environment that is evoking or maintaining the maladaptive behavior.
3. The intervention must be tailored to fit the unique interaction between the child and his or her particular ecological niche. An *ecological niche* is the role an organism fulfills in any of the various ecosystems available to it (Swap et al., 1982).

For example, an ecological intervention plan for a child with an attending deficit disorder (ADD) could include any or all of the following treatments: medication; a behavioral program to increase attending in a regular classroom setting; a study carrel; family counseling; placement in a special education, or resource, classroom for individualized academic instruction, including a number of behavioral interventions; regular physical education with a token economy; or an advanced swim class at the local community center.

Assessment of the Ecology of Behavior

Swap et al. (1982, p. 83) have stated: "There is no single assessment tool that could be used to evaluate each relevant child-setting-system variable in a faulty encounter. Each instrument selects certain variables for attention; different assessment tools are generally used in combination to create as complete a picture of the interaction as possible." It is a complex task to analyze all of the discernable factors that determine the ecology of a given behavior. We must first understand what the term *ecology* means, because our definition will determine what we will analyze and change to affect the target behavior. The ecology, or ecosystem, of a behavior is the complex social, cultural, and physical matrix in which it is embedded and which affects the student's behavior. The factors in this matrix are: (1) physical, (2) social and emotional, (3) curricular, (4) familial, and (5) community and national. Another way to identify these factors is to investigate the five "W's" of the behavior: who, what, when, where, with whom, and

possibly why. Like Sherlock Holmes, we must use deductive and inductive reasoning, and perhaps a little creative inspiration, to understand and change a child's behavior.

Traditional assessment.

A model for ecobehavioral analysis can be likened to a game of Chinese checkers: The object of the game is to affect students' choices in behavior by changing the encircling environmental factors that encompass their ecology (see Figure 5.1). Starting from the outermost ring, in descending, overlapping rings, the factors are:

1. The students' culture and the social and legal protections and sanctions of their society
2. The community and its resources and services; the family's socioeconomic status and relationship to the community, neighborhood, and church
3. The family and its internal dynamics and expectations; the marital status of caregivers, birth order, siblings, and gender
4. The school and its resources and physical plant, its staff, the student population, and its behavioral and curricular expectations
5. The classroom and its physical layout, curriculum, schedule, equipment, and materials
6. Classmates and other peers, their values and styles of interaction, social perceptions and skills, and tolerance for deviance
7. The teacher and his or her teaching style, behavioral and curricular expectations, biases, and perceptions and tolerance for deviance

Ecological assessment.

8. The students themselves, their physical and emotional state, their perception of themselves and others, and their skills in interpreting and responding to any or all of the factors that affect their environment, on any given day

It's no wonder that there are poor fits. Students must find their ecological niche in all of these areas.

After the ecobehavioral analyst (most often, the teacher) has carefully defined the environmental factors to be examined, he or she must garner all relevant information needed to plan the intervention. The first decision to be made is which behavior to analyze, what contexts to use, and which assessments to employ. The type of assessment conducted will depend upon the behavior, the setting, and the data needed to plan the intervention. The rule of thumb is to take baseline data on the behavior that is interfering the most with school success, since this is our focus.

There are a number of informal assessment tools available commercially. Figures 5.2 and 5.3 illustrate baseline assessments I have developed. It is important to observe, as closely and uncritically as you can, the behavior of the student and others in various behavior settings. Then choose the behavior that is showing the poorest fit.

Obviously, aggression leading to physical endangerment of self and others is the first concern. This behavior is usually the one that evokes the most negative feedback from the environment. It is usually embedded in a constellation of problems: poor communication and social skills; aggressive interactions with peers; positive reinforcement for previous aggression; and family or neighborhood relationships that value aggression, such as a positive self-image for "macho" behavior. Changing this type of behavior ecologically will take extensive analysis. Behavior does not occur in a vacuum. Assessing which settings, persons, and attitudes evoke aggression in the student will give clues to the interventions needed.

The goal of the interventions is to teach the student to solve his or her problems of self-protection or self-expression without the use of physical aggression. Ecological intervention encompasses the individuals in the peer group; all the students are expected to avoid behavior such as taunting that would lead to aggression.

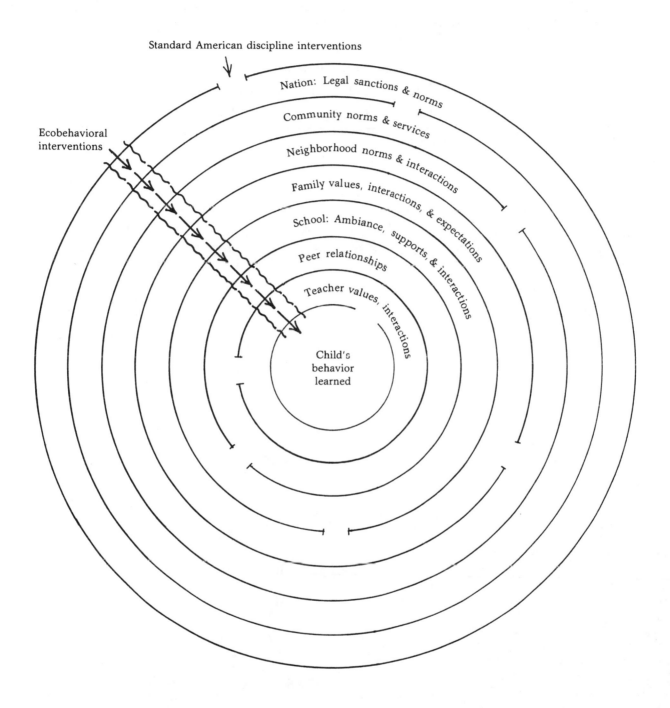

Standard American discipline interventions

Ecobehavioral
interventions

Nation: Legal sanctions & norms

Community norms & services

Neighborhood norms & interactions

Family values, interactions, & expectations

School: Ambiance, supports, & interactions

Peer relationships

Teacher values, interactions

Child's
behavior
learned

Ecobehavioral analysis makes the alignment between the child's ecological niches better to improve learning of adaptive behavior.

Figure 5.1. Model for ecobehavioral analysis. *Note.* Copyright 1988 by Barbara L. Drainville.

Directions: Place a hash mark next to each incidence of behavior under the time of day's scheduled activity. For example, if a student pushes in line going out to recess at 10:15, make a mark next to "pushes," between the numbers 10:00 and 10:30. This grid will enable you to pinpoint the times and behaviors you'll wish to investigate further.

Behavior/Schedule Grid

Time:	8:30	9:00	9:30	10:00	10:30	11:00	11:30	Noon	1:00	1:30	2:00	2:30	3:00
Action:	Opening		Reading		RR	Math	Spllg	LR	Lang.		Soc/Sci		End

argues
asks
complains
cries
curses
defaces
defecates
demands
destroys
fights
flaps
hits
ignores
isolates
jumps
kicks
laughs
leaves
lies
looks
makes faces
makes noise
masturbates
pinches
pokes
pouts
is proximate to
pushes
raises hand
reclines
runs
screams
sings
sits
spits
stands
talks
teases
threatens
throws
urinates
whines
whistles

Figure 5.2. Behavior/schedule grid. *Note.* Copyright 1988 by Barbara L. Drainville.

Name _____ Date _____ Grade _____

D.O.B. _____ C.A. _____ Referred by _____

Reason _____

	Yes	No	Notes:

1. understands expectations?   Y   N   _____

2. developmentally ready?   Y   N   _____

3. cognitively able?   Y   N   _____

4. receptive language OK?   Y   N   _____

5. expressive language OK?   Y   N   _____

6. hearing OK?   Y   N   _____

7. vision OK?   Y   N   _____

8. attending skills OK?   Y   N   _____

9. perceptual skills OK?   Y   N   _____

10. tool skills OK?   Y   N   _____

11. fine motor skills OK?   Y   N   _____

12. gross motor skills OK?   Y   N   _____

13. relationship with teacher OK?   Y   N   _____

14. relationships with peers OK?   Y   N   _____

15. family data pertinent?   Y   N   _____

16. siblings?   Y   N   _____

17. birth order?   Y   N   _____

18. most favored modality?   Y   N   _____

19. least favored modality?   Y   N   _____

20. strong likes?   Y   N   _____

21. strong dislikes?   Y   N   _____

What is the concern? Define the behaviors. _____

What? _____

When? _____

Where? _____

With whom? _____

Under what conditions? _____

Why? (guess) _____

Interventions tried: 1. _____

2. _____   3. _____

Recommendations: _____

Figure 5.3.   Mrs. D.'s Child Data Checklist. *Note.* Copyright 1988 by Barbara L. Drainville.

The assessment may identify, for example, which peers taunt the student, which taunts are "fighting words," which sports activities have evoked aggression in the student, and with which gang members the student invariably fights.

Initial Screening

Obviously, the type of baseline data you take will depend on the student's behavior. Chapters 3 and 4 will help you specify and assess this behavior. It is important to look at the ecological factors affecting behavior. A number of helpful tools for doing this are described later in this chapter. Taking informal anecdotal observation data such as ABC (antecedent, behavior, consequence) or a running record will help pinpoint what you're analyzing (Figure 5.4). Measuring the frequency, duration, and intensity of the behavior (Figure 5.5) is the initial step in an ecobehavioral analysis.

During the initial screening, these data will help the student study team to document which strategies, if any, the teacher has found effective. There's no sense in duplicating ineffective interventions. If nothing else, this allows us to exclude factors that obviously have no impact. It helps to know if anything has exacerbated the behavior. Other important information includes the student's date of birth, which is a crucial part of determining developmental level; the student's previous school experience, if any; his or her achievement level; and the attendance record. This allows us to judge if it is reasonable to expect the student to perform in a different way.

Once we have a basic picture of the child's developmental level, we can look at the ecosystem and determine what to do next. An efficient way to check these informal data is to grid the information, as on a 6-cycle chart, a time chart, or a percentage chart, and compare the data both to the teacher's expectations of performance and to a proficient peer's performance. It may be that one time of day or subject will leap out as the pivotal point because of an exceptionally good or exceptionally poor fit. It may be that the teacher's expectations are out of line with the child's developmental level or tool skills. It may be that the student is having difficulties in a number of behavioral settings. These data will help us choose the assessments needed for a more detailed look.

Consideration must be given to the behavioral settings in which the behavior occurs. Gump (1977) defines a behavioral setting as having the following factors: a physical milieu, a specific time and space, a set activity, and specific inhabitants. The behavioral setting is a crucial factor in any analysis of the behavior fit between the child and the evoking environment. For example, Jay's fit in the resource room's reading class may be good: He sits with three other peers and the learning specialist, reading his primer with 90% on-task behavior. Thirty minutes later, in physical education, he's whooping and climbing the basketball pole. The unstructured play and large, noisy gym are an ecological fit that evokes disruptive behavior in Jay.

Swap et al. (1982) define three levels of ecological systems. Level 1 is a narrowly defined, single milieu that evokes deviant behavior; for example, a child may "act out" or behave dysfunctionally in physical education class. In level 2, the scope is broader and the deviant behavior occurs across a number of level 1 settings; the child may display the same deviant behavior in the gym, in the lunchroom, at latchkey, and on the bus. Level 3 is much broader and encompasses the community or perhaps even the culture at large, its values, and its perceptions of normality; socioeconomic status (SES); racial, religious, or gender expectations; and tolerance for deviance from these norms. The legal and social sanctions for deviance vary with these factors, and expectations, which profoundly influence performance, are largely based on these often-unspoken values.

For example, Jesse Jackson has pointed out that the same socioeconomic factors that are cited to explain poor black students' lack of academic achievement are ignored when discussing these same students' phenomenal sports achievements. He contends that the critical environmental factor in these cases is not socioeconomic, but a lack of both high expectations for academic achievement and an appropriate curriculum. Like Jackson, the ecobehavioral analyst must look with critical eyes on the entire range of ecosystems that evoke or maintain the deviant behavior.

Swap et al. (1982, p. 79) state: "An ecological niche is the role an organism fulfills in any of the various ecosystems available to it." The potential tension between ecological niches is shown by the fact that the fight that blackens Suzie's eye and horrifies her father makes her a hero to the kids in her class, especially since she "decked" the class bully.

In a school environment, it is likely that among the staff, the families, the neighborhood, and the community at large, there will be values and expectations that are at odds. Even the most sophisticated adult cannot adapt to every environment without offending someone. Students, who are often impulsive and unsophisticated, are more prone to giving offense by virtue of their inexperience. The educators who deal with these students have a serious obligation to clarify their own values. This will ensure that their expectations are reasonable and not based on value judgments. It will also

The following checklist allows you to describe your student's problems in various situations. The situations are listed in the column at left and common problem behaviors are listed in the row at the top. Examine *each* situation in the column and decide if one or more of the problem behaviors in the row fit your student. Check those that fit the best—if any:

	Out of seat	Talks to others	Always has to be told	Doesn't pay attention	Forgets	Dawdles	Refuses	Argues	Complains	Demands	Fights	Is selfish	Destroys toys or property	Steals	Lies	Cries	Hangs on or stays close to adult	Stays alone	Whines	Acts silly	Mopes around	Has to keep things in order	Uses sexual play
Morning:																							
Teacher explains lesson																							
Teacher discusses with group																							
Silent work time																							
Cooperative work with other students																							
Oral reading or class presentation																							
Line up for lunch or recess																							
Hall																							
Playground																							
Lunch																							
Afternoon:																							
Teacher explains lesson																							
Teacher discusses with group																							
Silent work time																							
Cooperative work with other students																							
Oral reading or class presentation																							
Line up for recess or dismissal																							
Hall																							
Playground																							

Figure 5.4. Child-school behavior checklist. *Note.* From "The Ecological Interview: A First Step in Out-Patient Child Behavior Therapy" by R. G. Wahler and W. H. Cormier, 1970, *Journal of Behavior Therapy and Experimental Psychiatry, 1*, p. 283. Copyright 1970 by Pergamon Press, Ltd. Reprinted by permission.

This ecological baseline card, developed by Prieto and Rutherford, is useful for recording ABC data.

Child's Name _____ Date _____

Antecedents to problem: Statement of problem: Consequences of problem:

_____   _____   _____

_____   _____   _____

_____   _____   _____

_____   _____   _____

_____   _____   _____

Time (When does problem occur?):   Frequency (How often or long does problem occur?):

_____   Day 1 _____   Day 6 _____

_____   Day 2 _____   Day 7 _____

Place (Activities/location problem occurs):   Day 3 _____   Day 8 _____

_____   Day 4 _____   Day 9 _____

_____   Day 5 _____   Day 10 _____

Figure 5.5. Ecological baseline card. *Note.* From "An Ecological Assessment Technique for Behavior Disordered and Learning Disabled Children" by A. G. Prieto and R. B. Rutherford, Jr., 1977, *Behavior Disorders, 2,* p. 172. Reprinted by permission.

ensure that any behavioral interventions will be to the students' benefit, and will not be the source of conflicts in their other ecological niches. This is an important factor in the emotional climate of the classroom.

Survey of Ecobehavioral Measures

Since no one assessment will provide all the necessary data, it is helpful to become familiar with some of the measures that have been developed. Systematic and structured observations of the child behaving in a variety of settings can provide necessary data useful in planning, monitoring, and generalizing effective interventions. Success in acquiring and maintaining behavior change is more likely with a good ecological fit.

Rogers-Warren (1984) suggested an ecobehavioral matrix that incorporates an analysis of the context of the behavior as well as larger units of behavioral sequences that have natural beginnings and ends. She defines these levels of behavior as *discrete behavior, exchanges, episodes,* and *standing patterns.* Discrete behavior is a singular action that is the usual focus of behavior analysis; for example, an observer may count the frequency of verbal initiations the child makes. The exchange behavior is reciprocal within the behavior set-

ting: An observer may take ABC data on the child asking for and receiving a block from a peer. An episode is an extended form of exchange, as when a student builds a block structure with a peer. A standing pattern is a series of episodes that occur in different settings or over time. An example is the transition between home and school: putting on the appropriate outerwear, leave-taking, the bus ride, and greeting others upon arrival. Rogers-Warren recommended analyzing these four types of behavior within three contexts:

1. Behavior to environment—for example, the child may initiate verbally more often in the classroom than at home. Analysis of the anecdotal records may indicate that the classroom environment is structured to create a need to talk, whereas at home the student has older siblings who speak for him.

2. Behavior to behavior—for example, ABC data may reveal that when a child must ask her neighbor to pass the juice, she will then continue to talk to that peer during snack time.

3. Environment to environment—for example, if a student is successful in physical education, he is compliant during the ensuing period in the regular classroom setting.

In each case, the question remains the same: Do these factors strengthen, weaken, or simply occur at the same time as the behavior being observed? Following is an example of an exchange in which Jackie (J.) is encouraged by her teacher (T.) to initiate verbally:

J. reaches for and can't get doll.

J. initiates to T. by tugging on her skirt.

T. looks at J. and says, "What do you want?"

J. smiles and points to doll on high shelf.

T. pretends not to understand J.'s gesture and says, "Tell me again."

J. says, "My doll," and points to doll and then to herself.

T. gives doll to J. and says, "That's the way to tell me, 'I want the doll!'"

J. nods, says, "My doll," and hugs it.

These data show that Jackie's verbal initiation was evoked and strengthened (reinforced) by the exchange with the teacher during the activity. The teacher knew that Jackie often chose to play with a certain doll. When she placed the doll on a high shelf, the teacher created a need in Jackie to communicate her desire for the doll. By pretending not to understand Jackie's pointing, the teacher created a need for Jackie to expand her communication; in this case, she chose to say, "My doll" and point. The teacher then praised Jackie for using a verbal request; used an expanded model, "I want the doll"; and gave her the doll. We can assume that these environmental factors reinforced Jackie's verbal initiations if she uses a verbal request to get the doll another time or uses a verbal request to acquire other toys and activities.

The Classroom as a Behavioral Setting

Swap (1974) outlined an ecological and developmental approach to analyzing disturbing classroom behaviors. She suggested using the developmental schema of Hewett (1964) and Erickson (1963, 1964) to pinpoint the developmental stage of the child's responses to the environment. She then suggested adaptations of the environment based upon this identified stage, to design a better ecological fit between the child's behavior and environment. Using the chart in Figure 5.6 as a guideline, a teacher can individualize the classroom activities for students who are having difficulty with a particular stage.

Swap et al. (1982) describe a method of ecobehavioral analysis using the concept of *behavior setting* as the basic unit of analysis. By *behavior setting*, we mean the people and the physical environment, or milieu, in which they interact in standing patterns of behavior. Some crucial factors of the classroom behavior setting are:

1. Physical arrangement, size, and comfort of the furniture or equipment
2. Sensory climate: temperature, ventilation, lighting, colors, and odors
3. Traffic flow and amount of physical activity
4. Schedule and time of day
5. Social climate including the teacher and peers
6. Daily curriculum and related school activities
7. Physical and emotional health of the student, teacher, and peers
8. Teaching style and expectations of the teacher
9. Learning styles and self-esteem of the students

For example, if a child consistently acts out just before lunch, regardless of the activity scheduled at that time, we can speculate that it is the time of day, or perhaps hunger, rather than the curriculum content that is affecting the behavior. Taking data and then varying the antecedents will help to pinpoint the factors evoking the behavior. Interviewing the child will also help to pinpoint critical factors. A student recently told me that she was able to learn improved study skills when I made permission to sit with her friend contingent upon completion of her work. Proximity to a favored peer can be a cue to talk instead of work, *or* a reward for success. The act of sitting next to a friend remains the same, but how a teacher uses it will make a difference to the student.

Prieto and Rutherford (1977) developed an Ecological Niche Breadth Assessment (Figure 5.7) to screen learning-disabled and behaviorally disordered students within the behavior setting of the classroom. The teacher rates the child's "niche fit" as positive or negative in each factor, such as transitions, math, or the student's relationship with the teacher. First, the teacher hypothesizes whether each factor is a positive or a negative fit; then he pinpoints the factors with a negative fit and takes baseline data on the target behavior, its antecedents, and its consequences. The teacher then plans an intervention.

Thurman (1977) suggested a number of factors to assess the target behavior in its ecological niche: environmental tolerance, child competence, and child deviance. He suggested examining behavior settings, ecological niches, or "microecologies" to develop inventories of critical behaviors particular to the behavior setting. When the child's ability to perform these needed skills is assessed, the areas of poor fit will be pinpointed. This analysis will facilitate planning interventions to reinforce the desired behaviors and improve ecological fit.

Developmental Stages		Triggering Behaviors	Adaptive Environmental Response
Erikson	Hewett		
Basic trust versus mistrust	Attention	Withdrawal Self-stimulation Inability to focus attention Preoccupation with fantasy Inability to form close relationships	Establish climate of safety and predictability Accept and reward child's limited responses Provide one-to-one relationship
	Response	Inability or unwillingness to respond to unfamiliar stimuli Fear of failure, phobias	Limit competition Provide simple tasks at which child can be successful
Autonomy versus shame and doubt	Order	Inability to complete tasks Compulsive rituals Disruptive outbursts Intolerance of frustration Defiance of authority Distractibility Destruction of products	Provide structured learning environment Set clear expectations for student behavior and follow through consistently Require finished products Establish a firm one-to-one relationship Design a curriculum activity with a specific starting point in a series of steps leading to a conclusion Set up peer activities of a simple design
Initiative versus guilt	Exploratory	Extreme dependence Fear of looking, exploring Overzealous exploration	Provide multisensory experiences Build a framework for "orderly exploration" Teach child to plan and evaluate Encourage "discovery" activities
Industry versus inferiority	Social	Low self-esteem Isolation Difficulty with sharing, competition Inappropriate social behaviors Aggression, teasing	Set up group projects Experiment with cross-age teaching Educate children about their own values and attitudes Provide communication exercises
	Mastery, achievement	Low achievement Overly dependent on others' approval or initiative	Provide wide range of learning activities and methods Cultivate students' interests Encourage self-evaluation

Figure 5.6. Developmental view of behaviors and teacher responses. *Note.* From "Disturbing Classroom Behaviors: A Developmental and Ecological View" by S. M. Swap, 1974, *Exceptional Children, 41,* p. 166. Reprinted by permission.

Smith et al. (1978) developed comprehensive checklists to assess the social environment, the physical environment, and the curriculum, methods and materials of the classroom setting. The checklists are then used to develop an environmental profile, which can pinpoint factors that facilitate, inhibit, or have no effect on the child's deviant behavior. They believe that the three factors with the most impact on the child's deviant behavior are teacher behavior, peer culture, and curriculum. The Teacher Attention Scale (Figure 5.8) is a self-administered assessment used to measure the teacher's social reinforcement of appropriate and inappropriate student behavior. This tool can also be used by an impartial observer. The data analysis is relatively simple and enables the teacher to modify the social reinforcement evoked by deviant student behavior.

The purpose of the Interaction Analysis Model developed by Flanders (Flanders, 1964) is to assess the degree of freedom teachers allow students in the classroom (see Figure 5.9). A trained observer records at 3-second intervals the type of verbal interaction occurring in the classroom. These data are later analyzed to identify the predominant types of interaction taking place. Smith et al. (1978) suggested that the teacher tape-record an activity and later conduct a self-assessment, using the same format. This enables the teacher to modify as needed the type of verbal interaction and social reinforcement given to student behavior. Videotapes can be used for the same purpose and give additional information on nonverbal interaction.

The Washington Social Code (Figure 5.10), developed by Bijou and Baer (1961), is another interval-

	Positive	Negative
Child's Name ___Jay___ Date _Feb., '89_		
Interface		
Teacher relations		X
Peer relations		X
Other adult relations		X
Math	X	
Science	X	
Social studies	X	
Reading		X
Language		X

Figure 5.7. Ecological Niche Breadth Assessment card. *Note.* From "An Ecological Assessment Technique for Behavior Disordered and Learning Disabled Children" by A. G. Prieto and R. B. Rutherford, Jr., 1977, *Behavior Disorders, 2,* p. 172. Reprinted by permission.

observation tool that enables the observer to code the interactive and verbal behavior of a child, the teacher, and peers. It is particularly useful when analyzing interactions during unstructured time, when the child has a choice of activities and can initiate interactions with the teacher and peers.

The following description shows how the Washington Social Code can be used to describe social interaction in a classroom. I have adapted its use slightly by adding notations, but the basic format is standard. Figure 5.10 shows samples of the play behavior of Sue Z., a 4-year-old with expressive language delay. She was observed during choice time on 3 consecutive days, in order to gather baseline data on her social interactions during a less structured activity, choice time, in her preschool class.

Each block of boxes is a record of 1 minute of observation, in which the observer notes the child's behavior every 10 seconds. The "/" mark at the top of the boxes indicates teacher attention given to Sue Z. The top line of boxes is used to record Sue Z.'s initiating behaviors to others: "T" for touch, "V" for verbal interactions, and "N" for nondirectional verbalizations. The middle line is used to record Sue Z.'s play behavior: a dot for playing alone (isolate), "P" for playing nearby and watching someone else (parallel), and "C" for playing with someone else (cooperative). The bottom line is used to record abbreviations for activity (i.e., "H" for household play).

This observation shows that Sue Z. played alone 34% of the time; she watched others and played nearby 35% of the time and played cooperatively 31% of the time. Her interactions were verbal 11% of the time, compared to peer verbal interactions at 26%. Her interactions were physical 6% of the time, compared to a peer's at 11%. These data show a gain in social interaction for Sue Z., as well as an increase in her verbal initiations. When she first enrolled in the class, most of her play was isolate (78%) and she did not initiate verbally at all. The teacher has created opportunities for her to interact by setting up role-playing situations, such as being the checker in the grocery store, that enable Sue Z. to practice her verbal and cooperative play skills in a natural way. The Washington Social Code provided the teacher with information that helped her to identify the types of interactions Sue Z. engaged in most of the time and to plan interventions to increase her verbal and cooperative interactions.

Another important factor of teacher behavior is teaching style. One of the most common ecological factors in poor fit between the student and the environment is the discrepancy between the teacher's style and expectations and the student's style. We've probably all known of cases where the fit was poor. For example, a teacher's brilliant, hard-driving style can overwhelm a fragile and contemplative learner, or a laissez-faire teacher may drive an overachieving student to misbehave. There has been little research in this area, yet many professionals acknowledge that personality factors can play a large role in school success for students.

In recent years, some educators have speculated that a teacher's instructional style is related to his or her favored learning modality. The term *learning modality* in this case means the specific sensory mode through which an individual learns best. For example, one student may learn best when the material is presented with visual cues, such as charts or pictures. Another student may be distracted by such visual cues, and will learn best by having the material explained verbally. The neuropsycholinguistic theory describes how these modalities affect learning. Direct observation in a variety of settings may enable a teacher to identify the favored learning modalities of his or her students. The Swassing-Barbe checklist (Figure 5.11) is an observation checklist designed to identify the favored learning modalities of students—visual, auditory, or kinesthetic. The relationship between preferred learning mode and teaching style has not been extensively researched as yet. Informal studies of teachers, the classroom settings they create, and their favored learning modalities have shown that there is some relationship. A teacher whose teaching style emphasizes a visual mode is bound to have difficulty understanding the student who is com-

The Teacher Attention Scale was developed by Neisworth, Smith, and Greer. It is easy to use and enables the teacher to monitor her or his own behavior, a critical factor in managing the behavioral ecology.

Reinforcing Actions	Punishing Actions	Extinguishing Actions
(Positive, pleasant)	(Aversive, unpleasant)	(Ignoring, overlooking)
Supportive encouraging remarks	Criticism	Deliberately not answering a
Expressing satisfaction/pleasure	Ridicule	question
Smiling at student	Verbal reprimands	Looking away
Physical signs of affection (pat on	Facial expressions indicating	Turning back to child
the back, a hug)	disapproval (frowns, scowls)	Leaving an area of the room
Acknowledging use of student's idea	Body movement indicating hostility,	Redirecting attention to another child
Verbal praise	dislike, irritation	

The teacher behaviors are related to two general categories of student behavior: appropriate and inappropriate. While the definition of what is appropriate or inappropriate depends largely on the teacher, the circumstances, and the type of students, these examples are typical.

Appropriate Student Behavior	Inappropriate Student Behavior
Working quietly at seat	Talking loudly
Cooperating with a peer	Calling others names
Raising hand to ask a question	Running in the building
Participating in class activities	Daydreaming
Finishing assignments	Refusing to do assigned work

Record of Teacher and Student Behavior

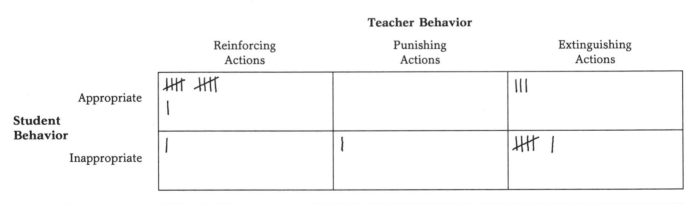

Figure 5.8. Teacher Attention Scale. *Note.* From ''Evaluating the Social Environment,'' chapter 4 in *Evaluating Educational Environments* (pp. 88–89) by R. M. Smith, J. T. Neisworth, and J. G. Greer, 1978. Columbus, OH: Merrill. Reprinted by permission.

pelled by a kinesthetic learning style to touch every teaching aid. With knowledge of learning modalities and some adaptations, the two can probably learn to work well together.

Student evaluations and checklists offer another valuable measure of teacher effectiveness, teaching style, and ecological fit with the students. A sample questionnaire is shown in Figure 5.12. These evaluations must be safeguarded by eliminating both peer pressure and fear of the teacher's response to criticism. Using a sentence completion or true-false format is a quick way to assess teacher effectiveness from the students' perspective. It is important to keep in mind the various influences that will affect the outcome of these questionnaires. Some students are nervous about what the teacher or their friends will think about their responses. It is often difficult for an adult to comprehend the particular social milieu students experience with their peers. This milieu will shape the students' view of the questionnaire and their responses.

One informal way I assess the climate in my room on a daily basis is the ''telling can.'' This is a large can

Categories for Interaction Analysis, 1959

Teacher Talk	Indirect Influence	1.* Accepts Feeling: Accepts and clarifies the tone of feeling of the students in an unthreatening manner. Feelings may be positive or negative. Predicting or recalling feelings is included. 2.* Praises or Encourages: Praises or encourages student action or behavior. Jokes that release tension, but not at the expense of another individual, nodding head, or saying "Um-hm?" or "Go on," are included. 3.* Accepts or Uses Ideas of Student: Clarifying, building, or developing ideas suggested by a student. As teacher brings more of his own ideas into play, shift to category 5.
	Direct Influence	4.* Asks Questions: Asking a question about content or procedure with the intent that a student answer. 5.* Lecturing: Giving facts or opinions about content or procedure; expressing own ideas, asking rhetorical questions. 6.* Giving Directions: Giving directions, commands, or orders that students are expected to comply with. 7.* Criticizing or Justifying Authority: Statements intended to change student behavior from unacceptable to acceptable pattern; bawling someone out; stating why the teacher is doing what he is doing; extreme self-reference.
Student Talk		8.* Student Talk—Response: Talk by students in response to teacher. Teacher initiates the contact or solicits student statement. 9.* Student Talk—Initiation: Talk initiated by students. If "calling on" student is only to indicate who may talk next, observer must decide whether student wanted to talk.
Silence		10.* Silence or Confusion: Pauses, short periods of silence, and periods of confusion in which communication cannot be understood by the observer.

*There is *no* scale implied by these numbers. Each number is classificatory, designating a particular kind of communication event. To write numbers down during observation is merely to identify and enumerate communication events, not to judge them.

Using an audio- or videotape recorder and this model, the teacher will be able to analyze the class or group interactions to identify ecological factors reinforcing student behaviors.

Figure 5.9. Flanders' Interaction Analysis Model. *Note.* From *Teacher Influence, Pupil Attitudes, and Achievement* (p. 20) by N. A. Flanders, 1964. Washington, D.C.: Department of Health, Education and Welfare.

I've decorated and labeled for the students. There's a pad of brightly colored paper under the can; each student also has a small sheaf of these papers in her or his bin. The purpose of the can is to tell me what is bothering, or pleasing, the students. I've told them that anything is open for discussion through the telling can, even criticism of me. My behavior has certainly been modified by some of the messages from my students. I've been told what has worked as an intervention and what has not! It's been amazing to see the messages, and the children's entrance into the classroom is no longer stormy with bids for my attention. We take 5 minutes to write our thoughts the first time we convene each day. I read the notes as soon as we've finished the instructional phase of the period and have begun the practice phase, unless there's an emergency. I've seen children back away from a fight and grab their paper and pencils, venting their anger on paper. The language is unique, the spelling is creative, and sometimes the paper looks like it's been through the wars. But they know I read them, and if it says "Talk" at the end, we do. I've changed seats, modified reading programs, and altered the way I handle teasing, as well as my schedule, since the beginning of the quarter, based on this feedback from the students. There have been times when I've conferred with the child, and times when I've written notes. Some I don't respond to at all, like the ones Jay writes about himself: "_____ Jay." But I save all of the notes, and have a running record of our student-teacher and peer relationships. It takes almost no effort to gather these data, but they've been extremely helpful. The best part is that the students trust the system; they know that someone is listening but that their confidences will be kept.

Social Code Data Sheet

Time begun: _____1:05_____

Time stopped: _____1:21_____

Where: _____Room 4_____

Child: _____Sue Z._____

Observer: _____Drainville_____

Date: _____2-14-89_____

above top line /: teacher interaction

top line
V: verbal address or answer to peer
/: verbal address or answer to adult
N: nondirectional verbal
Z: observer-defined verbal (e.g., giggle)

middle line
•: isolate play
P: proximate or parallel play
T: touch (momentary) to/from peer
Ⓣ: aggressive touch to peer
C: cooperative play

bottom line   Activities in which the child is engaged
H: housekeeping; grocery store
A: art
Bk: books
B: blocks
]: not engaged in any activity

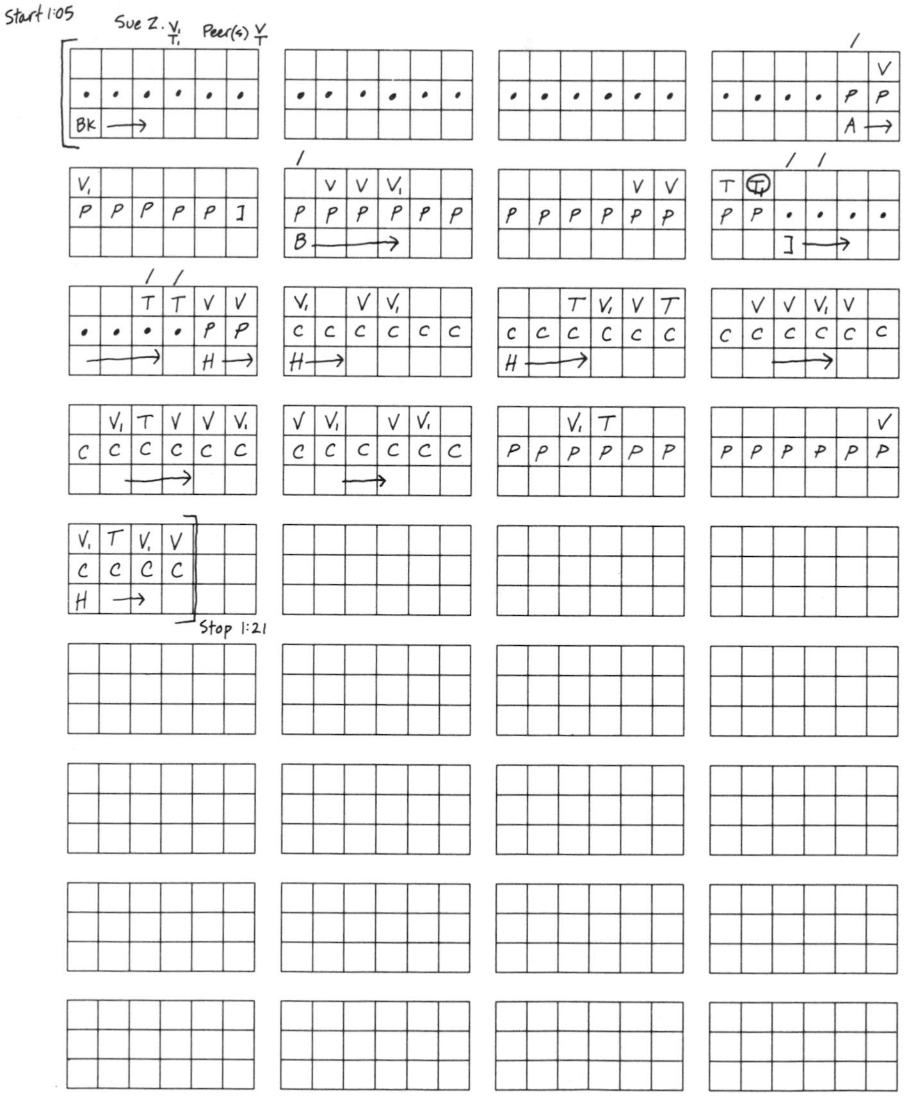

Figure 5.10. Washington Social Code. *Note.* From "Washington Social Code" by Bijou, S. W.; Peterson, R. F.; Harris, F. H.; Allen, K. E.; and Johnston, M. S., 1969, *Psychological Record, 19,* pp. 177–210. Reprinted by permission.

Area Observed	Visual	Auditory	Kinesthetic
Learning Style	☐ Learns by seeing; watching demonstrations	☐ Learns through verbal instructions from others or self	☐ Learns by doing; direct involvement
Reading	☐ Likes description; sometimes stops reading to stare into space and imagine scene; intense concentration	☐ Enjoys dialogue, plays; avoids lengthy description, unaware of illustrations; moves lips or subvocalizes	☐ Prefers stories where action occurs early; fidgets when reading, handles books; not an avid reader
Spelling	☐ Recognizes words by sight; relies on configuration of words	☐ Uses a phonics approach; has auditory word attack skills	☐ Often is a poor speller; writes words to determine if they "feel" right
Handwriting	☐ Tends to be good, particularly when young; spacing and size are good; appearance is important	☐ Has more difficulty learning in initial stages; tends to write lightly; says strokes when writing	☐ Good initially, deteriorates when space becomes smaller; pushes harder on writing instrument
Memory	☐ Remembers faces, forgets names; writes things down, takes notes	☐ Remembers names, forgets faces; remembers by auditory repetition	☐ Remembers best what was done, not what was seen or talked about
Imagery	☐ Vivid imagination; thinks in pictures, visualizes in detail	☐ Subvocalizes, thinks in sounds; details less important	☐ Imagery not important; images that do occur are accompanied by movement
Distractibility	☐ Generally unaware of sounds; distracted by visual disorder or movement	☐ Easily distracted by sounds	☐ Not attentive to visual, auditory presentation so seems distractible
Problem solving	☐ Deliberate; plans in advance; organizes thoughts by writing them; lists problems	☐ Talks problems out, tries solutions verbally, subvocally; talks self through problem	☐ Attacks problems physically; impulsive; often selects solution involving greatest activity
Response to periods of inactivity	☐ Stares; doodles; finds something to watch	☐ Hums; talks to self or to others	☐ Fidgets; finds reasons to move; holds up hand
Response to new situations	☐ Looks around; examines structure	☐ Talks about situation, pros and cons, what to do	☐ Tries things out; touches, feels; manipulates
Emotionality	☐ Somewhat repressed; stares when angry; cries easily, beams when happy; facial expression is a good index of emotion	☐ Shouts with joy or anger; blows up verbally but soon calms down; expresses emotion verbally and through changes in tone, volume, pitch of voice	☐ Jumps for joy; hugs, tugs, and pulls when happy; stamps, jumps, and pounds when angry, stomps off; general body tone is a good index of emotion
Communication	☐ Quiet; does not talk at length; becomes impatient when extensive listening is required; may use words clumsily; describes without embellishment; uses words such as *see, look*	☐ Enjoys listening but cannot wait to talk; descriptions are long but repetitive; likes hearing self and others talk; uses words such as *listen, hear*	☐ Gestures when speaking; does not listen well; stands close when speaking or listening; quickly loses interest in detailed verbal discourse; uses words such as *get, take*
General appearance	☐ Neat, meticulous, likes order; may choose not to vary appearance	☐ Matching clothes not so important, can explain choices of clothes	☐ Neat but soon becomes wrinkled through activity
Response to the arts	☐ Not particularly responsive to music; prefers the visual arts; tends not to voice appreciation of art of any kind, but can be deeply affected by visual displays; focuses on details and components rather than the work as a whole	☐ Favors music; finds less appeal in visual art, but is readily able to discuss it; misses significant detail, but appreciates the work as a whole; is able to develop verbal association for all art forms; spends more time talking about pieces than looking at them	☐ Responds to music by physical movement; prefers sculpture; touches statues and paintings; at exhibits stops only at those in which he or she can become physically involved; comments very little on any art form

Figure 5.11. Swassing-Barbe checklist. *Note.* Excerpted from *Teaching Through Modality Strengths: Concepts and Practices* by W. B. Barbe and R. H. Swassing, with M. N. Milone, Jr., 1980. Columbus, OH: Zaner-Bloser. Used by permission of the publisher, Zaner-Bloser, Inc., Columbus, OH. Copyright, 1979, 1988.

1. Who is your favorite work partner? _____

2. Who is the person who helps you the most? _____

3. Who is your least favored work partner? _____

4. List three classmates for your work group:

    a. _____

    b. _____

    c. _____

5. Why did you pick each person?

    a. _____

    b. _____

    c. _____

6. If you could pick your own seat, where would you sit and why? _____

    _____

7. Whose list will you *never* be on? _____

8. Whose list will you *always* be on? _____

9. Is our class friendly: why or why not? _____

    _____

10. Does teaching kids about being caring help? _____

    _____

11. What is the best thing about our class? _____

    _____

12. What is the worst thing about our class? _____

    _____

13. What else would you like to tell me? _____

    _____

Figure 5.12.   Mrs. D.'s student questionnaire. *Note.* Copyright 1988 by Barbara L. Drainville.

Peer influence has been shown to be affected by (1) developmental age (Shinn, 1972), (2) socioeconomic status (Tasseigne, 1975), (3) family stability (Rice, 1975), (4) gender (Gilligan, 1987), and (5) in some cases race (Winkler, 1975). While peer values and norms affect both academic achievement and social behavior, they are notoriously hard to measure because of their fluidity and the differences in perception between adults and children. Each group of students will develop its own pattern of social interaction with leaders, followers, and those excluded from group alliances. Generally, it is easier to observe these relationships with younger children, before peer pressure becomes significant to the students. If an intervention is to modify a student's behavior, especially in the area of social behavior, these factors must be considered. Questionnaires and sociometric devices can be effective measures of the peer norms and alliances in the classroom setting, as long as safeguards are used to question in a positive, nonthreatening manner (Fishe & Cox, 1960; Fox et al., 1966; Hollander, 1964; Moreno, 1953; Reynolds, 1966).

In her book *In a Different Voice* (1987), Gilligan has analyzed the research done by Erickson and Kohlberg on the development of social conscience. Because she found that all of their subjects were male, she has been conducting research on the same subject, using both female and male subjects. Her preliminary research has shown significant differences between girls and boys. For example, she has found that girls will give up a game rather than exclude one member of their social group. In contrast, boys will adhere strictly to the rules of the game and will exclude a member of their group who does not adhere to those rules. Gilligan is currently conducting further research into gender differences in social norms; this new research could have a profound impact on the types of ecological interventions developed in the area of social skills.

Ecobehavioral Assessment of Disturbing Behavior in School

Assessment of the ecological factors of the target behavior consists of a series of task analyses for the child's various ecological niches. First we have to know what the behavior is and what it isn't. Then we can analyze the ecological factors supporting that behavior and change them. This will change the behavior. Analysis of the ecological supports will also provide the information needed to plan for generalization and maintenance of new behaviors.

Step 1: Pinpointing the Behavior
An assessment of a child's disturbing behavior is an integral part of planning an intervention to change the ecology of that behavior. The first task is to define, or pinpoint, the behavior of concern—that is, the particular behavior that is the poorest fit in the child's ecological niche. It is impossible to observe the behavior unless it is clearly defined to all observers. Often there is a constellation of behaviors that set the child apart from his peers and make his "match" with his learning environment dysfunctional. There is also a reciprocal spiral of reinforcement from the environment; these behaviors become overwhelming as they escalate. At this point, the child becomes a focus of concern and the specialists are called in. Using a multidisciplinary team approach, the classroom teacher, the specialists, the principal, and others involved with the child can define the target behavior by answering the following "W" questions: who; what; where; when; with whom; under what conditions; and, at times, why. These questions provide a shorthand investigative outline with which to pinpoint the behavior and define the ecology in which it occurs.

Step 2: Observing the Behavior Across Settings
Once the behavior has been clearly defined, structured baseline observations can be conducted. It is crucial that the behavioral/ecological match be carefully observed across behavioral settings. The intervention may already be present in another setting. For example, Johnny's screams on the bus caused him to be suspended, and he was in danger of losing his transportation to school. In a similar unstructured situation with a large group of cross-age peers, Johnny did not scream and was a model student, as well as a group leader. By observing Johnny behaving appropriately in a different setting with similar evocative conditions, the teacher has an indication (1) that Johnny can behave appropriately and (2) that having a leadership role may reinforce Johnny's self-control. Across-setting observations can also rule out possible interventions; if Johnny were to scream every time he was with more than three other children, we could assume that a leadership role would not be the first intervention of choice.

Step 3: Analysis of the Environmental Reinforcers
This phase is unique to the ecobehavioral analysis of the behavior. It requires extensive baseline data from the variety of ecological niches in which the child behaves. The baseline data include information about the child, teachers, classrooms, peer relationships, curriculum, schedule, family, neighborhood, and community services available to the child.

When identifying the events that support deviant behavior, it is important to keep in mind the purpose of our investigation. It isn't helpful to assess a child as having ADD without looking at the behavior settings that precipitate or reinforce distracted as well as attending behavior. A child with ADD is not always flying around the room; there are times when she demonstrates self-control and attends to *something*.

Children with ADD and any other learning disability or, as I term it, "learning difference," must learn to cope with the real world. That is our purpose: to reinforce survival skills (i.e., behavior appropriate to their behavior settings). In chapter 12, I describe types of interventions we developed using these ecological baselines. The examples I've used are the students who have been in our resource room; in most cases, the interventions were shared with the regular classroom teachers. Often, these baseline data were the basis of the interventions used. In many cases, we had to modify our behavior, teaching style, values, or mode of interacting with children because these particular students needed something different from us. Much of the ecological niche fit is based upon the fit between the child and the teacher. The teacher is the significant other; he or she can have a tremendous impact on the student. It's hard to be "all things to all people," but ecobehavioral analysis will help a teacher observe each student's needs and meet them more efficiently.

Focus 1: The Child

The child is an obvious starting point in analyzing a poor fit with his or her ecological niches. This does not mean that the child is viewed as the sole "owner" of the problem. Pinpointing the behavior can only be done by observations. Since the child has become the focus of concern, it is important to see if he or she has the following basic skills to meet the expectations of the environment:

1. The ability to understand what those expectations are
2. The aptitudes to meet those expectations
3. The developmental and cognitive ability to perform as expected
4. The receptive language required to understand his environment and the expressive language necessary to demonstrate that understanding
5. The motor skills needed to demonstrate her ability
6. The sensory and perceptual information required to extract needed cues from the ecological niche
7. The techniques to manage distractions in the environment in order to focus on what is expected
8. The ability to cope with his emotional state, so that it doesn't interfere with his adaptation to his environment
9. The ability to perceive and adapt to the social relationships with her family, her teachers, her peers, and the neighborhood

It is also important to realize that this is not a static situation, but one that changes and adapts to circumstances. This would be a tall order for any individual; it's a wonder that most children adapt so well. Or is it that we do not notice their difficulties until they become overwhelming?

All of these factors obviously cannot be tested by one measure. It is important to realize that any standardized test is going to provide a very narrow view of a child. The results are only as good as the match between the child and the ecological niche, which consists of the test situation and the examiner on that particular day and in that specific environment. Normative data are static; these data have recently come under a lot of criticism for racial, gender, cultural, and socioeconomic bias. There is no magic in these tests; an IQ or achievement score is not cast in bronze! Figure 5.13 shows a summary of test data from standardized tests.

With this in mind, the focus can be on the child's performance on a number of different measures: criterion referenced, standardized, structured behavioral observations across settings; sensory, perceptual, and motor evaluations; interviews with significant others; and an often neglected part of the workup—an interview with the child. In many cases, the child will tell you why there is a poor fit. It is important to hear what the child says, because these comments often will tell you how to intervene.

Focus 2: The Teacher

The second factor that must be analyzed is the teacher; it requires a good deal of professionalism for a teacher to recognize that he or she is part of the problem. The basic premise of ecobehavioral analysis is that the poor fit is the result of ecological reinforcement of the disturbing behavior. Since the teacher is the most reinforcing element in the child's classroom environment, this is the next logical factor to analyze. It may be a problem of style or of personality; not every teacher and child dyad is a happy one. It may be the result of the teacher's lack of perception of other stressors that are affecting the child's behavior. Perhaps the teacher lacks training in behavior management strategies. In an effort to help, many teachers give inadvertent reinforcement by repeatedly "counseling" the child about his inappropriate behavior.

This reinforcement, in fact, is the norm in "standard American discipline" (S.A.D.) and is certainly not limited to teachers! Parents, principals, counselors, coaches, bus drivers, and specialists—anyone, in fact, who comes into contact with the child—may reinforce the very behavior he or she is trying to extinguish or change. That is because these people don't know one of the basic tenets of behaviorism: What earns atten-

NOTES:

VMI																		
WRAT-R: MATH																		
WRAT-R: SP																		
WRAT-R: RDG																		
W/J: W. EXP.																		
W/J: MATH																		
W/J: RDG																		
WEPMAN:																		
TOWL																		
TONI																		
TERA																		
TEMA																		
TWS																		
SORT																		
PPVT																		
MATH INV: ×/×																		
MATH INV: ÷																		
MATH INV: ×																		
MATH INV: −																		
MATH INV: +																		
KEYMATH																		
IRI: TEXTS																		
IRI: WD. LISTS																		
DOLCH PHRASES																		
DOLCH #138																		
BRIG. SURV. WRDS.																		
BRIG. MATH																		
BEH. RTG. SCALE																		
BARNELL-LOFT SP																		

Figure 5.13. Summary of test data. *Note.* Copyright 1988 by Barbara L. Drainville.

tion is likely to be reinforced; what is reinforced is likely to be repeated. This creates a dilemma for many adults, because they want to be sure the child understands what is expected and how to be successful. The child's understanding can be checked once by asking, "What are you supposed to be doing?" or "What is the rule?" Once it's been established that the child knows what's expected, any further discussion is unnecessary. It is imperative, at that point, to implement whatever intervention has been chosen to change the environmental support of the deviant behavior. It is no easy task to change a mindset that is ingrained by the way we have been raised, but that is what is needed, if we are going to change the way the school environment evokes and maintains deviant behavior.

This process must include several steps. First, the teacher must perceive that she or he is part of the problem. Second, the teacher must be aware of the specific types of cues and reinforcement he or she is giving. And third, the teacher must systematically reinforce changes in his or her own behavior that will change those cues or reinforcers. This is actually easier than it sounds, and most teachers are relieved by the release from the spiral of negative interactions with the child.

For example, every time Jane slammed into the room, the teacher would cue her to come in quietly. Jane's continued disruptive entrances drove the teacher and the class to distraction. A number of factors had to be analyzed. First, it was imperative for Jane to understand the teacher's expectation that she come in quietly. The quickest way to determine if she knew that expectation was to ask, at a later time, what she thought the expectation was. If she knew she was expected to come in quietly, any cue to her would be reinforcement. Once the teacher determined that Jane understood the rule, he knew that her behavior was reinforced by the individual attention. The teacher then had a number of options.

One, he could reinforce other students who came in quietly and ignore Jane. He could also reinforce the other students for ignoring Jane's noisy entrances. This would probably precipitate even louder entrances from Jane, because most extinction data curves escalate before they fall. The student may feel that if a little of the behavior that worked before is no longer "buying" the payoff (attention), then perhaps a lot of the behavior will! It is important for the teacher and other students to realize this and persist in the intervention. Escalation therefore is a sign that the intervention is working.

A second option would be to give Jane some responsibility, such as helping the teacher set up the next activity, so that she would get individual attention for appropriate behavior. This also enables the teacher to establish a more positive relationship with Jane, so that

she becomes invested in the teacher's reinforcement and in the success of the activity.

A third option would be for Jane to be the "data taker" and take data on which peers are coming into the room quietly. This intervention has some added benefits. Not only is Jane practicing coming in quietly, she is modeling the appropriate behavior for her peers and is being reinforced for doing so. Another potential benefit is that her peers may view her in a more positive light—first, because she is using appropriate behavior and has the responsible role of data taker, and second, because she has become a source of reinforcement for them. There is some merit in teaching the students data-based instruction, because it teaches them who is responsible for each part of the learning interaction.

These interventions will work as long as there is no lapse into the old pattern of paying attention to noisy entrances. In addition to being consistent, the teacher must take data, if for no other reason than to reinforce the change in his own behavior.

I used a simple data collection technique to find out why there were so many interruptions during a large-group period in one of my self-contained classes. The students in this class were 6 to 8 years old; they were functioning from 2 to 3 years below expectations for their age and grade level. Five of the 11 students had entered my class from a program for behavior-disordered students. My goal for this large-group instruction was twofold: to improve social and language skills. It was important first to reduce talk-outs; the constant interruptions were rendering this group period useless. I developed a chart with which the aide observed me as I interacted with the students. The baseline phase showed that I was reinforcing talk-outs by attending to them at a rate of 75%. I corrected out-of-seat and kicking behavior with a redirect cue that was effective only 30% of the time. I praised on-task behavior about 35% of the time. The behaviors decreased in frequency by almost 50% when I led an activity that involved some motor response (i.e., standing up to talk). I then implemented a program to increase my praise of on-task behavior and my extinction response (ignoring, paired with praise to a peer for on-task behavior). The aide took data and after three incorrect responses, she would cue me: "ignore" or "praise." These data were taken twice a day for 10 minutes. The result was a decrease in interruptions by more than 80%; the on-task behaviors increased to 95% for all but one student. (See Figure 5.14.)

When I first explained the data I wanted and the intent of the intervention, the aide reacted with surprise and disbelief. It is awkward, at first, to run a program to modify one's own behavior. It makes you vulnerable and self-critical. But the results are usually rewarding,

Date: _____/_____/_____

Recorder: Student Behavior: Teacher Behavior:

A.M.   P.M.   Goal: –   –   –   +

Name:	Talk-Out	Out of Seat	Kicks	Hand	R+	R–	Ignore
Alice							
Brent							
Clark							
Danielle							
Janine							
Emily							
Linda							
Mark							
Mickie							
Susie							
Jamar							
Totals:							

Figure 5.14. Large-group data. *Note.* Copyright 1986 by Barbara L. Drainville.

not only for the students' skills, but also for the teacher's. If you don't have an aide, use a volunteer, a tape recorder, or a video recorder. I was assisted by a volunteer from a local teachers' retirement home.

Another type of data I found useful in analyzing social interaction was self-reported in a self-contained resource program for elementary students. The class was a reentry point for at least half of the students who had been placed in a facility for behavior-disabled students and who were returning to the public school system. One of the main difficulties was social interaction outside of the classroom.

Figure 5.15 shows a recess evaluation form which I developed to gather data on the types of recess behavior the students reported to me after each recess. We sat in a large circle and each child would report on his or her recess. Then the other students shared their observations with that student. A happy or sad face was recorded next to each child's name on the board. If a student got a sad face, we met before the next recess so that we could make a plan to solve that child's particular challenge. A happy face was earned by playing

cooperatively and safely, using words to solve conflicts, and asking for help with problems. A sad face was earned for fighting, playing unsafely, calling names, and other uncooperative behaviors. We practiced safe and cooperative play and repeated the rules before and after each recess: play safe, use words, and ask for help. We also recorded activities chosen by the students, so that they could identify activities in which they were successful. We used the honor system to report, and the students kept each other honest with feedback. This program increased appropriate play by over 60% and had an added benefit of creating camaraderie among children who had been complete isolates at one time.

Most teachers are reluctant to use data collection methods that are unwieldly and time consuming. Professionals from outside the classroom have been notorious for designing data systems that don't work for that reason. It is imperative that the data collection system be accurate and easily administered across settings.

One of the informal measures I've developed is the teacher tolerance scale (Figure 5.16). It helps me to focus on the areas of the classroom ecology that I can control

Happy 😊 Unhappy 🙁	A.M.	Lunch	P.M.
Alice			
Emily			
Brent			
Clark			
Donna			
Jamar			
Danielle			
Mark			
Mickie			
Susie			

Activity: Sand: Balls: Room 8 peers: Climbers:

Other-room peers: Tutor:

Code: CP = Cooperative play with peer   F = Fight   B = Broke rules

Skills: Help asked from: T = Teacher   TU = Tutor   P = Peer

W = Used words   I = Ignore   WA = Walk away   NG = New game

Interventions: TO = Time out   LR = Lost recess   O = Other

Notes _____

_____

_____

Figure 5.15.   Recess evaluation data. *Note.* Copyright 1986 by Barbara L. Drainville.

and reminds me what my tolerance is for deviance from my expectations for each factor. I've discovered that my tolerance has varied as the year has progressed. I attribute this, in part, to the rise in expectations that comes with familiarity. I've also discovered that changes in the student population have changed my tolerance for certain behaviors. This knowledge is helpful in alerting me to problem areas or times, and has prompted me to make changes in the schedule and curriculum. Using this scale in conjunction with other assessments has enabled me to monitor the ecology of behavior in the resource room.

For example, I began to have little tolerance for talking during language arts for intermediate students. This was one period of the day I usually enjoyed, because the students had made good progress and I'd been able to introduce cooperative learning activities to them. Both cooperative small-group and large-group instruc-

tion were less effective than they had been due to a high number of disruptions (an average of 95 per period). I instituted small-group activities and individual instruction while I analyzed the situation.

I found that three new students had completely changed the configuration of the group. When all three were present the disruptions (talk-out, out-of-seat, and off-task behaviors) rose from an average of 8 to 95 during an 85-minute period. Their off-task and disruptive behaviors made cooperative learning activities impractical. In addition to using the teacher tolerance self-assessment and sociogram, I assessed these new students individually on a criterion-referenced skills assessment to determine their reference and writing skills, and took data on on-task behavior during some structured writing tasks.

I discovered that the new students did not have the same "tool" skills as the other students: They were

---

Tolerance Scale:

0 = none 1 = little 2 = some 3 = more 4 = much

During transitions, I have this much tolerance for:

activity:	0	1	2	3	4
delay of response:	0	1	2	3	4
dependence:	0	1	2	3	4
independence:	0	1	2	3	4
individual attention:	0	1	2	3	4
noise:	0	1	2	3	4
off-task behavior:	0	1	2	3	4
peer interaction:	0	1	2	3	4
physical proximity:	0	1	2	3	4
talking:	0	1	2	3	4

During instructional periods, I have this much tolerance for:

activity:	0	1	2	3	4
delay of response:	0	1	2	3	4
dependence:	0	1	2	3	4
independence:	0	1	2	3	4
individual attention:	0	1	2	3	4
noise:	0	1	2	3	4
off-task behavior:	0	1	2	3	4
peer interaction:	0	1	2	3	4
physical proximity:	0	1	2	3	4
talking:	0	1	2	3	4

Expectations for:

entering: _____

leaving: _____

large-group instruction: _____

small-group instruction: _____

independent work: _____

Figure 5.16. Teacher self-assessment: Tolerance. *Note.* Copyright 1988 by Barbara L. Drainville.

unable to structure sentences and paragraphs, they did not know how to use a dictionary or encyclopedia, and they could not tell me the rules and expectations of cooperative learning. Although they'd been in three dif-

ferent resource settings around the state, none of them had ever been required to write original or research material. My students write every day, and the new students found my expectations too high.

Two of the students were seated individually to cut down their off-task behavior. For part of each period, they each were placed with two proficient students to practice their tool skills and to produce written assignments with the group. These students have since written some good stories and reports. The third student showed no change in his disruptive behavior, and it continued to escalate. We had numerous conferences with his parents, who were divorced, and with the various staff members who worked with him. After analyzing all of the data from the numerous interventions tried, we referred the student for drug testing. He was subsequently returned to his father's custody in another city. His father obtained treatment as well as behavior intervention through the school. The student is currently achieving at grade level, with no behavior problems.

Teachers other than the homeroom teacher are important in analyzing behavior for two reasons. First, these teachers give another view of the child, and second, they manage a different ecological niche for the child. The physical education teacher who sees Lisa as a fine athlete and a compliant group member may be describing the kinesthetic learner who bulldozes through every quiet activity the classroom teacher plans. In ecobehavioral analysis, teachers must be included in every phase as an integral part of the process. Often they have the knowledge and insights into the child that will provide the key intervention and break the pattern of the deviant interaction.

Focus 3: Peer Interactions

The next factor to be analyzed consists of the social interaction patterns in the ecological niches where the child misbehaves. A child's peer relationships cannot be underestimated, since these relationships provide increasingly important reinforcement for appropriate or deviant behavior. Sociograms and other measures can help the teacher arrange interactions by changing seating patterns and by assigning cooperative learning activities. For example, a specific cooperative learning activity, in which the group earns one grade, or points, for work done together, can assist the child by changing the expectations and reinforcement of on-task behavior. The same students who snickered at Johnny's off-task antics become very invested in helping him complete his work when their points depend on his performance. The teacher can facilitate this interaction by teaching her students how to reinforce on-task work positively and ignore off-task behavior. Children often feel unable to cope with aggressive behavior on the playground. They can be empowered to handle that behavior by not engaging with the aggressive child. This will decrease the number of times they are victimized. A child who finds that no one will play with her while she is being aggressive may find another way to play.

Assessing peer relationships and using them to plan interventions takes a delicate touch. To minimize the social cues for deviant behavior, the teacher must work to create a classroom environment in which every child is valued and feels safe. This can only be accomplished by asking questions about peer relations.

Focus 4: The Physical Setting

The fourth factor in the ecology of the behavior is the physical setting, or the classroom. The arrangement of desks, traffic patterns, and overcrowding all have an impact on the way children interact in the classroom. Generally, when a teacher designs her classroom, she does it without the children present. The arrangement may look efficient or appealing but it doesn't take into account the unique characteristics of the class and the interactions they develop.

Physical factors such as temperature, light, noise level, and even odors can have a profound effect on the children's ability to concentrate. The rumble of the radiator may be torture to one child, while it provides pleasant background noise to another. The sizes and developmental levels of the students must also be considered. Have you ever sat through a movie where the seat was uncomfortable? Think how excruciating it would be to sit like that every day for hours. Sometimes out-of-seat behavior is simply discomfort, a prime example of poor fit! Seasonal and even daily shifts in the weather, amount of sunlight (glare), and temperature may affect a child's comfort in his ecological niche. Many experienced teachers have said that windy days make all their students excited and distractible. So it is important to assess the classroom environment not as a static ecology, but as one that changes frequently. Ask about comfort levels (Figure 5.17); sit at their desks or, for younger students, on the floor. The best way to assess their physical environment is kinesthetically.

Proximity is the critical factor in peer interaction in the classroom. If you want children to interact, put them together. A child's proximity to the teacher or a favored peer can change that child's behavior. A few minutes in the quiet corner can be a lifesaver for a distractible and physical student.

The benefits of asking students about their comfort level, where and with whom they'd like to sit, and other such factors are numerous. Unknown problems come to light; rewards and contingencies are easy to spot. If students state a preference for working together, cooperative learning activities are more likely to succeed.

Focus 5: The Curriculum

The term *curriculum* means all of the activities that encompass instruction, including guided practice, independent work, the materials used to instruct, and practice learning. A child's success with the curriculum is dependent on three factors: her ability to extract information from the curriculum, her motivation to do so, and the teacher's expectations. The similarity between the teacher's and student's styles of learning is important, as is the content of the lessons. A child's perception of the lesson will affect his motivation. The child who is a defeated learner, and who feels the task is too hard, may misbehave or act out to get attention or distract himself from the frustration of the work.

Remember that the focus of the curriculum is to teach the student needed skills and concepts. If it is too hard or does not meet the child's needs, she will not benefit from it. Scrap it or change it, but don't waste your time and frustrate the student with a poor curriculum fit.

Assessment of the child's ability and analysis of the curricular expectations can provide significant insight into deviant behavior. Adaptations can then be designed to enable the student to be successful while performing tasks within the curriculum. For example, the kindergarten teacher is demonstrating how to blend the primary colors to make secondary colors. Steve doesn't know the names of the colors, but he can match them. The teacher may allow Steve to match the colors as he demonstrates. This allows Steve to participate, without disrupting the class, and provides him with practice that will lead eventually to naming the colors.

Adaptation of the curriculum is something teachers do on a daily basis. It requires creativity and finesse to fine tune the curriculum to stimulate the advanced students, while meeting the needs of the less able. Although the idea of adapting the curriculum as an intervention for disruptive behavior may be disturbing to teachers, often a simple change in how the student demonstrates mastery can eliminate a whole constellation of deviant behavior. It has been my observation that teachers spend more time and anguish on management problems than on any other single issue. Wouldn't it be nice to spend that time and energy on more productive activities?

As an example, if a student's lack of visual motor skills would interfere with her success on a written test, a peer tutor or a tape recorder might be used to test her ability to spell the spelling list. The question in this case is: What is the purpose of the activity? Is it to teach spelling or writing? There are a few important questions to be raised in assessing the curriculum:

1. Is the child able to do the work?

This can be used as an individual pencil-and-paper activity or as an overhead interview of the group. The items can be tailored to your class.

 1. Do you like your seat?   Y   N   Why? _____

 2. Is it comfortable?   Y   N   Why? _____

 3. Do you have enough space?   Y   N   Why? _____

 4. Is it too cold or hot?   Y   N   Why? _____

 5. Is it too noisy?   Y   N   Why? _____

 6. Is there enough air?   Y   N   Why? _____

 7. Does it smell OK?   Y   N   Why? _____

 8. Is the light OK?   Y   N   Why? _____

 9. Is the traffic OK?   Y   N   Why? _____

10. Can you see OK?   Y   N   Why? _____

11. Can you hear OK?   Y   N   Why? _____

What do you like best about the classroom? _____

_____

What do you like least about the classroom? _____

_____

How can we fix it? _____

_____

_____

Figure 5.17. Comfort check. *Note.* Copyright 1988 by Barbara L. Drainville.

2. Can the work be adapted so that the child can do it?
3. Is the work critical to the child's long-term success in school?

These questions are practical considerations, but they also are value laden. The teacher who is heavily invested in a particular methodology or content area will answer these questions differently from one who is not. There lies the value judgment. It is not only, or always, the teacher who is invested; it may be the principal, the special education director, the superintendent who purchased the curriculum materials, or the local university that developed the materials and provided student teachers to be trained in their use. The needs of the child must be considered in light of these value judgments. The important safeguard is to know your biases and those of the others who affect the curriculum and the student. This analysis gives us a small glimpse into the interconnections in the educational ecosystem.

Focus 6: The Schedule
The daily schedule is of primary concern because of the way it affects the child's physical state and the curriculum. Common sense tells us that if a child acts out during the period before lunch, regardless of the activity, she is probably hungry. This may sound simplistic, but it is amazing how many "behavior problems" are cured by a snack at recess. If there is a subject with dif-

ficult content just after physical education or lunch recess, the chances are great that there will be disruptive behavior. In early-childhood programs, it is helpful to alternate quiet and active periods. An average 4-year-old's lung capacity will sustain him for about 20 minutes of high activity. By working with the physical and developmental ages of the students, the teacher can avoid precipitating unnecessary disruptions.

A teacher can also use the schedule to make a highly motivating activity contingent upon completion of a less motivating task. For example, the teacher may schedule an art activity after the class has completed the math seatwork. Adaptation of the schedule is dependent upon other schedules in the building, such as physical education, the resource center, speech therapy, and music. Sometimes the amount of disruption caused by these interruptions can lead to deviant behavior. The assessment of the schedule must take the teacher's and students' tolerance for disruption into account.

Tinkering with the schedule can be a never-ending process; I try to limit it by asking the students to decide when to do one or two subjects. Then we choose a student or two to take frequency data on late starts and off-task behavior. After a week or so, we meet again to discuss the change. If the data suggest another change, we repeat the process. The content remains the same; only the times are changed. Giving the students some control over their day can increase their commitment to the class. I've had students tell me that over and over: "You let us decide, Ms. D.," or "You listen."

Ecobehavioral Assessment Outside of the School Environment

Focus 1: The Family

Many factors outside of the school environment have a strong impact on the student's behavior. In fact, the family is normally the primary educator of the child, while the school is secondary. Parents are often the models of learning behavior. They teach the child values and methods of social interaction. Every family has its own style and norms; these will shape the way a child interacts with new ecosystems. If there is a poor fit at school, the parent or caregiver may be able to give valuable insight and assistance in helping with deviant behavior. I would say that the parents and the teacher are the two most critical agents of change in a child's ecology until adolescence.

A child's world view, approach to new situations, and style of learning are well established by the age of 5 or 6. Early-childhood programs should be especially sensitive to the developmental needs of the students because of the formative nature of those early experi-

ences. It is imperative to maintain good communication with the parents so that a problem can be addressed as soon as it arises.

Family values and expectations may differ from those held by school personnel. It may be more important for the child to be compliant at home by doing chores or caring for siblings than it is to do homework. This factor will certainly affect an after-school intervention for incomplete homework!

The family is also a critical factor in generalization of new skills and expectations; programs to change behavior must consider the hours at home as integral to a change in the ecology of a behavior. After all, the child may spend 6½ to 7 hours at school; the rest of the 24 hours are spent at home.

Focus 2: The Neighborhood

The socioeconomic status of the neighborhood and that of the child's family will have an impact on the child's before-school and after-school adaptation in the neighborhood. The child's relationships in the neighborhood will affect the way she enters and leaves school and the kinds of peer relationships she develops. Knowing the dynamics of the neighborhood and anticipating alliances and conflicts makes a teacher wise. She will then be able to avoid evoking deviant behavior. She may also be able to assist the student in dealing with a potential problem before it becomes a school problem.

For example, if Joaquín gets into fights before school or anticipates a fight after school, he's not going to care about this week's art lesson. He's also going to be more likely to carry over aggression to the playground as well as the classroom.

Focus 3: The Community and Beyond

The impact of the school district, the community, the state, and the nation is largely outside the influence of school personnel. There are times when the teacher is obliged to contact other social service agencies, such as child protective services, the police, or probation officers. In some states, there are legal mandates for teachers to do so when they suspect a problem within those provinces. No one can ethically stand by while a child suffers; there've been too many cases of that in the news.

The ecological management of behavior is teaching children and adults to work together toward a goal: the success of each child in learning how best to survive in the ecological niches she or he encounters. Humans are not static beings, and teaching children to live adaptively is the best gift we can give them. Most teachers enter the field of education because they care about children and want to help them learn to live well in the world. The ecological management of behavior helps teachers do so in an ethical and efficient manner. And since management skills are the critical factor in successful learning, both teachers and children benefit from ecobehavioral analysis.

In conclusion, the interventions you choose should be based on what the child does in the context of his or her environment. For a discussion of interventions and case histories, refer to chapter 12.

Chapter Five Self-Assessment

See Appendix A for acceptable responses.

1. Write a definition of ecobehavioral analysis.

2. Describe the difference between ecobehavioral analysis and the medical and psychodynamic models.

3. List the factors of the ecology of behavior.

   a.

   b.

   c.

   d.

   e.

4. Match the definitions of the following terms in column A with those in column B:

   <u>Column A</u>

   a. behavior setting

   b. ecological niche

   c. the three levels of behavior

   d. poor fit

   <u>Column B</u>

   1. single, multiple, cultural

   2. maladaptive relationship between behavior and the behavioral setting

   3. the physical setting, time and place, with specific activities and inhabitants

   4. the role that one fulfills in any given ecosystem

5. List the types of assessments useful in ecobehavioral analysis.

Part III
Creating Change in Students

chapter 6

Strategies for Strengthening Behaviors

Upon successful completion of this chapter, the learner should be able to:

1. State rules regarding reinforcement
2. Label examples of social, token, primary, tangible, and activity reinforcers
3. Describe methods used to choose reinforcers
4. Answer multiple-choice questions regarding schedules of reinforcement
5. Draw diagrams of schedules of reinforcement
6. Write a shaping program for a student given the target behavior and the student's current level of functioning
7. Describe the difference between shaping and fading
8. List the steps in the chaining process
9. List questions to consider when planning a token economy
10. State how to avoid (or solve) four problems common to the token economy
11. Write a definition of the Premack Principle
12. List high- and low-frequency behaviors that apply to himself or herself
13. Write a self-management contract to perform a low-frequency behavior with a high-frequency behavior as the consequent stimulus event (CSE)
14. Describe the trouble-shooting procedure to use if a given reinforcement program does not achieve the desired objective

---

As has been stated in an earlier chapter, there are only two ways to strengthen behavior: (1) positive reinforcement, in which a behavior may be strengthened by consequating it with the presentation of a pleasing stimulus or reward, and (2) negative reinforcement, in which a behavior may be strengthened by consequating it with the removal of an aversive stimulus.

I don't intend to spend much time discussing negative reinforcement (R–). I think it is overused in our society. Most of us learn to obey society's laws, not necessarily because they are good laws that should be obeyed or because we will be rewarded if we obey them, but because of the bad things that might happen to us if we disobeyed them. The Internal Revenue Service does not give out rewards for people who file their income tax returns on time or without error, intentional or otherwise. The police do not reward drivers who obey the traffic laws. It is no different in our schools. Many of them seem to run on the principle of negative reinforcement. You obey the rules in order to avoid aversives such as detention, failing grades, negative attention, or suspension, not to receive rewards. Go into almost any classroom and collect data on the number of negative and positive comments teachers give to their students and you will probably find the ratio to be as high as 4:1, negative to positive. We have enough R– going on in the schools and I don't think we need any more. However, just in case you need to use R–, you might as well know when and how.

First, use R– when you want to strengthen desirable behavior with little or no behavior to reward. You can't reward being in seat or on task if the student is seldom in her seat or on task. If it's too difficult to catch the student being "good," catch her being "bad" and use R– (e.g., "If you don't sit down, you're going to lose _____ of the points you've earned" or "If you don't finish your math by dismissal, you will have to finish it after school"). There is nothing wrong with using R– in this situation. You can't use R+ because there isn't enough appropriate behavior to reinforce. You could always punish her out-of-seat and off-task behavior, but punishment has so many disadvantages (see chapter 7) that you would be better off using R–. Another rule of thumb is to always make sure you can do what you say you'll do. If you tell the student she will stay after school if she doesn't sit down, you had better be able to back up that statement. If you know ahead of time that you will be responsible for her if she stays after school, you should be able to stay as long as she does. The point is, don't make any threats you can't keep.

Finally, always make sure that all avenues of retreat are closed for the student. In other words, the only way Joey can avoid detention is to sit down. He can't avoid it by being quiet (and still being out of his seat) or by running an errand for you or by going back to his seat and not sitting in it. If you make sitting down the only way he can avoid detention and he wants to avoid it, he will sit down. The only time you might want to leave some room for negotiation or flexibility is when you anticipate a power struggle. If Joey refuses to sit in his seat and you anticipate a power struggle, give him a choice, such as "You can either sit down in your seat or find another seat of your choice but you must sit down now." A psychologist friend of mine has suggested that teachers use this technique and they have met with some success. It seems that being given a choice makes the student feel more in control of the situation and thus he or she is more likely to choose.

I should also mention at this time that no special strategies for reinforcing specific behaviors are discussed in this chapter. Teachers often ask me how to reinforce specific student behaviors such as staying on task, complying with directives, staying in seat, initiating conversations with peers, establishing eye contact, completing assignments, and feeding self, among others. I have no compunction about sitting down with a teacher to help design a reinforcement program for a specific behavior. However, I think it would be a redundant, not to mention lengthy, process to present a reinforcement program for each and every one of those behaviors in this chapter. I also believe that in the long run it is more beneficial for teachers to learn some basic reinforcement strategies they can apply to any number of behaviors instead of relying on someone to tell them exactly what to do in each special case. I am a firm believer in the adage, "Give someone a fish and he eats for a day, teach him to fish and he eats for a lifetime."

Whether catching fish or changing behavior, it is best to start out simply. Therefore, I will limit your "fishing" lessons to those basic competencies needed to successfully reinforce any student behavior. These are: (1) knowing the basic, empirically tested rules regarding reinforcement; (2) knowing the different types of reinforcers available; (3) being able to choose the right reinforcer for a given student; (4) knowing the different schedules of reinforcement as well as when and how to use each; (5) designing and implementing shaping, fading, chaining, contingency contracting, and token reinforcement; and (6) being able to "trouble-shoot" (i.e., determine why your reinforcement program is not working and what to do about it). Let's begin with some basic rules regarding reinforcement.

Rules Regarding Reinforcement

The following are a few guidelines to remember when implementing a reinforcement program:

1. *The latency between the student's response and the reinforcer presented by the teacher must be as short as possible.* Older and more developmentally able students can usually make the association between their response and the CSE even when the latter is delayed. For example, graduate students can make the connection between their studying behavior and the passing grade they receive on a test even though a week might intervene between the two. On the other hand, very young or handicapped students must receive positive reinforcement immediately following a response in order to understand that they are being rewarded for it.

Reinforce immediately whenever possible.

2. *Reinforcement must be given systematically according to a schedule.* This is one of the reasons behavior modification is referred to as the systematic application of rewards and punishment. New (unlearned) behavior cannot be randomly reinforced or it may never be learned. Instead, it must be reinforced on a continuous schedule. Conversely, behavior that has been learned and is fairly well established should no longer be reinforced continuously or the student may become satiated or so dependent upon the extrinsic reward that she or he never internalizes the behavior. Instead, learned behaviors should be randomly reinforced on a variable schedule. Because the change from the continuous to the variable schedule must be gradual, a fixed schedule of reinforcement should be used as a bridge between the two. These three schedules of reinforcement are discussed in detail later in this chapter.

3. *Reinforce behavior that is a step in the right direction.* If you wait until the student emits the exact response you want before you reinforce her, you may be waiting a long, long time. For example, if you want

a student who never turns in assignments to complete all of her work, you should begin your reinforcement program by rewarding her for turning in parts of assignments. Reinforcing behavior that is a step in the right direction is called *shaping;* it should be used whenever there is a wide gap between the student's present level of functioning and the terminal or target behavior. Shaping is also discussed in detail later in the chapter.

4. *Model the behavior you want from your students.* A great deal of human behavior is learned by watching and imitating significant others in the environment. Children learn by modeling their parents, peers, and teachers. It has also been said that we teach more by our deeds than by our words. Therefore, if you want a student to persevere at a difficult task, you should not just tell him to "hang in there." You should demonstrate perseverance by your actions or point out examples of perseverance in the environment. The worst thing you can do when you want to reinforce a behavior in a student is to model the opposite of that behavior. You don't help a screaming student learn self-control by yelling at him to be quiet.

5. *A state of deprivation must exist in order for a reinforcer to maintain its reinforcing properties.* In order for a reinforcer to be effective in strengthening a student's behavior, the student has to want the reinforcer enough to emit the behavior for it. The more she wants the reinforcer, the more inclined she will be to engage in the contingent behavior. The student's desire is related to her state of deprivation. If she feels deprived (i.e., lacking the reinforcer), she will work harder to overcome this deficit. From a practical standpoint, this will require the teacher to create a situation in which the student always feels deprived of the reinforcer so that she will constantly work to get it. Imagine that you were using a token economy in which students earned tokens such as chips or points for work completed or for socially acceptable behavior. Then imagine that a student earned more than enough tokens for a favored activity at the end of the day. It is entirely possible that she might stop working or behaving properly for those tokens an hour or more before the activity period; because she does not feel deprived of the tokens she will not feel that she must continue to work hard to overcome this deficit. In order to avoid this situation, the teacher must create a state of deprivation by removing some of the tokens the student has previously earned. More will be said about this practice in the section on token economies.

6. *Use rewards because they are reinforcing to your students, not because they are reinforcing to you.* Looking at old copies of *National Geographic* or *Boy's Life* may have been fun for you when you were younger but your students may not enjoy this activity. To find out what

your students do enjoy, follow the directions in the following section.

Reinforcers

Reinforcers may be classified for purposes of discussion into the following categories: primary, social, tangible, activity, and token. Each type has characteristics that make it appropriate to certain students and certain situations.

Primary reinforcers satisfy an individual's biological or physical needs. An example of a commonly used primary reinforcer is food. Unfortunately, the type of food most often used as a primary reinforcer is junk! I have a strong aversion to the use of candy, cookies, cupcakes, doughnuts, potato chips, and soft drinks as primary reinforcers. Children do not need all of the sugar, salt, and artificial ingredients in these foods. There are plenty of natural and nutritious foods available, such as fresh or dried fruits, unsalted nuts (dry toasted in the oven instead of being roasted in oil), granola, yogurt with fruit, and carob, which is a substitute for chocolate. Using junk foods high in sugar as reinforcers can have negative side effects. First, students' poor eating habits are reinforced. They get enough junk food at home; they don't need it in school. Second, you are setting them (and subsequently yourself) up for the maladaptive behavior that usually accompanies the drop in blood sugar after the "quick high." The children may love candy, but if you really have their best interests at heart, you'll find something better to use as a primary reinforcer.

Social reinforcers are by far the cheapest kind to give and among the most effective. Examples are verbal praise, smiles, attention (e.g., looking at someone when they are speaking), nodding your head (as if in agreement with the speaker), and physical contact such as hugs, pats, and touches. While praise should be dispensed freely, be careful not to satiate your students. Too much praise tends to lose its importance. Also, try to sound sincere. Don't be unctuous or patronizing. Students who can't read a word can spot a phony a mile away! Try to avoid making comments about the student. Instead, praise his behavior. Many students have heard nothing but derisive remarks from their teachers. By the time they get to your class, they are convinced that they are lazy, crazy, stupid, or just plain no good. However, they can still tell when they have done something correctly. By confining your praise to their response, you are merely stating the obvious. If you start generalizing, such as by saying, "Boy, are you smart!" your credibility will suffer. If you program for success by giving them many opportunities to respond correctly and to receive praise for their correct responses, eventually their self-image may improve enough so that you can make some value judgments without losing any credibility. It's really very simple. Instead of saying, "That's right! Boy, you're smart!" simply say, "You're right! That was a good answer." Even if you don't like the student, try to give praise with some feeling. Think of it this way: You are actually praising yourself. If you weren't such a good teacher, your students wouldn't be giving you all those opportunities to praise them. Also, try to vary your comments from time to time so that they don't get repetitive and lose their power to reinforce. Make sure your students understand you. Be aware of your vocabulary. Don't use comments that are too babyish or too adult for them. You wouldn't want to reward a high school student with "Good boy!" or a first grader with "Now you're cooking!" Refer to the list of approval responses found in Figure 6.1 if you find yourself running out of things to say.

Teachers should also use positive physical contact to reinforce student behavior whenever it's appropriate. We don't touch each other enough. A pat on the back or a hand on the shoulder can be as powerful a reinforcer as verbal praise. Just be careful not to use it with a student who might misinterpret your intentions. I once made the mistake of putting my arm around an adolescent to reinforce him for being on task. He proceeded to push my arm away with the admonition, "Hey, man. I'm no queer!" Later that day in recess, after this same student hit a home run in a softball game, I slapped him on the behind. This time, my gesture was not only accepted, it was returned! A hard slap on the behind after a display of physical prowess was considered macho and, therefore, acceptable. However, soft touching or holding as a reward for a cerebral activity was taboo! This doesn't mean that you should avoid using physical contact to reinforce behavior in the classroom. By all means, try it. You may make some

---

Verbal or Written

yes	oh boy	delicious	neato
good	correct	fabulous	very good
neat	excellent	splendid	well done
nice	that's right	smart thinking	nicely done
OK	perfect	right on	congratulations
great	how true	wow	superior
uh-huh	absolutely right	good choice	yeh
positively	keep going	on target	
go ahead	good responses	now you're cooking	
yeah	beautiful	that's the way	
all right	wonderful job	keep it up	
exactly	fantastic	thank you	
of course	terrific	fine	
cool	super	I like it	
wonderful	swell	I love it	
outstanding	tasty	the best yet	
exciting	marvelous	bravo	

Nonverbal

smiling	widening eyes	signaling OK with fingers	touching nose
winking	wrinkling nose	giving thumbs up	patting back
nodding	whistling	shaking head	giving quick squeeze
grinning	cheering	circling hand	touching arm
raising eyebrows	licking lips	touching head (student's)	hugging
forming kiss	rolling eyes	patting head	putting hand on hand
opening eyes wide	clapping hands	pinching cheek	shaking hands
slowly closing eyes	raising arms		giving "high five"
laughing	shaking fist		

Figure 6.1. Approval responses.

mistakes along the way but you will also be adding a powerful reinforcer to your repertoire.

Tangible reinforcers are like those little prizes you get in cereal or Cracker Jack boxes. They are relatively inexpensive and easy to give. Students from low socioeconomic status (SES) backgrounds especially enjoy earning tangibles. However, be careful that the tangibles don't become too distracting to the student and interfere with the behavior you are trying to strengthen. Some students play with these items so much that they do little else. The teacher winds up in a power struggle trying to take the distracting item away. For this reason, tangibles should be dispensed so that the student can see what she's earned but can't handle it until her work is finished or the school day is over. Also, try to use tangibles that serve a constructive purpose. Pencils, pens, writing and drawing pads, loose-leaf books, paperbacks, modeling clay, inexpensive puzzles, games, shoelaces, toothbrushes, and combs all serve a more constructive purpose as tangible rewards than do water pistols, cap guns, fake spiders, and rubber knives. If you find you must use tangibles as reinforcers, try not to get trapped into buying them yourself. Many of these items can be donated by the school store or one of the local merchants. The parents or Parent Teacher Organization group in your school or district is another likely funding source. If you can't find anyone to subsidize your reinforcement program with tangibles, change to another type of reinforcer. In my opinion, social reinforcement and favored activities are preferable to tangible reinforcers.

Activity reinforcers actually provide double benefits because participation in the activity may give the student an opportunity to receive "bonus" reinforcement in the form of verbal praise. For example, when a student earns free time to draw a picture, he not only gets to enjoy the activity of drawing but also has the opportunity to receive social reinforcement from the environment when his picture is hung up on the bulletin board. Aside from giving the student an opportunity to develop lifelong skills and interests, activity reinforcers also allow him to experience intrinsic reinforcement. Everybody enjoys doing things well. The average school setting provides many opportunities for a variety of activity reinforcers such as helping the building maintenance people, working in the kitchen or helping in the office, serving as a messenger or peer tutor, working in the shop or playing in the gym (in addition to regularly scheduled times), taking over as teacher of the class, listening to recorded music, reading material from the school library, and being a school monitor. The list of activities can be as long as the teacher's imagination and resourcefulness and the rest of the school's cooperation.

Also, don't be afraid to use activity reinforcers that you would normally consider undesirable. Many years ago, I let some of my students write on a "graffiti board" in the classroom as a payoff for low-frequency (desirable) behavior. Normally they spent more time writing on walls outside of class than on paper in class. These students were mainly low achievers from the inner city who lived in buildings with graffiti-covered walls, rode on graffiti-covered subway trains, and walked on graffiti-covered sidewalks. Notice the power of modeling. After numerous complaints from the school maintenance people and several ineffective attempts at punishing this behavior, I decided that if they liked writing on walls so much, I would let them do it in class, provided that they earned the privilege by first writing on paper. This practice not only increased the number of written assignments completed; it also resulted in a marked decrease in graffiti writing outside of class. This is merely one example of an otherwise undesirable activity being used as a payoff for a desirable low-frequency behavior. I have listed others in Figure 6.2. Don't be afraid to use them if the more conventional reinforcers don't work. You can't expect all of your students to work for a smile or a Twinkie.

---

1. Sleeping (i.e., allowing student to put head down on desk to rest)
2. Graffiti board (should be covered when not in use to avoid distracting students)
3. Reading comic books
4. Playing cards or rolling dice (acceptable as long as no money changes hands)
5. Eating in class (as long as students clean up after themselves)
6. Chewing gum (as long as it isn't stuck on chairs, tables, or desks)
7. Listening to transistor radio (as long as it doesn't disrupt learning environment)
8. Wandering around room (same as number 7)
9. Talking to peers (same as number 7)
10. Daydreaming
11. Taking things apart (as long as they are put back together)
12. Passing notes to peers
13. Making a mess (as long as it is cleaned up)
14. Playing with puzzle or game (e.g., Rubik's Cube)
15. Ignoring teacher when she or he is talking (not attending)
16. Talking loudly
17. Engaging in self-stimulation (e.g., rocking in seat, waving hands)
18. Singing or whistling
19. Leaving the classroom (to go to another supervised area)

Figure 6.2. Acceptable undesirable behaviors for use as reinforcers.

Token reinforcers are dispensed in place of backup reinforcers such as primaries, tangibles, or favored activities. Some examples of token reinforcers are points, stars, check marks, and chips. Students seldom tire of receiving tokens because they can be turned in for a variety of reinforcers. This allows the tokens to keep their reinforcing properties. Token reinforcers, like most social reinforcers, tangibles, and favored activities, are considered secondary (i.e., learned or conditioned) reinforcers because the student has to learn the connection between the token and the backup reinforcer before the former acquires any reinforcing properties. Much more will be said about tokens and token reinforcement later in the chapter. First, let's talk about how to go about choosing the right reinforcer.

Observe students during their free time to identify potential reinforcers.

Choosing Reinforcers

You won't know whether or not you have chosen the right reinforcer until after you have used it with your student. If the behavior you wish to strengthen gets stronger, you may say that you have chosen the right reinforcer. On the other hand, if the behavior stays the same or weakens, you might not have chosen the right reinforcer. I say "might not" because there are other reasons for a behavior weakening besides using the wrong reinforcer. These will be discussed at the end of the chapter. A rule of thumb is to choose the least artificial reinforcer possible. By "artificial" I mean a reinforcer that is so contrived that it differs markedly from the reinforcers typically used in the learner's environment. A young severely handicapped student may need to be rewarded with food or toys, but an older and more able student would probably work for a more common school activity or social reinforcement. You don't want to create the problem for yourself of having to "wean" the students.

Basically, there are two ways to choose a reinforcer. The first is to simply observe the student during her free time to see how she elects to use it. This is especially helpful when you are planning to use an activity reinforcer. Watch the student to see if she spends her free time daydreaming; coloring; talking to peers, you, or herself; sleeping; listening to music; reading comics or magazines; or writing. Try to provide her with as many activities as possible during her free time from which to choose. If you limit these choices to coloring, playing with puzzles, or looking at magazines, you won't necessarily know what the student considers reinforcing. All you will know is which of the three available activities she considers the most reinforcing (or the least boring).

A second method for choosing a reinforcer is to ask the student what he likes. Assuming that he can read and write, have him complete an interest inventory

such as the one in Appendix D. If he can't read or write, ask him the questions and let him dictate the answers. If possible, consult with parents, siblings, past teachers, and friends to find out what the student considers reinforcing in the way of activity, primary, tangible, or social reinforcers. It goes without saying that the items on the interest inventory should be appropriate for the student's age and developmental level. If you feel that they are too babyish or too sophisticated, make the necessary modifications. Once you determine what the student will work for, it is time to place him on a schedule of reinforcement.

Schedules of Reinforcement

A *continuous schedule of reinforcement* should be used whenever you are beginning to modify a new (i.e., unlearned) behavior. In order for the student to learn this behavior, she will have to be reinforced every time she engages in it. Diagrams of continuous reinforcement may be seen in Figures 6.3 and 6.4. Of all the schedules, continuous reinforcement is the most easily affected by change. This means that if you forget to reward the student from time to time, the chances are that extinction will occur.

A *fixed schedule of reinforcement* should be used when the student has demonstrated that he is capable of engaging in the new behavior and you want to begin to wean him from continuous reinforcement. Simply move from rewarding every desired response to every second, third, fourth, or more. While your reinforcement pattern is still predictable, you are making the student work harder to obtain the same reward. A diagram of a fixed schedule of reinforcement may be seen in Figures 6.5 and 6.6.

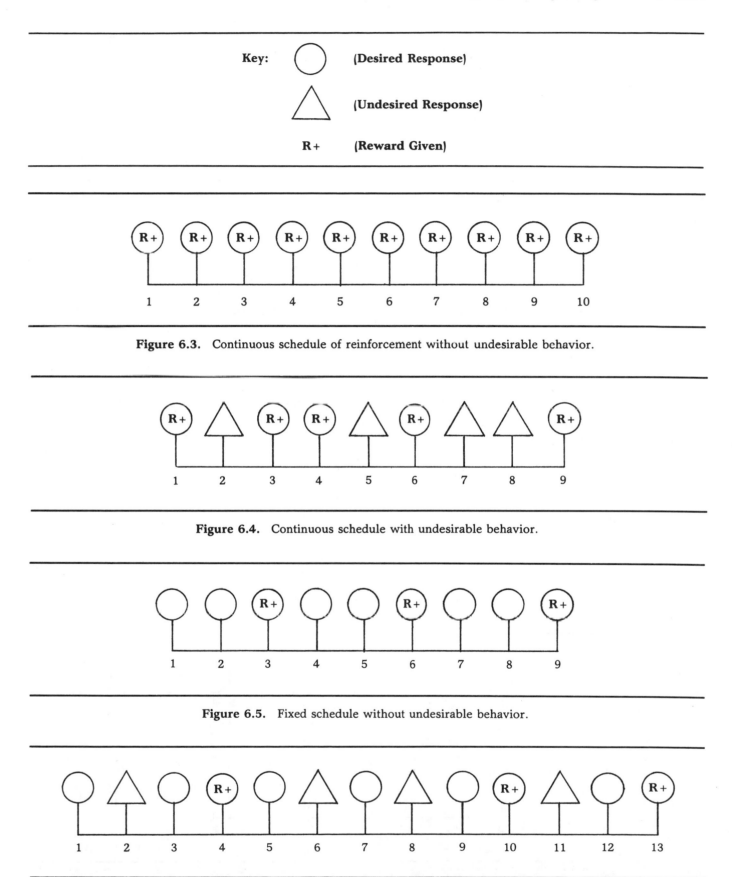

Figure 6.3. Continuous schedule of reinforcement without undesirable behavior.

Figure 6.4. Continuous schedule with undesirable behavior.

Figure 6.5. Fixed schedule without undesirable behavior.

Figure 6.6. Fixed schedule with undesirable behavior.

A *variable schedule of reinforcement* is similar to the fixed schedule except that it is not predictable. Because the student never knows when she is going to get a reward, she must behave appropriately all the time if she wants the reinforcer. This type of schedule is used as a maintenance schedule after the behavior has been learned and after the student has been sufficiently weaned from the continuous reinforcement with the fixed schedule. A diagram of a variable schedule of reinforcement may be seen in Figure 6.7. Of the three schedules, it is by far the least affected by change in reinforcement. This means that if you were to forget to reinforce the student from time to time, extinction would not take place (i.e., the student would continue to behave appropriately).

Ratio and Interval Schedules

Two aspects of behavior that the teacher can reinforce are *frequency* (the number of times a behavior occurs) and *duration of response* (the length of time the behavior lasts). It is possible to reinforce frequency or duration of response for each of the three schedules of reinforcement that have been discussed. Response (frequency) schedules are referred to as *ratio schedules*. These include continuous-, fixed-, and variable-ratio schedules. Duration (time) schedules are called *interval schedules*. There are continuous-, fixed-, and variable-interval schedules.

In Figure 6.8 the student is being reinforced on a fixed-ratio (FR) schedule. The number of consecutive correct responses necessary for presenting the reinforcer is known as the *arrangement*. In Figure 6.8 the arrangement is 2. In other words, the student has to make two consecutive correct responses before the teacher will present the reinforcer. Note that these must be *consecutive* responses. Figure 6.9 is also an FR sched-

ule with a 2:1 arrangement. However, in this example, the student is still engaging in some occasional undesirable behavior. Notice that the student was not reinforced for his third response even though it was his second correct response. This was because it was not his second *consecutive* correct response. Don't think that all FR schedules of reinforcement call for the student to be reinforced after two consecutive correct responses. Some require three, four, five, and more. The number of consecutive correct responses required changes as the student's behavior changes.

Figure 6.10 is an example of a variable-ratio (VR) schedule with a 4:1 arrangement. This means that the student is reinforced once on the average of every four consecutive correct responses. In this case, the teacher knew ahead of time that she wanted the student to make 20 responses so she gave her 20 cues or opportunities to respond. Because she also wanted her on a VR schedule of 4:1, she divided the average (4) into the number of opportunities to respond (20) to get the number of times she would have to reinforce her (5). Then she presented the reinforcer five times on a random (unpredictable) basis.

An example of a fixed-interval (FI) schedule may be seen in Figure 6.11. Notice that we have arbitrarily made the "sticks," or vertical lines, in this diagram stand for minutes instead of responses. The arrangement is 4:1. In other words, the student is being reinforced once at the end of each 4-minute block of time. As in the FR schedule, the contingency is consecutive behavior. In Figure 6.12, the student is not reinforced for his second minute of on-task behavior because it wasn't consecutive.

Finally, Figure 6.13 shows an example of a variable-interval (VI) schedule of reinforcement. Here the student is being reinforced once on the average of every

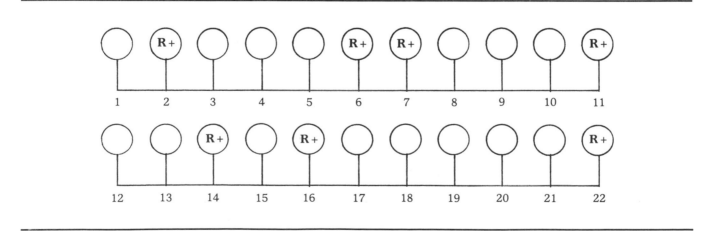

Figure 6.7. Variable schedule without undesirable behavior.

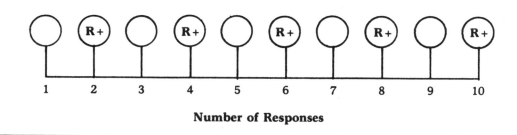

Figure 6.8. Fixed-ratio (FR) schedule without undesirable behavior and with 2:1 arrangement.

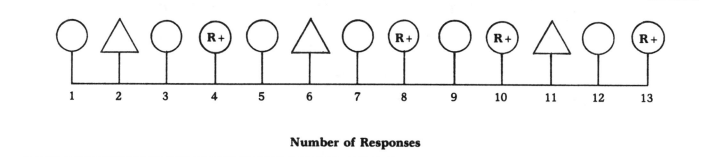

Figure 6.9. Fixed-ratio (FR) schedule with undesirable behavior and with 2:1 arrangement.

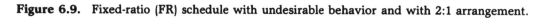
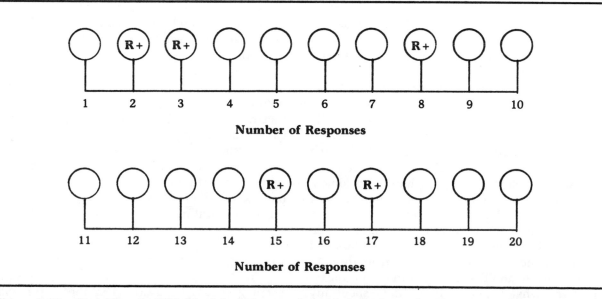

Figure 6.10. Variable-ratio (VR) schedule without undesirable behavior and with average of 4:1 arrangement.

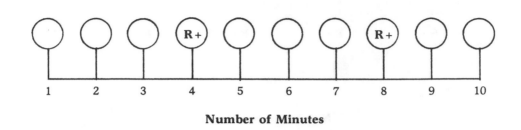

Figure 6.11. Fixed-interval (FI) schedule without undesirable behavior and with 4:1 arrangement.

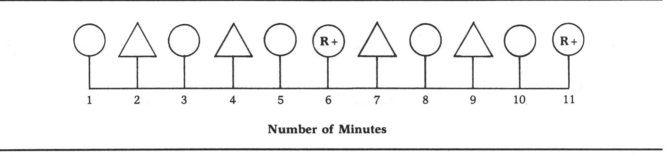

Figure 6.12. Fixed-interval (FI) schedule with undesirable behavior and with 2:1 arrangement.

5 consecutive minutes that she engages in the target behavior. In this case the teacher knew ahead of time that the student's assignment would take her 20 minutes if she stayed on task all of the time. Because the teacher wanted the student on a VI schedule of 5:1, he divided the average (5 minutes) into the total number of minutes to behave (20 minutes) to get the number of times he would need to reinforce her (4). Then he presented the reinforcer four times on a random (unpredictable) basis.

While we have already discussed when you should use each of the three schedules of reinforcement, we have not talked about moving from one schedule to the next. There is no hard and fast rule that would apply to every student with whom you work. Generally speaking, you should be guided by the student's behavior. For example, if you are reinforcing hand-raising behavior on a ratio schedule and baseline data indicate that the student seldom raises his hand and almost always calls out, you should assume that hand-raising behavior is new and reinforce it on a continuous schedule (i.e., every time it occurs). When the intervention data show that the student is beginning to raise his hand more often than he calls out, try moving from the continuous schedule to an FR schedule with a 2:1 arrangement and see what happens. If the data show any regression, you can always go back to your continuous

schedule. If, however, the level of desirable behavior continues to improve, change the contingency for reinforcement by increasing the arrangement from 2:1 to 3:1 and so on. Do this until the data show that the student always raises his hand. At this point, begin using a VR schedule and gradually increase the average in the arrangement. If you have done all of this, eventually the student's hand-raising behavior should maintain even if you don't attend to him on all occasions.

Although the transition from schedule to schedule is the same when you are reinforcing behaviors based on duration (i.e., interval), you don't have to make your reinforcement contingent upon the number of minutes that have passed. For example, baseline data might show that the longest period of time a given student is able to stay on task is 30 seconds. In this case, you would begin with a continuous-interval schedule and reinforce the student for every 30 seconds of sustained on-task behavior. Now, let's take a look at another important reinforcement strategy.

Shaping

Shaping should be used when there is a wide gap between a student's present level of functioning and the

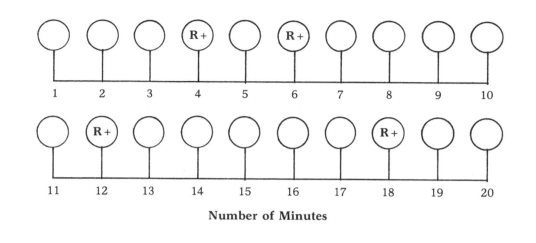

Figure 6.13. Variable-interval (VI) schedule without undesirable behavior and with average of 5:1 arrangement.

target behavior. It is unrealistic to expect a student who has been misbehaving for years to suddenly change overnight. Similarly, since students need to be positively reinforced for desirable behavior, you cannot always wait until a student's behavior is exactly the way you want it before reinforcing it. Therefore, you must reinforce change in the right direction (i.e., improvement). A shaping program has three basic components: *successive approximations, differential reinforcement,* and *shifting criteria for reinforcement.* Let's examine each.

Successive Approximations

An *approximation* is "something like" a given behavior. In shaping, you choose a target behavior that you want the student to engage in and reward each successive approximation of the behavior until the student is able to engage in the target behavior. While the student may not be able to engage in the target behavior in the beginning, she will most likely be able to engage in behavior that is something like (i.e., an approximation of) it. As the student progresses through the conditioning (i.e., learning) process she will be able to engage in behavior that is a closer approximation of (more like) the target behavior. Each behavior that moves closer and closer to the target behavior is referred to as a *successive approximation: approximation* because each is not the target behavior but something like it and *successive* because each behavior is more like the target behavior than the one that preceded it.

For example, let's suppose that the target behavior for a student who is always near his seat but never in it is to stay in his seat for 10 minutes at a time. If you waited until he stayed in his seat for 10 minutes at a time before you rewarded him, you would probably

never reward him. However, you could start by rewarding him for "being near his seat." Simply put a small rug remnant under his desk and whenever he's on the rug, reward him for being near his seat. Eventually, you could reward him for "being next to his seat," then for "being in physical contact with his seat," for "sitting in his seat in any fashion," for "sitting in his seat properly" (i.e., with both legs under his desk), for "sitting in his seat properly for 1 minute," then "for 2 minutes," "5 minutes," and finally, "10 minutes," the target behavior. Beginning with "being near his seat" up through "sitting in his seat properly for 5 minutes," you would have rewarded eight successive approximations of the target behavior. Notice that each approximation was more like the target behavior than the preceding one. This is critical. If you are merely rewarding several different behaviors that are not successive approximations of the target behavior, you are not using shaping and may never reach your goal.

Differential Reinforcement

When you reward a student for an approximation of a target behavior the chances are that she will repeat that approximation. However, if you reward the student for all or any approximation of the target behavior, you will probably confuse her because she won't know which approximation you want her to make. By being careful to reinforce only the desired approximation and not earlier approximations, you eventually will teach the student what it is you expect from her. This process is referred to as *differential reinforcement: differential* because you want the student to be able to differentiate between behavior that results in the presentation of a reward and behavior that does not.

In the out-of-seat example, if you want to strengthen "being next to his seat" (approximation 2) instead of "being near his seat" (approximation 1), you should only reinforce the student when he is next to his seat and not when he is near it. When you strengthen both behaviors the student may assume (correctly) that he can do either and still get reinforced. Since approximation 1 is probably easier for the student than approximation 2, if you reinforce him for both approximations, he will probably revert back to the easier behavior (1). If the student engages in a more difficult (i.e., closer) approximation such as approximation 3 ("being in physical contact with his seat") when you were looking for approximation 2, reinforce him for the more difficult behavior. There is no rule that requires the student to go through the successive approximations one at a time. If he can successfully skip some along the way, more power to him!

Shifting Criteria for Reinforcement

Remember that the teacher should reward successive approximations of the target behavior. But how will you know when a student has been on one approximation long enough and needs to move on to the next? One rule of thumb, especially with cognitively slow students, is to move on to the next approximation when the student is able to successfully engage in a behavior on a variable schedule of reinforcement. For example, in the out-of-seat example, the student is reinforced for being near his seat on a continuous schedule, then on a fixed schedule, and finally on a variable schedule of reinforcement. When he is able to stay near his seat on a variable schedule, for however long you deem necessary, you shift criteria for reinforcement and move to the next approximation. Again, you first reinforce him continuously for being next to his seat, then on a fixed schedule, then a variable one, and so on. The reason you want the student doing one approximation on a variable schedule before moving to the next (closer) approximation is that cognitively slow students may not understand that the contingency for receiving reinforcement has changed and they may not emit the next approximation for a while. Since you are practicing differential reinforcement, you will no longer reinforce the preceding approximation when it occurs. In other words, you do not reinforce approximation 1 while you wait for him to engage in approximation 2. In this case, extinction of approximation 1 may occur while you are waiting for the student to engage in approximation 2. By waiting until approximation 1 is well established (on a variable schedule) before moving on to approximation 2, you lessen the probability of extinction.

Another rule of thumb, more appropriate for cognitively able students, is simply to spend an arbitrary amount of time at a given approximation, then inform the student that the contingency for receiving reinforcement is going to change. Let's say that you are shaping the number of assignments completed. You can shift from one approximation to the next when your student is able to perform an approximation for 2 consecutive days. In this instance, it doesn't matter whether or not the student is being reinforced on a variable schedule before moving on to the next approximation. You are assuming that the student understands that the contingency for receiving reinforcement is going to change.

How To Shape Behavior

The first step is to decide upon the target behavior, the point where you will stop intervening. Let's suppose that you have a student who doesn't speak at all unless she's spoken to by one particular student in your class; even then, she only makes one-word responses like "yes" or "no" and never establishes eye contact. Your target behavior might be for her to initiate conversations with her peers.

The second step in the program is to decide where to start. This means establishing which behavior the student has in her present repertoire that you are going to reinforce now. For example, in our hypothetical case of the withdrawn student, you would begin the shaping program by reinforcing her when she talks to her one friend whenever her friend asks a question, without requiring eye contact.

The third step is to decide what you are going to use to reward the student. Let's suppose that after using the interest inventory or observation method you decide to reinforce her with tokens that can be turned in later for time spent coloring.

The next step is to make a list of successive approximations. You might list the first approximation of the target behavior as "verbally responds to questions from her friend requiring one-word answers (e.g., 'yes' or 'no') without eye contact." This is the behavior you decided to start with in step 2 because the student is already engaging in it. The rest of the approximations appear in Figure 6.14 where the entire shaping program for this hypothetical case is outlined.

After implementing your program, you may find that your approximations are too far apart, requiring rather severe jumps. There is no rule that prevents you from adding new approximations in between those originally listed.

Once you have listed your approximations you may begin implementing the program by rewarding the first approximation. Whenever the student talks to her friend she is given a token. When she's not talking to her friend, she receives no tokens. This is *differential rein-*

Where To Stop: When student initiates conversations (i.e., is able to get a student's attention by calling his or her name and asking a question while maintaining eye contact with that person) with all classmates

Where To Start: When she verbally responds to questions from her friend requiring one-word answers (e.g., "yes" or "no") without eye contact

Reward: Token dispensed by peers, to be turned in for time spent coloring

Approximations:

1. When she verbally responds to questions from her friend requiring one-word answers (e.g., "yes" or "no") without eye contact
2. When she verbally responds to questions from her friend requiring two- or three-word answers without eye contact
3. Same as approximation 2 with brief eye contact
4. Same as approximation 3 maintaining eye contact while speaking
5. When she initiates verbal communication with her friend by calling her name to get her attention when prompted by teacher
6. Same as approximation 5 without prompting by teacher
7. When she gets her friend's attention and asks her a question when prompted by teacher
8. Same as approximation 7 without prompting by teacher
9. Same as approximation 7 with a second student (other than her friend)

Continue adding students until target student is able to initiate conversation with all classmates.

Shift criterion for reinforcement when she is able to perform an approximation on a variable-ratio schedule for one full day.

Figure 6.14. Shaping program.

forcement. When the student is able to talk to her friend on a variable schedule of reinforcement or is able to demonstrate this behavior over a prespecified period of time (e.g., 1 day, 1 week), you may decide to go on to the next approximation. This is *shifting criteria for reinforcement.* You continue to move through each successive approximation until the student is able to engage in the target behavior on a variable schedule of reinforcement or to demonstrate each over a prespecified period of time. If the student has difficulty performing at any one of the approximations, you can always return to an earlier (preceding) approximation and continue to work on it or add a new approximation that is harder than the old one but not as hard as the new one with which she is having trouble.

Fading

Fading is often confused with shaping. According to Mikulas, fading involves "taking a behavior that occurs in one situation and getting it to occur in a second situation by gradually changing the first situation into the second" (1978, p. 85). Notice that the situation is gradually changed, not the student's behavior, as is the case in shaping. In other words, shaping involves approximations of responses, while fading involves approximations of stimuli. Shaping provides an effective means of changing behavior from one response to another;

fading helps facilitate the generalization of that behavior change from one setting to another.

For example, suppose that you are teaching in a resource room for handicapped learners and want to mainstream one of your students. However, you have some concerns about his ability to generalize his on-task behavior from the resource room to the regular classroom. Through shaping, you have gotten your student to attend to task in the resource room 90% of the time observed. But, your resource room allows the student to work in a relatively distraction-free environment and to earn tokens for backup activity reinforcers for on-task behavior. Unfortunately, the "real world" of the mainstream classroom is filled with distractions and the only payoffs for on-task behavior are passing grades, social praise, and avoiding reprimands and other aversives. In the resource room, your student is seated facing a wall with a portable study carrel on his desk limiting visual distractions from the front and sides. In addition, he is wearing a headset hooked to a tape recorder playing classical music, which reduces the distraction of extraneous auditory stimuli in the room. A laminated countoon (see chapter 14) is taped to the student's desk and he is given check marks on a VI schedule for on-task behavior. Since you have an aide and a smaller number of students than the mainstream teacher, you are usually able to provide the student with attention very quickly. He also has "dispatch" material (i.e., busywork) to do if he has to wait for you. Because it

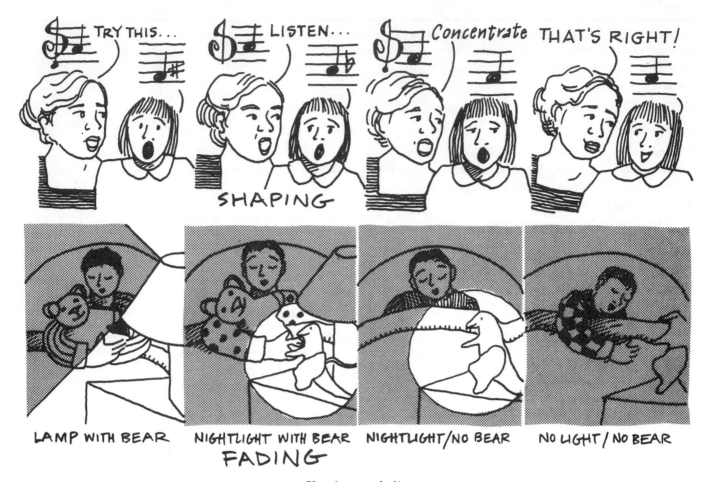

Shaping vs. fading.

is impossible to expect the mainstream teacher to replicate all of this in her classroom, it is therefore necessary to gradually change (i.e., fade) the environmental variables in your room so that it more closely resembles the mainstream classroom. If your student is able to maintain his on-task behavior at or near 90% in the presence of these new environmental variables, he should be ready for his new class. One of the first things you might do is change the classical music on his headset to class noise from a room with 25 to 30 students. Ask the mainstream teacher if she will tape-record the noise in her room during activity periods. In addition to fading out the classical music, you are providing the student with an audio distraction that he will have to become used to.

The second step might be to remove the headset completely, requiring the student to listen to the class noise directly from the tape recorder in your room. Next, you might remove one or both of the side panels on the desktop study carrel. This will allow your student to handle peripheral visual distractions. After this you might have him turn his desk around so that he is no longer facing the wall but has visual access to the

entire room. Your next step might be to train your student to wait for adult attention for longer and longer periods of time—first with dispatch work, then without. Your goal here is to teach patience, the ability to stay out of trouble while waiting with nothing to do. That's what the students in the regular class have learned how to do. Continue to use your token economy throughout the fading process. Eventually, you will begin to wean your student from the token economy and use more of the consequences found in the regular classroom, such as grades, reprimands, social reinforcement, and response cost. Finally, when you think he is ready, let him attend the mainstream classroom for brief periods at a time, gradually increasing this time until he has been completely mainstreamed. This entire fading process is outlined in Figure 6.15. Notice that the gradual change is in the environment (stimuli), while the student's behavior (response) stays the same.

Chaining

The technique of chaining may be used to strengthen new responses by helping students to remember to

Problem: Student C. is a handicapped learner currently placed in a resource room. His teacher wants to mainstream him into the regular fifth-grade classroom. However, while C. is able to attend to task in the resource room (on task 90% of time observed), trial placement in the regular classroom indicates that this behavior has not generalized (on task 10% of time observed).

1. *Where to stop:* When C. is able to attend to task 90% of the time observed in the regular fifth-grade classroom without using any of the instructional variables operating in the resource room (e.g., headset with music, token economy).

2. *Where to start:* When C. is able to attend to task 90% of the time observed in the resource room while listening to classical music on a tape recorder headset.

3. *Reward:* Token (check marks) to be dispensed by C.'s teacher on a card attached to his desk; to be turned in at the end of each period for a free time activity of his choice.

4. *Successive approximations:*
   a. When C. is able to attend to task 90% of the time observed in the resource room while listening to classical music on a tape recorder headset.
   b. When C. is able to maintain 90% on-task behavior listening to class noise on headset instead of classical music.
   c. When C. is able to maintain 90% on-task behavior listening to class noise on tape recorder without headset.
   d. When C. is able to maintain 90% on-task behavior without study carrel, but with class noise on tape recorder without headset.
   e. When C. is able to maintain 90% on-task behavior with desk facing peers, with no study carrel, and with class noise.
   f. When C. is able to maintain 90% on-task behavior with delay in teacher or aide attention but with dispatch work available.
   g. When C. is able to maintain 90% on-task behavior with delay in teacher or aide attention without dispatch work available.
   h. When C. is able to maintain 90% on-task behavior without token economy operating.
   i. When C. is able to maintain 90% on-task behavior in the regular fifth-grade classroom for gradually increasing periods of time.

5. *Criteria for shifting reinforcement* (to next approximation): When C. is able to maintain 90% on-task behavior on a variable-interval schedule for a 3-hour period.

Figure 6.15. Fading program.

engage in the target behavior. Similarly, chaining may also be used to weaken old maladaptive behaviors that have become so habitual that the student cannot stop engaging in them even if he or she wants to.

Students often have difficulty changing their behavior because they can't remember to behave differently. Their old, unwanted behavior is the result of a behavior chain practiced over and over again for years. One might say that it has become a habit for some students to behave the way they do. For example, when my daughter Kim was a child, she would often forget to put her bike away in the garage at the end of the day. It would sit by the front door each night providing a temptation to any would-be bicycle thief. I'm not talking about a little tricycle. This was a relatively expensive ten-speed bike. I tried a number of interventions before I thought about chaining. I put her bike away for her and reminded her to put it away herself next time. I yelled at her to put her bike away. I hid her bike and told her that it was stolen. I took away her bike. I grounded her. On those few occasions when she would remember to put her bike away without being told to do so, I would praise her to the skies. Once, I even woke

her up in the middle of the night to make her go outside and put her bike away. None of these interventions worked. Why? Kim had practiced this behavior so many times in the past that it was virtually impossible for her to behave any other way. I had to come up with a new behavior chain and teach it to her before I could get rid of the old one. The old chain was: ride bike home → stop bike in driveway → get off bike → walk bike to front door → put down kick stand → enter house through front door. Each response in this chain served as a stimulus for the next response. I had to teach her a new chain of behaviors that would end up with the bike in the garage. The new chain was: ride bike home → stop bike in driveway → get off bike → walk bike to garage → open garage door → put bike in garage → close garage door → enter house through garage.

Needless to say, writing a new behavior chain did not automatically change Kim's behavior. Kim first had to be taught the new chain. Whenever she came home on her bike and left it in front of the house, I would have her get back on it, ride around the block, come home again, stop the bike in the driveway, get off the bike, walk it to the garage, open the garage door, put the bike in the garage, close the garage door, and enter the house through the garage. I continued to do this with Kim, praising her for her new behavior, until she was able to go through the new chain by herself (i.e., without being reminded). I won't say that her behavior changed overnight, but eventually, it did.

Chaining can be used to strengthen new, incompatible, or competing behaviors in place of old, unwanted behavior chains. The steps in the process are:

1. Identify the responses in the old behavior chain, starting back far enough to include responses that serve as stimuli to the unwanted behavior.

2. Write a new behavior chain, again starting well before the target behavior.

3. Model the new behavior chain for the student.

4. Have the student go through the new chain to demonstrate that she knows what to do.

5. Reinforce the student whenever she engages in the new behavior.

6. If the student reverts back to the old chain, start the new chain from the beginning again.

In some instances, it may be necessary to employ a self-instruction technique similar to the material discussed in chapter 9. After telling the student what to do, have her demonstrate each response as she gives herself the direction to do so. At first, she does this out loud; then she merely whispers the directions or thinks them. Finally, the behavior should become automatic and she will not have to think about it at all.

Contingency Contracting

Another approach to add to your repertoire of behavior management skills is contingency contracting. Contingency contracting is based on the Premack Principle: If a high-frequency response is made contingent upon a low-frequency response often enough, the low-frequency response is likely to become more frequent in the future (Premack, 1959). For example, if a low-achieving student is left to choose between reading a comic book and a history text, he will probably choose the comic book. We may, therefore, say that the high-frequency (Hi-F) behavior is comic book reading while history-text reading is the low-frequency (Lo-F) behavior. According to the Premack Principle, if comic book reading (Hi-F) is made contingent upon reading the history text (Lo-F), the student will be more inclined to read the history text in the future without any prompting from his teacher.

Actually many teachers and most parents have been using the Premack Principle for years without know-ing it. My own grandmother, a Russian immigrant with little education, never heard of behavior modification, let alone the Premack Principle. Yet she used Premack all the time. Whenever my cousins and I ate at Grandma's house, we were required to drink our milk before we could have soda pop and finish all of our vegetables if we wanted to get our dessert. Since we knew that was the rule at Grandma's, we never argued or complained the way we did at home, where soda pop or dessert might be dispensed on a noncontingent basis. Today, I use Premack on my own behavior whenever I am faced with an aversive task. For example, I do not like grading students' papers at all! However, I do like to watch television and read fiction or magazines. Therefore, whenever I have a pile of student papers to grade, I make an informal (unwritten) contract with myself that I will do so much paper grading (Lo-F) before I allow myself a certain amount of television or reading (Hi-F) time. I might grade five papers and then reward myself with 30 minutes of reading or television watching. In fact, if it were not for Premack, this book would never have been written. Writing is a low-frequency behavior for me.

Premack can also be used to strengthen a number of other Lo-F student behaviors, such as staying in seat, studying, completing work assigned, doing homework, coming to class prepared, and sharing work materials with peers. It is not as difficult to find Hi-F student behavior to use as reinforcement. If you watch a student closely during her free time, you will be able to identify something she enjoys doing. As mentioned earlier in this chapter, don't be afraid to use Hi-F behavior that is undesirable in some settings as a payoff for Lo-F behavior, as long as the "cure" is not worse than the "disease." For example, just because one of your students spends more time beating up his peers than he does working on his math, you shouldn't make beating up peers contingent upon working on math. However, if a student spends more time daydreaming than working, there is nothing wrong with using daydreaming as a payoff for working behavior. In this instance, simply tell the student that for every assignment she completes, she will receive 2 minutes to daydream. For students who are less able, you could incorporate shaping into the program by having them start with 2 minutes of daydreaming for every example computed or sentence written, instead of requiring the entire assignment to be completed.

With older or more developmentally able students, you might wish to expand on the Premack Principle by actually writing up a contract. A sample set of negotiations might sound like this: (Teacher) "I know you would rather color than practice your cursive writing, but we both know that if I let you color now and write later, you probably won't get much writing done without my nagging, and we both hate that! So I want you to do your writing first, and for every five letters written correctly, I'll give you 1 minute of coloring time when you've finished all of the writing." (Student) "Five letters for 1 minute is too hard! I can't do that!" (T.) "Well, what do you think you could do for the 1 minute of coloring?" (S.) "I guess I could do three." (T.) "Well, I think you could do the five letters but I'd be willing to let you do only four letters correctly for each minute of coloring. That's the best I can do. You can always sit and do nothing at all. No writing and no coloring. The choice is yours." Once the teacher and the student agree on the contingency and the payoff, the contract may be written up. An example of a simple contract based on these negotiations may be seen in Figure 6.16.

The following rules of thumb regarding contracts have been suggested by Homme and his associates in their excellent book on contingency contracting (Homme et al., 1969).

1. Beginning contracts should call for and reward small approximations of the target behavior. In other words, use shaping whenever appropriate.
2. Reward frequently with small amounts rather than with one big reward given later.
3. The contract should call for and reward accomplishment, not blind obedience. Have the student work on adaptive or target behaviors such as assignments completed, coming to class on time and prepared, "getting along" with peers, working independently, and accepting criticism from others.
4. Reward the student's performance only after it occurs. Do not give noncontingent reinforcement.
5. The contract should be fair and written in positive terms. In other words, something good will happen to the student if he engages in desirable behavior. Avoid statements such as "The student will stay after school for 1 hour if he fails to complete his work" or "If the student goes all day without fighting, she gets to take home a library book." Instead, write "The student will receive 10 minutes of free time during the last hour of the school day for each work assignment successfully completed, up to six assignments."
6. The terms of the contract should be clear. Make the student paraphrase the terms to be sure that he understands them.
7. The intervention (i.e., the contingency and the payoff) must be used systematically. This means that any changes in the contingency or the payoff should be based upon data collected by the teacher, and that decisions regarding the program should not

The teacher will *let Bobby color for one minute for each four letters written correctly*

if the student *Bobby Brown* will *finish all of his writing*

Signed *John Kimball* Date *4-30-89*

Signed *Bobby B.* Date *4-3-89*

Witnessed by *Joey J.* Date *4-3-89*

Figure 6.16. Contract used in contingency contracting program.

be made in a haphazard fashion. Be consistent and follow through!

Contracts may be written for long- or short-term behavior. You may write up a new contract for a student's behavior in your class every day. At the beginning of school or the beginning of the class period, simply take a blank contract form like the one illustrated in Figure 6.16 and fill it in, have the student fill it in, or do it jointly. It then becomes the student's responsibility to live up to her part of the contract for the school day or for the class period and it is your responsibility to "pay up" according to the agreement. If you don't want to bother writing new contracts daily, they can be written for the week, month, term, or even school year, if appropriate.

Contracts can also include other parties in addition to the student and the teacher. For example, you could include the student's parents on a contract in which Hi-F behavior at home, such as television watching, snacking, staying up late, going to movies, sleeping over at a friend's house, or earning allowance, is made contingent upon Lo-F behavior at school (e.g., assignments completed, coming to class prepared or on time, or staying on task). Parents can monitor the student's behavior at school with a daily "report card" like the one shown in Figure 6.17, which the student takes back and forth between home and school every day. Failure to bring

Name _CASEY_   Week _5-6-89_

Date	What Student Did (Behavior)	Signature	What Parent Did (Consequence)	Signature
5-7-89	came to school on time	B.A.M.	T.V.	J.S.K.
5-8-89	came to school one hour late	B.A.M.	No T.V.	J.S.K.
5-9-89	came to school on time	B.A.M.	T.V.	J.S.K.
5-10-89	came to school on time	B.A.M.	T.V.	J.S.K.
5-11-89	came to school on time	B.A.M.	T.V. snack popcorn	J.S.K.

If found, please return to _FERNWOOD ELEMENTARY SCHOOL_
1625 S.W. 9th St., MILLVILLE 444-2772

Figure 6.17. Daily report card.

the card home results in the loss of one or more Hi-F behaviors. This approach requires a great deal of communication and cooperation between parents and the school but it is well worth the effort because it works! It is especially effective if the parents enter into a contractual agreement with the school (see Figure 6.18) agreeing to provide the appropriate consequences for their child's behavior at school. In this way, everyone knows what he or she is responsible for in the program; somehow, the signing of the formal agreement (while not legally binding on any party) results in a more permanent commitment from everyone involved.

The Token Economy

A *token economy* is an entire behavior management system that makes use of token reinforcers. Behavior modification is often confused with the token economy. People often think that behavior modification is nothing more than rewarding desirable student behavior with tokens that are turned in later for some favored activity, food, or toy. Fortunately, there is more to behavior modification than token reinforcement. What you may not know is that there is more to token reinforcement than rewarding desirable student behavior with tokens that are turned in later for a backup reinforcer. Let's examine all of the questions that must be considered before a token system can even get off the ground.

1. *What are the contingencies for the tokens?* In other words, what does the student have to do to earn tokens? This should be made clear at the very outset. If more than one student is working on the same contingencies, the contingencies should be posted somewhere in the classroom so that everyone will know what he or she has to do to earn tokens. Figure 6.19 is an example of a set of group contingencies for earning tokens. When a student is working on an individual contingency or a set of contingencies, a list of these contingencies should be attached to the student's desk to serve as a constant reminder of what is expected. Figure 6.20 provides an example of a set of individual contingencies for earning tokens.

2. *What are you going to use for tokens?* Check marks? Stamps or stick-ons? A ticket punch like the one train conductors use? Play money? Try to use a variety of tokens whenever possible, since students tend to get bored if the same type is used over and over again. The tokens should appeal to the particular age group with which you are working. Younger students tend to prefer stick-ons with stars, animals, or hero figures such as cowboys, astronauts, or cartoon characters. Play money, poker chips, or just plain points are popular with older students. You can have your students make or design the tokens themselves, as long as they don't get into the business of using "black market" tokens, where students who have access to the tokens take

It is understood by all parties (signed below) that the following responsibilities must be attended to:

1. It is the *school's responsibility* to fill out Casey's daily report card regarding tardy and attending behavior. All of Casey's teachers will do so. If the card is not brought to school the parents must be notified.

2. It is the *parents' responsibility* to look at Casey's card daily, initial it, and indicate in writing what consequences occurred. If the card is not brought home, the school should be notified and the consequences agreed upon should occur.

3. It is *Casey's responsibility* to be on time to class, every class, each and every day. It is also his responsibility to bring his card back and forth (home and school) and to see that his teachers and parents sign it.

Signed _____   _____
                               Parent   Date

_____   _____
                                School   Date

_____   _____
                         Program Manager   Date

_____   _____
                                Casey   Date

_____   _____
                                                                               Date

Figure 6.18. Contract between student, family, and school.

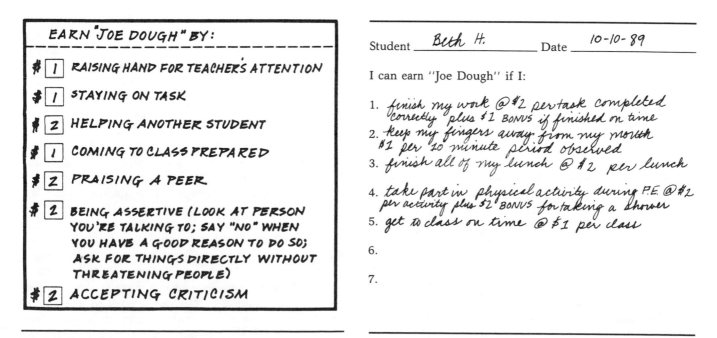

Figure 6.19. Group contingencies for earning tokens.

Figure 6.20. Individual contingencies for earning tokens.

advantage of the situation by "selling" them to their peers for favors or a share in the backup reinforcers. This situation can be avoided easily if you validate each token with a special stamp or your signature and only accept validated tokens from students when they are turned in for backup reinforcers. Figure 6.21 is an example of a simple token I have used in the past called "Joe Dough." You can make it in different denominations such as ones, fives, tens, twenties, fifties, and hundreds. Older students, especially those in upper elementary and junior high school, enjoy this type of token. It gives them the impression that they are actually earning money, like adults, for their work and behavior. Whatever tokens you decide to use, be sure that they can be given quickly and easily, are cheap and durable, and cannot be obtained without being earned.

3. *What is the ratio between student behavior and tokens dispersed?* In other words, how much are you going to "pay" your students for their work and behavior and what are you going to "charge" them for the backup reinforcers? Figures 6.19, 6.20, and 6.22 provide examples of "wages" and "prices" in a token economy.

4. *What are you going to use for backup reinforcers?* Most token economies use prizes as backup reinforcers. A prize is something that the average student would not normally receive in school, such as a gift certificate to McDonald's. Other token economies use entitlements as backup reinforcers. These include rewards that students would normally receive, such as eating lunch in the cafeteria with their peers, attending assemblies, and belonging to school clubs. While entitlements are provided to the average student "free of charge," the student in the entitlement token system must "buy" them with tokens earned for appropriate behavior. Whichever system you use, it is unlikely that it will work effectively unless you have backup reinforcers that are, in fact, reinforcing to your students as well as feasible to dispense. So unless you know someone in the travel business, don't promise to provide paid vacations to Disneyland or ski trips to Aspen. Be realistic about what students can earn with their tokens and, above all, make sure that the prize is something they want.

Figure 6.21. Token (play money) used in token economy.

SPEND "JOE DOUGH" ON:

TAPE RECORDER & TAPES
$5 PER RECORDER AND
$1 PER TAPE

PAPERBACKS, MAGAZINES, COMICS
$1 EACH

SUPPLIES—PAPER, PENCILS,
COMBS, ERASERS, RULERS,
CRAYONS (SEE PRICE EACH ITEM)

GAMES, PUZZLES, CRAFTS
$5 RENTAL
$20 PURCHASE

Figure 6.22. Reinforcing event "menu" for use in token economy.

5. *Who dispenses the tokens?* Tokens should always be given by an authority figure in the student's environment such as a teacher, aide, or peer tutor.

6. *When should they be given?* Tokens should be used when it is not feasible or appropriate to give the student the backup reinforcer for desirable behavior. However, like any reinforcer, tokens must be dispensed immediately following the contingency for reinforcement. For this reason, they should be dispensed quickly and easily according to whatever reinforcement schedule a teacher may be following with a given student.

7. *How will the tokens be given?* This depends upon the type of token used. Check marks can be made by the teacher on his copy of the student's token sheet. Stars and stick-ons can be given to the student for him to paste on his token sheet. Many of these stick-ons have other reinforcing properties such as a pleasing smell or taste. Chips or play money may be given directly to the student or placed in the student's "bank" by the teacher. Two criteria for deciding how the tokens will be dispensed are (1) what is reinforcing for the student (she should be aware that she is getting a token or tokens) and (2) what is easiest for the teacher (she should dispense the tokens so that it won't interfere with her teaching). You don't want to become a bookkeeper or an accountant, so keep it simple.

8. *When will the tokens be redeemed (i.e., turned in for the backup reinforcer)?* This depends upon the stu-

dent's need. Some may be able to wait until the end of the day or even the end of the week before redeeming their tokens. Others may need the backup reinforcer sooner. Obviously, the longer the student can wait, the better. When the tokens are redeemed will also depend upon the backup reinforcer that is being used. For example, if reading comic books is the backup reinforcer, the student could conceivably turn in his tokens virtually any time during the day. Since comic book reading does not require any elaborate involvement on the part of the teacher, he is free to continue to teach while the student cashes in his tokens for free time reading comics. However, if the backup reinforcer is teacher attention, a special event such as a class auction, or any other activity that might disrupt the learning environment, it will be necessary for the teacher to set up a special time for the redemption of tokens. Again, this time would be determined by the teacher's schedule and the students' ability to delay gratification.

Implementation

Once you have attended to all of these questions, you are ready to implement your token economy. If you have planned accordingly, you should not encounter many problems. However, as a firm believer in Murphy's Law (If something can go wrong, it will), I would be on the lookout for one or more of the following:

1. *A student has earned all of the tokens she needs before the school day or class period is over.* This student may then begin to misbehave, since she already has enough points for the backup reinforcer she wants. She should be told at the beginning of the program that while she can earn points for appropriate behavior, she can also lose them for inappropriate behavior. Losing points for inappropriate behavior is called *response cost* and will be discussed in more detail in the next chapter. Response cost helps to keep the student's behavior under control because she doesn't want to lose what she has worked so hard to earn. It goes without saying that once response cost is put into effect and tokens are taken away for misbehavior, the student must have the opportunity to earn them back again. If the student feels she doesn't have the opportunity to earn back lost tokens, she may no longer be motivated to behave appropriately.

2. *A student complains because he has to do more to earn the same number of tokens as his peers.* Because your students will vary in terms of their ability, two of them may be earning the same number of tokens while one is required to do twice as much work as the other. To solve this problem you might try one of the following techniques. First, have the "slow" student perform five jobs; if each is done correctly, he will receive 10 tokens apiece, for a total of 50 tokens for the day. In the mean-

time, have the "fast" student complete 10 jobs at 10 tokens apiece, or 100 tokens for the day. In this way, you do not penalize the fast student for his greater ability and you provide incentive for the slow student to work harder and faster, so that he too can add more jobs (and more tokens) each day. A second option is to limit both the fast and slow students to the same number of jobs per day but "pay" the fast student more for his work since his jobs are more difficult. Again, this provides the slow student with an incentive to work harder in order to get more difficult assignments and the opportunity to earn higher "pay."

3. *A student uses extortion to get tokens or backup reinforcers from peers.* While this sounds more ominous than it actually is, extortion can make your token system fail. What usually happens is that one student who is bigger or tougher than the others extorts tokens or backup reinforcers from them under threat of physical harm. This usually occurs when the extortionist is not getting enough tokens in the classroom, either because she fails to participate in the token economy or because the teacher has made it too difficult for her to earn as many tokens as her peers. To avoid extortion in your classroom make sure that all of your students have the opportunity to earn as many tokens as they feel they need. Sit down and contract with them at the beginning of the program to determine the contingency required, tokens received, backup reinforcers available, and cost for each. Contracts in the classroom can be similar to those between employer and employee in the business world. When the employee perceives this agreement as fair and the payoffs as equitable and attainable, he is less likely to take advantage of his employer or his colleagues. You can also discourage extortion in your classroom by keeping close track of the tokens earned by your students. If one or more of them feel that they need to extort tokens from their peers, don't let this behavior lead to a payoff. You can stop extortion simply by knowing how many tokens each of your students should have. Unfortunately, there is little you can do to discourage the extortion of backup reinforcers outside of the classroom if you are using tangible or primary reinforcers such as books, toys, or granola bars. Unless one of your students lets you know what's happening, you may not even know that any extortion has occurred. This is one good reason for avoiding the use of tangible items as backup reinforcers. If you stick with social reinforcers as well as activity reinforcers awarded during school hours, keep close track of the tokens your students have earned, and make sure that everyone has ample opportunity to share in the "wealth," extortion should not be a problem.

4. *A student refuses to go off the token economy.* What student in her right mind would voluntarily give up Big

Macs, comic books, and toys for pats on the back, smiling faces, and passing grades? What do you say to your students when you feel that they no longer need prizes for behaving properly? If you tell them that they no longer need them because their behavior is so good, won't they revert back to their old tricks in order to get the prizes again? I don't know about your students, but mine certainly would! The message you are communicating to them is that crime does pay. If you are bad in school, you get tokens. If you are good in school, you don't. While I'm not suggesting that this situation is inevitable, it does occur and you should take some necessary precautions to avoid it. First of all, the problem is not weaning students from the tokens as much as it is weaning them from the backup reinforcers. The students don't mind giving up the tokens, but they don't want to give up what they can buy with them. In order to avoid this situation, have your students redeem tokens for backup reinforcers that the average student gets for "free." Instead of using junk food, toys, or trips to the local pizza parlor or skating rink as prizes for work and good behavior, have your students earn the privilege of eating lunch with their peers in the school cafeteria, attending school assemblies, joining school clubs, participating in intramural or interscholastic athletic programs, and going on field trips, among others. Please keep in mind that I am not talking about having students earn tokens to buy basic instruction or entry into classes that are part of their individualized education program. I am talking about using tokens to purchase those extracurricular privileges which are not part of the prescribed educational program. I do not believe that these are God-given rights protected by the Constitution. They are privileges that all students can earn only by behaving like students. The fastest way to wean any student from a token economy is not to make her give up something good that she has access to only if she misbehaves. The fastest way to wean a student from a token economy is to make her earn something good that she thinks her peers get for free.

If you must use prizes, you can still wean students from a token economy if you pay close attention to the following guidelines. First, remember to keep increasing the contingencies for earning tokens. Make it more and more difficult for the student to earn the same number of tokens as she improves. If she had to stay in her seat 10 minutes in order to earn 10 tokens before, when her behavior changes, make her stay in her seat 15 minutes to earn the same number, then 20, 30, and so on. If she balks at having to do more or work harder to earn the same number of tokens, tell her she has other options. She can always go off the token economy and work for "nothing." She can stay on the token economy and buy entitlements instead of prizes.

She can stop working altogether and watch her peers earn and spend their tokens. She can become disruptive and be punished every day instead of being rewarded. The decision is hers to make. I would also try very hard to convince her that while the tokens are a crutch she needs now to help her change her behavior, by working for longer and longer periods of time without receiving tokens she eventually will be able to work without them.

Second, remember to keep giving the student social reinforcement in liberal amounts even though you are giving fewer tokens. Make sure your praise focuses on his behavior (i.e., the contingency for the tokens). Never praise him for the number of tokens he has earned but for the completed work or behavior change that led to the token reinforcement. Make him more aware of the change in his behavior and less aware of the tokens he has earned as a result of that change. Your goal is to make him value his new behavior more than the tokens he receives for it. If you accomplish this goal, weaning him from the token economy should become a relatively simple process.

If you are going to use a token economy for all of your students, the most practical way to wean them away from tokens is probably the levels system. Each level in the system is a closer approximation of the "real world" or the mainstream. For example, students on level 1 ("freshman") might be given reinforcement frequently because they need it more than their peers. In addition, they might be given tokens that are quite unusual compared with those used at a higher level. Poker chips or play money might be used instead of grades on a report card. At the "freshman" level, students might only have access to certain backup reinforcers such as records or tapes or arts and crafts materials, which they would be required to "purchase" with their tokens. "Sophomores" would not be given tokens as often as "freshmen" and the tokens would more closely resemble those of the mainstream school (e.g., points on a card instead of poker chips or play money). "Sophomores" would also have the privilege of receiving backup reinforcers such as tapes and crafts materials for free; in addition, they would be able to "purchase" a wider variety of backup reinforcers including class jobs, such as being a teacher assistant or paper monitor.

Students at the "junior" level would receive tokens on a less frequent basis than "sophomores" and "freshmen" and their tokens would more closely resemble those used in the mainstream. In addition, "juniors" would have free access to the same backup reinforcers that "freshmen" and "sophomores" were required to purchase (e.g., crafts, tapes, and class jobs) and they would be allowed to purchase school privileges such as attending assemblies, school movies, athletic events, and the like. Finally, "seniors" would be reinforced still less often (perhaps once at the end of the week); this reinforcement would be in the form of grades on a report card. Students at the "senior" level would also have free access to everything at the first three levels and would be able to use their tokens to purchase school jobs such as safety patrol officer or work in the office or cafeteria.

As you can visualize from this description, as students move through the levels system they gradually are weaned away from the token economy. Levels systems require a great deal of work to set up and operate, but in the long run they can be quite beneficial. An example of another levels system may be seen in Figure 6.23.

Trouble Shooting

What should you do if your reinforcement program isn't working? The first thing to do is to find out why. This is called *trouble shooting*. It's not unlike that section in the operator's manual for a dishwasher or stereo system.

1. *Does the student have all of the essential prerequisites for the target behavior?* Did you do an assessment on the student before you designed and implemented your reinforcement program? If not, it must be done now. If you did do an assessment and concluded that the student had all of the prerequisites for the target behavior, take another look at your assessment. Did you leave out any prerequisites in your task analysis? Were you in error about the status of any of these prerequisites? Were any of your assessments invalid? If you are convinced that your assessment was valid and that the student has all of the essential prerequisites for the target behavior, go on to another area.

2. *Are you using the correct schedules of reinforcement and, if so, are you using them correctly?* Did you stay on one schedule too long or not long enough? Did you use any schedules of reinforcement at all? Did you have the correct schedules written on paper but fail to implement them correctly?

3. *Are you presenting your reinforcers appropriately?* Is the latency between the student's behavior and the reinforcer too long? Are you being enthusiastic enough in your use of social reinforcement so that the student accepts it as sincere? Are you overdoing the use of the reinforcer to the point where it is beginning to lose its reinforcing properties?

4. *Are you using the right reinforcer?* How did you decide to use this particular reinforcer? Observation? Interview? How many people did you interview and how well do they know the student?

Program Guide
for the Parkrose Middle School Project

The Middle School Project is designed to meet the needs of students with behaviors which interfere with the educational process. The goal of the program is to mainstream students gradually as they learn behaviors which enable them to be successful in the regular classroom setting.

Levels System: The classroom operates on a levels basis, where students work to earn their way up the levels and out into mainstream classes.

Level 1 is for students who are unsuccessful at Level 2. In order to assure success, students at this level attend school the first four periods only. They do not eat lunch at school and have no passing privileges. They go to their regular Advisory three times a week.

If a student on Level 1 earns 80% of his possible points in 15 out of 20 consecutive days, he can graduate into Level 2. He must also display appropriate out-of-class behavior and have no significant problems in Advisory.

Those at *Level 2* have a six-period day, with Advisory and one other period mainstreamed. All other classes are in the self-contained setting but there are passing and lunch privileges. If the student at Level 2 is suspended for repeated noncompliance he will go to Level 1. He can also be put in Level 1 if, at mid-term or at the end of the term, he has an average of less than 75% and/or if at any point there are numerous reports about poor behavior outside the classroom.

On the other hand, if at mid-term or at end-of-term the Level 2 student has earned 85% for 25 days or 80% for 50 days he will be considered a candidate for Level 3.

Level 3 is a transition time, where the student is in school for seven periods and mainstreamed for two to six classes per day. This student has all the rights and responsibilities of any other student in the school. As long as he maintains an 80% average and is getting good reports from his mainstream classes, the student is a candidate for further mainstreaming. Evaluations are made every three weeks to determine whether the student should remain at this level.

Reasons for demotion could be suspension, failure in mainstream classes, problems with lunch or hallway behavior, or low percentage on the point system in the self-contained classroom.

Figure 6.23. Example of levels system used in schools. *Note.* Reprinted by permission of Peter Nordby, Parkrose School District, Portland, OR.

5. *Should you have used a shaping program?* Are you expecting too much from the student too soon? If you did use a shaping program, did you make too great a jump between successive approximations? Did you wait until the student was engaging in an approximation on a variable schedule for a period of time before moving on to the next one?

6. *Are you or anyone else in the student's environment modeling a behavior that is incompatible with the target behavior?* In other words, if you wanted to reinforce staying on task or being in seat, is off-task behavior or out-of-seat behavior being modeled by the student's peers? If it is not being modeled by all of his peers, is it being modeled by a peer considered important enough to emulate?

7. *Are the reinforcers themselves interfering with the target behavior?* Is the student spending time playing with her earned tangibles when she should be doing her work?

8. *If you are using a shaping program, did you remember to use differential reinforcement or did you accidentally reinforce old approximations instead of (or in addition to) new approximations?*

9. *If the behavior has been learned (i.e., reinforced) but has not generalized to other settings, have you taken the time to program for generalization through fading?*

Chapter Six Self-Assessment

See Appendix A for acceptable responses.

1.   When would you use positive reinforcement?

2.   When would you use negative reinforcement?

3.   State two rules of thumb to follow if you want to use R– effectively.

    a.

    b.

4.   State six rules to follow if you want to use R+ effectively.

    a.

    b.

    c.

    d.

    e.

    f.

5.   List two examples each for social, token, primary, tangible, and activity reinforcers.

    a.   Social:

    b.   Token:

continued next page

c. Primary:

d. Tangible:

e. Activity:

6. Describe two methods used to choose reinforcers.

   a.

   b.

7. Underline the correct answer in the parentheses.

   a. The best schedule to use when you are first starting to build a new behavior is the (continuous, fixed, variable) schedule.

   b. The schedule that is most resistant to change is the (continuous, fixed, variable) schedule.

   c. The schedule that is least resistant to change is the (continuous, fixed, variable) schedule.

   d. The schedule used with behavior reinforced over time is the (variable, interval, ratio) schedule.

   e. The schedule used with behavior reinforced according to responses is the (variable, interval, ratio) schedule.

   f. The best schedule to use for maintenance is the (variable, fixed, continuous) schedule.

   g. An intermittent schedule of reinforcement that is predictable is the (variable, ratio, fixed) schedule.

   h. An intermittent schedule of reinforcement that is unpredictable is the (variable, ratio, fixed) schedule.

8. Draw a diagram showing each of the following schedules of reinforcement, using the key that is given.

   ◯ desirable behavior

   △ undesirable behavior

     positive reinforcement

continued next page

a.   Variable interval (2:1) without undesirable behavior:

b.   Fixed ratio (3:1) with undesirable behavior:

c.   Fixed interval (2:1) without undesirable behavior:

d.   Continuous (ratio) with undesirable behavior:

9.   Write a shaping program for a student that will strengthen in-seat behavior. Right now, the student is never in his seat unless the teacher tells him to sit down. At such times he complies, but after a few minutes he gets up to wander again. Your goal is for him to stay in his seat for 30 minutes at a time while on a variable-interval schedule of reinforcement. He loves peanuts.

Stop:

Start:

Reward:

Successive Approximations:

a.

b.

c.

d.

e.

When would you shift criteria for reinforcement?

continued next page

10. Explain the difference between shaping and fading.

11. List the steps in a chaining program.

12. List eight questions to consider when planning a token economy.

    a.

    b.

    c.

    d.

    e.

    f.

    g.

    h.

13. State how you would avoid or solve each of the following problems common to a token economy.

    a.   The student who has earned all of the tokens she needs before the school day or class period is over.

    b.   The student who complains because he has to do more to earn the same number of tokens as his peers.

    c.   The student who uses extortion to get tokens or backup reinforcers from peers.

    d.   The student who refuses to go off the token economy.

14. Write the definition of the Premack Principle.

15. Describe the trouble-shooting procedure you would use if one of your reinforcement programs did not achieve the desired objective.

chapter 7

Strategies for Weakening Behaviors

Upon successful completion of this chapter, the learner should be able to:

1. Explain how to use RIBs, response cost, extinction, time out, negative practice, overcorrection, and a hierarchy of escalating consequences to weaken hypothetical maladaptive behaviors
2. State incompatible or competing behaviors for given maladaptive behaviors
3. State the disadvantages of punishment
4. State when to use punishment
5. State how to use punishment effectively
6. State how to use reprimands effectively

Reinforcing Incompatible Behaviors (RIBs)

Even though reinforcing means strengthening, reinforcing an incompatible response is, in my opinion, the best way to weaken a student's maladaptive behavior. Obviously, it is only possible to use this strategy when there is an incompatible behavior to reinforce. If a student is never in her seat, you can't very well weaken out-of-seat behavior by reinforcing in-seat behavior. If a student never uses appropriate language, you can't weaken cursing by reinforcing him when he speaks appropriately. If a student is never on task, you can't weaken off-task behavior by strengthening on-task behavior. However, in my experience with children, in most instances, a student will engage in some behavior which, if not incompatible, at least competes with the maladaptive behavior. It may not occur very often, but when it does, be ready to reinforce it! The following is an example of how I used RIBs to weaken a maladaptive behavior.

I once worked with a young severely retarded girl who constantly sucked on the backs of her hands until the upper layer of skin came off. Fearing infection, the hospital staff where she lived wrapped her hands in sterile gauze bandages every day. However, this didn't stop the girl from sucking on her hand through the gauze. The next intervention tried was corporal punish-ment. Every time she had her hands in her mouth, someone would finger-flick her cheek hard enough to hurt her. Unfortunately, this intervention caused her to become anxious in the presence of any adult and the anxiety resulted in more frequent and intense hand-sucking behavior. It was finally decided to reinforce all instances of hand-out-of-mouth behavior. Whenever she had her hand out of her mouth, someone rewarded her with a primary reinforcer (a piece of a cookie), rubbed her head, and said, "Good girl!" Unfortunately, we didn't have the patient-staff ratio that would allow us to keep an aide next to this girl at all times. Since her hand-out-of-mouth behavior was so infrequent, it was next to impossible for us to catch her being "good" on a continuous basis. We therefore had to create a situation where she would be inclined to keep her hands out of her mouth more often. When we thought about the reinforcement she was getting out of sucking on her hands, we concluded that the feeling of sucking (the tactile pressure of the skin) plus the warmth and wetness from her mouth and her saliva were all part of what she liked about the activity. At first, we tried to simulate these reinforcing qualities by giving her a doll to "bathe" in a bowl of warm water. The idea was to keep her hands on the doll in the bath water as often and as long as possible so that we would have more opportunities to reinforce her with the primary and social reinforcement. We quickly discovered that the warm bath water was doing as much damage to her hands as was her sucking. Our next intervention was to give her a hot-water bottle tied to a metal rod attached to her wheelchair with a doll painted on it to simulate a baby and a baby bottle. She liked sucking on the bottle (even when there was nothing in it) and holding the "baby." We made the string short enough so that she could not bring the bottle near her mouth and suck on her hands while she held it. From time to time, an adult would walk by her wheelchair; if she was sucking on the bottle and holding the "baby," the adult would gently rub the back of her head and say, "Good girl!" By strengthening an incompatible behavior (or set of behaviors), we managed to weaken a maladaptive behavior.

Other examples of the use of incompatible and competing behaviors are reinforcing in-seat behavior to weaken out-of-seat behavior; asking questions of and listening to others to weaken constant "I" talk; reading or writing to weaken television watching; using on-task behavior to weaken off-task behavior; reinforcing hands-in-lap behavior to weaken thumb sucking or hitting neighbors; covering mouth and raising hand to weaken calling-out behavior; reinforcing compliance to weaken noncompliance; using appropriate language to weaken use of provocative language; and being assertive to weaken physically aggressive behavior. The strategy is simple. Find an incompatible or competing behavior and reinforce it when it occurs. This must be a behavior that is already in the student's response repertoire; it also must be a behavior that is likely to be maintained by the environment (i.e., a practical behavior that is apt to be maintained through natural consequences). If you don't see a change in the student's maladaptive behavior after a while, you may have to punish it as long as you remember to continue to reinforce the adaptive (incompatible) behavior at the same time.

Extinction

As stated earlier in the text, extinction occurs when you withhold or remove the consequent stimulus event (CSE) that is reinforcing the student's maladaptive behavior. If you find a student engaging in a behavior you wish to weaken, ask yourself if that behavior is being reinforced by something in the environment. For example, Ronnie engaged in behavior I will refer to as "personal narratives." He constantly told the teacher how he felt, what he was doing, and what was happening in the room or outside the window. At first, Ronnie's teacher would come to his desk and put her hand on his shoulder and her finger to her mouth to indicate that he should be silent. However, when the teacher found herself doing this at a rate of once every 5 minutes, she realized that something had to be done about Ronnie's behavior. By collecting some baseline data on what occurred in the environment immediately after Ronnie's narratives, she was able to see that her attending behavior was actually reinforcing his maladaptive behavior instead of weakening it. She was then able to withhold this reinforcer and extinguish his personal narrative behavior.

However, sometimes the known reinforcer is not under the teacher's control. For example, B.J. spent a great deal of time acting as class clown. She did this because the other students laughed at her and B.J. liked the attention she got from them. Her teacher recognized this but felt that he had little control over B.J.'s peers' attending behavior. B.J. did some outrageous things and although the teacher tried to get B.J.'s peers to stop laughing at her and simply ignore her, they found her antics too funny to do so. Once the teacher even tried to reinforce any student who could ignore B.J. Unfortunately, as much as her peers liked the reinforcement from the teacher, they just couldn't help themselves when B.J. started her act. She was a born comedian. In desperation, B.J.'s teacher removed her from the class to a special time out room near the school's office where she would receive none of the peer attention that reinforced her behavior.

There are other reinforcers in the environment besides attention. For example, I once worked with a young blind student who, when given a puzzle or form board to work with, would drop the pieces on the floor or table top because the sound they made was very stimulating for her. If you took the puzzles away from her, she would sit and rock back and forth on her chair, make a banging sound on the wooden floor, and screech like an animal. After an hour of this, the rest of the students were so stimulated that they would begin a chorus of sounds until the room seemed to quake with the sound track of a Tarzan movie! Time out didn't help to weaken her behavior in the classroom because she could screech there all she wanted. For her, time out wasn't punishing; it was actually reinforcing! I suggested to the teacher that since the sound of the falling wooden and plastic pieces from the puzzles was reinforcing the student's behavior, we would have to devise a way of removing this reinforcer without removing the puzzles. The teacher had an ingenious idea. She placed a padded tablecloth on top of the table where the student sat and a piece of rug remnant under the student's chair. After dropping several puzzle pieces on the table and the floor and not hearing any sound, the student stopped dropping them. I wish I could report that she then put the puzzles together. Unfortunately, her next trick was to throw the pieces across the room. We finally wound up punishing this behavior, since it was considered potentially harmful to her peers; at the same time we reinforced her when she put a piece where it belonged. I mention this case only because it serves to illustrate a situation where extinction occurred by withholding a known reinforcer other than attention.

Here are some things you should know about extinction:

1. When using extinction, the maladaptive behavior often gets worse before it gets better. This phenomenon was discussed in chapter 1. Be aware of this and do not give up too soon. Extinction may also produce a brief period of aggression in the early stages. This is probably a result of the discontinuation of reinforcement. Again, if you are aware of it, you will be better able to "tough it out."

2. Extinction, of all the methods in this text, probably requires the most patience. It takes a long time to see results. Collect data. Even the smallest changes in behavior can reinforce your desire to stay the course.

3. Extinction, like punishment, should be combined with the positive reinforcement of an adaptive behavior that is incompatible with the behavior you wish to weaken (i.e., RIBs).

Punishment

When teachers think about strategies for weakening student behavior, the first thing that comes to mind is usually punishment. However, punishment is not the only way to weaken undesirable student behavior; in fact, in most instances, it should be the last strategy used. Let's examine some of the reasons why punishment should only be considered when all else fails.

For one thing, punishment can lead to avoidance or escape behavior such as sneaking, stealing, cheating, lying, running away, and truancy. Here are a few examples. Mr. X. always yells at his students if he catches them talking in class. The children have gotten around this by whispering when his back is turned or by passing notes. Bobby knows he's going to be punished for not being prepared for gym class so he "borrows" Rafael's sneakers from his locker without Rafael's permission. Katy didn't study for the big test in math and her Dad is going to ground her if she gets "one more failing grade." To avoid this, she copies from Aletia's paper during the exam. Shelly knows she will be sent to the office if she confesses her part in some vandalism in the girl's lavatory, so she lies and blames it on someone else. Ralph knows he is going to be reprimanded for not doing his homework so he tells his mother he is sick and doesn't go to school. All of these students have one thing in common: They are all trying to avoid or escape punishment. Unfortunately, the only way they can think of to accomplish this end is to engage in behavior that is often just as undesirable as the behavior the teacher wants to punish.

Another reason for not using punishment as the strategy of choice in weakening undesirable behavior is that the punisher is often perceived by the student as a model of aggression. It is not uncommon for a student to be paddled for fighting or ridiculed for teasing. Children pay more attention to what we do than to what we say. Telling a student not to fight because she might be hurt or might hurt someone else makes no sense if you are proffering this wisdom while you are paddling her. You are really teaching the student, by your actions, that it is all right to hurt others. You are also teaching her to be careful not to get caught in an act of physical aggression. If she had been sneakier about it, she wouldn't have to endure the paddling. Of course, if she were caught again, she could always try to lie her way out.

One of the best reasons for not using punishment is the lack of supportive data regarding its long-term efficacy. Because punishment does not have a long-lasting effect on behavior, we are forced to use it again and again. Behaviors that are no longer punished or that are replaced by incompatible or competing behaviors tend to return to their prepunished state. True, the immediate effect of punishment is to weaken the response that it follows. Tell a student who is out of his seat to sit down. If he finds the reprimand aversive, he will comply. Out-of-seat behavior has been weakened. Punishment has occurred. However, unless you reinforce in-seat behavior, the chances are that the student will get out of his seat again in the very near future. The problem with this chain of events is that the teacher often believes that the punisher (i.e., the reprimand, "Sit down!") is working. Because of its short-term effectiveness, punishment tends to reinforce the teacher's expectation that it always works. Becker et al. refer to this as the "criticism trap" (1971). The teacher uses criticism to "punish" out-of-seat behavior. The immediate effect of the criticism makes the teacher think that it works. Because it is only a stopgap measure, the student continues to get out of his seat. But because the teacher has been rewarded (negatively) in the past for criticizing this behavior when the student sat down, she will continue to behave this way. The cycle repeats itself over and over again, day after day. If you showed the teacher data indicating the frequency of the student's out-of-seat behavior in relation to her criticizing behavior, she would realize that her reprimands do not have the desired effect of weakening the behavior over time and, technically, punishment has not occurred.

There can also be emotional side effects with punishment. Many teachers use it for their own benefit, rather than the student's. Punishing becomes a release for pent-up frustrations over mounting professional or personal stress. When this happens, it is often difficult to punish without showing some emotion; while such venting may aid the teacher emotionally, it often can produce anger, fear, or hurt feelings in the student. These feelings are counterproductive to learning and to the establishment of a positive, trusting relationship between teacher and student. I am not suggesting that all teachers who punish their students will necessarily give them a psychological trauma. I am simply saying that punishment delivered in a highly emotional state often leads to undesirable emotional side effects in the student. The result of all this is that the person doing the punishing may become an aversive stimulus to the student. In addition, the setting in which the punishment occurs, the subject matter being taught, and the peer group witnessing the punishing event can all become aversive stimuli.

Put simply, if punishment occurs often enough during the school day and across enough settings in the school, students will view the entire school experience as aversive and, seeking to escape from these aversive stimuli, they may become truant, or just drop out.

Kids can learn a lot from punishment.

When To Use Punishment

While punishment should be avoided because of the reasons that have been mentioned, there are two situations in which punishment may be necessary.

Punishment may be unavoidable when the maladaptive behavior is so intense or severe that someone might be hurt, including the child with the maladaptive behavior, or when you have tried everything else without success. Remember that it is your responsibility to weaken and, if possible, eliminate maladaptive behavior as long as the punishment used doesn't create problems for the student or those in the student's environment that are worse than the problem currently caused by the maladaptive behavior.

How To Use Punishment Effectively

Let's assume that you are facing one of the two situations just described and you have to use punishment. While this is bad enough, you don't want to become

one of the millions of teachers who use punishment incorrectly. To avoid this, follow these rules of thumb:

1. To be effective, punishment must prevent avoidance and escape from the source of the punishment. If the student can successfully escape from the punishment through sneaking, hiding, cheating, lying, or stealing, punishment will lose much of its potency.

2. Minimize the need for future punishment by positively reinforcing adaptive behaviors that are incompatible or in competition with the maladaptive behaviors you punish. Don't simply punish out-of-seat behavior. Positively reinforce in-seat behavior. Don't simply punish hitting behavior. Positively reinforce gentle touching behavior. If the student doesn't know how to touch gently, teach her. Don't simply punish cursing and abusive or aggressive language. Positively reinforce the use of appropriate assertive language. Again, if the student doesn't know how to speak in an assertive, nonaggressive manner, teach him.

3. Never be a model of aggressive behavior. Don't "attack" students verbally or physically when you punish them.

4. Never hold a grudge. It's not healthy for you or your students. If the student feels that you have a grudge against him he will be less inclined to try and change his behavior. Why should he bother if your feelings toward him prevent you from rewarding him when he's behaving properly?

5. Punishment, like reinforcement, should be administered immediately. The longer the latency, the less likely it is that learning will take place.

6. Communicate to the student, in terms she can understand, exactly how she may earn back whatever reinforcers you might have taken away from her.

7. Try to use a warning signal of some kind before punishing a student. Even a look is better than nothing. Give the student one, and only one, opportunity to change his behavior before you punish him. If he doesn't stop, then punish him.

8. Always do what you say you will do. Never threaten if you can't produce. Don't tell a student she is going to have to leave school if she doesn't behave if you don't know whether or not her parent is available to come and get her. Don't threaten detention on a day when you have to leave school early.

9. Try to carry out your punishment in a calm manner, without losing your temper. Besides making you look foolish, weak, scared, immature, and insecure, losing your cool can teach the student that self-control is impossible. If an adult can't attain it, how can the student be expected to?

10. Be consistent and always punish the same behavior. The student who can't remember his own

name somehow always manages to remember all the details of other students' punishments.

11. Be certain that the intensity of the punishment is high enough to ensure that the behavior is weakened. At the same time, try not to gradually increase the intensity of the punishment, or the child may develop a tolerance for it.

12. Use a variety of punishers. Just as a student can become satiated from the use of the same reinforcer over and over again, so she can become desensitized to the use of the same punisher used continuously.

Types of Punishment

Five strategies which may be categorized as punishment are: *reprimands, response cost, negative practice, overcorrection,* and *time out*. Let's examine each.

Reprimands. A reprimand is a simple word or statement the teacher says to stop the student from doing whatever behavior the teacher objects to. Examples are "No," "Stop," "Don't do that," and "I want you to stop _____." Reprimands are usually the first punisher a teacher uses to weaken a behavior. To be effective, the teacher must be aware of all of the following:

1. Get as close to the student as possible, without being threatening, so that your physical presence will help attract the student's attention. Don't shout across the room and further disrupt the learning environment. A "private" reprimand is less likely to result in face-saving defiance before the peer group.

2. If you cannot get close to the student, use an attention signal such as calling her name before giving the reprimand. Sometimes the attention signal ("Amy!") is aversive enough to the student to punish her behavior.

3. Look directly at the student while talking to him, even if he's not looking at you. Eye contact is important in asserting yourself.

4. Make the reprimand as short and succinct as possible, using one or two sentences at the most.

5. Use simple vocabulary. It is incorrect to say, "Stop procrastinating." A student can't follow a directive unless she understands it. Instead, say, "Stop putting off doing your work" or "Stop daydreaming."

6. Specify the behavior you want the student to stop (or start) engaging in. Don't use terms that are open to interpretation. It is incorrect to say, "Stop bothering him." The word "bothering" is open to interpretation. Instead, say, "Stop talking to him." The stranger test applies to the use of reprimands the same way it does to pinpointing behaviors.

7. Under no circumstances use sarcasm. Some students won't understand you and you will also be

serving as a model for students who enjoy making fun of others.

8. Use an if-then statement when reprimanding the student. Specify what you want the student to do and let him know exactly what the consequences will be if he doesn't do it. It's wrong to say, "Stop talking" and "If you don't stop talking, you are going to be punished." It's correct to say, "If you don't stop talking to Pete, you'll lose 10 points."

9. Deliver the reprimand in your normal teaching voice. If you speak too softly, the student might not hear you or might think you don't mean what you say. If you speak too loudly, aside from disrupting the entire class, you may also communicate anxiety, fear, or loss of self-control. Speaking too loudly may stimulate the student (i.e., make her anxious) to the point where she can't respond appropriately even if she wants to, or it may reinforce her maladaptive behavior if she thinks she's gotten under your skin. It is also ludicrous to expect a student to demonstrate self-control in the presence of an adult who has lost it.

10. Always finish what you have to say to one student before addressing another. Try to ignore the second student until you have reprimanded the first. Students can manipulate your verbal behavior and reduce the effectiveness of your reprimands.

11. Students are also good at reading body language and facial expressions. Never fold your arms across your chest when reprimanding a student; it conveys aggression (or at the very least, defensiveness) and tends to make some students anxious, while others perceive it as a challenge. Pointing, especially when up close, and standing with hands on hips may also convey the same aggressive or hostile message. Try to communicate as little of your feelings as possible through facial expression. Students tend to focus on the way you speak to them rather than on what you actually say. If your mouth says one thing and your body says something else, they will attend to your body. Force them to focus on your words rather than reading your expression or posture. Remember that a low-key, calm demeanor will be more effective in the long run than blowing off steam. The latter approach will make you feel better for the moment but it may serve to prolong or escalate the student's disruptive behavior.

12. Give the student enough time to comply with the request. You should determine what constitutes "enough" based upon (1) your past experiences with the student, (2) how upset he is now, and (3) how difficult your request is for him to comply with. Compliance time will vary from student to student and from situation to situation. Whatever you do, never repeat a request unless you are certain that the student did not hear you the first time. You will only be teaching him

not to pay attention to you; he will feel that he doesn't have to comply the first time because you will repeat the directive. Ignore back talk such as "What ya pickin' on me for?" or "I'm not doin' nothin'." Compliance is the important thing. As long as the student does as he is told, it doesn't make any difference whether he does it with or without comment. However, when profanity is used, you may wish to punish the behavior with response cost; other provocative language such as threats to the teacher or peers may be consequated with a more severe punishment, such as time out.

13. If the student has complied with your request within a reasonable amount of time, thank her for her actions and remember to praise her for any behavior that is incompatible with her maladaptive behavior. If the student continues to engage in her maladaptive behavior and does not comply with your request (i.e., your reprimand doesn't work), proceed to a more severe consequence; do not use reprimands over and over again.

Response Cost. Response cost is sometimes also referred to as *cost contingency*. It involves the removal of a potentially rewarding event (e.g., leaving school at dismissal) or the removal of an earned reinforcer (e.g., losing tokens earned for past behavior) contingent upon an undesirable behavior. Grounding a teenager for coming home late from a dance is an example of response cost used to punish staying-out-late behavior or disobeying rules. Paying a fine for a parking violation is an example of response cost used to punish "bad" driving behavior. Any time you are taking something away from the student that she or he has or expects to have, in order to punish a behavior, you may say that you are using response cost. Do not confuse respose cost with extinction. In the latter, you are withholding or removing the object or event that is reinforcing the student's maladaptive behavior. For example, a student may be distracted all day by a puzzle he brought to school. Instead of attending to his tasks, he spends most of his time playing with his Rubik's Cube. It is the Cube that is reinforcing his off-task behavior. By removing the Cube, you have removed the known reinforcer of the maladaptive behavior. Without this reinforcer, he must either find some other reinforcing object to keep himself off task, or stay on task. If he stops being off task, we may say that his off-task behavior has been "extinguished" by the removal of the known reinforcer. This is an example of extinction. In response cost, the teacher might take back some tokens the student had previously earned or take away his recess or free time period as a punishment for his off-task behavior. Keep in mind that the tokens he earned or the recess or free time period are not the known reinforcer for his off-

task behavior. It is still the Cube that is reinforcing the off-task behavior. Therefore, we may not say that by removing his tokens, recess, or free time, the teacher is practicing extinction. Instead, he is practicing response cost, a form of punishment.

Response cost is probably most useful in a token economy. Students need to know that "bad" behavior can result in the subsequent loss of points. Having a student stop work because she knows that she already has enough points for the backup reinforcer needs to be discouraged. If you are not using a token economy and don't have the option of removing tokens earned, there are still some other potentially rewarding events or earned reinforcers you can remove. Unfortunately, you may run out of reinforcers to remove before you weaken the student's behavior. How many times in one day can you tell a student he's going to miss recess or get detention? If you remove recess or give him detention for days on end, you will be defeating your purpose in the long run. The student, knowing that he's "bankrupt" for the next week, may decide that he has nothing to lose as far as his behavior is concerned.

For this reason, I advocate more parent-teacher agreements for the consequation of a student's school behavior at home. There are many potential reinforcers available in the home that the parents might remove to punish maladaptive behavior at school. Removal of television privileges, staying up late, eating favored desserts, having snacks, having friends sleep over, going out to play after school, using the family car, going out on dates, going on family outings, going to the movies or sporting events with the family, getting an allowance, and using the stereo are just a few of the potentially reinforcing events that a parent might remove through a response cost program. Don't get me wrong. I still prefer to use a positive program of reinforcement rather than a negative program of punishment to change a student's behavior. However, as I have stated before, when all else fails, punishment may be your only hope.

If you decide upon a strategy of response cost, make sure you follow these rules of thumb:

1. Remove whatever you told the student she would lose as quickly and quietly as possible. Do this without any dramatics. Do not communicate to the student that you are glad that she is losing something she wants, even if you actually feel this way.

2. Let the student know what he is losing, why he is losing it, how he might earn it back, and what will happen if he continues to misbehave. For example, "Rudy, I'm taking ten of the points you have earned because you are still talking to Tina. If you stop talking and get back to work, you can start earning those points back. If you continue talking to Tina, you will have to

go to time out and you won't be able to earn any points for five minutes no matter how hard you try."

3. Because response cost is so convenient to use, teachers tend to use it too often. Overuse, however, may limit its effectiveness.

4. Collect data ahead of time to determine the severity of the cost or fine. You don't want the fine to be too heavy. This might result in the student completely giving up and not trying to earn back reinforcers through adaptive behavior. It might also provoke an emotional reaction (e.g., anger) in the student, which could exacerbate the situation. On the other hand, if the fine is too light, it will not have the desired effect of weakening the maladaptive behavior. If you have initially settled on a fine that is too light, by all means increase it. However, do not increase it gradually or you may find that the student will adapt to it and it therefore will not serve to weaken the maladaptive behavior. Either return to baseline for a while or implement a much heavier fine immediately. For example, Harriet's teacher wants to weaken her swearing behavior through response cost. Since Harriet is on a token economy, the teacher decides to fine Harriet so many tokens earned for each swearing episode. At first she fines Harriet 10 tokens for each episode. This doesn't seem to have any effect, so she immediately moves to a fine of 25 tokens per episode. This fine produces the desired effect and Harriet starts to limit her swearing.

5. If the student becomes upset at the fine, try to ignore any emotional outbursts. If they become serious, you might consider fining the student for these reactions. You could even begin charging students for the privilege of a tantrum in the same way that you would charge for listening to a rock-and-roll tape. On the other hand, if the student behaves in an accepting and responsible manner, you might consider returning a portion of the fine you assessed.

Negative Practice. This punishment procedure requires that the student perform or engage in the maladaptive behavior so many times that it becomes aversive to him. For example, little Marshall was a multiply handicapped youngster who was mentally retarded and confined to a wheelchair. Marshall was also very spoiled. If he didn't want to drink his milk he would simply knock the container off his tray. This behavior was repeated three times a day, at each meal. After trying positive means to modify Marshall's behavior, we decided on a trial run of negative practice. We kept putting paper cups on Marshall's tray and made him knock them off one by one. This was done over and over again until it was obvious that it was becoming extremely aversive to him. This procedure was repeated every time Marshall knocked a carton of milk off his tray until he

finally tired of the practice and the maladaptive behavior stopped. At that point, we were able to successfully implement a positive reinforcement program to get Marshall to drink his milk with every meal.

There are two things you must consider when using negative practice:

1. Avoid using it with students who are starved for attention. Negative practice requires that you spend a great deal of time with a student. I spent something like 15 minutes with Marshall the first time we tried negative practice with him! Even though the time may be spent engaging in behavior that is aversive to the student, we know that most students seek attention. If they can't get it through positive means, they will work for it through negative means. Nobody likes to be ignored. Therefore, the time you spend with a student performing or engaging in the maladaptive behavior you wish to weaken may instead serve to reinforce that behavior.

2. Remember to go beyond the point of satiation. At first, Marshall thought it was great fun to keep knocking cups off the tray. It was a game to him and he laughed and laughed. After about 25 cups, however, he began to tire of the game and would simply sit still with his hands in his lap. At this point, if we had stopped, we would have let Marshall control the situation by determining when he had had enough. We also didn't feel that "cup knocking" was aversive for him yet. True, he was tired of it, but it had to be aversive in order to be effective as a punisher. Therefore, we continued with the cup knocking by taking his hand and providing some firm guidance (i.e., forcing him to knock cups off the tray). After some 15 or 20 additional cups, it was obvious to us that Marshall found this practice extremely aversive. At this point, we stopped.

Overcorrection. This is one of the oldest methods used to punish maladaptive behavior in school children. Remember how you were made to write a misspelled word over and over until you learned it? That's overcorrection. Or we make students write, "I will come to class prepared," one hundred times. Other examples are requiring students with messy desks to clean up their own desks and all the other desks in the classroom, or requiring students caught writing on school walls or furniture to wash all the walls in the school or refinish all the desks in their classroom as a punishment.

Overcorrection has two basic components: (1) restitution, which requires the individual to restore the environment to its original state prior to the maladaptive behavior; and (2) positive practice, the repeated practice of a positive behavior incompatible with the maladaptive behavior. Here is an example: Jane gets angry and sometimes throws her desk or another student's over, scattering materials everywhere. In applying the restitution component of overcorrection, Jane's teacher makes her pick up the overturned desks as well as the spilled materials. For the positive practice component of overcorrection, Jane is required to stack all classroom furniture (i.e., seats on desks) for the maintenance crew prior to dismissal for 1 week.

Time Out.   Technically speaking, time out (TO) is closer to extinction than it is to punishment. You might say that TO is extinction in the extreme. Instead of withholding one reinforcer for one particular response, you withhold all reinforcement for all behavior. For example, Sandy curses at the rate of five curses every 10 minutes. In the past, this behavior has gotten her all the attention she wanted, even though most of it was negative. Now, her peers and the teacher ignore her cursing but they attend to her whenever she uses appropriate language. Eventually, Sandy's cursing will become extinguished because the known reinforcer, attention, is being withheld. In this case, a specific reinforcer is withheld for a specific response. However, reinforcement is being presented for other behavior (appropriate language). Let's suppose that Sandy's cursing behavior gets worse and eventually becomes so disruptive to the learning environment that she has to be removed. Once Sandy is removed from the environment, she will receive no reinforcement for any behavior, cursing or appropriate language. TO means time out from all reinforcement for all behavior.

Sometimes it may be possible to place a student in TO without having him leave his seat. This is a modified TO sometimes referred to as *contingent observation.* You might simply tell a student who is being disruptive in a group setting to leave that setting and go back to his seat for a period of time. He can return contingent upon his quiet behavior away from the group. You can also have a student simply put his head down on his desk. If your students were on a token economy you could put a student on a modified TO by simply removing his point card from his desk. This would alert the student to the fact that for a prespecified period of time, he will not be earning points regardless of what he does. In this case, TO is like being laid off from work. No matter what you do, you aren't going to earn any money from your employer.

For TO to be effective, it is necessary for the teacher to observe the following rules of thumb:

1. Be sure to put the student into an environment that is virtually free of reinforcement. Putting a student out into the hall where there are other rooms to look into as well as hallway traffic does not provide a reinforcement-free environment. There are too many opportunities to interact with peers and engage in more mischief. Sending a child to her room where she can

play with her toys is also not appropriate. Try to set up a TO space in your room or somewhere in the school building where a student will receive no reinforcement for any behavior, but where he or she can be observed from time to time. This may be difficult but it will save you grief later on. Sticking a child in the cloakroom or walk-in closet of a classroom is not only cruel; it's downright risky business. Students have been forgotten in closets and some have developed real psychological traumas as a result of such treatment. A student sent to the hall for TO can inflict serious physical damage on peers who happen to walk by. He might also be fair game for physical abuse himself. Aside from the obvious damage to the student, the teacher in this situation is wide open to litigation from the student's parents. In the past, I have simply put a student in a chair facing the corner and set a timer so he would know when he might be free to leave TO and return to his desk. In this way, I could see him but he could not see the rest of the class. He could still hear us and we could still hear him. If he attempted to take advantage of this situation, I could always reinforce his peers for ignoring him, or I could add more time on the timer. An ideal setup for the classroom would be to place a chair behind a screen in the back of the room. Here, the student would not be able to see his peers and, as long as their seats were facing the front of the room, they would not be able to see him. The teacher, however, could monitor the student by installing a wide-angle mirror above the TO area. If this is too expensive, the wide-angle stick-on mirrors sold in auto parts and recreational vehicle shops can do the job for much less money.

2. The student should not stay in TO for more than 1 minute for each of her chronological years. In other words, a 10-year-old should not stay in TO for more than 10 minutes. The student should always know how long she is "in for." You might have to add time on for disruptive behavior in TO, but I have found that longer time spent in TO results in more disruptive behavior later on. It then becomes a vicious cycle. The student in TO for more than 5 minutes usually becomes restless and agitated. She manifests this by attempting to communicate with the teacher ("How much longer do I have to stay here?" "When can I go back to my desk?"). While this behavior can be ignored by the teacher, it may eventually become disruptive to the other students, causing the teacher to add more time on the TO in order to punish the student's calling-out behavior. The more time the teacher adds on, the more restless and agitated the student becomes and the more disruptive behavior she's likely to engage in.

3. TO should not be used unless the student's behavior is disruptive to the learning environment. If the student's peers cannot learn and the teacher can-

not teach as a direct result of maladaptive behavior, the student should be placed in TO, assuming that other interventions have not been effective.

4. Ideally, the student should go to TO under his own power. Do not attempt to move him yourself unless you are convinced you can do so quickly and easily without providing a "show" for the student's peers. If he refuses to go, start a stopwatch in his presence and tell him that the time he takes to go to TO will be added to the time he already has to spend there. Do not discuss the situation with the student after you have started the watch. Turn around and walk away. Obviously, you don't want to let the watch run indefinitely or you will have a situation where the student will simply try to outwait you. If, after a few minutes, the student still has not gone to TO on his own, you will have to take him. Sometimes walking toward the student and standing by him while repeating the command ("Please go to time out") may be enough to convince him you mean business. If this doesn't work, move the student toward the TO area with one hand on the small of his back and the other on the elbow of his nearest arm. Again, if you have any compunctions about moving the student yourself, you will have to get some help. Under no circumstances should you let a student get away with not going to TO after he has been told to do so. Two ways to facilitate compliance are conducting "TO drills" and deducting time spent in TO when students comply immediately. A TO drill is simply having students rehearse going to TO periodically so that they will understand the procedure better.

5. If the student leaves TO for any reason without your permission before her time is up, she should be told to return and her time begun again.

6. If the student should engage in any disruptive behavior while in TO, try to ignore it and reinforce those students who ignore it. If it becomes disruptive to the learning environment, add more time to the timer and let the student know what's happening and why. Don't get into an argument or a dialogue with him; just tell him and go on with whatever you were doing before.

7. Make sure that before you put a student into TO, the environment from which she is being removed is reinforcing. If the student is supposed to be working on her math assignment and she hates it, she may engage in disruptive behavior just to "escape" from it. If you put her in TO every time she engages in disruptive behavior, you will have actually (negatively) reinforced her behavior by providing her with an escape from something she considers more aversive than TO. The obvious problem here is that the student's disruptive behavior will not weaken through the application of TO. Instead, it will actually be strengthened by it! TO means time out from reinforcement. Therefore, in order for it to be effective, you must be removing the student from a reinforcing environment.

Time out should be devoid of all reinforcement.

8. Finally, it should go without saying that when the student returns from TO, he should be reinforced immediately for appropriate behavior.

It is often difficult for the classroom teacher to find a physical setting within her classroom where she can both monitor and exercise some control over a student's behavior and, at the same time, be relatively certain that the student is not receiving any reinforcement. Also, as long as the student remains part of the learning environment, there is a chance that she will learn new behavior. Even when she is punished, as long as an attempt is made to model and subsequently reinforce positive responses, the student has an opportunity to learn from experience. However, when the student is isolated from the learning environment and receives no feedback (negative or positive) regarding her behavior, there is little chance for learning to occur. It is for these reasons that I suggest that TO only be used when (1) the student's behavior is disruptive to the learning environment and (2) all other interventions, including other punishments, have failed.

To help you better understand the differences between each of these strategies for weakening behavior, I have included examples of the application of each of them to the same behavior problems (see Fig. 7.1). Once you know how each strategy works in isolation, you should look at the application of these strategies in the structured plan.

Escalating Consequences

We have already made the point in chapter 4 that students misbehave for different reasons and that they may respond differently to the same management strategies. When I go into classrooms I find teachers using the same strategies over and over again. Most

Note: I'm not suggesting that you use any or all of the following techniques. The purpose of this table is simply to illustrate the differences between them.

Maladaptive Behavior: Student is disruptive (e.g., talks to peers) during math lesson.

Reinforcing Incompatible Behaviors (RIBs): Wait until the student is attending and reinforce that behavior.

Extinction: If peer attention is reinforcing disruptive behavior, reinforce peers for ignoring student when he talks to them or move him far enough away from them so that they can't attend to his talking.

Reprimands: Tell student, "If you don't stop talking and start listening . . ."

Response Cost: Take away points student has earned (or recess or some other entitlement) and tell her how she can earn them back (e.g., by attending to lesson).

Overcorrection: Have student apologize to you and to peers for disrupting lesson; he should then write down everything you said and everything from the blackboard, reproduce these notes, and make them available for any student who wants them.

Negative Practice: Have the student stay after school and talk to you over and over again while you play a tape recording of your math lesson.

Time Out: Have student go to time out (i.e., leave the math lesson and her peer group) for a predetermined time; during this time she is not to receive any reinforcement for any behavior.

Figure 7.1. Examples of techniques to weaken behaviors.

teachers I have observed tend to use some form of punishment to weaken maladaptive behavior. Some use reprimands ("Now I told you to stop doing that and I mean it!"), response cost (removing earned tokens or a valued activity like recess), or abusive-provocative language (sarcasm or yelling or threatening). They also often use negative reinforcement to reinforce an incompatible behavior. For example, they might use the threat of response cost to strengthen on-task behavior in order to weaken off-task behavior. They tend to use these same strategies over and over again whether they work in reducing maladaptive behavior or not. Nag, nag, nag. Threaten, threaten, threaten. Yell, yell, yell. Scold, scold, scold. Not only shouldn't you use the same strategies with all of your students; you shouldn't use the same strategies over and over again with the same student. Students can become desensitized to the same consequences when they are being used over and over. Although you should try to use a variety of strategies,

it would be wise to use them in a structured manner. The format I believe to be most effective is referred to as the *hierarchy of escalating consequences.* In this hierarchy, the first consequence is the least severe (to the student) and the last consequence, the most severe. Here is how it works.

When a student misbehaves, first ask yourself if the behavior passes the "So what?" test. If it doesn't pass, don't bother trying to weaken it. It's not worth the effort. If the behavior is not maladaptive but still bothers you, try using a self-management program to change your thinking, feelings, or behavior in the presence of this student and the student's behavior (see chapter 13).

If you determine that the student's behavior is maladaptive, try to weaken it with RIBs first. Ask yourself if there are any incompatible or competing behaviors you might reinforce in its place. If the student is talking to a peer, wait until she is quiet or on task and reinforce her for it. If there are no incompatible behaviors to reinforce or this strategy doesn't work, ask yourself if there is an obvious reinforcer in the environment that is maintaining the student's maladaptive behavior. Is it possible for you to withhold this reinforcer? If so, do it. If not, or if this strategy doesn't work, move on to the next consequence and punish the maladaptive behavior directly.

If you find that you must punish the maladaptive behavior, try to start with a reprimand unless the behavior is so disruptive or intense that someone is in danger of being physically hurt. Reprimanding two students who are fighting is totally ineffective unless neither of them wants to fight. Unfortunately, there is usually one (or sometimes both) who either loses his head or is having so much fun (he's obviously doing most of the damage) that reprimands are unrealistic. At this point, a physical intervention by you or someone who is physically able (and willing) is called for. When you do reprimand, follow all of the rules for reprimanding outlined in this chapter. Do not repeat the reprimand a second time if the behavior doesn't cease. Tell the student to stop what he's doing and let him know what will happen if he doesn't comply. Repeating yourself only teaches the student that he doesn't have to listen to you the first time.

If the reprimand doesn't weaken the maladaptive behavior, move on to the next more severe consequence. This may be response cost or, if you have the time or the manpower, overcorrection or negative practice. Use whichever you feel is most appropriate and feasible. If you use response cost, be sure to follow the guidelines in this chapter.

If these strategies do not weaken the maladaptive behavior and you consider the student's behavior disruptive to the learning environment, warn him that he will have to go to TO if his behavior doesn't change.

If that doesn't work, send him to TO. Be sure to follow the recommended guidelines for TO in this chapter. If he continues to misbehave in TO, either extend his time or remove him from the classroom. If he continues to be disruptive in the school office or in-school suspension area, he should be sent home. This should require a parent coming to school to pick him up. At this time, the teacher should be prepared to document to the parent what was done to try to bring the student's behavior under control.

When severe disruptive behavior is exhibited, such as actual or potential physical violence, the teacher should begin at whichever consequence he feels necessary. He might even consider immediate removal from the classroom. The teacher should not have to start over from the beginning (e.g., with RIBs and extinction) if the student starts behaving in a disruptive fashion again after a brief respite or if the student engages in a different disruptive behavior. The following example of a hypothetical interaction between a student, his peers, and his teacher illustrates the hierarchy of escalating consequences.

Response (What the Child Does)	Consequence (What the Teacher Does)
1. Johnny talks to Pete during a math lesson and keeps him from doing his work. Pete listens and laughs at Johnny but does not talk to him. In between Johnny's talking, Pete works on his math. Johnny does not work on his assignments at all.	
	2. Having decided that Johnny's behavior is maladaptive, the teacher looks for any incompatible or competing behavior to reinforce. When she can't find any, she focuses on the known reinforcer (Pete's attention) and reinforces him whenever she catches him doing his work ("Pete, give
3. Johnny continues to talk to Pete even though Pete is trying harder to ignore him.	yourself a point for being on task.").
	4. Although the teacher continues to reinforce Pete for being on task (and ignoring Johnny), she sees how difficult it is for him to concentrate and decides to intervene directly with Johnny. She walks to his desk and quietly reprimands him ("Johnny, Pete's trying to work. If you don't stop talking to him and start working, you're going to lose ten points.").
5. Johnny stops talking to Pete and gets his book out but after a few minutes, he starts talking to Pete again.	
	6. The teacher walks to Johnny's desk and quietly tells him that she's taking away 10 of the points he earned this morning. She tells him why and how he can earn them back. She also tells him that he'll have to move his seat if he doesn't stop.
7. Johnny complains loudly about losing his points ("That's not fair!").	
	8. The teacher ignores Johnny's complaining until she sees that it's disrupting the rest of the class. Then she quietly goes about

Response (What the Child Does)	Consequence (What the Teacher Does)	Response (What the Child Does)	Consequence (What the Teacher Does)
	reinforcing Johnny's peers when she catches them on task.		and watches for an opportunity to reinforce him.
9. After a while, Johnny stops complaining and puts his head down on the desk. After about 5 minutes, Johnny resumes talking to Pete.		17. Johnny's mutterings get louder and louder and he calls out to Pete.	
	10. The teacher quietly tells Johnny to move his seat ("Take your work and move to the desk in the back of the room. If you try to talk to anyone again, you'll have to go to time out."). Even though Johnny is being moved to a new desk, he may still earn points for being on task. Once he goes to time out, he earns nothing regardless of his behavior.		18. Johnny's teacher quietly tells him to move to the time out area (a small corner area in the back of the room with a chair and a desk covered by a screen).
		19. Johnny stops muttering but doesn't leave his seat ("I won't talk no more. Let me stay here.").	
11. Johnny changes seats with much complaining.			20. The teacher starts her stopwatch in full view of Johnny ("The longer it takes you to get to time out, the longer you'll have to stay there.").
	12. Again, the teacher ignores Johnny and reinforces his peers when she catches them on task.	21. After a few minutes of protesting, Johnny goes to time out.	
13. Johnny continues to complain loudly.			
	14. When she sees a number of his peers off task, the teacher quietly warns Johnny that he will have to stop his complaining and sit down at his desk or he will have to go to time out.		
15. Johnny sits down but continues to mutter under his breath.			
	16. Johnny's teacher ignores his muttering		

In this illustration, Johnny did stop engaging in disruptive behavior on occasion. However, these periods did not last very long. That is why his teacher did not return to the first or least severe consequence in the hierarchy each time Johnny resumed his disruptive behavior. Instead, she moved to the next (more severe) consequence. If a teacher starts over with the first or least severe consequence in the hierarchy each time the student resumes his disruptive behavior, it is conceivable that a student will engage in disruptive behavior all day long with the teacher using the same (least severe and ineffective) consequences over and over again. This is what typically happens in many classrooms now.

Knowing when to start over again and when to go on to the next more severe consequence is not always obvious. However, the following guidelines will provide you with some basis for making this decision.

1. When a student engages in disruptive behavior where there is the potential for physical harm to a peer or adult, begin your intervention with time out (i.e., isolation and removal from peers).

2. When a student engages in disruptive behavior where there is actual physical harm to a peer or adult, begin your intervention with removal from the classroom to the school office.

3. When a student engages in disruptive behavior that is not potentially or actually physically harmful on an intermittent basis during the same class period, begin your intervention with the least severe consequence (e.g., RIBs and extinction) for the first incident; from then on, progress through the other consequences without starting over at any time.

4. When a student engages in disruptive behavior that is not potentially or actually physically harmful on an intermittent basis during the school day approximately once or twice a class period, begin your intervention with the least severe consequence each time. Students are less likely to remember consequences from hour to hour or from class period to class period than from minute to minute.

Teachers who have used the hierarchy of escalating consequences over the years have told me that it afforded them a number of benefits. First of all, they didn't become as anxious or angry as they used to when they only used one or two strategies over and over again. The reason for this is simple. When you use the same strategies over again and they don't always work, you become frustrated and angry and, when you don't have anything else you can think of to do, you become scared. With the hierarchy you are bound to find something that works; even if it takes a while, you are less likely to panic knowing that if plan A won't work, there is always plan B, and so on. Another benefit that teachers derive from the hierarchy is the effect it has on their students and their students' behavior. Students are less likely to become desensitized to the same old strategies used again and again. They have to stop and decide if they really want to lose points, go to time out, or be removed from the classroom. They tend to show more respect for their teachers, especially when the teachers consequate their misbehavior in a calm, matter-of-fact manner rather than by showing fear or anger. If nothing else, the hierarchy will free you from the rut of using the same old strategies over and over again.

Chapter Seven Self-Assessment

See Appendix A for acceptable responses.

1. Describe how you would use reinforcing incompatible behaviors (RIBs) and extinction to weaken a disruptive behavior such as calling out without raising hand.

2. Write an incompatible or competing behavior for each of the following:

   a. Is out of seat:

   b. Bites self when frustrated:

   c. Hits peers when angry:

   d. Calls out without raising hand:

   e. Takes things from others without asking:

   f. Is off task (i.e., looks around room):

   g. Leaves room without permission:

   h. Swears for attention:

   i. Refuses to comply with request:

   j. Comes to class late:

3. State four disadvantages of punishment:

   a.

   b.

   c.

   d.

continued next page

4. Describe two situations when it would be permissible (even appropriate) to use punishment:

   a.

   b.

5. State 10 rules of thumb to follow in order to punish effectively:

   a.

   b.

   c.

   d.

   e.

   f.

   g.

   h.

   i.

   j.

6. Explain how you would use response cost to weaken out-of-seat behavior.

7. Explain how you would use time out to weaken tantrum behavior.

8. Explain how you would use negative practice to weaken self-stimulating behavior (e.g., hand waving, rocking, or chin touching).

continued next page

9.   State eight rules of thumb to follow in order to use reprimands effectively:

   a.

   b.

   c.

   d.

   e.

   f.

   g.

   h.

10.   Explain how you would use overcorrection to weaken the behavior of a student who insults his or her peers.

11.   Write an example of how you would use a hierarchy of escalating consequences to weaken disruptive behavior such as yelling abusive and provocative language at peers. Include time out, response cost, reprimands, extinction, removal from classroom, and RIBs.

chapter 8

Self-Management Skills for Students

Upon successful completion of this chapter, the learner should be able to:

1. State a rationale for teaching self-management skills to children and youth
2. Name and describe the components of self-management
3. Describe how to keep students from cheating in a self-management program

Rationale

There are several reasons for teaching students how to manage their own behavior. First of all, it has been empirically demonstrated that teaching self-management skills to students can result in improved generalization and maintenance of behaviors (Bornstein & Quevillon, 1976; Wood & Flynn, 1978). From a behavioral standpoint, anything that will improve the maintenance and generalization of behavior is worth trying.

There is also some empirical evidence that teaching students self-management skills can change their locus of control (Bradley & Gaa, 1977; Pawlicki, 1976). Since so many students with behavior problems have been conditioned to rely on external controls such as medication or token economies for much of their school life, it is not surprising that as a group, they tend toward externality. Both John Dewey (1938) and Robert Gagne (1965) have touted self-reliance as the ultimate goal of education. What better way to teach self-reliance than to train students to manage their own behavior? With self-reliance comes responsibility for one's actions and, consequently, a more internal locus of control.

Another reason for teaching self-management skills is cost effectiveness. It is virtually impossible for teachers to run several different behavioral interventions on several different students at the same time. As student behavior changes, students may no longer need the teacher to provide the necessary antecedents or consequences, and students themselves can begin to assume responsibility for running the interventions. Walker (1979) has suggested that generalization and maintenance of behavioral interventions might be improved by requiring students to take over the responsibility for monitoring and reinforcing their own behavior. Figure 8.1 illustrates the sequence of Walker's approach.

During the baseline phase, the student's behavior is maladaptive and the management strategy used is either ineffective or nonexistent. During the first intervention phase, the teacher operates the management strategy; as you can see, it has a positive effect on the student's behavior. In the second intervention phase, the teacher gives the responsibility of operating the program to the student and it continues to be effective. Finally, in phase 3, the student internalizes the behavior to the point of being able to function in the school setting with naturally occurring consequences (e.g., social praise, grades, the work itself) to maintain the behavior. Notice how Walker's three-phase approach differs from the traditional two-phase sequence illustrated in Figure 8.2. In the latter, the teacher intervenes and may change the student's behavior to the extent that it will become internalized and maintained by the naturally occurring consequences in the student's school environment. Given what we know about maintenance of newly learned behavior, this is probably the exception rather than the rule. In Walker's sequence, there is a transition (or bridge) between the first phase, in which the teacher manages a change in the student's behavior, and the last phase, where it miraculously becomes internalized and maintained over time. Training in self-management skills can help students (and their teachers) to implement this transition phase.

Finally, it can be argued that training in self-management skills is actually more relevant than many of the other skills we teach our students. When was the last time you had an occasion to use the Pythagorean theorem or any of those dates you learned in history class? On the other hand, self-management skills can be used in countless situations during a student's life, both in and out of school.

Components

There are three basic self-management skills to learn: self-assessment (SA), self-monitoring (SM), and self-

PHASE	BASELINE Ø	1	2	3
Student Behavior	Maladaptive 😈	Target 😊	Target 😊	Target 😊
Management (structured program)	None (or ineffective)	Teacher Operated (e.g., behavior modification program)	Student (i.e., self) Operated (e.g., behavior modification program)	None Naturally occurring consequences (e.g., praise, grades, enjoyment of task)

Figure 8.1. Walker's three-phase approach to behavior management.

PHASE	BASELINE Ø	1	2
Student Behavior	Maladaptive 😈	Target 😇	Target 😇
Management (structured program)	None (or ineffective)	Teacher Operated (e.g., behavior modification program)	None Naturally occurring consequences (e.g., praise, grades, enjoyment of task)

Figure 8.2. Traditional two-phase approach to behavior management.

reinforcement (SR). These skills are not very different from those used in traditional (teacher-operated) behavior modification programs. In SA, instead of the teacher assessing the student's behavior to determine whether or not it should be reinforced, the student assesses his or her own behavior and makes that decision. In SM, progress is monitored by the student, not the teacher. And in SR, instead of the teacher reinforcing the student as a consequence of the behavior, the student does it.

For example, suppose that a student we'll call George was off task 90% of the times observed and was put on a token economy which, initially, was run by his teacher. Since George's teacher was the primary change agent responsible for assessing, rewarding, and monitoring George's on-task behavior, this was a teacher-operated intervention, or *TOI*. George was given work he could successfully complete and was told

that the teacher would look at him at different times during the day to see if he was on task. If he was on task, the teacher would record a plus in a box on a card in her pocket. *On task* was defined as any one or a combination of the following: (1) looking at the task, (2) being actively involved in the task (e.g., writing), and (3) engaging in task-related talk with peers or the teacher. If George was not engaged in any of these behaviors, he was considered to be off task and his teacher would record a zero in a box on the card. At the end of a designated period of time (e.g., class period or school day), the teacher computed George's percentage of on-task behavior; if he had reached the designated goal for the day, he would receive a predetermined amount of time to engage in a favored activity. George's on-task behavior improved quickly and a new goal was set for each day until he reached the overall IEP (individualized education program) goal of 80%. Eventually, George's teacher found that she no longer had time to run the program. There were too many other students in George's class who were more in need of her attention. At this point, many teachers would simply stop the TOI and hope that George's behavior would maintain over time and even transfer across settings. However, George's teacher decided not to risk a relapse and kept the token economy in place, but she gave the responsibility of running the program to George. This freed her to work with other students in the class and also ensured that George's newly acquired behavior would maintain.

In a student-operated intervention, or *SOI*, the student may start out being responsible for all three components (SA, SM, and SR) or may take on the responsibility for the components one at a time. For example, George's teacher might continue to assess and monitor his on-task behavior and only give George the responsibility for dispensing reinforcement. If this situation worked out satisfactorily, George might then be given the responsibility of assessing as well as reinforcing his own behavior while the teacher continued to monitor it. Finally, he would take over all three components. Let's assume that George's teacher gave him the responsibility for all three components at the outset. The first thing she did was make sure George understood exactly what constituted on- and off-task behavior so that he would be able to accurately assess whether or not he was engaging in one or the other. Again, *on task* was defined as any one or a combination of (1) looking at the task; (2) being actively involved in the task (e.g., writing); (3) engaging in task-related talk with peers or the teacher; and, since George would be able to assess his thoughts as well as his behavior, (4) thinking task-related thoughts. To help George remember the difference between being on and off task, his teacher provided him with a form (see Figure 8.3) to keep on his desk that graphically depicted examples of each.

George used the same signal system as his teacher had when she was assessing his behavior. A tape recorder on the teacher's desk played a tape of music. When the music stopped, that was the signal for George to assess his current behavior as on or off task. Let's say that George was signaled approximately 2 minutes after starting work on his math. At that time, George looked at the pictures of on- and off-task behaviors and asked himself if he was on or off task. He decided that he was engaging in at least one of the behaviors and marked a plus on his rating sheet (see Figure 8.4). George continued to assess his behavior each time he was signaled by the tape recorder to do so. At the end of the period (or day), he counted the total number of boxes marked and the total number of pluses and then computed his percentage of on-task behavior for that period of time (see Figure 8.5). He then compared his attained percentage of on-task behavior with his desig-

NAME _____ DATE _____

ON TASK = +   OFF TASK = O

TOTAL INTERVALS = ___

TOTAL ON TASK (+) = ___

PERCENTAGE ON TASK = ___ %

Figure 8.4. Rating sheet for use in self-assessment (blank).

nated goal. Being at or over this goal would earn George minutes of free time with a favored activity at the end of the school day. If necessary, a self-punishment component could be added in the form of response cost where George would lose minutes earned earlier in the day if he began to slack off during the afternoon. Again, he would be responsible for computing the deductions.

George then used the data from his self-rating form to monitor his progress. He marked the percentage from the form on a chart (see Figure 8.6). This not only helped him and his teacher see how he was progressing; it also helped to keep him motivated to stay on task.

At this point you are probably wondering what would keep students you wouldn't normally turn your back on from cheating. There is some empirical evi-

Figure 8.3. "Cheat" sheet for on- and off-task behavior (to aid in self-assessment of behavior).

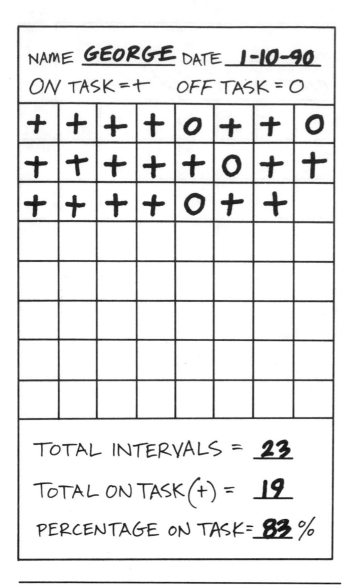

NAME **GEORGE** DATE **1-10-90**

ON TASK = + OFF TASK = 0

+	+	+	+	0	+	+	0
+	+	+	+	+	0	+	+
+	+	+	+	0	+	+	

TOTAL INTERVALS = **23**

TOTAL ON TASK (+) = **19**

PERCENTAGE ON TASK = **83**%

Figure 8.5. Rating sheet for use in self-assessment (completed).

dence that contradicts the assumption that students can't be trusted to reinforce themselves without cheating (Workman & Hector, 1978). In fact, in some instances, students responsible for their own behavior management programs either were not giving themselves enough reinforcement or were being too rigorous in their self-assessment (Workman & Hector, 1978). There are ways to keep students honest. You can practice random surveillance and periodically assess student behavior or check the student's records against the amount of reinforcement given. In other words, do an audit—check the books from time to time. If you find discrepancies in the student's favor, fine her. On the other hand, if you find that the student has been run-

ning an honest program, give her a bonus. Show her that honesty pays. If you don't have the time to practice this surveillance you might merely suggest that you are going to do it. Planting the idea that Big Brother (or Sister) is watching can be just as effective as actually watching (Hundert & Bastone, 1978).

Perhaps some of you are still not convinced that children can learn self-management skills or that they can benefit from learning them. Let's take a quick look at some of the research findings. Glynn et al. (1973) examined the effects of SR on on-task behavior in an entire classroom of second-grade students. Subjects were taught to notice if they were on task when a signal was emitted by a tape recorder. Those students who were on task rewarded themselves with points that were later turned in for extra recess. During baseline (no SR), the on-task behavior of the average student was 58%. By the end of the intervention (SR), the on-task behavior of the average student was 93%. It should be noted that a teacher-operated token system was used prior to the SR program; it resulted in an on-task rate of 81%. When the tokens were removed, the students' on-task behavior decreased to an average of 55%. When the SR program was removed, the students' on-task behavior dropped to an average of 75%.

Glynn (1970) examined the effect of SR on the accuracy of responses to daily quizzes in history and geography classes by 128 ninth-grade students. The students rewarded themselves with one token for each set of four correct answers on each quiz. The results indicated a significant increase in the number of items each student answered correctly.

Humphrey & Karoly (1978) studied the effects of SR on reading performance (task completion) in second graders who were taught to reward themselves with colored plastic chips when they appropriately completed daily reading assignments (e.g., reading passages and answering questions). Results showed an increase in the number of daily assignments completed by each student from an average of fewer than two assignments completed during baseline to four assignments after baseline with no difference in accuracy of response. The same study also examined the effect of self-punishment (SP) (i.e., response cost for incorrect answers). Increased rates of assignments completed with SP were not as high as those completed with SR.

In 1972, Bolstad and Johnson compared the effects of SR and a traditional teacher-operated token system on the disruptive behavior of first- and second-grade students. Both groups had been exposed first to the traditional program of reinforcement. The experimental group was taught how to use SR with tokens for not exceeding a prespecified number of disruptive behaviors per day, while the control group continued to

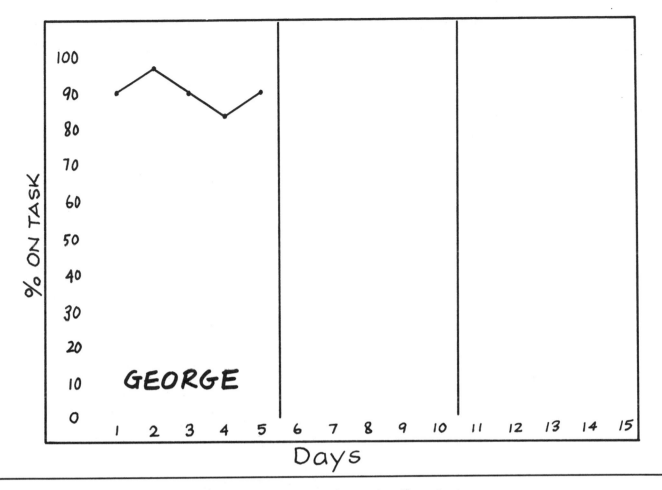

Figure 8.6. Data display for use in self-monitoring.

operate under the traditional system of reinforcement. Results indicated that both programs were effective in decreasing disruptive behaviors, with the SR program slightly more effective than the control program.

Moletzky (1974) studied the effects of SM on a 9-year-old who raised his hand energetically even when he couldn't respond to the teacher's questions. The child was taught how to use SM on his disruptive behavior with a wrist counter. The result was that hand-raising behavior dropped to zero times per day and stayed at zero throughout a 6-month followup. A second case focused on an 11-year-old's out-of-seat behavior. Also using a wrist counter, this child was able to decrease disruptive out-of-seat behaviors from 23 per day during baseline to 2 per day. Behavior maintained over a 6-month period.

Workman et al. (1982) taught a preschooler to assess on-task behavior (during assignments) on an interval basis. The subject placed a mark on a sheet of paper if on task when a kitchen timer buzzed every 5 minutes. SA raised the subject's average rate of on-task behavior from an 8-day baseline of 37% to an intervention aver-age of 64%. This improvement in on-task behavior also generalized to the subject's compliance behavior, with a 30% increase in compliance with teacher directives.

Can students with limited cognitive ability learn to use self-management skills? Yes. Both educable mentally retarded (IQs from 50 to 70) and trainable mentally retarded (IQs from 30 to 50) were successfully taught to use SM on their behavior (Litrownik et al., 1978; Mahoney & Mahoney, 1976).

Certain conclusions can be drawn from these studies as well as from extensive reviews of the self-management literature (Rueda et al., 1980; Workman & Hector, 1978).

1. Self-management skills can be successfully taught to a wide range of students as young as preschoolers and as cognitively limited as the trainable mentally retarded.

2. Self-management skills can be successfully used by these students to significantly improve a wide variety of behaviors.

3. SR appears to be more effective than SP.

4. Students are not apt to cheat, especially if they believe they are under surveillance.

5. Teaching self-management skills to students appears to be most effective if they have first been exposed to a traditional teacher-operated management program.

6. Self-management programs appear to work best when the teacher: (a) lists the steps the student will follow, (b) explains and models these steps for the student, and (c) provides the student with an opportunity to demonstrate that he or she knows what to do and how to do it.

Method

If you're now convinced that students should and could learn self-management skills, how can you help your students to learn them? What follows is a detailed look at each skill. Although they are not listed in any special order, I recommend that you introduce them (i.e., teach and let the student use them) one at a time; introduce first the skill you believe the student will have the least difficulty learning and using, and introduce last the skill with which the student might have the most difficulty.

Self-Assessment (SA)

In SA, the first step is to select a target behavior. Sit down with the student and identify and specify the maladaptive and fair-pair target behavior. If the SOI program is following a TOI, this will already have been done. It's important that the student be involved in the process, especially when the "So what?" test is applied. The student should understand why her behavior is maladaptive and why it is in her best interests to engage in the target behavior. The behavior should also be pinpointed so that it passes the stranger test and so that the student has no problem recognizing the behavior when she engages in it. If necessary, use pictures as examples of appropriate and inappropriate behaviors. These may be drawn by the student or you can use Polaroid snapshots.

The second step in teaching the student how to use SA on his behavior is to devise a rating system. This refers to the process by which the student will assess, evaluate, or rate his behavior. It must include a description of what he does and how and when he does it. Be sure you involve the student in the process. He is the one who is going to have to use the system. Getting the student's input in devising the system, or any other component in the program, will improve the chances of his understanding how it works as well as his willingness to cooperate and use it. Again, if you are following a TOI, you may not want to reinvent the wheel; simply use the rating system already in place. If it is

too complex for the student to use, don't dump it—simply modify it until the student can use it and you can still have confidence in its reliability.

The third step in the process of SA is to design and produce any of the rating forms (or other materials) the student may be required to use. An excellent source for rating forms is Workman (1982). In addition to pencil-and-paper forms you may need to produce a signal that will cue the student to assess her behavior. One idea is to make a tape recording of a sound, such as a beep emitted at varying intervals. I have had good success using the timer signal on a microwave oven. The obvious advantage of using a prerecorded signal is that the student can't predict when it will be emitted.

Next, list all of the steps the student will follow in assessing his own behavior. This is essentially an operationally defined task analysis, showing what he does first, second, third, and so on. Finally, these steps must be explained to and modeled for the student. This is probably the most critical part of the process. If the student does not understand when and how he is to assess his own behavior, he will do it either incorrectly or not at all. Make sure you use vocabulary that the student can understand. Use a direct teaching approach. Get feedback from the student to make sure that he heard you, understood what you said, and can do what you want him to.

Self-Monitoring (SM)

The first step in SM is pinpointing the target behavior. Use the same procedure here as you would in a TOI program. Describe the behavior you want the student to monitor so that it passes the stranger test. Make sure the student understands what aspect of her behavior she is recording. In most instances, it will be less complicated if the student simply records frequency of response. Even if you want her to spend more time engaged in a target behavior such as being in seat or on task, you can have her record the number of times (i.e., intervals) she rated her behavior as in seat or on task when cued to do so. If the number of intervals changes daily, make sure the student understands that she will need to summarize her data as a percentage. The student also must know how to compute percentage. Don't take anything for granted. The student won't cooperate if she doesn't understand what to do or how to do it.

Next, set the intervention goals. What percentage of the time should the student be in seat or on task? What percentage of assignments should he complete? What percentage of accuracy should he strive for? How many times should he use "socially appropriate" language (i.e., without using threats or swear words) in communicating with the teacher or a peer? These may be the same goals you used in your TOI or they may be renegotiated with the student. It is important that the student know what he is aiming for so that he can monitor his progress daily.

Next, design and produce the necessary forms such as the observation and recording (O & R) form and the data display or chart. In many instances, the O & R form can be the same as the rating form on which the student assesses her behavior. Check Workman (1982) for examples of O & R forms and data displays. Finally, list the steps the student will follow in monitoring her own behavior and explain and model them for her.

Self-Reinforcement (SR)

The first step in SR is to determine the reinforcer. Again, if your SOI program is following a TOI, you might simply continue using the same reinforcer. The process for determining a reinforcer is no different from that used in the TOI program (interview, observation, interest inventory). Next, determine the contingencies. In other words, how much of the target behavior must the student engage in to earn X amount of reinforcement? Again, this can be negotiated with the student. Finally, list the steps in the process and explain and model them for the student.

Grandma's Rule

So far we have been talking about self-management in the context of a transitional phase between TOI and the internalization (and maintenance) of behavior. This is not the only way to use self-management. For years, parents and teachers have been telling children that they could change their behavior if they just had more willpower. No wonder they've given up. We've made it sound as if the only way one can change is to have been born with some magical trait, a blessing obviously not bestowed on these particular children. These students don't need willpower. What they need is "skillpower." They need to know *how* to change. One simple self-management skill you can teach them is how to apply Grandma's Rule. Grandma's Rule says, "Children who don't eat their vegetables don't get any dessert." Grandmas understand that for most children, eating vegetables is a low-frequency activity, while eating dessert is a high-frequency activity. In other words, left on their own, children will spend more time eating desserts than they will eating vegetables. However, when children are required to eat their vegetables in order to get their dessert, vegetable-eating behavior increases in frequency. If Grandma's Rule sounds familiar, it should. It's based on the Premack Principle discussed in chapter 6: When a high-frequency behavior is made contingent upon the emission of a low-frequency behavior, the low-frequency behavior

increases in frequency (Premack, 1959). Your goal is to get your students to use Grandma's Rule by themselves to modify their own behavior (i.e., to increase low-frequency responses). You want them to start making high-frequency behaviors such as television watching contingent upon low-frequency behaviors such as doing homework, so that the low-frequency behaviors will increase in frequency.

Grandma's Rule.

How can you get students to use Grandma's Rule voluntarily? First, explain what Grandma's Rule is. The rule may be stated any number of ways depending on the age and cognitive ability of your students. For example, it might be expressed as "When I do something I *don't* like doing, then I may do something I *do* like doing" or it could be as simple as "business before pleasure" or "work before play." Relate specific examples of how people used Grandma's Rule to change their behavior. Use yourself as an example. You've probably used Grandma's Rule at least once in your life to change a behavior. Perhaps some of your students have, too. Even if neither you nor your students have ever heard of the rule or David Premack before, that shouldn't keep either you or them from using it. What you want to do in this first stage is to get your students to know the rule and understand how it works.

Next, have your students brainstorm high- and low-frequency activities. Try to limit them to school-related activities. For example, a student-generated list of *low-*

frequency school-related activities might include reading, doing classwork, sitting at desk, answering questions, having to share, doing math, preparing homework, typing, practicing music, having to read aloud, taking group showers, going to science class, and doing what the teacher says. Examples of *high-frequency* school-related activities might include going to recess, eating lunch, doing silent reading, talking with friends, playing video games, shooting baskets in physical education, listening to music, being a messenger, and running errands.

When your students have generated a list of high- and low-frequency behaviors, have them choose one behavior from the low-frequency list that they would like to change into a high-frequency behavior. Some of your students might want to increase the frequency of completing assignments or answering questions or spending time studying for tests. Next, have them pick a behavior from the high-frequency list that they are willing to use as a payoff for engaging in the low-frequency behavior. For example, students might use an easy task (e.g., reading) as a reward for doing a difficult task (e.g., math). You can take it one step further and have them contract with themselves (see Figure 8.7).

The final stage, of course, is to get your students to actually implement Grandma's Rule. You can keep them accountable by having them relate to you and their peers on a daily basis how they used Grandma's Rule in your class, in school, or outside of school. In the beginning, you might want to use some extrinsic reinforcement to strengthen their use of Grandma's Rule; but soon they will realize how effective it is in changing their own behavior and will enjoy the intrinsic thrill of being able to change themselves.

I, _Jerry Jones_ promise that before I _go outside to recess today_ (at 11 AM),
Student   (Hi-F behavior)

I will _finish my assignments in math and reading_.
(Lo-F behavior)

Signed _Jerry Jones_   Date _5/1/89_
Witnessed by _Mr. Augustine_   Date _5/1/89_

Figure 8.7. Student contract for use in self-management program.

Chapter Eight Self-Assessment

See Appendix A for acceptable responses.

1. State three reasons for teaching students self-management skills:

   a.

   b.

   c.

2. List and describe each of the three components of self-management:

   a.

   b.

   c.

3. Describe how you would keep students from cheating in a self-management program.

chapter 9

Cognitive Behavior Management Skills for Students

Upon successful completion of this chapter, the learner should be able to:

1. Describe the characteristics that distinguish CBM from traditional behavior modification
2. Describe the types of cognitions CBM strategies focus on
3. State reasons for teaching problem-solving skills to children and youth
4. Describe the competencies required in problem solving
5. Write an example of how beliefs are learned
6. Describe how beliefs affect our behavior
7. Describe how to assess beliefs
8. Describe how to modify beliefs using DIBs for KIDs
9. List and describe the steps in the self-instruction training process
10. List and describe the steps in the verbal mediation process
11. Describe how to facilitate generalization of CBM skills in students

Cognitive Behavior Modification

Behaviorists are beginning to realize the importance of focusing their interventions on covert behaviors such as thoughts and feelings. This change in philosophy has come about primarily because of (1) the need for behavior management strategies other than (or in addition to) conventional behavior modification for use with older and more developmentally able students, and (2) the emergence of effective intervention strategies reported in the cognitive behavior modification (CBM) literature (Bem, 1967; Bornstein & Quevillon, 1976; Camp et al., 1976; De Voge, 1977; Di Giuseppe, 1977; Finch et al., 1975; Gottman et al., 1974; Karnes et al., 1970; Knaus & Block, 1976; Knaus & McKeever, 1977; Meichenbaum & Goodman, 1971; Novaco, 1975;

O'Leary, 1968; Palkes et al., 1972; Schneider, 1974; and Spivack & Shure, 1974). As you can see, CBM has been around for a number of years, but only recently, with the popularity of social skills training, has it become more widely used by teachers. In 1985, an entire issue of the *Journal of Abnormal Child Psychology* was devoted to CBM. To quote from the foreword of that issue, "CBM is not just another fad. . . . In its brief history to date it has evidenced strong links to data and empirical verification" (Harris et al., 1985, p. 329).

What is CBM?

CBM has five characteristics that distinguish it from other forms of behavior management. First, in CBM programs, the subjects themselves rather than external agents such as the classroom teacher are the primary change agents, if not at the beginning of the program, certainly by the end. Second, verbalization—on an overt level, then on a covert level—is the primary component. CBM requires that the subject talk to himself or herself, first out loud, then using silent speech. Third, subjects are taught to identify and use a series of steps to solve their problems. Fourth, modeling is used as an instructional procedure. And fifth, most of the CBM literature focuses on helping the individual to gain self-control. These characteristics will be described more fully when we discuss different CBM strategies.

Cognitions

Before we look at these strategies I will define exactly what "cognition" means in CBM. Behavior doesn't lend itself to much interpretation, but there is more than one type of cognition and they relate differently to CBM. Simply, cognitions may be divided into four categories: cognitive events, cognitive processes, cognitive structures, and inner speech.

1. *Cognitive events* are those thoughts or images occurring in an individual's stream of consciousness. Those of you who have tried to meditate know how difficult it is to modify cognitive events. Even experienced meditators admit that it is virtually impossible to completely shut down this stream of consciousness for any

appreciable amount of time. None of the CBM strategies are effective in modifying cognitive events.

2. *Cognitive processes* are ways in which external stimuli are appraised and transformed. A cognitive process has to do with the way in which we think about something rather than what it is we think about it (e.g., the "how," not the "what" of thinking). Problem solving is an example of a CBM strategy used to modify cognitive processes.

3. *Cognitive structures* are beliefs or attitudes. They can have a profound influence over our behavior. They are not thoughts per se, but foundations that influence cognitive processes and inner speech. Fortunately, since they are learned, cognitive structures can be unlearned through a CBM strategy called *cognitive restructuring*, which will be described later in this chapter.

4. *Inner speech* is the fourth type of cognition. It is sometimes referred to as *self-talk, automatic thoughts,* or *covert self-instruction.* Inner speech may vary in the degree to which the individual is aware of what it is she is saying to herself. The CBM strategies that have been effective in modifying inner speech are self-instructional training (Meichenbaum & Goodman, 1971) and verbal mediation (Blackwood, 1970).

Problem Solving

Students with behavior problems tend not to perceive the same numbers or types of behavioral options that others do and are more likely to engage in rigid thinking (Spivack & Shure, 1974). One reason for this may be the *availability heuristic,* the theory that people are apt to select those behavioral options which are easiest for them to remember (Tuersky & Kahneman, 1973). Obviously, the easiest events for them to remember are those that most dramatically aroused emotions or occurred most frequently. For example, if a student has seen force applied frequently or dramatically to solve problems, he is most likely to recall this "solution" when he is faced with a problem to solve. When he experiences a new situation, he may search for options, but because of his specially trained perception, he may only recognize the ones involving force. Because he fails to perceive nonforceful options, he has fewer choices to make and therefore has less freedom to act (Howell & Kaplan, 1980). A student who comes from a home where disagreements are settled by fighting is most likely to perceive fighting as the only viable option available to her when she finds herself in a dispute at school. This may explain why many students persist in engaging in maladaptive behavior such as fighting even though they are repeatedly punished for their actions. They simply can't perceive any other behavioral alter-

natives. These students need to be taught how to problem solve.

Why? First of all, problem-solving skills are valuable to adjustment. It has been said that "psychological health is related to a problem-solving sequence consisting of the ability to recognize and admit a problem, to reflect on problem solutions, to make a decision, and to take action" (Kendall & Braswell, 1982, p. 116). There is also some research which suggests that improvement in problem solving can lead to improved classroom behavior (Spivack & Shure, 1974).

Second, we need to encourage children and youth to think of their own solutions to their own problems rather than always telling them what we think they should do. Students are more likely to use an idea if it is their own. Researchers found that when children were allowed to think of their own solutions, they were less likely to resist than when suggestions were offered or demanded by an adult (Spivack & Shure, 1974). We must stop thinking for children if we want them to think for themselves.

Third, problem solving is a lifetime skill, something the student can use in or out of school, today or five years from today. Problem solving, truly, is probably more important than a lot of the curriculum we currently teach.

What Is Problem Solving?

Problem solving has been defined as "a behavioral process . . . which a) makes available a variety of potentially effective response alternatives for dealing with the problematic situation and b) increases the probability of selecting the most effective response from among these various alternatives" (D'Zurrilla & Goldfried, 1971, p. 108). In terms that children might understand, problem solving is what you do to find the solution to a problem that is most likely to work.

Most of the research in the area of problem solving has been done by George Spivack and his associates. They have divided problem solving into five separate competencies: (1) recognizing a problem, (2) defining the problem and the goal, (3) generating alternative solutions, (4) evaluating the solutions, and (5) designing a plan. Let's take a look at each.

Recognizing a Problem. Not everyone recognizes a problem when it exists. In order to have this competency, a student must be able to differentiate between instances and not-instances of problems. It would help a great deal if your students knew the characteristics of a problem. Kendall and Braswell define a problem as "a situation to which a person must respond in order to function effectively but for which no effective response alternative is readily available" (1982). In simpler terms, you have a problem when you need to do something to get what you want but you don't know what to do or how to do it. Problems can be interpersonal or intrapersonal. The former always involve another person. For a student, having a bigger student extort lunch money is an example of an interpersonal problem. On the other hand, an intrapersonal problem does not involve anyone but the student. An example of this is when a student loses his or her lunch money.

If you want to assess whether or not your students are able to recognize a problem when they see one, give them instances and not-instances of problems and see if they can differentiate between them. Consider the following example:

Teacher (T.): "You get home from school on Monday and find that you left your math book in your desk at school and you have an assignment due on Wednesday. Is that a problem?"

Student (S.): "No."

T.: "Why not?"

S.: "Because there is something you can do to get what you want and you know what it is." (in other words, there is an effective response alternative readily available)

T.: "What is that?"

S.: "You can get the book on Tuesday and still have time to finish the assignment."

T.: "Here's another. You get home from school on Monday and find that you left your math book at school, which is locked up for the evening, and you have an assignment due on Tuesday. Your math class meets first period. Is that a problem?"

S.: "Yes, because if you wait until Tuesday to get the book, you won't have time to finish the assignment."

T.: "You get home from school on Monday and find that you left your math book at school, which is locked up for the night, and you have an assignment due on Tuesday. Your math class meets third period after a study hall. Is that a problem?"

S.: "No, because you can get your book on Tuesday and finish the assignment during study hall."

An alternative for younger students might be to use pictures of instances and not-instances of problems.

Students can be taught to recognize instances of problems by following the same procedure used to assess them. I recommend using a direct instruction approach similar to the following one.

T.: "We have a problem when we need to do something to get what we want, but at the time we need to do something, we don't know what to do. What's a problem?"

Students (Ss.): (state definition of a problem)

T.: "Good! Now here's an example of a problem. Some bigger kids are picking on you on the playground. You want them to stop but you don't know how to do this. You have a problem because you need to do something to get the kids to stop picking on you but you don't know what to do. Why is this a problem?"

Ss.: "Because you want them to stop picking on you but you don't know what to do."

T.: "Good. Here's another example of a problem." (gives several more instances of problems and, in each case, asks the students why each one is a problem)

T.: "Here are some examples of situations that are not problems. See if you can tell me why each is not a problem. Your best friend at school stops talking to you. You want to know why so you decide to ask her why. Why isn't this a problem?"

Ss.: "Because you want to know why she won't talk to you and you ask her."

T.: "Right. You need to do something to get what you want and you knew right away what to do. What did you want?"

Ss.: "To find out why she stopped talking to you."

T.: "Good. And did you know right away how to get what you wanted?"

Ss.: "Yes."

T.: (continues giving other not-instances of problems and, again, in each case, asks the students why each is not a problem)

Before moving on to the second competency, be sure your students pass an assessment on identifying (i.e., labeling) instances and not-instances of problems.

Defining the Problem and Stating the Goals. This competency is especially important since many students who have difficulty with problem solving know that a problem exists but misdefine it. The most common error seems to be leaving themselves out of the problem. Consider the following:

T.: "It's lunchtime; you're hungry and are on the way to the cafeteria with two of your classmates. The school bully stops you all and asks each of you in turn to give him money. The first classmate is not afraid, refuses the bully, and walks away. The second classmate pulls his pockets inside out, holds up his lunch bag, and tells the bully he's brought his lunch and has no money. The bully looks at you. By this time, he's good and angry. You are afraid of him and you did bring money for lunch. What's the problem?"

S.: "The problem is the bully."

T.: "And what is your goal?" (or "What would you like to have happen?")

S.: "That he would leave me alone."

What's wrong with this? The student has misdefined the problem. The problem is not simply the bully. He's only part of the problem. The bully tried to extort money from three students. The first one wasn't afraid of him and refused. Did this student have a problem? No. The second student didn't have any money to give to the bully. Did he have a problem? No. The third student had money that he could lose and was afraid of the bully. Did this student have a problem? Yes. What is the problem? Well, it isn't simply the bully, or the bully extorting money, because the bully wasn't a problem for two other students. Only the third student had a problem: The bully was extorting money from him, he didn't want to give the bully his money, and he didn't know what to do about it. This definition of the problem is different from the original definition, which only included the bully and the bully's behavior. By defining the problem only as the bully, the goal becomes one of simply getting rid of him. This goal won't solve the student's problem because it doesn't give him enough information with which to generate a viable alternative solution. It is also very external. It puts the responsibility for what happens to the student on parties or forces outside of him, over which he has no control. Maybe my luck will change one day and the bully will die, move to a new neighborhood, or take pity on me and decide to leave me alone. Learning how to deal effectively with extortion is a more viable solution to this student's problem than wishing the bully would disappear or spontaneously change his behavior.

In teaching the skill of defining problems and goals, first generate a list of student problems to draw from. This may be done simply by asking your students to brainstorm problems they encounter in or out of school. Remember, brainstorming requires no censorship on your part. Once you have this list, take each problem from the list and give it to your students to define; then give them each a defined problem and have them write a goal for it. Examples of defined problems and their corresponding goals are shown in Figure 9.1.

Generating Alternative Solutions. Spivack and his associates consider this the most critical or essential problem-solving skill because knowing what to do in case of failure is the cognitive skill that best prevents, or at least diminishes, the student's continued frustration and subsequent need for impulsive behaviors or withdrawal. They consider it (1) the single most powerful predictor of maladaptive behavior; (2) the one that is most enhanced by training; and (3) the one which, when enhanced, seems to result in the greatest concomitant improvement in student behavior (Spivack & Shure, 1974). Knowing how to turn to another solution may

---

1. The problem is that you lose your homework assignment by the time you get home from school and you need to turn it in first thing next day. Your goal is to turn in your homework on time.

2. Some bigger kids start picking on you at school; you want them to stop but you don't know what to do to make them stop. Your goal is to get the bigger kids to stop picking on you.

3. You like some girl (boy) at school but she (he) doesn't pay any attention to you. Your goal is to get her (him) to pay attention to you.

4. You are having trouble with an assignment in class and you need (want) to get a good grade on it but you don't know how. Your goal is to successfully complete the assignment.

5. You forget where your next class meets and your name will be sent to the office for cutting class if you don't get there on time. Your goal is to get to class as quickly as possible.

6. Some kids offer you a cigarette (dope, alcohol). You don't want to take it but you're afraid of what they'll think of you if you don't. Your goal is to refuse the offer without losing face.

Figure 9.1. Examples of defined problems and goals.

be all the encouragement a student needs not to give up. This results in resiliency instead of frustration.

The ability to generate alternative solutions is assessed in much the same way as it is taught, through brainstorming. Simply take a list of defined problems with corresponding goals, present each to a student or group of students, and have them brainstorm possible solutions. Consider the following:

T.: "I am going to give you a defined problem with a goal and I want you to tell me as many possible solutions as you can. Remember, a solution is anything you do that will get you what you want without causing any new problems for you. Don't bother to think about each solution before you give it to me. It can be anything you want. It might turn out to be silly or wrong or something you wouldn't even try. I still want you to tell me what it is. Any questions? (pause) OK. The problem as defined is: When you come back to your seat after sharpening your pencil, you find another student sitting in it and you know you'll get into trouble if you're not in your seat. Your goal is to sit in your seat as soon as possible. Tell me what you could do to solve this problem."

Ss.: (the students yell these out one by one, and the teacher writes them on the board, overhead projector, or easel)

"Pull him out of my seat."

"Tell the teacher."

"Ask him to get out of my seat."

"Find another seat to sit in."

"Go sit in his seat."

"Share my seat with him."

"Sit down on top of him."

"Beat him up."

"Sit on the floor."

"Hide so the teacher won't see you."

"Go back to the pencil sharpener and make believe you're still sharpening your pencil." (stall)

"Stand there until he moves."

"Keep asking him to move until he moves." (broken record)

T.: (keeps encouraging the students to produce more "solutions" until it appears that they have dried up)

Spivack and his associates found that the number of different solutions generated by a student considered competent at this skill is at least three or four and that children as young as 4 years old are considered capable of developing this skill.

Evaluating Solutions. Once your students are able to generate a number of alternative solutions to a problem, they need to evaluate each solution according to the following criteria: (1) *efficacy* (will this solution help me reach my goal without creating more problems for me?) and (2) *feasibility* (will I be able to take the action cited in my solution?). Starting with the list of solutions generated through brainstorming, help your students go through each and evaluate it with regard to efficacy and feasibility. If they think it will help them get what they want without creating new problems for them, they can label the solution "E" for effective. If they aren't certain the solution will help them get what they want without creating new problems, they can label it "e" to indicate their doubt. If they know the solution would definitely not get them what they want, they can cross out (eliminate) the solution. If they think they could definitely do it, they can label the solution "F" for feasible. If they aren't sure, they can label the solution with an "f." If they know they couldn't do it, they can eliminate the solution. When they are all finished with each solution, they should first look for any solutions labeled both "E" and "F." These are the solutions with the best chance of working since they are both effective and feasible; they should be tried first. If there aren't any solutions designated both effective and feasible, you can brainstorm again to see if there was anything you missed, reevaluate the solutions you have, or try one of the solutions you have some doubts about. The goal is to generate as many possible (i.e., "E" and

"F") solutions as you can. The more you have, the more likely it is that you will find one that really works. The teacher must act as a facilitator. This means that you don't tell your students which solutions are effective or feasible and which are not. You ask them and let them tell you. If it becomes obvious that they are having difficulty evaluating solutions, then you should help them, but only help—do not give them the answer. They must arrive at the answer themselves. Be prepared to ask pointed questions. For example:

T.: "OK, let's look at the first solution, 'pull him out of my seat.' Would this work? Would this get you what you want (to sit in your seat as soon as possible) without creating any new problems for you?" (waits for response)

Ss.: "Yes, it would get you what you want."

T.: "It could get you in your seat as soon as possible. Could it also create some new problems for you?"

Ss.: "Maybe, maybe not."

T.: "How many of you think it might create some new problems?"

Ss.: (a few students raise their hands)

T.: (addresses question to these students) "OK, why do you think pulling the student out of your seat might make new problems for you?"

Ss.: (no response)

T.: "Who can tell me what might happen if you tried to pull the student out of your seat?"

Ss.: "He might put up a fight and you could get hurt (or hurt him) and get into trouble for fighting (or hurting him)."

T.: "OK, how many of you still think that the first solution is effective (would get you what you wanted without creating new problems for you)?"

Ss.: (no students raise hands)

T.: "How should we label this: 'E' or 'e,' or should we cross it out?"

Ss.: "Cross it out!"

T.: "Why did we get rid of it?"

Ss.: "'Cause it wouldn't help us get what we wanted without making new problems for us."

Making a Plan. The last step in the problem-solving process is to take the best solution from the list of solutions generated and make a new list of things you would have to do to implement that solution. This skill requires the ability to identify obstacles that might have to be overcome as well as the understanding that goal satisfaction may not occur immediately. This can also be accomplished through brainstorming. Consider the following:

T.: "Now that we have decided to try the solution of being assertive (using broken record) and asking the student in our seat to move over and over again until he does, let's make a plan to help us carry out this solution. What's the first thing we need to do?''

Ss.: ''Think about what we're going to say.''

T.: ''Good. (writes it down) After we decide what to say, what should we do next?''

Ss.: ''Think about how we are going to say it over and over again.''

T.: ''Good. In other words, use broken record. (writes this down) What else?''

Ss.: ''Try to stay calm.''

T.: ''OK, and what can we do to stay calm?''

Ss.: ''Do some belly breathing.''

T.: ''Good. (writes this down) Is there anything else we need to include in our plan?'' (pause)

After this first go-around, you might want to look at each of the steps in the plan and ask your students if there are any obstacles that might arise and how long they expect it will take to arrive at goal satisfaction (i.e., get the other student out of the seat). For example:

T.: ''Can you think of anything that might keep you from reaching your goal?''

Ss.: ''Yeh, the kid might get mad and try to hurt you.''

T.: ''OK, what should you do if that happens?''

Ss.: ''Walk away.''

''Protect yourself so you don't get hurt.''

''Tell the teacher.''

T.: ''Those are all good ideas. How long do you think it might take to reach your goal?''

Ss.: ''A few seconds.''

''Two days.''

''A week.''

''Five, ten minutes.''

T.: ''Why do you think it might take days to get the student out of your seat? (discusses this question) Why do you think it might only take a few seconds?''

Cognitive Restructuring

The term *cognitive restructuring* as it is used here simply means modifying one's beliefs. A belief may be any rule that a person applies to all situations regardless of his or her current experiences (Howell & Kaplan, 1980). Cognitive restructuring is used to modify irrational beliefs. A belief may be considered irrational if (1) it has no factual basis (i.e., there is no evidence to support its validity) or is illogical, and (2) it is harmful to the person who endorses it. For example, a student might believe that all teachers are her enemies because (she believes) they always pick on her. This belief is not factual, since the student has had a number of teachers over the years who demonstrated caring and concern

for her welfare. Still, because she endorses this irrational belief, it influences her feelings and her behavior toward her teachers and school to the extent that she is on the verge of expulsion; not incidentally, this is harmful to her. Other examples of irrational beliefs common to many children and youth can be seen in Figure 9.2. If, like me, you have trouble remembering all of these beliefs, Roush offers an abridged version in his excellent article on teaching cognitive restructuring to low-functioning students (1984). Roush's abridged version appears in Figure 9.3.

Where do children get their beliefs? Are they born with them? Do they get them from their environment? Fortunately, beliefs are learned. I say ''fortunately'' because this means that like overt behavior, beliefs can be unlearned. Let's take a look at how beliefs are learned so that we may be better able to help students unlearn them.

Kids say the darndest things (to themselves).

According to the Russian psychologist Luria, the acquisition of a belief system is an integral part of the development of language (1961). Children learn language through a combination of modeling and operant conditioning. A child's father picks him up and says, ''Da Da.'' The infant then imitates the father and says, ''Da Da.'' The consequence of this response is a smile and a hug, which reinforce the child's verbal behavior. Luria postulated that as the child grows older, he begins to incorporate a sublanguage that De Voge refers to as ''the meaning of the facts'' (1977). This sublanguage eventually becomes the child's belief system. It develops the same way his language does, through modeling and positive reinforcement. A child's mother points to fire and says, ''Bad! No touch!'' The child then imitates the mother by pointing to the fire and verbalizing an approximation of ''Bad! No touch!'' Mommy rewards this behavior by smiling and hugging the child. This reward not only reinforces the child's actions; it also reinforces her sublanguage or belief system. In this manner, the belief system of the significant person or persons in the child's life will largely determine whether she thinks rationally or irrationally about the facts of her environment. A child walking with his mother sud-

1. I must be good at everything I do.
2. Everyone must like me.
3. If people do things I don't like, they have to be bad people and they must be punished.
4. Everything must go my way all the time.
5. Everyone must treat me fairly all the time.
6. I never have any control over what happens to me in my life.
7. I should never have to wait for anything I want.
8. When something bad happens to me, I must never forget it and I must think about it all the time.
9. I must be stupid if I make mistakes.
10. I should never have to do anything I don't want to do.

Figure 9.2. Common irrational beliefs of children and youth.

1. Robot thinking ("It's not my fault.")
2. I Stink thinking ("It's all my fault.")
3. You Stink! thinking ("It's all your fault!")
4. Fairy Tale thinking ("That's not fair!")
5. Namby Pamby thinking ("I can't stand it!")
6. Doomsday thinking ("Woe is me!")

Figure 9.3. Common classes of irrational thinking in children and youth. *Note.* From Roush, 1984.

How beliefs are learned.

denly trips and falls down on the sidewalk. This is a fact. The meaning attached to this fact is taught to the child by his mother's reaction to it. Let's assume that the child is more surprised than hurt. He looks up at his mother as if to say, "What happened? Is this something I should be worried about?" Let's also assume that his mother becomes upset over the fall and picks him up in an agitated state. Her actions and words convey alarm. The mother's reaction not only produces anxiety in the child because it is dramatically different from her normal behavior; it is also interpreted as a model of how he should behave under similar circumstances. The fact is that he fell down. The meaning of that fact, as conveyed by his mother, is that falling down is a bad thing, and one must become upset when one falls down. Obviously, this meaning of the fact, or belief, is taught over a period of time and not after one occurrence.

Suppose that instead of becoming agitated over the fact of her child's fall, the mother, seeing that he is not hurt, reacts in a calm, reassuring manner. Let's assume that she simply tells him to get up and assures him that he's all right. The fact is the same. However, the new meaning of that fact as conveyed by his mother is that

falling down is not always a bad thing and that one should not get upset about it unless one is seriously injured. Again, this is learned after several similar experiences and not just one occurrence. The point of all this is that children learn rational and irrational thinking or beliefs by observing significant adults. If a child misbehaves and her parent says, "What's wrong with you?" or "The next time you do that I'm going to give you a beating you'll never forget," the child will probably grow up believing "It's terrible when you make a mistake" or "I must be stupid if I make mistakes." If a child, riding in his parent's car, observes his father yelling and cursing at the driver ahead of him because he's going too slowly, he is likely to grow up believing "It's terrible if things don't go your way" or "People who don't behave the way you want them to must be terrible people" (De Voge, 1977). How these and other beliefs affect the way children behave is the crucial issue.

Beliefs and Behavior

It has been postulated that much of our behavior is influenced by the way we feel and that our feelings are initially produced by our beliefs (Ellis, 1962). According to Ellis, if we hold an irrational belief, we are likely to behave inappropriately because our irrational thinking produces strong negative feelings (i.e., emotional states such as rage or extreme anxiety) that are manifested by irrational behavior. The whole sequence is set in motion by an external event (something that happens to us), which I shall refer to as "A" in the sequence. The event (A) triggers the irrational thinking or unfounded, counterproductive belief, which is referred to as "B." This thinking, by the way, is not necessarily done on a conscious level as when a student might say to herself, "All teachers are mean. She's a teacher. Therefore, she's mean." Nevertheless, the thought is close enough to the surface to allow the individual to make the connection between it and the event. Once the connection is made, strong emotions or feelings emerge. These are referred to as "C" in the sequence. They are usually manifested in some form of behavior, usually maladaptive. The A-B-C sequence may be seen in Figure 9.4.

Look at example 5 in Figure 9.4. If you have ever worked in an inner-city school with low-income minority students, you have probably encountered this type of irrational thinking. Roush calls it "robot" thinking. It is one of the most damaging of the many irrational beliefs we find in students. For one thing, they don't seem to outgrow it. According to a study by Kassinove et al., robot thinking is the only irrational belief that doesn't change (i.e., improve) with age (1977). Students who believe they have little or no control over what happens to them are said to have an *external locus of control*. The term "locus of control" refers to the degree to which individuals believe that they are able to influence the outcome of situations in their lives (Rotter, 1966). People with an external locus of control believe that the reinforcements and punishments they experience are not under their personal control but rather under the control of powerful others, luck, fate, or a supreme being. On the opposite end of the locus of control spectrum are people with an *internal locus of control*, who believe that their actions produce the reinforcement and punishment that follow their efforts. For example, an "internal" student who did not study for a difficult test, and who subsequently failed it, would be likely to accept responsibility for his grade and believe that he got what he deserved. The same would hold true if the internal student had studied for the test and subsequently passed it. In this case, he would probably believe his hard work paid off. Meanwhile, the external student who finds herself in the same situation would either blame the teacher if she failed the test or consider herself lucky if she passed it. Keep in mind that I am not talking about false modesty here. Many of us have been conditioned to act humble even when we don't feel humble. However, the true external isn't acting. She actually believes she was lucky! She does not see the relationship between her hard work and the rewards it produces. Neither is this a case of sour grapes. Many of us tend to rationalize or make excuses or alibis for our behavior when we know in our hearts that we have no one to blame but ourselves. However, the true external actually believes that negative experiences are caused by some outside force over which he or she has no control.

What does all of this have to do with beliefs and behavior? It has been suggested that students who are

Event (A)	Thinking (B)	Feelings/Behavior (C)
1. Peers tattle on him	"If people do things to me that I don't like, they must be rotten and deserve to be punished."	Anger/verbal and/or physical attacks on peers
2. Asked to do something new and/or difficult	"I must be competent at everything."	Anxiety attack/noncompliance
3. Loses a game at recess	"Things must always go my way."	Anger/tantrum
4. Peers tease her	"Everyone must like me."	Depression/truancy
5. Asked to change his behavior	"I can't help the way I am."	Apathy/negativism/frustration/noncompliance

Figure 9.4. Ellis's A-B-C Model applied to school situations.

convinced that they have little control over the rewards and punishments they receive from their environment will probably have little or no reason to modify their behavior in an attempt to alter the probability that those events will occur (Crandall et al., 1965, p. 92). It therefore becomes critical for the teacher to identify students with an external locus of control before attempting to modify these students' behavior. Methods of identifying external students will be discussed next. The important thing to remember is that irrational thinking or beliefs often trigger powerful emotional states (feelings) that may be manifested by maladaptive behavior.

External locus of control.

Assessing Beliefs

Before attempting to modify a person's beliefs, determine (1) what they are; (2) whether or not they need

changing; and (3) if they do, what specific changes are required. How do you find out what another person believes? This is no easy task, but one well worth the effort. The traditional method has been the pencil-and-paper test. This is still an acceptable approach as long as the following guidelines are adhered to.

1. *The testing should be direct.* This means that it should be a direct measure of the student's beliefs without relying on esoteric interpretations. Projective tests are not direct measures of a person's beliefs. Completing a sentence can be a direct measure of a person's beliefs if the sentence relates to the beliefs you wish to measure. For example, if you want to ascertain the student's belief about school, you could have him complete the sentence, "I think that school is . . ."

2. *The testing should be continuous.* In other words, give the test more than once. This helps to ensure reliability or consistency of response. It is a good idea to give your entire class a pencil-and-paper beliefs inventory once a week or once a month. In this way, you can see how their thinking changes over time or how persistent they are in their thinking. You can also see how each student's mood affects her thinking.

3. *A number of test items should be included for each belief you wish to assess.* If you want to determine a student's locus of control, include more than one item—for example, "If I get a passing grade on a test: (a) it's more likely to be because I studied for it; (b) it's more likely to be because I was lucky." Include several items that differentiate between internals and externals. If a student chose "b" (i.e., "because I was lucky") in the only item measuring locus of control, it doesn't prove that he's an external. However, if a student consistently chose the external-oriented responses from a number of locus of control items, you could assume that he does, in fact, have an external locus of control.

4. *Use commercially available tests that present evidence of validity and reliability whenever possible.* Two such instruments for assessing locus of control in students are the Nowicki-Strickland Locus of Control Scale (Nowicki & Strickland, 1973) and the Intellectual Achievement Responsibility (IAR) questionnaire (Crandall et al., 1965). More general student belief inventories you might use include the Children's Survey of Rational Beliefs found in *Rational Emotive Education: A Manual for Elementary School Teachers* (Knaus, 1974) and the belief inventories from the PRE-MOD program (Kaplan & Kent, 1986); also refer to chapter 4.

5. *Always compare the student's performance on the pencil-and-paper assessment with her observable behavior.* When there is a discrepancy between the student's behavior and her responses on the pencil-and-paper test, I prefer to give more weight to behavior. By "behavior," I mean what the student usually says or does at school.

If, for example, a student consistently makes negative comments about school, tends to be tardy or truant, and is seldom observed being successful or having positive experiences at school, I assume she believes that school is aversive. If her responses on a pencil-and-paper test suggested the opposite, I would not be inclined to give them any credence.

6. *Try to conduct the pencil-and-paper assessment without being present.* If the student has difficulty reading or writing, it may be necessary to provide him with a tape-recorded version of the test. He can listen to the items and either mark his responses if they are multiple choice, or tape-record them if necessary. Your presence during the testing session may have some effect on the student's performance. It might inhibit him from responding in a truthful (i.e., valid) manner.

Constructing Beliefs Assessments

If there is no beliefs assessment readily available, you may wish to construct your own. The procedure is neither difficult nor time consuming. Your objective in assessing beliefs will be to identify the beliefs a student endorses that might support her maladaptive behavior or interfere with her engaging in the target behavior. The best way to achieve this objective is to provide the student with a list of statements reflective of beliefs or ideas and have her indicate which ones she agrees with (believes to be true) and which ones she disagrees with (believes to be false).

First, take a piece of paper and fold it in half. At the top of one half, write down the maladaptive behavior the student engages in, and at the top of the other half, the target behavior you would like her to engage in. Next, write down as many ideas or beliefs as you can that would support the maladaptive behavior. Do the same for the target behavior. Now go over each statement and reword it so that it will be easy for your student to understand it. Your list might resemble Figure 9.5.

Second, make a list of neutral beliefs that have nothing to do with the maladaptive or target behavior. Include these items in your beliefs assessment as distractors so that what you are attempting to measure will not be too obvious to the student. After rewording them, add them to your list of beliefs. Add a set of directions; the final product might look like the beliefs assessment in Figure 9.6.

Remember that this process is not very scientific and doesn't prove anything. However, if you follow the guidelines listed here, the results will give you some indication of what the student's beliefs are and if they might contribute to her maladaptive behavior.

Maladaptive Behavior: When criticized by teacher, S. gets angry and has tantrums (e.g., screams, curses, cries)	Target Behavior: When criticized by teacher, S. will interact with her without getting angry and having tantrums
I must be stupid if I make mistakes	It's a teacher's job to tell students when they're wrong.
I feel like I'm being picked on when I'm criticized by my teacher	I feel good about myself
I never make mistakes	If at first you don't succeed, try, try again
If people say things to me that I don't like, they must be rotten	Mistakes are part of learning

Figure 9.5. Beginning a beliefs assessment.

Modifying Beliefs

Ellis argues that if behavior is a manifestation of the feelings produced by one's thinking, the best way to change a person's maladaptive behavior is to modify the irrational thinking that led to the behavior in the first place. Ellis's intervention program is called Rational Emotive Therapy (Ellis, 1962) and one of its strategies is disputing irrational beliefs (DIBs). I have taken the liberty of adapting this strategy to the problems of children and youth. I will refer to it from now on as "DIBs for KIDs." The teacher can go through the process with the student or, if possible, the student should do it alone.

The first step is to describe the event (A) associated with the maladaptive behavior. Step 2 is to identify the thinking (B) triggered by the event. In other words, when this particular event or a similar event occurs, what does the student usually think or say to himself? This is probably the most difficult step in the DIBs process, primarily because students don't actually speak to themselves when a particular event occurs in their lives. Many students get stuck on this step and require some prompting. One way to prompt is to provide a list of irrational beliefs and have the students choose the ones they think are probably associated with the event. Another approach is to give a student a beliefs assessment ahead of time, identify any irrational beliefs she may have, and ask her if any of these go with the event.

Name: _____ Date: _____

Directions: Read each statement below and decide whether it is true or false. If you believe the statement is true, write the letter "T" next to the number of the statement. If you think that it is false, write the letter "F" next to the number. It is not necessary to think about each one for very long. Be honest. You are not going to be graded on this and no one but you and your teacher will ever see it. Don't answer the way you think your teacher might want you to or the way you think you are supposed to. You won't get into any trouble because of your answers so *answer the way you really believe.*

1. Everyone should treat me fairly and it's awful if they don't.

2. Everyone must like me and it's awful if they don't.

3. I always have to win and it's terrible if I don't.

4. I never make mistakes.

5. People should not have to do anything they don't want to.

6. If people say things to me that I don't like, they must be rotten.

7. School is fun.

8. It's part of a teacher's job to tell a student when he or she is wrong.

9. I like school.

10. When people find fault with you, it usually means they don't like you.

11. I must be stupid if I make mistakes.

12. I can't help the way I act around others. That's just the way I am and there's nothing I can do about it.

13. People who find fault with me are usually nit-picking.

14. Being criticized makes me feel like I'm being picked on.

15. It's important to go to school and get an education.

16. It's awful when things don't go my way.

17. I feel good about myself.

18. Teachers like to find fault with their students.

19. If at first you don't succeed, you should try, try again.

20. With a little effort, one can change his or her behavior.

21. I must be good at everything I do and it's terrible if I'm not.

22. Mistakes are a part of learning and should be expected.

23. One can learn a lot from the criticism of others.

24. When bad things happen to you, you should think about them all the time.

25. It's never right for one person to criticize another person.

26. You should never admit when you're wrong.

Figure 9.6. Sample beliefs assessment.

If the student is still unable to identify the irrational thinking associated with the event, you will probably have to help her. For example, if she has indicated on her beliefs assessment that teachers always pick on her, she must be made to recognize the relationship between this belief and the event of her teacher reprimanding her. It may be necessary to speak in the third person. You might say, "Let's suppose that a student named Jon believes that all of his teachers pick on him. One day his teacher tells Jon to stop talking and get to work. What do you suppose Jon thinks when his teacher says that to him?" Continuing in the same vein, ask her, "What do you suppose Jon thinks when his teacher tells him to sit down and stop wandering around the room?" and "What do you suppose Jon thinks when his teacher has him stay after school?" The obvious response to all of these questions is that Jon probably thinks that his teacher is picking on him. Next, ask the student, "How do you know that Jon is thinking that?" She should reply, "Because you said that Jon believes that all of his teachers pick on him." Now switch to the first person and ask her, "Do you believe that teachers pick on you?" If she answers in the affirmative, ask her, "When I tell you to sit down or stop talking, do you think that I am picking on you?" Again, if she feels secure enough to answer honestly, point out to her the relationship between her belief and the event. Show her how the event (A) leads to the belief (B). To restate the first two steps in DIBs for KIDs: the first step is to describe the event (A) associated with the student's maladaptive behavior. Step 2 is to identify the thinking or belief (B) triggered by, or associated with, the event.

The third step is to describe how the student feels (C) when she thinks about her belief (B) and the event (A). Again, if she has any difficulty describing her feelings, you may have to prompt her. Ask her if she feels happy, sad, angry, annoyed, nervous, excited, disappointed, depressed, guilty, concerned, embarrassed. If she can't remember how she feels, you may have to resort to role playing where you both re-create the event, or include some imagery where you have the student imagine the event taking place. It may be necessary for you to describe the event for her as a sort of guide through the imagery phase. After she is able to describe how she feels, she is ready for step 4. This step requires her to describe her behavior. Leading questions or prompts may also be necessary here. "What did you do when I told you to stop talking to Dee and sit down?" These first four steps comprise the reporting stage of DIBs for KIDs. Steps 5 and 6 make up the evaluating (or reevaluating) stage.

In step 5, the student is asked to provide evidence (i.e., facts) that supports his belief (B). "What makes you think teachers always pick on you?" He should be prodded to cite specific past experiences. In step 6, the student is asked if there is any evidence that his belief (B) might not be true. If he denies any evidence of falseness, be prepared to cite such evidence yourself. Describe events in the student's recent past where you or another teacher interacted with him in a positive manner or where you were justified in reprimanding him. Point out those instances where you have consistently reprimanded all of the students in the same manner for the same behavior. This is probably the most critical step in the program. If you can't come up with any evidence that the student's thinking (B) is irrational, you may have to admit that it is justified. In this case, you should be secure enough and professional enough not only to admit that the student is right but also to do something about changing your behavior. This is covered specifically in chapter 13. On the other hand, if you do come up with evidence that the student's thinking is irrational but can't convince him of it, you are probably looking forward to a lengthy intervention. Have the student collect evidence that his belief is true while you collect evidence that it is false. When it is appropriate to do so, sit down with him and compare data. It might not be a bad idea also to do a perception check in order to determine whether or not both of you have the same interpretation of "being picked on." If your perceptions differ, you will not generate the same data regarding the event and you will be unable to change the student's irrational thinking.

Assume that you convince the student that her thinking is irrational (if it is). In step 7, she must think of a rational thought or belief to substitute for the old, irrational one. She should begin practicing saying the new belief to herself several times a day. Figure 9.7 includes a number of common irrational beliefs of students and corresponding rational beliefs. It might be helpful for the student to tape-record her new rational belief and play it back several times a day or she might read the rational statements from one or more cards she carries with her. Have her reinforce this behavior herself, if possible (see chapter 8 for more information on self-reinforcement). Otherwise, be available to reinforce her on those occasions when you hear her saying her new belief aloud. Don't laugh! It is entirely possible to reinforce students for rational ideas that they verbalize. De Voge (1977) conducted research on a group of severely emotionally disturbed persons between the ages of 8 and 13 in which she measured the effects of reinforcing rational statements on their emotions and behavior. Her findings indicate that the technique works!

DIBs for KIDs can be done in a group or on a one-to-one basis. It can be done verbally or in writing. Figure

1. I must be good at everything I do./Nobody's perfect.
2. Everyone must like me./You can please some of the people some of the time but you can't please all the people all the time.
3. If people do things that I don't like, they must be bad people and must be punished./I've done things that other people don't like but I'm not a bad person and I don't think I deserve to be punished.
4. Everything must go my way all the time./You can't always get what you want (but if you try some time, you just might find, you get what you need) (Mick Jagger).
5. Everyone must treat me fairly all the time./Who said life is fair?
6. I never have any control over what happens to me in my life./Nobody has control over everything that happens but you can control some things (e.g., the grades you earn in school or your relationships).
7. I should never have to wait for anything I want./Waiting for something sometimes makes the getting all the more special.
8. When something bad happens to me, I must never forget it and I must think about it all the time./Don't worry, be happy! (Bobby McFerrin).
9. I must be stupid if I make mistakes./Nobody's perfect.
10. I should never have to do anything I don't want to./Nobody is free to do whatever he or she wants.

Figure 9.7. Examples of fair-pair thoughts.

9.8 is a sample of a DIBs for KIDs form that a student might fill out with or without the teacher's help.

One word of caution. A student's thinking is not going to change overnight. Although he may be "practicing" his new thinking each day, it is highly probable that certain events will occur and trigger his old thinking again. Therefore, until his new thinking becomes established, it will be necessary to have him review for you ahead of time what he plans to do if an event occurs that is likely to trigger old thinking. Have him rehearse his plan of action in a role-playing situation. When the event or a similar event does occur and he puts his plan into action, reinforce him for his efforts. For example, if you should happen to reprimand the student and you observe him switching on the tape recorder to listen to his new thinking (e.g., "He's just doing his job. Don't take it personally.") or you see him mouth or whisper these words to himself or read them from his cards, praise him for it. It will take a while, but eventually he will come to believe what he's telling himself. Once he reaches this stage in the intervention, you should begin to see a marked reduction in maladaptive behavior due primarily to the reduced intensity of his emotional state. While before the intervention, a reprimand from the teacher produced anger or even rage, the change in his

thinking will now allow him to accept a reprimand with only annoyance or concern.

An alternative approach to DIBs for KIDs is described by Roush (1984). Roush's procedure is more appropriate for use with younger or less cognitively able students and it's worth discussing here. Roush has made it easier for students to remember the different types of irrational thinking by condensing them into the six types that were listed and described in Figure 9.3. He recommends that students become familiar with these types of irrational thinking to the point where they can recognize them in others and, ultimately, in themselves. Instead of Ellis's DIBs, Roush uses the five questions from Maultsby's *Rational Behavior Therapy* (1984). Roush has added the acronym "A FROG" as a mnemonic device to help students remember these questions (see Figure 9.9). Roush's version of cognitive restructuring works in the following way.

Let's say that a student is engaging in some verbally aggressive behavior when she is teased by her peers. Each time this occurs, the teacher might cue her with a comment such as, "It sounds like you're doing some 'You stink!' thinking. Are you? Think about it." If and when the student is able to agree that (1) she would like to change her behavior and (2) her "You stink!" thinking is contributing to it, the teacher may suggest that she dispute this thinking by addressing each of the five questions. If the student answers "yes" to one or more of the questions, she concludes that her thinking is helpful and does not attempt to change it. On the other hand, if she answers "no" to all five questions, she concludes that her thinking is harmful and tries to change it.

Obviously, this is easier said than done. In reality, it is a difficult task to get a student to dispute and give up a belief he may have endorsed for years. For one thing, the student may not want to give up his belief even if he knows in his heart of hearts it is irrational. His belief may serve an important purpose for him. For example, a student who is rather small in stature compared to his peers may need to hold on to his "You stink!" thinking because it fuels the anger he needs to make him seem intimidating to his peers instead of being seen as a helpless victim. You could actually be doing this student a disservice by getting him to modify his belief. In this case, you would be better off trying to teach the student as well as his peer group some prosocial skills they could use so that they could all get along better. Another reason why disputing a belief is so difficult is that many students lack the necessary cognitive development. If this is the case, follow Roush's suggestions. Always start by using a logical argument with a student. If she has difficulty grasping the logic of this argument, move to an empirical argument. Have her look for physical evidence of the validity or fallacy

---

Completed by _TODD A. w/help from his teacher_ Date _Nov., 1989_

Directions: Fill out this sheet by answering each of the questions below. Ask your teacher for help if you need it. Be honest. You are not going to be graded on this. Don't answer the way you think your teacher might want you to. Answer the way you really feel.

1. What happened to me? *"I MADE A MISTAKE ON MY WORK"*

2. What did I think when this happened? *"I'M STUPID"* (This took quite a lot of coaxing from me.)

3. How did I feel when this happened? *"ANGRY"*

4. How did I behave when this happened? *"TORE UP MY WORK"*

5. How do I know that what I thought in #2 is actually true? *"I ALWAYS MAKE MISTAKES ON MY WORK SO I MUST BE STUPID"*

6. Is there any reason why my thinking in #2 might be false? *After many leading questions and much prompting from his teacher, Todd volunteered that he couldn't be stupid because he has managed to learn many difficult things (eg., telling time, how to read, make small purchases, fix his own bike...)*

7. If my thinking in #2 is false, what should I think instead? *"I'M NOT STUPID" "I'VE LEARNED LOTS OF THINGS" "MAKING MISTAKES IS A PART OF LEARNING" "IF AT FIRST YOU DON'T SUCCEED, TRY, TRY AGAIN"*

Figure 9.8. Example of completed DIBs for KIDs form.

A — DOES IT HELP KEEP ME ALIVE?

F — DOES IT MAKE ME FEEL BETTER?

R — IS IT BASED ON REALITY?

O — DOES IT HELP ME GET ALONG WITH OTHERS?

G — DOES IT HELP ME REACH MY GOALS?

Figure 9.9. Roush's five questions for challenging beliefs.

of her belief. If this fails, appeal to the student's basic hedonism and see if she is willing to continue to endorse a belief that makes her feel bad. Examples of arguments at each of the three levels of disputation may be seen in Figure 9.10.

My approach to cognitive restructuring borrows heavily from both Ellis and Roush but includes some new wrinkles. I do not take it for granted that students are able to identify what happens to them, how they feel and behave, or what they are thinking. Most students aren't that aware. Before I had them attempt to dispute a belief I would train them to become aware of the events (A), mediating beliefs (B), and feelings and behaviors (C) they experience on a daily basis. The process is relatively simple. Using a form such as the one illustrated in Figure 9.11, first have them spend several days monitoring their feelings, focusing on intense negative feelings such as anger or anxiety. Since they might not remember to do so in the beginning, prompt them at predetermined intervals by asking them if they were angry during the last half-hour. If this doesn't work, prompt them on a continuous basis (i.e., whenever you catch them being angry) and tell them to write down on their form how they feel and what they are doing. Eventually, the practice of self-monitoring can become so natural that they will be able to do it without prompting. After they get to the point where they are able to

Belief Type	Argument Type
"You stink!"	**Logical:** "Do you do bad things (or things others don't like) sometimes? Are you a bad person? Should you always be punished for doing something that others don't like?" Have the student try to give you an example of his doing something to someone that they didn't like or that they thought was bad (e.g., calling someone a name they didn't like or taking something away from them or disappointing another person). The point you want to get across is that people are fallible and we often do things that hurt or disappoint others; if we do such things and we don't consider ourselves bad or deserving of punishment, why should we consider others bad and deserving of punishment?
	Empirical: Have the student collect data to support (or disprove) his argument. For example, if he believes that *all* of his teachers are *always* picking on him, have him collect data for a few days on positive and negative comments his teachers direct at him; hopefully, these data will show that not all (but some) of his teachers pick on him some (not all) of the time.
	Functional: Simply ask the student if his thinking makes him feel better or worse: "How do you feel when you think that all of your teachers always pick on you? Does that make you feel good or bad? Do you like feeling bad? Maybe if you changed your thinking you might start feeling better—would you like to feel better?"
"I stink!"	**Logical:** Where performance anxiety is the issue and the student is reluctant to try new tasks, you can use the argument that everyone makes mistakes; nobody's perfect. Where low self-esteem is the issue and the student is a social isolate, you can use the argument that everyone has value or self-worth simply by virtue of being a person.
	Empirical: Have the student list all the tasks she learned to do over the years, such as feed herself, dress herself, and learn language. We take many of these for granted but they are not all easy to learn. Have the student list some things she learned to do that not everybody else can do, such as use a personal computer, take her bike apart and put it together, draw, and do well at math. Have the student make a list of all the people who like her including family members, teachers, and peers; if she can't think of people who like her, have her collect data on the number of times people at school (peers or teachers) greet her, compliment her, smile at her, or try to help or "be nice" to her over a 3-day period.
	Functional: The same as for "You stink!"
"Robot"	**Logical:** "People are not machines. Look at all the ways you have changed already; therefore, you can't say that it's impossible for you to change the way you are or that you have little or no control over how you behave."
	Empirical: Have the student monitor his own behavior. Use a behavior that he is changing, such as the number of math facts computed correctly on daily quizzes; have him plot data (e.g., test scores) on a chart and call his attention to the change in his behavior.
	Functional: The same as for "You stink!"
"Namby Pamby"	**Logical:** "You can stand it; you're still alive, here, and not crazy. Think of the worst thing that could happen to you—how does this compare?"
	Empirical: Have the student collect data on events in her life (for 1 week) that are threatening and also write down whether or not the threat ever materialized (i.e., whether it was actually as bad as she thought it would be) and what happened to her (i.e., if she got hurt, sick, died, or whatever she thought would happen to her).
	Functional: The same as for "You stink!"
"Fairy Tale"	**Logical:** "Life is not fair, so (logically) you can't expect things always to turn out the way you want them to."
	Empirical: Have the student collect data on events in his life over a 1-week period that he considers fair (i.e., turned out the way he wanted) or unfair (i.e., didn't turn out the way he wanted).

Figure 9.10. Sample disputations.

Belief Type	Argument Type
"Doomsday"	Functional: The same as for "You stink!"
	Logical: "Bad things are always happening to good people; if they worried about that prospect all the time, they would never experience any joy in their lives. It doesn't pay to worry about things over which you have little control."
	Empirical: Have the student collect data about good or positive things that happened to her over a 1-week period.
	Functional: The same as for "You stink!"

Figure 9.10. *Continued*

Name _____ J. R. _____ Date __ 2-11-88 _____

Directions: Fill out in the following order: 1. C 2. A 3. B

A—Events (What happened?)	B—Thoughts (What did I think about?)	C—Feelings/Behaviors (How did I feel/act?)
		(10:00) I got angry at R. and told him to shut up.
		(11:00) I got mad at S. and called her a bitch.
		(1:30) I got mad at R. and told him he better stop calling me names or I will kick his butt.
		(2:30) I got mad at T. and called him a dick face.

Figure 9.11. The A-B-C form with feelings/behavior data.

collect valid data on their feelings and behaviors, have them add events to the process (see Figure 9.12). When they are able to self-monitor events, feelings, and behaviors accurately and without prompting, add mediating beliefs to the process (see Figure 9.13). It should be noted that students are to record their observations in the following order: (1) how they feel and behave, (2) what happens to them that they associate with their feelings and behavior, and (3) the thinking or belief that

mediates between the event and their feelings and behavior. The reason for following this sequence is simple. You do not want students to become aware of and record everything that happens to them or every thought that comes into their heads. You only want them to become aware of those events and thoughts associated with intense negative feelings and maladaptive behavior. Therefore, they have to record their feelings and behaviors first. "I'm shouting. I must be angry.

Name __J. R._____ Date __2-17-88__

Directions: Fill out in the following order: 1. C   2. A   3. B

A—Events (What happened?)	B—Thoughts (What did I think about?)	C—Feelings/Behaviors (How did I feel/act?)
(11:00) S. laughed at me when I asked T. a question.		(11:00) I got mad at S. but I didn't do anything about it.
(1:00) T. bumped into my desk when he went by.		(1:00) I got mad at T. and yelled for him to watch his big butt.
(2:00) S. called me a butt.		(2:00) Got mad at S. and flipped her off.

Figure 9.12. The A-B-C form with feelings/behavior and events data.

Name __J. R._____ Date __2-21-88__

Directions: Fill out in the following order: 1. C   2. A   3. B

A—Events (What happened?)	B—Thoughts (What did I think about?)	C—Feelings/Behaviors (How did I feel/act?)
(11:00) S. laughed at me.	You stink I hate her for laughing at me.	(11:00) I got mad at S. and called her retardo woman.
(11:30) T. took my ruler from my desk without asking me.	You stink I hate it when people steal from me.	(11:30) I got mad at T. and hit him when Mr. B wasn't looking.
(2:00) T. said I was dopey looking.	You stink cause he called me names.	(2:00) I got mad at T. and told him to shut up.

Figure 9.13. The A-B-C form with feelings/behavior, events, and thoughts data.

What happened and what am I thinking about what happened to make me angry?"

Once students have had the opportunity to self-monitor their feelings, behaviors, events, and mediating beliefs, I think they will develop an awareness that is essential for them to successfully use cognitive restructuring, on their own or with our help.

Self-Instructional Training

Self-instructional training (SIT) is based on research in the development of socialization and language in young children by two Soviet psychologists, Luria (1961) and Vygotsky (1962). Their findings suggested three stages by which the initiation and inhibition of voluntary motor behaviors come under verbal control. In the first stage, the speech of others in the child's environment (e.g., his parents) controls and directs his behavior. In the second stage, the child's own overt speech becomes an effective regulator of his behavior. He begins telling himself out loud what he should or should not do. In stage 3, the child's covert (i.e., inner) speech assumes a self-governing role. He stops telling himself what to do out loud and begins to think about it instead. Eventually, he no longer needs to think about what he should or should not do. He simply does it automatically (Meichenbaum, 1977, pp. 18–19).

This sequence may be experienced by adults as well as children. For example, when I first learned how to drive a manual shift automobile, my Uncle Syd would take me out in his old Chevy convertible and tell me what to do. I would repeat these directions out loud as I followed them. "Push in clutch with left foot. Shift down into first. Ease up on clutch and down on gas until it catches." My driving behavior was being regulated by my uncle. After several trials, I began to regulate my own behavior by telling myself what to do. Again, I spoke the directions out loud. Uncle Syd would simply nod his approval and say things like, "That's the way. Good!" By the time I reached the third stage, my self-instructions had gone "underground." I was thinking out my actions before I acted. Today, of course, I shift from gear to gear automatically and concentrate instead on the traffic, road conditions, and my destination. I no longer have to think about pushing in the clutch and shifting gears.

Borrowing on the theoretical work of Vygotsky and Luria, Meichenbaum developed a practical program of self-instruction to help hyperactive, impulsive children bring their behavior under their own control (1977). The first step requires the adult model to perform the task while talking to himself out loud. This step is referred to as *cognitive modeling*. The second step, *overt external*

guidance, requires the child to perform the same task under the adult's direction. In *overt self-guidance*, step 3, the child performs the task while instructing herself aloud. Step 4 requires the child to whisper the instructions to herself as she performs the task. This is *faded, overt self-guidance*. Finally, in step 5, *covert self-instruction*, the child performs the task while guiding her own performance through inner speech.

Meichenbaum's work in self-instruction eventually led to the development of the Think Aloud materials, a commercially available program in SIT (Camp & Bash, 1981). These materials have been used effectively with hyperactive, impulsive, and aggressive students (Camp, 1980) and clearly represent a future trend in behavior management. While much of the research has focused on the effects of SIT on academic behaviors, there is research to suggest that it is also effective in improving social behaviors in problem children (Drummond, 1974; Monohan & O'Leary, 1971; O'Leary, 1968) and in prolonging a student's tolerance for resisting temptation (Hartig & Kanfer, 1973). In particular, SIT can be effective in dealing with low frustration tolerance or personal narrative behavior, and in helping students to listen to directions before acting and to sit or stand next to peers without engaging in any provocative physical contact. Figure 9.14 is an example of a SIT program to help a student with low frustration tolerance. By the time the student has gone through steps 1 through 5, he is able to talk himself through frustrating work situations without external assistance. If necessary, the teacher can provide the student with a card (see Figure 9.15). This card not only acts as a reminder to talk through the problem; it also helps remind the student what to say and do.

Some helpful hints in using SIT:

1. Whenever possible, use peer teaching by having children cognitively model while performing for another child.
2. Facilitate remembering in your students by having them move through the program at their own rate, building up the number of self-statements little by little. You can also use written cues or prompts such as the first few words of a statement on a card at the student's desk.
3. Students should not simply repeat the self-statement in a rote, mechanical fashion but should rehearse meaningful self-talk through paraphrasing. Whenever possible, have them give the self-statement you have given them in their own words or have them generate the self-statements themselves.
4. In the beginning, when you are first introducing a student to SIT, use it to modify simple psychomotor or academic behaviors such as learning long division or putting a puzzle together. Do not use it to change

Step 1. Teacher (T.) models and talks out loud while student (S.) watches and listens.

   a. T. imitates S. doing work and starting to get upset; T. says out loud, "My muscles are getting tense and my face feels hot. I must be starting to get upset. What am I supposed to do when I get upset about my work?" T. pauses as if thinking.

   b. T. says out loud, "I know. First, I'm supposed to take a few deep breaths."

   c. T. models diaphragmatic breathing with her hand on her abdomen.

   d. T. says out loud, "That feels better. What should I do next?" T. pauses as if thinking.

   e. T. says out loud, "I know. I'll raise my hand and ask for help."

   f. T. models proper hand-raising and waiting-for-attention behavior.

   g. T. says out loud, "Good! I kept control over my behavior. I can do it!"

Step 2. S. performs task while teacher gives him instructions out loud.

   a. S. role plays self doing work and starting to get upset; T. says out loud, "My muscles are getting tense and my face feels hot. I must be starting to get upset. What am I supposed to do when I start to get upset about my work?" S. pauses as if thinking.

   b. T. says out loud, "I know. First, I'm supposed to take a few deep breaths."

   c. S. does diaphragmatic breathing with his hand on his abdomen.

   d. T. says out loud, "That feels better. What should I do next?" S. pauses as if thinking.

   e. T. says out loud, "I know. I'll raise my hand and ask for help."

   f. S. models proper hand-raising and waiting-for-attention behavior.

   g. T. says, "Good! I kept control over my behavior. I can do it!"

Step 3. S. performs task while he repeats steps out loud.

   a. S. role plays self doing work and starting to get upset; S. says out loud, "What am I supposed to do when I get upset while I'm doing my work?" S. thinks.

   b. S. says out loud, "I know. First, I'm supposed to take a few deep breaths."

   c. S. does diaphragmatic breathing with his hand on his abdomen.

   d. S. says out loud, "That feels better. What should I do next?" S. thinks.

   e. S. says out loud, "I know. I'll raise my hand and ask for help."

   f. S. models proper hand-raising and waiting-for-attention behavior.

   g. S. says out loud, "Good! I kept control over my behavior. I can do it!"

Step 4. S. performs task while he whispers steps. Steps 4a through 4g are the same as steps 3a through 3g.

Step 5. S. performs task while he thinks them (i.e., says them to himself). Steps 5a through 5g are the same as steps 4a through 4g.

Figure 9.14. Example of self-instructional training.

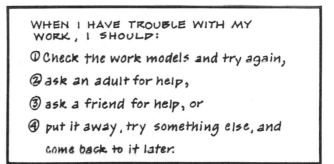

WHEN I HAVE TROUBLE WITH MY WORK, I SHOULD:

① Check the work models and try again,

② ask an adult for help,

③ ask a friend for help, or

④ put it away, try something else, and come back to it later.

Figure 9.15. Alternative self-talk and responses for student who destroys work out of frustration.

behaviors associated with intense emotional states such as anger or anxiety. After students have had a successful experience with SIT, then you may use it to modify behaviors in the affective domain.

5. At the beginning of each SIT session, ask the students to recall their self-instructions. Students who cannot do this should practice their statements while you work with those who can remember. Let your students use scripts or tapes, but don't let them become dependent upon them. Eventually, they must memorize their self-talk.

6. Encourage your students to use their self-statements outside of the classroom, for homework. Ask them to remember one instance when they used it and describe it at the beginning of the next lesson.

Verbal Mediation

It has been said, "When a child is tempted to misbehave, he often thinks before, while, and after acting. When he thinks in words, overt or covert, the words mediate between the temptation (i.e., the stimulus situation which tends to evoke the misbehavior) and the target response" (Blackwood, 1970, pp. 251–252). This is essentially what verbal mediation is all about—teaching students to talk themselves out of "bad" behavior and into "good" behavior. This skill may be particularly important in helping students deal with tempting situations. Consider the following: You have a student in your class who is engaging in off-task behavior (e.g., talking to peers) when she should be doing her work. She knows she will have to stay after school to finish her work if it is not finished by dismissal. Although talking to her peers is positively reinforcing, detention is extremely aversive to her. The temptation to talk to her peers, however, occurs in the morning and she doesn't have to experience detention until hours later in the afternoon. If, when she is tempted to talk to her peers, she is willing and able to use verbal mediation, she can describe the consequences of her off-task behavior to herself, which might serve as a warning strong enough to suppress the misbehavior. In addition, she can describe the consequences of a competing response: finishing her work, riding home on the school bus at dismissal, and being with her friends. Traditionally, in this type of situation, we would rely on extrinsic controls such as telling the student what will happen if she doesn't stop talking and get back on task, but this does not help the student learn self-control. We need instead to condition the student to produce her own verbal stimulus at the time of the temptation in order for her to eventually bring her behavior under her own control. We can teach the student to do this through the use of mediation essays.

With mediation essays, the teacher has the off-task student dictate an essay ahead of time regarding her misbehavior. "Ahead of time" means before the misbehavior occurs. The essay contains the six questions

shown in Figure 9.16. When the student misbehaves (i.e., is off task talking to peers), the teacher places a copy of the essay on her desk without any verbal interaction. The student is required to write two copies of the essay by the next day. If she doesn't complain at

---

1. What am I doing (or did I do) that I'm not supposed to do?
   I'm talking to my friends instead of working on my assignment.

2. Why shouldn't I be doing this?
   Because talking to my friends will get me into trouble with the teacher. It will keep them from doing their work. It will keep me from doing my work and if I don't do my work, I will fail in school.

3. What will probably happen if I continue doing it?
   I will probably have to stay after school until my work is finished. I'll miss the school bus and my parents will be called to come get me or else I'll have to walk home. My parents will be angry with me if they have to come get me. They might take away my TV and ground me. My friends might be angry with me if they get detention too.

4. What should I be doing instead?
   I should be doing my work without talking to anybody.

5. Why should I be doing it instead?
   So I won't get into trouble in school or at home. So I won't have to stay after school. So I'll pass my subjects at school and learn something. So my friends can get their work done.

6. What will probably happen if I do what I'm supposed to?
   I'll get my work done and leave school at dismissal. I'll be able to take the bus home and not have to walk.

Figure 9.16. Sample essay used in verbal mediation program.

Verbal mediation.

the time she receives the essay and she stops engaging in the off-task behavior, the assignment is decreased to one copy by the next day. If the student complains or the misbehavior continues, the number of copies is increased. If the assignment is not turned in by the following day, the number of copies is doubled. If the assignment is still not done, a detention slip is sent home for the parents to sign. If the student does not stay for detention, detention is doubled. If she still doesn't stay for detention, she is sent to the principal. This is an example of a hierarchy of escalating consequences similar to those discussed in chapter 7. If the student does the essay and gives it to the teacher upon entering class the following day, the teacher compliments and praises her. If it is not turned in the next day, the teacher waits until she has a chance to discuss the matter privately with the student. Detention is made highly aversive and the student may only leave detention if and when she cooperates by copying the essay.

For the first two misbehaviors, the student is required to copy the essay at home. For the third misbehavior, the student is kept after school to paraphrase the essay; if she continues to misbehave, she is required to write the essay from memory. Finally, she is required to describe orally the situation that typically stimulates her misbehavior and how she will think (i.e., what she will say to herself) when she is tempted again.

Does verbal mediation work? It appears to. There have been a number of studies comparing the efficacy of verbal mediation and other traditional behavior modification approaches such as token reinforcement on a wide range of behaviors and subjects; these findings suggest that verbal mediation is more effective (Blackwood, 1970; Miller et al., 1987).

Encouraging Students To Use CBM Strategies

Throughout this chapter I have described ways to teach your students how to use CBM strategies—cognitive restructuring, problem solving, SIT, and verbal mediation. While students are often able to use these strategies, they are not necessarily willing to use them. What good is having a skill if you need to use it and choose not to? The following is a list of helpful hints that may enhance the probability of your students using CBM strategies outside of their CBM lessons.

1. You—the teacher—must be a model for your students. You should use these CBM strategies yourself whenever it is appropriate to do so. Share with your students how you are using or have used cognitive restructuring to help you modify your thinking about them, about your job, about teaching, about yourself. Don't be afraid of self-disclosure. It will go a long way toward humanizing you in the eyes of your students. Use problem-solving skills in front of your students. Ask

them to help you brainstorm some alternative solutions. Let them see how you use this technique to solve your own problems. Don't worry about making mistakes. You are a coping model, not a mastery model. Nobody learns much from a mastery model. People think mastery models are perfect and never make mistakes; they therefore have trouble identifying with them. If there is some bonding between you and your students (if they can identify with you or relate to you, or even care about you), they are going to be more likely to do as you do.

2. Teach each skill and subskill in each CBM strategy to the mastery level. You wouldn't teach multiplication tables to your students without assessing whether or not they had learned them. Do the same with CBM skills. Be sure your students have learned them as well as they have learned their times tables. Give assessments and make sure that each student has learned a skill well enough to be able to use it if he wants to. When skills or knowledge are learned at the mastery level (i.e., when the student is both fast and accurate), the learner is more likely to choose to use that skill or knowledge than if he learned it only at the acquisition level (i.e., when the student is accurate but slow).

3. Any time you observe a student using any of the CBM skills outside of the CBM lesson, reinforce her. Use her as a model for her peers. "Janey, do you want to share with the class how you used your problem-solving skills to help you solve a problem you had on the playground today?" Encourage Janey's peers to praise her behavior and encourage them to follow suit. If you wish, use more tangible reinforcement. Set up a token economy system and reward students who use CBM skills outside of the CBM lesson with points or tokens that can be turned in for backup reinforcers.

4. Be sure you program for generalization by having your students use CBM skills outside of the CBM lesson. Give them homework assignments requiring them to use CBM skills in your classroom, in other classrooms, in other parts of the school, or outside of school. Role play these situations at first. For example, role play using verbal mediation to help deal with temptation or peer pressure, using SIT to deal with frustration in trying to master difficult skills or knowledge, or using problem solving to solve a problem with a family member.

5. Discuss the relevance of each strategy when you teach it. Children tend to think that much of what we teach them in school is irrelevant, and they are probably right. Remember, it doesn't matter how important we think our curriculum is. If our students don't see any relevance in what we're teaching them, they probably won't use it outside of our classroom without some form of extrinsic controls. Then we're right back where we were before: with the student learning to rely on his environment rather than on himself.

Chapter Nine Self-Assessment

See Appendix A for acceptable responses.

1. State the five characteristics that distinguish CBM from traditional behavior modification.

    a.

    b.

    c.

    d.

    e.

2. List and describe the three types of cognitions CBM strategies focus on as well as the CBM strategy that focuses on each.

    a.

    b.

    c.

3. State three reasons for teaching problem-solving skills to children and youth.

    a.

    b.

    c.

4. Describe each of the five problem-solving competencies.

    a.

    b.

continued next page

c.

d.

e.

5. Write an example showing how beliefs are learned.

6. Write an example showing how our beliefs influence our behavior.

7. Describe how you would assess beliefs.

8. Describe how you would modify beliefs using DIBs for KIDs.

9. List and describe the steps in the self-instructional training process.

   a.

   b.

   c.

   d.

   e.

continued next page

10. List and describe the steps in the verbal mediation process.

   a.

   b.

   c.

   d.

   e.

11. Describe how you would attempt to facilitate the generalization of CBM skills in students.

chapter 10

Social Skills Training for Students

Upon successful completion of this chapter, the learner should be able to:

1. State why social skills should be taught to children and youth
2. List a dozen social skills that might be taught in a social skills curriculum
3. Describe how to assess social skills deficits
4. Describe how to teach a social skill

Despite the fact that social skills training is the hottest topic in behavior management today, this chapter is going to be very short. Why? First, there are a large number of commercial social skills programs currently available and there is little purpose served by my reinventing the wheel. A fairly complete listing of these programs may be found in Appendix E. Second, if you look at enough of these programs you will find that what they refer to as ''social skills'' often includes what I have covered in this text under different headings, such as problem solving, SIT, and anger management. Because social skills training is so popular these days, anything that remotely relates to the modification of behavior, cognitions, or emotions has been loosely classified under that rubric. Since I have discussed the modification of cognitions and emotions in other chapters within this text, I will limit the scope of this chapter to those behaviors that help children and youth ''get along with'' their peer group and with adult authority figures; as a psychologist friend of mine has said, ''Social skills training is teaching kids how to keep people from getting mad at them.''

For those of you who might not be able to use one of the commercially available programs listed in Appendix E, I will provide a list of social skills you might include in a social skills curriculum as well as a sample lesson and some assessment and teaching strategies. This should be enough to get you started.

Why Teach Social Skills?

When our students do poorly in math, we administer a diagnostic math test to determine what the problem is. If we find the problem, we remediate it. Over the years, we have followed this procedure for reading, writing, and a myriad of academic skills taught in school. Why has it taken us so long to apply the same procedure to the area of social behavior? Is it because we simply assumed that if a student had a social behavior problem, it was probably because he was a ''bad'' boy, emotionally disturbed, or the product of poor parenting? Or was it because we didn't feel that social behaviors should be assessed (let alone taught) in school? Whatever the reason, times have changed; we now know that students who misbehave in school may do so because of social skills deficits and that we have a responsibility to assess and remediate these deficits as well.

The benefits of social skills training include: (1) the building and maintenance of relationships, (2) the ability to handle the unreasonable behavior of others (e.g., peers or siblings who tease), and (3) those secondary benefits derived from being able to ''get along with'' people we work with or for in our school and work lives (Matson & Ollendick, 1988).

Assessment of Social Skills

There are two objectives in assessing social skills: (1) identifying those students who may have social skills deficits and (2) identifying the deficits these students have. If you are a special education teacher it is likely that many of your students have social skills deficits. This is especially true if you teach students with behavior disorders. One of the current theories regarding the etiology of behavior disorders is that these students are not necessarily emotionally disturbed but, rather, are so deficient in social skills that they engage in the maladaptive behavior which eventually gets them labeled and placed in special education classes. In case you have difficulty identifying a student with a social skills deficit, the socially unskilled person has been described as ''one who often fights with peers, is unpopular with peers and adults, and doesn't get along well with his or her teacher or other authority figures'' (Matson & Ollendick, 1988, p. 5). They also tend not to be concerned about the rights and privileges of others and are self-centered in their behavior. On the other hand, the socially skilled person is one ''who can adapt well to his or her environment and who can (particularly in the case of children) avoid conflict of both a verbal and physical nature through communications with others'' (1988, p. 5). Let's assume that you are a special education teacher, that most of your students have social skills deficits, and that your objective is to identify what those deficits are.

Identifying the individual with a social skills deficit.

One way to assess social skills deficits is to have an ''expert'' on the student, such as the teacher, complete a social skills checklist. Examples of standardized checklists include the Matson Evaluation of Social Skills with Youngsters (MESSY) (Matson et al., 1983), the TROSS-C (Clark et al., 1985), the Behavioral Assertiveness Test for Children (BAT-C) (Bornstein et al., 1977), and the Social Skills Test for Children (SST-C) (Williamson et al., 1983). In addition, many commercially available social skills programs already come with assessment measures to identify skill deficits. Another way to identify deficits is through direct observation of behavior. This involves taking a frequency count of student behaviors in natural settings such as classrooms, school playgrounds, and cafeterias. Behaviors to observe include frequency of eye contact, socially appropriate (vs. inappropriate) language, conversations initiated, and assertive behaviors used. Figure 10.1 lists a few discrete behaviors that might be assessed by a direct observation of behavior. Notice that I started with

a list of maladaptive behaviors typically seen in the schools and added to that a list of corresponding target behaviors and the requisite social skills for each.

Since there are no standards or norms to use with this method, you will probably have to establish your own. In other words, you will have to determine what is an appropriate (i.e., ''normal'') rate of eye contact or number of conversations initiated. It is probably better that you develop your own set of norms since this method requires you to use a sample of subjects who are most representative of the students you will be assessing. This is especially true if you are working with minority group students such as blacks, Hispanics, Native Americans, or Southeast Asians. Developing your own norms can best be accomplished by identifying a small group of students from among the larger sample of students that is similar to your target population and that has the skill being assessed, then collecting direct observational data on this group's behavior. This technique, referred to in the literature as *social validation,* is described in detail in chapter 3. If there is a discrepancy between the target student's data and those of her peer group, you may assume that she has a skill deficit. Notice that I said ''*may* assume.'' Matson and Ollendick caution that mood and rewards for performance may be important factors in the student's use of social skills (1988). In other words, the fact that a student doesn't use a social skill does not automatically indicate a skill deficit. It might be that the student has the social skill but chooses either because of his mood or a lack of extrinsic rewards not to use it. This makes the assessment of social skills more difficult, but not impossible. Once you have compiled a set of ''norms'' for one or more social skills, you can use them to write a performance objective for the student's individualized education program (IEP) using the data from your direct observation as criteria for acceptable performance (CAP).

You can also assess social skill deficits through role playing. A procedure described in Matson and Ollendick is to narrate a particular hypothetical social situation to the student such as, ''You are standing in the lunch line in the school cafeteria and another student cuts in front of you. You say . . .''; the student is required to finish the statement. Matson and Ollendick caution against using role playing alone in assessing social skill deficits since students may have a limited ability to generalize to the natural environment (1988). Still, if you suspect a social skill deficit in one or more of your students, you might have them use that particular skill in a role-playing situation to confirm your suspicions.

As for the problem of factoring out motivation, continue to collect direct observation data over a period of

Maladaptive Behavior	Target Behavior	Social Skills
1. Is aggressive (or passive) when provoked by peers	Is assertive when provoked by peers	a. Establishes and maintains eye contact b. Communicates wants and feelings (e.g., "I don't like that. Stop it.") c. Is able to accept criticism
2. Steals or takes without asking	Acquires things by asking	Asks permission to use, handle, see someone else's property (i.e., can ask without grabbing or threatening)
3. Is aggressive toward others without provocation	Interacts with peers without provocation	a. Gives compliments to peers b. Gives apologies c. Greets peers in socially appropriate manner
4. Is disruptive in group	Interacts in group without disruptive behavior	a. Waits turn b. Shares materials c. Can be assertive to get what he or she wants d. Speaks with appropriate volume

Figure 10.1. Social skills.

time and under a variety of conditions (i.e., different mood states in the student and different rewards from the environment). If the data are constant over time and across conditions, you may assume that a skill deficit exists. To support your assumption, I would also use a second assessment such as role playing to see if your student actually does not know how to engage in the target behavior.

Teaching Social Skills

Teaching social skills is not very different from teaching other skills in school. The same rules of thumb apply as those used for effective instruction. For example, use direct instruction as much as possible. This involves providing the student with direct input including explaining, demonstrating, and modeling appropriate behavior and giving her the opportunity to respond directly and as often as possible to demonstrate her understanding of the skill being taught. Modeling is particularly important in the teaching of social skills. For students to learn how to act in different situations they must see these behaviors acted out in each situation. It doesn't do any good simply to talk about these actions. They must be seen. In addition, your students must be given the opportunity to act out these behaviors as well as see them acted out. In other words, they will need to engage in role playing.

In addition to direct instruction, modeling, and role playing, your students should learn the more complex social skills in small pieces just as they would the more complex computational skills in arithmetic. It will also benefit students to learn each subskill to the mastery level before going on to the next level of skill. The more complex the skill, the more likely it is that you will need to incorporate behavior modification strategies such as shaping, fading, and chaining to teach that skill. Let's arbitrarily choose a social skill and examine the techniques that should be used to teach it.

I have chosen the social skill of assertiveness since it is one many students (not to mention adults) have difficulty with. The first thing to understand about teaching assertiveness is that it is a not a simple skill like saying "No." Assertiveness requires a person to endorse a particular cognitive structure or belief, such as "I have the right to disappoint others," "I have the right to get what I want as long as it doesn't infringe on the rights of others," and "I have the right to my feelings and to share them with others." Assertiveness requires a certain mind-set; however, this is not what we are going to attempt to teach in our social skills lesson. It also requires a person to act in an assertive way rather than acting aggressively or passively. Students with anger or anxiety management problems have difficulty coming across to others as assertive. Their anger makes them appear aggressive while their anxiety tends to communicate passivity. Therefore, part of learning to be assertive may require some anger or anxiety management on the part of the student, but this topic will not be covered in this lesson either.

This social skills lesson deals only with the behavioral component of being assertive: what the student should say and do and not what he or she thinks and feels. I also believe that teaching a social skill such as assertiveness must be undertaken in certain specific contexts and not as one skill that can be used across situations. Learning how to act assertively to handle criticism is a different skill from learning how to act assertively to handle manipulation; these skills should be taught separately. The sample lesson on assertiveness that follows teaches "acting assertively to handle criticism." More specifically, it focuses on handling unwarranted (i.e., undeserved or unjust) criticism from others—peers, teachers, siblings, or parents. The content of the criticism may not be accurate (e.g., one student calling another student of normal intellect "retarded") and the manner in which the criticism is given may be offensive. For example, a teacher might use sarcasm to criticize a student ("It's a pity you and your brothers have to share the same brain").

This particular social skills program may be used with any student or group of students who demonstrate difficulty in handling criticism from peers and others when it is obvious that the difficulty is the result of a skill deficit (i.e., not knowing how to act) rather than a problem with mood (e.g., anger or anxiety problems) or motivation. It doesn't matter whether or not everyone agrees that the criticism is or is not unwarranted. What matters is that the target of the criticism perceives it as being unwarranted. If the student believes it is unwarranted, he should be able to act in an assertive manner by (1) establishing eye contact with the critical party, (2) maintaining an assertive posture (body squared and hands at sides), and (3) using appropriate verbalization (proper vocal tone, volume, content, and articulation). He should be able to communicate how he feels ("That's not true" or "I don't like it when you say things like that") in a manner that does not convey aggression or defensiveness.

Begin by writing an instructional objective for this behavior; you will want to know when the student has mastered the skill so that you will know when to stop teaching him. For example, "given situations when the student is criticized and perceives that criticism to be unwarranted, he will act assertively 100% of the time over a 10-day period. To act 'assertively' means (1) to establish eye contact, (2) to maintain an assertive posture, and (3) to use appropriate verbalization." My reason for using 100% as the CAP is based on the belief that people should act assertively at all times. I know

I don't do it and neither do most people, but that's probably because we were never taught how to be assertive in school—or anywhere else, for that matter. Perhaps if we had been taught, we'd be able to reach the CAP today. Keep in mind that this is a long-range objective and, in the beginning, reinforce the student's assertive behavior at much lower CAP.

I would then assess each of the "subskills" (e.g., establishes eye contact, maintains assertive posture, and uses appropriate verbalization) to determine which, if any, the student already has. Teaching him skills he already has is a waste of time. The simplest way to assess these skills is to ask the student to demonstrate how he would perform each of them. For example, you might say, "Someone has just criticized you and you don't like it. You want to tell them how you feel. Make believe that I am the critic and show me how you would look at me when you spoke to me." The student should be able to establish and hold eye contact with you for a period of time long enough to tell you how he feels (at least 5 to 10 seconds). You might then say, "Show me how you would stand when you tell me how you feel [arms at sides, shoulders squared toward critic, back straight]. Now show me what you would say. I have just called you a 'retard' and you would say . . ." Here you would look for a number of things. First of all, the content should be appropriate. It should not communicate passivity ("I can't help it if I make mistakes") or aggressiveness ("Yeh, well so are you!"). It should communicate how the student feels ("I don't like it when you call me names") and what the student wants ("Don't call me that"). It should be stated in a calm but firm voice, not shaking with anger or disfluent from fear. Let's assume from our informal assessment that the student is able to establish and maintain eye contact and maintain an assertive posture but is unable to use appropriate verbalizations.

The first step is to have him listen to tape-recorded instances and not-instances of students using appropriate verbalizations. Have him listen to students using sarcastic or whining or threatening tones, or using a voice that is too loud or too soft, or being disfluent. Have him listen to students using proper tone and volume and a firm but calm voice but saying the wrong things. Discuss with him what is wrong with each instance and why. Then have him listen to students using appropriate voice tone and volume and appropriate content. Again, discuss each example with regard to what is good or correct about it and why. To assess his understanding of what you have taught, have him identify instances and not-instances of appropriate verbal behavior. Next, model appropriate verbalization and have him respond in kind. Use peers he likes (or at least feels comfortable with) who have the verbal skills being taught as models.

Teach and have him master one aspect of appropriate verbalization at a time. For example, you might work on his verbal content first. Use a script and have him read what he should say. Have him practice it until he is able to say what he needs to without any hesitation or disfluencies. Then work on tone of voice. Again, allow him to use the script if necessary but instead of focusing on content, make sure he uses an appropriate tone (i.e., one that is neither aggressive nor passive). Tape-record his readings and play them back. Compare them with a peer model's rendition and see if he notices any difference. When he has mastered both content and tone, work on volume. When he has mastered content, volume, tone, and fluency, have him practice this skill in a role-playing situation.

Chapter Ten Self-Assessment

See Appendix A for acceptable responses.

1. State the rationale for teaching social skills to children and youth.

2. List ten social skills that might be taught in a social skills curriculum.

    a.

    b.

    c.

    d.

    e.

    f.

    g.

    h.

    i.

    j.

3. Describe how to assess social skills deficits.

    a.

    b.

    c.

4. Describe how to teach a social skill.

    a.

    b.

    c.

    d.

Stress Management Strategies for Students

Upon successful completion of this chapter, the learner should be able to:

1. Explain the rationale for teaching stress management skills to children and youth

2. Explain the differences between stress and stressors, eustress and distress

3. Describe the physiological changes that occur during the alarm reaction (i.e., fight or flight) stage of Selye's general adaptation syndrome

4. Explain what a SUD level is and how it is determined

5. List at least one somatic-physiological stress management skill that could be used for each of the following: (a) before (in anticipation of) stress, (b) during stress, and (c) after stress

6. Make the same list as in item 5 for cognitive-psychological and social-behavioral stress management skills

7. List at least 10 stressors commonly experienced by children and youth

8. Describe Meichenbaum's stress inoculation approach to anger management

Why Teach Stress Management?

No one would deny that stress is a problem for adults. Is it also a problem for children and youth? Do we need to teach stress management strategies to them? The answer is "Yes." Today's young people seem to be more susceptible to stress and are less equipped to handle it than adults. Consider the following.

It has been estimated that 20% of the child population is negatively affected by biological (e.g., chronic disease) and psychological (e.g., parental divorce) stressors (Eisen, 1979). A much greater number of children are negatively affected by stressors that might be termed social, economic, and cultural (e.g., disadvantaged families and disadvantaged or high-pressure schools). One million 12- to 17-year-olds become pregnant each year and one in five uses drugs more than once a week. There are more and more runaways, more violent acts committed by adolescents, and more suicides. While suicide rates for adults have remained static, rates for adolescents and young adults 15 to 24 years old began rising in the mid-1950s and had tripled by 1978. Some 5,000 adolescents now take their lives each year. Suicide rates for 10- to 14-year-olds have tripled as well and psychiatrists report increased suicidal behavior—from fantasies and threats to attempts and deaths—in children ages 6 to 12.

What are some of the reasons for these alarming statistics? One reason offered by sociologists pertains to the family unit. Today's family is typically dual career, single parent, or step-parent. In 1950, 24% of wives worked outside of the home. In 1980, more than 50% of wives did so; 21% of families with children are single-parent families, 90% of which are headed by females. It has been suggested that a result of this change in the family unit is that child-mother dependency has been replaced by early independence. We have gone from the "age of protection" to the "age of preparation" (Winn, 1983). Elkind (1981) refers to today's children as "hurried children." They have to achieve success early or they are regarded as losers. "Schools divide the young into winners and losers and then train them to accept their roles" (Sebald, 1981, p. 53). Children suffer from fears and the consequences of failure. Unfortunately, it is predicted that this trend will continue well into the 21st century, which will be marked by an intensification of the pressures and fears that characterize contemporary times.

According to David Elkind, we have a society that puts emphasis on early achievement. Parents in turn require achievement from their children without offsetting these demands with a comparable level of support. This leads to a disequilibrium in the parent-child contract. Parents want and expect more from their children today than they did 30 years ago but they are less willing or able to help their children cope with the resultant stress.

In summary, what we have is a situation in which:

1. *The family unit is changing.* Because of several factors, such as the increase in divorce rates, unem-

ployment, and economic inflation, as well as the growing feminist awareness, the two-parent family where Dad works and Mom stays home to be with the children at least until they begin junior or senior high school (or, in some cases, until they begin college) is becoming the exception rather than the rule.

2. *There is more stress in the home.* Parents are exposed to more and more stress in the workplace and tend to bring this stress home (where it's safe to displace it) and thus create more stress for their children. This makes it especially difficult for single parents who have to deal with stress at work as well as in the home, usually without the support they need.

3. *Children are being exposed to more stress at an earlier age and are less able to cope with it.* As the family unit of the past (Dad the breadwinner and Mom the protector) evolves to the family unit of the present (either Dad or Mom is both breadwinner and protector), children in the family are exposed to more stress at an earlier age. And they are not able to cope. Their parents also serve as negative models. If Mom or Dad is coping with stress by yelling, drinking, being physically aggressive, or doing drugs, or is withdrawing in front the television, in back of a newspaper, or behind a closed door, children will probably learn to cope with their stress in much the same way. The problem is that adult society doesn't approve of children who yell at their parents or teachers or act physically aggressive or engage in substance abuse or act withdrawn. We tend to label them "behavior disordered" or "seriously emotionally disturbed."

Through commercialism and the media, society is putting more pressure on today's youth to grow up faster. Madison Avenue doesn't take the laws of nature into account. When you are young, you are less able to cope with stress by virtue of your limited experiences, cognitive ability, and skills, but that doesn't matter if you are insulated by your family from a great deal of life stress and don't have to worry about things like jobs and sex and being assertive with friends and getting a scholarship. As you grow older, you naturally will have more experiences, learn new skills, and develop cognitively, while at the same time, your family will insulate you from stress less and less. This is the natural order of things. Even during the Middle Ages when children left their homes in the country to live in the city and work as apprentices at 12 and 14 years of age, they still lived with a family, usually the family of the person they were apprenticed to. They had surrogate parents (a mother and a father) and surrogate siblings who assumed responsibility for insulating them from the stress of life until they were ready to cope. Today, this

is not the case. Many of today's adolescents have learned to expect the freedom they think comes with being an adult although they are unprepared to accept adult responsibilities. This attitude often puts them into direct conflict with the parent or parents who attempt to set limits. The result is more stress.

On one hand, they are getting messages from a number of sources (peer group, parents, society, media) telling them to grow up fast (how many times have you told a child, "Will you just grow up!"), while on the other hand, they are neither willing nor able to take on the responsibilities of being grown up. This brings them into conflict with their environment.

What I've presented so far is a broad, sociological view of the problem of stress in children. Now let's look at what this has to do with behavior management. There is evidence that a large number of students with chronic behavior problems have also experienced chronic life stress. For example, in an epidemiological study of the mental health of children in midtown Manhattan, Gersten et al. (1974) found that parent ratings of a variety of child adjustment problems correlated significantly with the parents' reports of stressful life events occurring during the previous year. Felner et al. (1975) found that 20% of students identified by teachers as having adjustment problems had a family history that included either a parental divorce, separation, or death. More specifically, students with a history of parent separation or divorce rated high in acting-out behaviors while students with a history of parent death rated high in shy-anxious behaviors. Sandler & Block (1979) investigated the relationship between life stress events and adjustment problems perceived in inner-city elementary students. They hypothesized that students identified by teachers as having adjustment problems had experienced more recent stress events than matched controls and that the amount of stress would correlate positively with both parent and teacher ratings of the child adjustment problems. They studied 99 students in kindergarten through third grade who had been identified by their teachers in four inner-city elementary schools as manifesting some social-emotional adjustment problem in the classroom. Results demonstrated evidence of a relationship between recent life stress events and the adjustment problems of young inner-city elementary students. Both hypotheses were supported by the results.

As further evidence of a link between stress and behavior problems in children and youth, when Johnson & McCutcheon (1980) developed and standardized their Life Events Checklist, they found that negative life stress, particularly among females, correlated significantly with general maladjustment.

While there is a great deal of evidence that stress and maladjustment in childhood go hand in hand, is there any evidence of a causal relationship? Chandler (1985) argues that much of the maladaptive behavior we see in the schools is the *direct result* of the life stress events that children experience both in and out of school. In many instances, these behaviors may actually be coping mechanisms, although inappropriate and inefficient ones; most likely they are coping mechanisms that have been modeled in frequent or dramatic fashion by a significant other (e.g., parent, teacher, peer, or sibling). If this theory is valid, we need to teach our students more appropriate ways of coping with stress. By doing this, we may not only help them to reduce the deleterious effects of stress but also weaken their maladaptive (coping) behavior.

Many benefits may be derived from teaching stress management to our students. Most of the stress coping skills are also self-management skills. They require that the individual apply the skill to and for himself. He can't rely on someone else to apply the skill for him. It's not like having a counselor or a doctor or teacher do something to you or for you. You must do it yourself. Therefore, in the process of learning how to cope with stress, students will also become more self-reliant. The more self-reliant they become, the less external their locus of control will be and the more responsibility they will ultimately take for their behavior.

Teaching Stress Management Strategies to Students

The following is a list of suggestions I have for teachers who wish to teach stress management strategies to their students.

1. First, you need to teach some basic concepts regarding stress and stress management. For example, you will need to define terms such as *stress, stressor, eustress,* and *distress.* Most people confuse *stress* with *stressor.* A stressor is an event (e.g., being teased by peers or failing a test) that usually leads to stress. Stress itself is the physiological response we experience depending upon how threatened we are by the stressor and how much control we believe we have over it. For example, some students are likely to feel more threatened by peer teasing than others; as a result, they will experience more stress than their peers. Students with an external locus of control will probably tend to experience more stress than their more internal peers simply because they believe they have less control over the stressors they encounter in their lives.

2. You also should teach your students that not all stress is bad. The stress we experience in scoring the winning touchdown or seeing our team score the winning touchdown is good stress. It's called *eustress,* as

in *euphoria.* However, the stress we feel when somebody teases us or we are taking a test we are sure we're going to fail is bad stress. It's called *distress* because it is negative or disabling. Students need to learn the difference between the two and also to understand that sometimes distress can be helpful. For example, when Jane is confronted by a bully, the distress she feels can produce the necessary changes in her body to help her escape the bully (i.e., run away so fast the bully can't catch her) or fight the bully (i.e., stand up for her rights and not get hurt). What we want to avoid is distress that is so disabling that it keeps us from escaping or fighting for our rights.

3. You should also teach your students about the physiological changes that occur during times of stress. The stress response is referred to in the literature as the general adaptation syndrome (G.A.S.) (Selye, 1976), and it is particularly important that your students understand the first stage in the G.A.S., the alarm reaction. An analogy often used to explain the alarm reaction describes the response of a primitive hunter following the trail of a wounded and dangerous predator. As the hunter follows the tracks of the predator, his stress level is high enough to keep him alert but not so high that he will run away or charge ahead at the sound of a broken twig. Finally, the trail ends at the entrance of a dark cave and the hunter's stress level increases. Again, it is not so high that he will charge into the cave or be frozen with indecision outside. As he enters the cave, he hears a low growling and can see the eyes of the wounded prehistoric cat glowing in the dark. As these eyes seem to move toward him and the growling gets louder, the hunter's stress level rises. He is now experiencing stage 1 of the G.A.S., the alarm reaction. This stage is commonly referred to as the fight or flight stage. Here are some of the things that are happening to his body: (a) his pupils dilate to let in more light so that he can see in the dark better, (b) his heart beats faster to pump more blood and life-giving oxygen to his muscles, (c) his muscles tense to better serve as armor protecting his vital organs in case of attack and also to better enable him to spring into action (either run away or stay and fight), (d) his blood undergoes chemical changes that increase clotting time just in case he is wounded, and (e) his throat and nasal passages dry up so that more oxygen can be taken in. There are several other changes that occur as well.

Your purpose in discussing all of this with your students is to communicate the important role stress plays in our lives. From early man to modern man, the fight or flight response has served us well as a survival mechanism when we have needed it. However, the average person in a highly industrialized society hasn't needed the fight or flight response as much as our early ancestors. We don't have to hunt for our food. We can go to the supermarket and buy it. There is usually nothing that happens at the supermarket that is so threatening to us that it evokes the fight or flight response required by the prehistoric hunter. Your students need to learn that while the fight or flight response is instinctive in all of us (i.e., we are born with it), we can learn to control it so that it doesn't disable us, and learning stress management skills is the way to do this.

4. Another concept you should teach your students is that we can't always escape from stress by running away from the stressor. You can't always run away from an angry dog on your paper route. Eventually, you will have to talk to the dog's owner. You can't always run away from the school bully. Sooner or later, you are going to have to confront your fear and do something about the bully. You can quit your paper route or fake being sick or play hooky from school but in the long run, these are poor solutions. There are too many angry dogs and bullies in this world. As soon as you get rid of one, you'll probably run into another. No matter where you go, you're bound to find similar stressors, and you'd better learn to deal with them or you'll be running all of your life. Some examples of stressors students typically run away from are (a) teachers ("If only I had a different teacher."), (b) schools ("If only I was in a different school."), (c) authority ("If only I didn't have to do what people tell me to."), and (d) responsibility ("If only I didn't have so much work."). Try to get your students to tell you why these are all unrealistic statements. For example, there is no place they can go where they won't find authority and responsibility. Even if they escaped from teachers and schoolwork by quitting school, they would just have to substitute a boss and work on a job, which might be harder. The basic idea you are teaching here is that stressors are everywhere and you can't escape them.

5. Effective stress management requires a holistic approach. You can't focus on one thing or keep trying old methods that work only with some stressors. Your students must learn a variety of strategies and know when to use them (as well as how). They will have to modify how they feel as well as what they think and how they act (behave). This holistic approach to stress management may be seen in Figure 11.1. Somatic-physiological interventions are used to modify stress directly and have a direct effect on the stress response. Cognitive-psychological interventions are used primarily to modify our thoughts, attitudes, beliefs, and self-talk with regard to stressors. Social-behavioral interventions are used to modify our overt responses to stressors. Your students should know how to use all three types of interventions. In addition, they must learn when to use them: before, during, and after encountering stressors. They also should learn that they can't use these strategies away from the stressor or after the stressful event is over. If they do not, they will develop an escapist attitude ("If only I wasn't here." "I can't wait to get outta here and smoke some dope." "Beam me up, Scotty.").

6. It is important for your students to understand that stress is cumulative and that people are often better able to deal with one big stressor than with several small stressors. Use the analogy of the straw breaking the camel's back or the boxer using several combinations of punches instead of one knockout punch. You can demonstrate the concept by having your students build a pyramid by piling objects of the same weight and size as high as they can. Eventually, something has to give. This concept is important to understand because any one stressor that can be eliminated from their daily lives may reduce the total stress they experience; since each stressor may be small, it should be relatively easy to eliminate just one. Once your students know that they are better off working on one stressor at a time, they can begin by working on the easiest one to fix.

7. Also, you should teach the conceptual framework behind cognitively mediated stress using Ellis's A-B-C model to illustrate that events (A) do not produce stress (C); it is what we say to ourselves (B) about the stressors that produces stress. Use pictures (cartoons) whenever possible to dramatize concepts. Examples may be seen in Figures 11.2 and 11.3.

8. Hold a brainstorming session early on to generate a list of as many student stressors as possible. Figure 11.4 is a sample list of stressors commonly experienced by children and youth. Ask your students to identify the two or three stressors that create the most stress for them. This should provide you with enough potential stressors to focus on during the school year. Once you have identified the stressors your students need to work on, you might have them list, name, or identify their affective (emotional or feeling) and behavioral responses to each stressor. You may first have to teach them how to monitor their emotional and behavioral responses to stressors and collect some baseline data. Show them how to monitor their stress levels by subjectively assigning values (numbers) to each level. One system for doing this is referred to as subjective units of distress, or SUD (Wolpe, 1969). Students are taught that their SUD level can be as low as 1 (very calm and relaxed) or as high as 10 (extremely distressed). They are shown how to calibrate this internal "instrument" so that at any given time, they can assign a number to their stress level. Sitting around the house at night watching television might produce a SUD level of 2 or 3; this number may be higher if they're watching something frightening or exciting or if their parents are fighting in the next room.

	To Create Least Stressful Environment	To Maintain Least Stressful Environment	To Restore Least Stressful Environment
Means / Ends	Situations in which potential stressors are kept to a minimum and/or individual is inoculated against deleterious effects of stress.	Situations in which stressors are present but individual is coping adequately.	Situations in which individual has experienced difficulty coping with stressors.
Somatic-Physiological	Exercise Progressive relaxation (PRT) Proper diet Stress inoculation	Diaphragmatic breathing Progressive relaxation (PRT) Stress inoculation	Exercise Diaphragmatic breathing
Cognitive-Psychological	Cognitive restructuring	Self-instruction Problem solving	Thought stopping
Social-Behavioral	Time management	Behavioral self-control Assertiveness training Social skills training	

Figure 11.1. "Holistic" stress management curriculum for children and youth.

Being asked to stand up in class and give a report or calling someone for a date might result in a SUD level of 8 or 9. Have your students keep logs on their SUD levels by writing down the stressor, when it occurred, and the SUD level it produced. They must do this over a period of several days in order to effectively calibrate their subjective measures. Ask them periodically during the day what their SUD levels are. This experience will put them in touch with their bodies and build an awareness of physiological stress, which is a prerequisite for change. In order to reduce their stress they must first become aware of it; the sooner they become aware of it, the easier it will be to reduce it. Keeping a log will also make your students more aware of the stressors they encounter and which ones produce the most stress for them.

Stress Coping Skills

Somatic-Physiological Skills

Somatic-physiological stress coping skills produce a direct effect on the body. They are the easiest skills to learn and they produce the fastest results. Three examples of somatic-physiological skills your students can learn are *diaphragmatic breathing, progressive relaxation training,* and *exercise.* Diaphragmatic breathing and progressive relaxation training may be used before (in anticipation of), during, or after experiences with stressors. Exercise can protect you against the harmful effects of stress and is especially beneficial after experiencing a stressor.

Diaphragmatic Breathing. I suggest you begin training your students in diaphragmatic breathing since it is the easiest technique to learn and requires the least amount of discipline to master. Some of your students may already engage in diaphragmatic breathing. In order to find out how your students breathe, have them close their eyes, put one hand on their chest and the other on their abdomen, and breathe naturally for 30 seconds or so. Ask them to notice whether their chest or their abdomen rises and falls when they breathe. Explain that diaphragmatic (abdominal) breathing is better than thoracic (chest) breathing because they obtain more oxygen by breathing through their diaphragm. If you are working with younger students and they have trouble remembering terms, you might want to refer to diaphragmatic breathing simply as "belly breathing." In belly breathing, the belly rises (pushes out) when you inhale and falls (pulls in) when you exhale. Have your students practice this regularly for several minutes during the day. If possible, they should lie on the floor when they do this as it will increase the relaxation

Figure 11.2. Example of picture used to illustrate concept of cognitively mediated stress (rational fear).

Figure 11.3. Example of picture used to illustrate concept of cognitively mediated stress (irrational fear).

death of parent
death of sibling or close friend
death of relative
divorce or separation of parents
sibling leaves home
moving
parent fighting
substance abuse (parent and/or sibling)
illness (of parent, sibling, child)
parent out of work
loss of pet
new school
failure in school
physical appearance problems (complexion, clothes, height, weight, sexual development, etc.)
poverty
victimization by peers
lack of proper nutrition
holidays
loss of friends (moved away)
test anxiety
new sibling (natural or step-siblings)
new parents
sports-related pressure
new job (of parent)
parent away from home often
puberty
injury to self or significant other
placement in special education
dating
learning to drive
peer pressure (drugs, sex, tobacco, alcohol, cheating, stealing, skipping classes or school, etc.)
witnessing traumatic events
graduation
punishment
finding job
control from authority
responsibility for siblings
homework
breaking up of relationship

Figure 11.4. Common stressors experienced by children and youth.

produced. Your next step will be to demonstrate how belly breathing can effectively produce relaxation. Put the students in some mild to moderate anxiety-provoking situations such as standing in front of their peers and talking or talking to someone in class they don't know very well. Have them concentrate on their SUD levels. When they feel their SUD level rising, have them stop what they are doing and practice their belly breathing while they continue to monitor their SUD levels. This simple but dramatic exercise demonstrates the efficacy of belly breathing and, more significantly, each student's ability to gain control over his or her stress level. Next, have your students make a list of situations when they might use belly breathing; again, have them keep a log over several days that includes stressors, SUD levels, and perceived efficacy in reducing stress and producing relaxation.

Progressive Relaxation Training (PRT). Once the students have mastered belly breathing and fully appreciate the effectiveness of relaxation in managing their stress, you can move on to training in progressive relaxation (Jacobson, 1929). PRT is more difficult to learn than belly breathing but once it has been mastered, it produces a deeper and longer-lasting state of relaxation. PRT is much more involved than belly breathing. It is based on the principle of reciprocal inhibition, which simply means that a muscle cannot be in a relaxed state and a tensed state at the same time (Wolpe, 1958). By alternately making your muscles tense and relaxed, you learn to recognize the sometimes subtle differences between the states; you also learn to relax all of your muscles. As it becomes easier to recognize tension in your body, you will be able to use PRT to achieve a more total and longer-lasting level of relaxation. Naturally, this takes time; the biggest problem you will have is getting your students to practice it to the point where its benefits will provide enough motivation to continue practicing it. I have included a relaxation script in Appendix F for teaching students progressive relaxation. Your students should receive 15 to 20 minutes of supervised practice daily (in class) over a period of several weeks in order to achieve the desired results.

Exercise. Exercise is also an effective stress coping skill. There is some evidence that aerobic exercise (i.e., rhythmic, reciprocal movement that keeps the heart working at a predetermined "training" rate) will not only have a "tranquilizing" effect in reducing stress; it will also lead to a concomitant reduction of maladaptive behaviors (Allen, 1980; Kobasa et al., 1982; Shipman, 1984). Exercises such as jogging, roller skating, cycling, and fast walking can all be done at school. Enlist the cooperation of your physical education teachers or do it yourself. Make sure you teach your students how to compute and monitor their training heart rate before beginning your exercise program (see Figure 11.5). Remember what I said earlier about your being a coping model and participate in the belly breathing, PRT, or exercise programs with your students.

Cognitive-Psychological Skills

Cognitive-psychological stress coping skills are more difficult to learn than somatic-physiological skills. They may even be more difficult to learn than many social-behavioral skills. This should not, however, deter you from teaching them to your students. If your stress management program is going to have a long-lasting effect on your students' stress, it is imperative that they learn how to change their minds as well as their bodies. Skills such as cognitive restructuring and problem solving, covered in chapter 9, may be applied to the reduc-

1. Begin with the number 220 (don't ask me why but this is the magic number).

2. Have students subtract their chronological age (CA) from 220. The result is the maximum heart rate (MHR).

3. Have students take their resting pulse. The best way to do this is to use the pulse in the wrist (or the neck) upon awakening in the morning and before getting out of bed. Otherwise, have them take their pulse after sitting quietly for a while and practicing diaphragmatic breathing until they perceive themselves to be relaxed.

4. Have students subtract their resting heart rate (RHR) from their MHR. The result is their resting heart rate reserve (RHR reserve).

5. Have students multiply their RHR reserve by 0.60 (60%) and 0.70 (70%) respectively.

6. Have students add their RHR to the respective products computed in step 5. This is their training heart rate (THR), lower and upper range. In order to gain the tranquilizing effect of exercise, your students should engage in aerobic exercise with their pulse rate somewhere between the lower and upper range of their THR for a minimum of 20 continuous minutes per day, 3 days per week.

Example: Joey is a 12-year-old student with a resting pulse rate of 72. Subtracting 12 (CA) from 220 = 208 (MHR) minus 72 (RHR) = 136 (RHR reserve) times 0.60 = 81.60 plus 72 (RHR) = 153.60 (rounded off to 154). This is the lower end of Joey's training heart rate (THR). Multiply Joey's RHR of 136 by 0.70 = 95.20 plus 72 (RHR) = 167.20 (rounded off to 167). This is the upper end of Joey's THR. When Joey exercises, he should try to keep his pulse rate somewhere between 154 and 167 in order to achieve the tranquilizing effect. A simple way for Joey to check his pulse during exercise is to take it (in his wrist or neck) for 6 seconds (count beats while looking at a sweep second hand) and multiply the number of beats he gets in 6 seconds by 10 to get his rate per minute. Ideally, it should be somewhere between 154 and 167.

Figure 11.5. Computing training heart rate for use in aerobic exercise program.

tion of stress. Students can learn how their beliefs and attitudes (i.e., self-talk) contribute to their high levels of anxiety or anger and how they can modify these debilitating emotions by disputing irrational beliefs and generating rational self-talk. They can also learn that proficiency in problem solving can lead to a reduction in stress levels, since they will be less likely to be threatened by stressors (i.e., problems) and more likely to feel in control of the situation or its outcome. Cognitive-psychological skills may be used before, during, or after encountering stressors.

Social-Behavioral Skills

These stress coping skills include all of the verbal and other overt behaviors required by the student to manage stress through the manipulation of his or her environment. They might include some social skills such as acting assertively in response to criticism (e.g., teasing) or manipulation (e.g., peer pressure). They might also include something as simple as time management. Students can be taught how to set both short- and long-term goals as well as to determine which activities to spend time on in order to realize those goals. Students should also be encouraged to monitor the activities they currently engage in as well as the time they spend on each. It may be that they need to reprioritize and spend less time on some activities, such as television watching or socializing on the telephone, and more time on others, such as homework, reading, and exercising.

Stress Inoculation: An Integrative Strategy

Two stress reactions that teachers most often observe in their students are anger and anxiety. Stress inoculation is a relatively new intervention that appears to be effective in managing anger and anxiety as well as depression in children and youth (Meichenbaum, 1985). It is considered an integrative strategy because it integrates or combines several different skills and involves a number of steps or stages. These are: (1) the *conceptual framework stage* where the student is taught basic concepts regarding stress and stress management; (2) the *relaxation training stage* where the student learns to master some form of relaxation training, usually PRT; (3) the *cognitive restructuring stage* where the student disputes any irrational beliefs that might be contributing to her high levels of anxiety or anger; (4) the *stress script stage* where the student writes down everything he needs to say or do to manage his stress before, during, and after being exposed to the stressor; and (5) the *inoculation stage* in which the student uses her stress script as she is gradually exposed to larger and larger "doses" of the stressor.

The conceptual framework stage involves teaching students some basic precepts regarding anger (or anxiety) and the relationship between what happens to us (A), what we believe about it (B), and how we feel and behave (C). Figure 11.6 is a list of anger management principles adapted from the work of Novaco (1975). After discussing these principles with your students, move on to the relaxation phase of stress inoculation. To save some time, you may want, initially, to limit this training to belly breathing, or you may begin this phase at the same time you start the conceptual framework phase.

1. Anger sometimes is a cover-up for feeling scared. You should ask yourself, "Am I angry or am I anxious (scared)?"

2. Don't take insults personally. Stay on task. Do what you must to get what you want without getting sidetracked. People will sometimes insult you to bait you into a quarrel in order to get you off task.

3. Sometimes we get angry because we don't know what to do. Once you learn other ways to act besides getting angry, you won't have to get angry.

4. Learn to recognize the signs of anger, such as dry mouth, hot skin, or tense muscles, as soon as they start. It will be easier to relax these feelings away if you catch them early.

5. Use your anger to work for you. Like pain, anger is a signal that something is wrong. It could be that your thinking is wrong and needs changing.

6. Sometimes we get angry because we are afraid that we're losing control. Remember, when you give in to your anger, you have already lost control.

7. It's not what happens to you that makes you angry. It's what you say to yourself about what happens that makes you angry. No one has the power to make you angry but you. No one has the power to get rid of your anger but you.

8. Be nice to yourself and others. Anger hurts.

Figure 11.6. Anger management principles for students. *Note.* Adapted from Novaco, 1975.

After the relaxation phase, introduce cognitive restructuring. During this phase your students monitor those events (A) that they associate with their anger and try to identify any cognitions (e.g., beliefs or automatic thoughts) that these events seem to trigger. This is difficult; prior exposure to cognitive restructuring is helpful. Once your students are able to identify the self-talk associated with their anger reactions, they need to dispute this thinking and generate fair-pair rational self-talk in place of the irrational self-talk. When your students have generated rational self-talk, they will be ready for the next stage of stress inoculation, writing the stress script. The stress script consists of everything the student says and does before, during, and after encountering the anger-provoking stressor. Figure 11.7 is a sample of a stress script a student might use to cope with anger provoked by peer teasing.

The final step in stress inoculation is actually to use the stress script in an anger-provoking situation. First, have the students simply sit and imagine themselves using the script in an anger-provoking situation, both before, during, and after the situation. They should visualize the script helping them control their anger. This will help them memorize the script as well as give them confidence in actually using it. A behavioral

How self-talk fuels anger.

The following is an example of a stress script that might be used to help a student manage her or his anger in the face of peer teasing (e.g., name-calling such as "retard," "faggot," "stupid").

Before (confrontations with peers):

"What do I have to do? Take a few belly breaths to get ready. This is going to be hard but I can do it. I just have to remember to take deep breaths and keep telling myself the magic words, 'saying it doesn't make it so.' Here they come. I'm ready for them."

During (confrontation):

"Stay cool. Saying it doesn't make it so. Take some deep breaths. Watch my SUD level. Saying it doesn't make it so. Just ignore them. Look away. Saying it doesn't make it so. Saying it doesn't make it so."

After (confrontation):

"I did it! I kept myself from getting angry. It worked. I can control myself. They didn't tease me as much as they usually do. Pretty soon they won't tease me at all. Now let's see . . . was there anything I could improve on for next time?"

Figure 11.7. Example of stress script for use in anger management (stress inoculation) program.

rehearsal follows in which the students use their scripts in a "safe" role-playing situation that simulates the anger-provoking event. If the students are able to use their scripts to keep their SUD levels down during several of the role-playing situations, they can be given the green light to use their scripts in a live situation. During the behavioral rehearsal, various elements or conditions can change gradually so that the role-playing situation more closely resembles the actual situation that produces anger in the students. Students might be exposed to a progressively larger group of peers who tease them, or a progressively longer period of teasing, or an increasing number of phrases used in teasing (i.e., insults). Another gradual change can be the types of insults used. Target students might be given the opportunity ahead of time to preview and censor the insults used. As students get better at controlling their anger, they might be given less (or no) opportunity to censor insults. Students should be encouraged to work with the teacher in developing a hierarchy of stress-provoking situations such as the one illustrated in Figure 11.8.

First Situation:

Students call me names but I get to choose the students and the names they call me.

I write the names on a list and they can't call me any names that aren't on the list.

They can't do this for more than 1 minute; if I say stop before the minute is up, they must stop.

Second Situation:

Students call me names; teacher chooses the students but I still get to choose the names they call me.

I write the names on a list and they can't call me any names that aren't on the list.

They can't do this for more than 1 minute; they don't have to stop before the minute is up even if I tell them to.

Third Situation:

Students call me names; teacher chooses the students and they get to choose the names they call me.

They write the names on a list and clear them with the teacher; they can't call me any names that aren't on the list.

Fourth Situation:

Students call me names; teacher chooses the students and they get to choose the names they call me.

They don't have to clear the names with the teacher ahead of time.

Fifth Situation:

(This is the same as the fourth situation, but it lasts longer.)

Figure 11.8. Example of a hierarchy of anger-provoking role-playing situations for use in a stress inoculation program.

Chapter Eleven Self-Assessment

See Appendix A for acceptable responses.

1. Explain the rationale for teaching stress management skills to children and youth.

2. Explain the differences between *stress* and *stressors, eustress* and *distress.*

3. Describe the physiological changes that occur during the alarm reaction (fight or flight) stage of Selye's general adaptation syndrome.

4. Explain what a SUD level is and how it is determined.

5. List at least one somatic-physiological stress management skill that could be used for each of the following:

    a.   Before (in anticipation of) stress:

    b.   During stress:

    c.   After stress:

6. List at least one cognitive-psychological stress management skill that could be used for each of the following:

    a.   Before (in anticipation of) stress:

    b.   During stress:

    c.   After stress:

continued next page

7. List at least one social-behavioral stress management skill that could be used for each of the following:

   a.   Before (in anticipation of) stress:

   b.   During stress:

8. List at least 10 stressors commonly experienced by children and youth.

9. Describe Meichenbaum's stress inoculation approach to anger management.

Part IV
Creating Change in Environments

chapter 12

Ecological Interventions
by Barbara L. Drainville

Upon successful completion of this chapter, the learner will be able to:

1. Define the term *ecological intervention*
2. Replicate the Anticipated Effect Chart
3. Give examples of each type of intervention on the Anticipated Effect Chart
4. Define natural and logical consequences and give examples
5. Describe prevention and intervention in the early-childhood classroom
6. Describe prevention and intervention in the elementary classroom
7. Describe prevention and intervention in the special education setting
8. Design an ecological intervention

Ecological interventions are based upon an analysis of the environment that supports maladaptive behavior. There are numerous ecological factors that affect a student's behavior in the classroom over which the teacher has little control. This chapter will focus on the factors within the classroom and school setting that the teacher can affect.

Intervention Decisions

There are a limited number of choices when it comes to goals for behavioral interventions: increasing or accelerating adaptive behaviors, decreasing or decelerating deviant behaviors, teaching incompatible behaviors (fair pair), or extinction. The creativity potential for designing these interventions is infinite. The basic principles are always the same: increase the adaptive, internally controlled behaviors that enable the child to be successful in all his or her ecological niches, and decrease or extinguish those behaviors that evoke negative environmental sanctions. To effect these behavioral changes,

the ecobehavioral analyst will look at what can be changed in the environment to help the child gain control of her or his behavior.

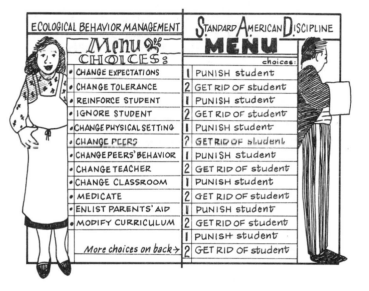

You pays your money . . . you takes your choice.

Figure 12.1 shows a handy chart to use for choosing interventions and stimulating creative interventions. I often use it with teams to develop ecological interventions. This chart enables you to graphically show the interventions you prefer, the ones that have been used in the past, and the ones that may be used next. I prefer to use rewards whenever possible, for a number of reasons—they are usually the most effective, they fit my particular set of biases, the options are almost infinite, and it usually is easy for children to see the connection between an action and its reaction. Cost reinforcement and negative reinforcement generally take some logical reasoning on the part of both the adult and the child; they require more effort for consistency, particularly in the fading stage on the schedule of reinforcement. Punishment options are very limited and should be used sparingly. Punishment is not the most effective way to get a student's attention and provide motivation for the

To Increase or Decrease a Behavior

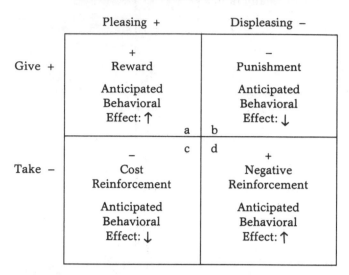

a. To give something pleasing is a reward, or positive reinforcement; it will tend to increase the behavior linked with it.

b. To give something displeasing is punishment; it will tend to decrease the behavior linked with it.

c. To take away something pleasing is a cost; it will tend to decrease the behavior linked with it.

d. To take away something displeasing is negative reinforcement; it will tend to increase the behavior linked with it.

Figure 12.1. Choices available for interventions.

student to find other solutions. Only so much punishment can be given, and it usually escalates, since negative emotions on the part of the child and the adult quickly become engaged.

There are a few types of increasing and decreasing interventions that are particularly effective. One is the fair-pair program: increasing an adaptive behavior that replaces or is incompatible with the deviant behavior, which is then decreased. See chapter 7 for an in-depth discussion of this strategy.

For example, during one school year, I was plagued by a group of boys who would throw balls at my windows. This frequently happened at lunch, while I was taking a break and doing data analysis in my classroom. Every time, I'd dash out to catch the offenders, but they were long gone by the time I got outside. Usually a group of boys was playing ball on the playground near my room. Since I was unable to catch the offender, I told the boys that if it happened again, I'd take the ball. In that way the group would put peer pressure on the

guilty student. The first time it happened, the boys quickly identified the offender in order to ransom their ball. Later that afternoon, I explained the situation to the ringleader's teacher and asked her to send him to my room. Imagine his surprise, and relief, when I asked for his help. I explained the problem with the ball on the window and asked him to watch for the guilty party for me. I told him that every day that I was able to work without the interruption of the ball hitting the window, I'd reward him after school. There was never another incident, and after a while, I faded the reinforcement.

Natural and Logical Consequences

Natural and logical consequences are an integral part of ecological interventions, because they can be built into the classroom environment. The antecedents and consequences can be designed to be as natural or as logical as possible. A *natural* consequence is one that occurs as a result of the behavior and the laws of nature; for example, if a child touches a hot stove, the natural consequence is that she will be burned. This type of consequence is very consistent; it is unlikely to require extraordinary intervention on the part of the teacher. In this case, the primary concern is the element of danger. No one would allow a child to be injured to teach her not to touch a hot stove!

A *logical* consequence is one that is a logical outcome of the student's behavior, allowing the behavior and consequence to be easily linked in the child's mind. A logical consequence may be planned and executed by someone else, but it is often the result of situational contingencies. For instance, a child may deliberately break his pencil and be unable to do his work. If the classroom contingency is that all students' work must be completed before they go out to recess, the student will suffer a logical consequence. He will miss recess because his work isn't done; his work isn't done because he broke his pencil.

This type of intervention is successful for a number of reasons: (1) it is fair, because it applies to all members of the class; (2) it is impersonal, because everyone has the same chance of earning recess; (3) it is consistent, because recess occurs every day; and (4) it is finite, because the time for recess is determined by the clock and not the teacher. One key to successful generalization is consistency. Both natural and logical consequences are likely to be consistent and therefore increase learning. They also are likely to be consistently implemented because they usually don't require extraordinary effort on the part of the teacher. Any intervention that is time consuming, unwieldy, or complicated is less likely to be used consistently; teachers are just too busy.

Generalization

Ecobehavioral analysis can solve one of the most frequent problems with behavioral interventions: generalization. Because the interventions designed with this method take into account all of the environmental factors affecting the behavior, generalization is easier to plan. Many ecobehavioral interventions must include multiple-setting interventions in order to ensure generalization.

Ethics

Using ecobehavioral analysis to change existing behavior is an ethical application of the principles of behavior management: It "blames" the environment or patterns of interactions, rather than the child. It also focuses on the various factors in the environment that can be changed to stop evoking or maintaining the behavior, and it may be less intrusive than other types of intervention. A rule of thumb that I use, "less is more," is very applicable in these types of interventions. Often, the last factor on which I impinge is the child. This minimalist philosophy is in the spirit of the "least restrictive environment" provision of Public Law 94-142, a federal law that mandates service to all handicapped students. This approach is also less likely to lead to a large number of individual programs for the regular classroom teachers.

When planning interventions, particularly with children, you must be absolutely clear on what your biases are, as they are bound to shape the types of interventions you choose. They will even affect the way you view the various factors that form the ecology of the child's behavior.

The Early Childhood Environment

Prevention

The creation of a positive classroom environment with fair and few rules goes a long way toward preventing rather than provoking disturbing behavior. The physical environment must reflect the developmental level of the students. An early-childhood program should look very different from a regular elementary classroom. For example, there should be smaller furniture and equipment reflecting the sensory-motor and preoperational levels of children aged 3 to 5.

The classroom should have discrete areas; the block or construction area should be easily distinguished from the manipulative and role-playing area. Children of this age need external organization and classification to order their thinking. Shelves and bins for storage of materials and supplies should be clearly marked with pictures. Many tantrums at this age are a result of feeling overwhelmed or overstimulated by the environment. Of course the materials should be attractive, complete, and developmentally geared for 2- to 7-year-olds. Having a range of developmental levels to choose from can prevent behaviors precipitated by feelings of boredom or inadequacy. There should always be something for the child to do that satisfies the drive to learn. Thwarting that drive is certainly a good way to evoke disruptive behavior!

There should be areas of the room where the children can use their large muscles, even during inclement weather, as the preschool years are geared for active play. Children of this age also need a sense of space so they do not feel crowded and aggressive. The body-image concepts of many preschool children are not yet firm. Some may not have developed lateral dominance. If you don't know which hand to use, how can you be expected to know where your feet are?

Children also need a quiet or rest area in which to read or dream or cuddle with a comfort toy. This is an appropriate way to teach time out, as a time away from others to avoid getting into conflicts and to sort out your feelings before you interact. And sometimes a child just needs to be shy.

The schedule should also reflect the needs of children this age, alternating between quiet and active periods. It's the rare preschooler who can sit for longer than 20 minutes, even during music. The greatest chunk of the schedule should be devoted to choice time, so that the children can pace themselves. This also means that the child who is focused on a developmentally critical activity will have time to repeat it as often as necessary. Adults have already completed their developmental stages and cannot feel the same rhythms and urges that children do. Allow them the time they need, and you'll have fewer behaviors to change. Piaget, Montessori, and other early-childhood theorists describe this as the "critical" or "sensitive" period, when children learn how to learn. By allowing the children to feel their own rhythms, you're shaping their lifelong learning habits. There are times when transitions will have to be made each day, but this can be eased by a number of strategies. An assurance that tomorrow is coming, with another choice time, will help. Preschool children often have little understanding of time. "It's time" is a cue that will take the onus away from the adult. In fact, the timer, a bonging clock, or some other timekeeper is a preschool teacher's friend. Transitions are difficult for all of us, especially when we're engaged in something really reinforcing. By giving the children a little forewarning: "This much time until cleanup," you enable them to gain a measure of predictability. Just think how frustrating it would be if you were always told what to do, when to do it, and how! Children have little control over their lives. By making life in the classroom more predictable, you're avoiding another setup for acting out.

Interventions

Rules should be explained, modeled, and represented pictorially. There should be clear consequences for each rule. It helps to have the rules stated positively whenever possible. Often the particulars of the rules will have to be demonstrated. Children of the preschool age do not always generalize.

One of the ways to create an environment that is not evocative of deviant behaviors is to anticipate potential—that is, developmentally likely—behaviors. Using inanimate objects is one way to demonstrate the consequences before the child acts deviantly. This is in keeping with the learning aspect of behaviorism. Another way to foster a "good behavior" ecology is to reinforce incompatible behaviors. If you want children to avoid aggression, teach them other ways to solve their problems. My rules reinforce those behaviors that are conducive to an aggression-free atmosphere: (1) share, (2) play safely, (3) use words, and (4) ask. Children have a difficult time sharing, particularly during the fourth year, as independence and competence blossom. They do not want anyone taking their possessions. This enables the teacher to plan an environment in which sharing and hanging on to one's belongings are paired. Guided practice works with little children, too!

For example, Tanya may know the rule "share" but she may have difficulty sharing a specific toy ("I want to share by myself."). The use of a timer may help all the students feel "safe from grabs" if they know that the timer is in charge of how long they play with specific toys. When the timer rings, all children exchange toys or change areas.

The rule "play safely" is easily demonstrated in the classroom with the use of a stuffed toy. The teddy that falls off the climber won't break any bones. But the doctors in the role-playing area will learn what could happen if a real person fell from the climber. There are a number of ways to teach safety; I praise it specifically so that the students get the kinesthetic feel of safe play.

"Generic" interventions, those I use regularly for young children, fall basically into these categories: redirection or distraction, overcorrection, and cost. Occasionally, I will use a contingency "when . . . then," but many young children don't have a firm enough grasp of time concepts to understand anything beyond the immediate. The most potent intervention remains, of course, adult attention. It's not unusual to see 20 pre-

schoolers sit up "straight as a tailor" if one child is praised for it.

Infractions such as hitting or kicking are easier to avoid if you show the children the "kicking shelf" with its lonely little shoe that kicked Joey last year. In my room, all hitting toys and kicking shoes must go to live on the shelf. And of course, it wouldn't be safe for anyone to go out to recess without a shoe. To earn the shoe back, the child has to "make friends"—that is, make a plan of restitution to the victim. A second infraction merits the parents' intervention. Since preschool children are very possessive of their things, kicking is usually reduced to one or two incidents.

On that shelf, there also lives a styrofoam cup with a thick red line two-thirds of the way up. This is the "spitting cup," which has to be filled by a spitter before she can get out of her chair. This cup ensures that *all* the spits are gone, never to come again! I've only had to use the cup intervention twice in over 20 years. Even discussions of negative practice can have a profound effect on young children. Older children, on the other hand, would probably sit there all day because spitting would be so reinforcing. Know your developmental expectations!

Hitting is harder to diminish, because it is so "handy." We role play "use words" many times, and practice comforting each other with hugs and "sorrys." I believe in restitution for this, too, so that the child can earn back his good name. Usually the children are very creative, and often they are much harder on themselves in their restitutions than I would be.

My rule of thumb, "remove the weapon, remove the victim, remove the perpetrator," is employed frequently (and in that order) for hitting with a toy. A teacher has to be alert, but the effectiveness of "disappearing" the weapon from behind the child, while it is on the upswing, will do wonders for your illusion of magic. It's a good idea for the teacher to "punish" the weapon for hitting, or threatening to hit, by scolding: "No hitting!" once in a powerfully disapproving voice and then asking all the children not to play with a block that hits. (I usually turn my back on it with a loud "Humpf!") I teach young children to ignore an object first, as it's a lot easier than ignoring a real live person. Also, ignoring and time out should be of short duration. I estimate that 1 minute per year of age is about the limit that children can tolerate, although this limit will vary with the child. Giving the weapon a time out is also good modeling. By removing the victim and, of course, the disputed toy if possible ("Come with me, Kim. We can play over here with this."), you are ignoring the potential hitter while rescuing the child. It is important to move on quickly or you'll have Kim, the ultimate victim, on your hands.

If a child does hurt another child, silent removal to an isolated spot is best. I use a timer and come to talk to the child very briefly when it rings. I ask, "Why are you here?" and wait. It is important that children know why they are removed and understand that it is a consequence of their behavior. If necessary I restate the rule: "Play safely; it's not safe to hit." Then I ask the child to make a plan to reenter the group. I do not believe it's wise to force children to apologize, because it teaches insincerity. But I will help the child feel what the other child felt and suggest possible restitution. I've found that most preschool children are impulsive and afterward feel sad that they've hurt someone.

Books have been written on the early-childhood environment, and there is not enough space here to develop this theme in great detail. However, the simple guidelines given here demonstrate the ecological approach: Work with the developmental level of the students, supply a positive and safe environment, and create a consistent behavioral ecology. Remember that there will still be the occasional "poor fit" that will require a more extensive ecobehavioral analysis. Some children are damaged by their environments even before preschool and will need help to learn that the world is a safe place.

The Elementary Classroom Environment

The guidelines discussed in the previous section also hold true for the regular classroom. It's more difficult to control all of the variables here because of curricular expectations; the school environment with its schedule coordination of grade levels, physical education, special services, music, and other classes; the greater freedom of the students in the neighborhood; and the stronger peer impact.

The teacher's style is a critical factor and may well make the difference between success and failure for each student. Every teacher needs to know his or her learning and teaching style; biases; values; and tolerance for stress, differences in children, and disruption. These are the factors that make or break teachers, not content mastery or pretty bulletin boards.

The physical environment is important in the prevention of disturbing behavior. It is imperative that the teacher analyze each year the relation of the classroom setting to the students' needs.

The schedule, given the contingencies that can't be changed, must also be reflective of the students' needs. If the children in the class have a difficult time with math, put it first in the day, even if you've always taught it later. This kind of consideration is worth the trouble of making an adaptation, because it is much easier to

change a schedule than to change a class pattern of acting out. The curriculum can be adapted to ease some of the difficulties of trying to fit one instructional medium to a wide range of skills. Boredom and creative vengeance on the part of one bright student can cause more havoc to your curriculum than any adaptation you might plan. At least you get to plan the change! Try cooperative learning or peer tutoring or cross-age tutoring or mentoring. It'll help all your students. It's much more fun to use your creativity to prevent problems than to solve them. Try developing a team approach with your colleagues. It's been my experience that teachers are some of the most creative people in the world. They can be positive or negative: Be positive! It takes less energy and is much more productive!

The Resource Room

The classroom environment that bears special mention is the resource room, or special education room (I hate that term because I think all education should be special). The resource room is an environment that children may view as different: a safe haven or a source of humiliation and shame. The school ambience, the regular education classroom (another favorite of mine!) teachers' attitudes, and the learning specialist have a profound effect on the students' views of this class. The following is a description of my classroom's rules and instructions to substitute teachers.

1. Do your best work.
2. Care for yourself.
3. Care for others.
4. Be safe.

The students are taught the rules and their implications immediately upon entering. Each new student's entry provides additional practice for the entire group. The class also reviews the rules intermittently, as well as when there's an infraction.

Students who obey these rules are reinforced during each period with praise, WOW's (chances to win a prize in the Friday lunchtime drawing), privileges such as tutoring, or free time for a choice of activities.

1. *Do your best work.* Each student is expected to stay on task and to use all of her or his resources to complete the assigned work. The students are also expected to take risks in solving problems, such as sounding out an unknown word or trying to figure it out from the context, or using reference materials like the dictionary. They should ask for help in understanding the assignment; they must ask permission to leave their seats, even if it is to get a reference book. Neatness and

legibility count. How can I know if a student understands if I can't read the answer? But the most important element is the process of completing the work and the content created in that process. I tell the students the purpose of each task, and I expect them to follow the specific assignment as accurately as possible. Corrective feedback and rewrites are an important part of each assignment, as the students need a great deal of practice in evaluating their own work.

2. *Care for yourself.* Every student who comes to the resource room has already experienced academic, and possibly behavioral, failure. The resource room must be a place where the student can feel safe again and where he or she can become able to take the risks necessary for growth. The students should not be reinforced for an ''I can't'' attitude. They are not allowed to denigrate themselves or their work. They are reinforced for using good work skills, trying to solve problems in a constructive manner, and any approximation thereof. They are reinforced for coming on time, for bringing *only* a pencil and homework, and for any behavior that reinforces their school success.

3. *Care for others.* Students are expected to treat each other, as well as the teacher and the aide, with courtesy, consideration, and respect. Every person in the resource room has a role to fill; the students are expected to enable others to fill their roles by refraining from hurtful or distracting behaviors, by using only given names, by allowing each person to solve her or his problems independently, by reinforcing appropriate rather than inappropriate behavior, and by modeling ''survival'' or caring behavior. The class works very hard on generalizing this skill to the regular classroom, the playground, the lunchroom, the bus, and the neighborhood. Students who show increased caring skills earn the right to tutor other students.

4. *Be safe.* Students must keep themselves from physical or emotional harm. This means staying healthy by using good hygiene; avoiding unsafe confrontations, such as taunting others, playground roughhousing, or mock fights; and refraining from unsafe habits such as chair tipping or pencil flipping. It also entails learning and using social skills to negotiate in times of conflict, build friendships, and establish positive relationships with the adults and children in the school environment.

This rule seems to evoke the most infractions on a day-to-day basis. I suspect that the low self-esteem of students with learning disabilities makes them vulnerable. The students are often impulsive and seem to lack judgment about appropriate ways to draw attention from others. There also seems to be an element of impulsivity or a lack of understanding about the connection between cause and effect. The students with

ADD (attending deficit disorders) or a kinesthetic learning style are often at risk for infringing on this rule.

Cues and Consequences

Reinforcement is given for compliance with the rules.

1. *Do your best work.*

- First cue: On-task students are given praise or other reinforcement, a WOW, or a punch in their punchcard for an extra minute of recess.
- Second cue (redirection): The student is told, ''Do your work.''
- Third cue (negative reinforcement): The student is given no recess or lunch break until the work is done (''My time, or yours?'').

There is an additional contingency/cost program for intermediate students. The are allowed 15 minutes of recess at the end of the day; every incident of off-task behavior by one member of the group costs the group 1 minute of recess. Off-task behavior is defined, for the group, as talk-outs, out-of-seat behavior, or arguing. These students also have punchcards: They receive a punch for each page of homework completed, each period with no off-task behavior, and helpfulness to others. Each punch earns the student a WOW or an additional minute of recess.

2. *Take care of yourself.*

- First cue (specific corrective feedback): The student is told, ''You need to bring a pencil when you come to resource.'' or ''You need to come at 9:00.''
- Second cue (restitution): The student is told, ''You owe me 2 minutes for being late or unprepared.'' The student must pay that at recess.
- Third cue (overcorrection): The student is escorted to class by a peer, who brings the pencil and the student on time.

3. *Take care of others.*

- First cue (redirection): The student is asked, ''Is that caring?''
- Second cue: The teacher stops and removes the student from class for 5 minutes, ignoring the student. A conference is held to discuss specific expectations.
- Third cue: The student is sent to time out for the remainder of the period; work is made up at recess.

4. *Be safe.*

- First cue (corrective feedback): The student is told, ''Sit centered.''
- Second cue: The teacher interrupts the behavior and removes the student's chair.
- Third cue: The student is sent to time out; work is made up at recess.

These are the guidelines for the types of interventions I usually employ. I tailor the specifics to the particular student. My biases show quite clearly and I do not apologize. In fact, I try to make my biases as obvious as possible to the students, my colleagues, and parents. Many elements of this type of intervention require an initial investment of reinforcement with a very gradual fading of the schedule of reinforcement. Students identified as learning disabled share some deficits in school survival skills and tool skills; however, it is hard to know at first the etiology of a student's problem. It could be an organic problem, a curriculum problem, or a constellation of deviant school behaviors. Each year, the behavior of new and returning students is consistently improved by these interventions. The highly structured class and consistent rules may "cost" in terms of the amount of reinforcement and feedback the teacher can give. I have always found this to be well worth the cost. If the students' behavior is under control and they know that the teacher will be consistent, they are more likely to take the academic risks they need to take in order to make progress. As their confidence grows, they can begin to take risks in other ecological niches. Nothing succeeds like success. By creating a microcosm of success for these students, we can effect changes in the learning ecology of the school. We also can design and test behavioral interventions that may be transferred to the regular classroom. An intervention that's had the bugs worked out and that has proven successful is more likely to be implemented by the busy classroom teacher.

A Case Study: Jay

Jay is a fourth-grade student aged 9-4 who has been assessed as learning disabled; he has ADD, and takes ritalin at school at noon. He is in the regular classroom for approximately 70% of the school day, including lunch, physical education, and recess. He receives special services during the remaining 30% of his day: speech therapy three times per week for 30 minutes, and instruction in reading, spelling, language arts, and math in the resource room for 75 minutes in the morning and 60 minutes each afternoon.

His initial evaluation showed that he had good potential for learning, yet his reading achievement was preprimer and he had not mastered basic addition and subtraction facts. We conducted observations of him in the resource and regular classroom, at lunch, on the playground, in the gym, and during music and library time. We found that few activities held Jay's interest for more than a minute, particularly if he was required to sit still. He was disruptive in the library and music, but was on task while eating lunch. In the classroom

and the resource room, his behavior significantly interfered with his learning; baseline data showed him to be off task 95% of the time. His off-task behaviors included being out of seat, jumping up and down, physically poking or hitting peers, crawling under desks, tearing or poking holes in his papers, looking out of the window, and eating his pencil. His behavior also was disruptive to the regular and resource classes. The initial observations showed that his behavior became more extreme in the gym, where he ran, screamed, flapped his arms, climbed on and jumped off equipment, and physically attacked any peers who were in his path.

Both Jay and his mother reported that open, noisy environments excited and overwhelmed him. In the previous school year, he had broken his arm twice by climbing and jumping out of trees in the park; his mother no longer allowed him to play outside because of this tendency to get "wound-up" by open spaces and unstructured activities. Jay and his mother reported that he needed his medication to control his impulsivity; Jay would often excuse his behavior by saying, "I forgot to take my medication."

Using the Swassing-Barbe observation form, I determined that his kinesthetic learning style was causing a high number of self-interruptions while he was doing a task. Or he'd sharpen his pencil to a 1-inch stub by perseverating on the action of the pencil sharpener. His auditory memory skills were good, and I set up his first intervention to strengthen his ability to listen to and follow directions.

In gathering baseline data on Jay, even an approximation of successful work was helpful information to build on. It was also helpful to know which precise events sent him flying and which had no impact on his behavior. This information was vital to planning an ecological intervention. Our intervention had to provide him with further practice in attending; finding a behavior setting that evoked that attending behavior provided an opportunity to reinforce it. The next step was to take data and communicate the information so that we could modify the program as Jay progressed. A description of Jay's intervention program follows:

1. A classroom intervention included a punchcard for on-task, in-seat work with no talk-outs. Regular classwork was replaced by materials from the resource room.

2. The resource room used the same punchcard and provided achievement-level academic work, a training program for tool skills, and a program to increase social skills.

3. Jay's transportation was provided by the special education bus rather than the regular one. Jay remained in his regular class until the bus came; the

secretary then buzzed his room and his teacher escorted him to the bus. The punchcard was also used on the bus.

4. Jay's mother rewarded him for any punches he'd earned.

5. Jay's mother and the resource teacher documented changes in his behavior related to his medication. The doctor requested these data to regulate his medication. Jay's prescription was changed and he began to take it midday.

A Case Study: Eric

Eric, a third-grade student aged 8-7, was referred to special education in the first grade; he was retained but continued to have difficulty with his behavior and skills. He was certified learning disabled and placed in the resource room for reading, written expression, and math. By the time he entered second grade, he displayed a constellation of disruptive behaviors that was quite impressive. He ran away from school regularly; he had catastrophic tantrums during which he screamed, threw chairs and desks, and attacked anyone who tried to restrain him; he wet and soiled his pants; he refused to work on any task that involved pencils and paper; and he would throw his book whenever he made a mistake in reading, which was frequently, since he had mastered only seven consonant sounds. His compliance rate to teacher directions was about 50%, as long as it did not involve any of the skills in which he was weak. His area of strength was addition facts on the computer, which he would do willingly. Eric did respond to primary reinforcers (candy and peanuts) and he would work for the teacher for short periods (10 minutes) on a one-to-one basis.

I had been given much of this information before resource room classes started and was able to arrange some preentry time with Eric during the second week of school before I started the other primary students. During this time, I used the primary reinforcers to conduct some testing, using a criterion-referenced skills test; gave him a Beery Visual Motor Integration (VMI) test and the Wepman auditory battery; and did some other informal visual perceptual activities. I discovered that Eric had a significant deficit (below the first percentile) in visual motor integration, and that his auditory memory was below average. He also seemed to be a kinesthetic learner, according to the Swassing-Barbe criteria. He disliked coloring and complained that he had trouble focusing his eyes and that close work gave him headaches. In conducting the personal information interview that's part of the criterion-referenced skills test, I found that he did not know his birthdate, that

his brother "beat me up every night," that he went to bed when he wanted to, and that he did not eat regularly. He spoke with a tremor in his voice at times, and it sounded hoarse. When I asked him if his throat hurt, he said he yelled a lot. He also told me he hated school and all the kids and teachers hated him. When I asked him if he wanted to come back to the resource room later, he said that he did, so we began instruction that same afternoon. His teacher was very cooperative and concerned; he had also been transferred that year and had no history with Eric. He was quite startled when Eric ran away from school on the second day. Although the interventions we implemented have taken some effort and modification in the year and a half we have worked with Eric, his progress has been significant.

Eric's program included the following ecological interventions:

1. He was placed in the resource room for reading and written expression; his classwork was supplemented by the resource room. In the resource room, he earned WOW's on a 1:1 reinforcement schedule for in-seat, on-task work. We designed writing paper and tracking aids to help his visual motor integration. He was given responsibility for helping the teacher or a peer after an agreed-upon assignment was completed. He earned computer time for good work.

2. The regular classroom teacher implemented an intervention for cooperation in the classroom (no fighting and no disrupting); he also earned time on the computer or at another favored activity for each period he complied with these directions.

3. Every day, his teacher gave him a chit with a happy, so-so, or unhappy face noted on it. He then made the rounds to his "mentors": the librarian, the office staff, the resource teacher and aide, and the other specialists and aides. He received hugs and other rewards from each. We felt that embedding him in a "family" at school would help him try hard to earn the card.

4. The resource aide gave him a special treat for a number of days of happy faces; the number of days was increased over time, so that, during the last quarter, he worked for 60 days of happy day cards for his treat.

5. Running away from school was sanctioned by in-house suspension; we decreased the severity of this behavior by pairing it with a cooling-off time out which was self-administered. The rule was that he had to tell the adult he was going to the hall or the closet. He did not run away during the last 7 months of school. In addition, his tantrums and catastrophic reactions decreased from an average of 4.5 per week to 1 per month.

6. Community services were sought for neglect and physical abuse, which has continued throughout the year. The resource teacher monitors his hygiene and has provided instruction in this area.

A Case Study: Julie

Julie was a learning-disabled third-grade student, aged 9-7, who had a history of child abuse and neglect. She'd been burned as an infant over 30% of her body by her mother's boyfriend. Her mother had custody of her during most of the year, but was working with the Children's Services Department to maintain Julie and her two younger brothers in the home. Julie complained daily about being tired and hungry; she often came to school with no socks, shoelaces, or coat. Sometimes she would wear ill-fitting or damaged clothes that interfered with her work because they distracted her. Julie complained that her hair itched, and she missed school because of head lice on two occasions.

According to the Swassing-Barbe criteria, Julie was a kinesthetic learner who stood every time she came to a word or a math problem that was hard for her. She spent 72% of her class time out of her seat, at the aide's station, or at the teacher's side. Her reading achievement was at the preprimer level, and she did not write legible letters. It was difficult to get her to complete written work because of her interfering behaviors: being out of seat, putting her head down and sleeping, or complaining about her discomfort. We spent much of the time she was in class adjusting her clothing, finding her donated clothing, or providing food for breakfast. This is a case where the ecological intervention involved outreach to community agencies. The interventions we implemented are as follows:

1. The teacher and the resource teacher, the school nurse, and the school counselor worked with Children's Services to monitor Julie's physical well-being. We often provided food or clothing to Julie, and allowed her to sleep as needed.
2. The classroom teacher gave Julie attention for being on task while she worked on replacement materials from the resource room.
3. The resource room provided academic training, tool training, and social skills training.
4. Julie was removed from her home after 17 months of monitoring.
5. She returned to school after an absence of 8 months, including summer, during which time she was in a foster setting.
6. Julie had made significant gains during that time, but stopped progressing after she returned to her mother.
7. The same ecological interventions continued after her return.

The more you become familiar with an ecological approach to behavior management, the freer you will become with using it. It will give you the confidence to be creative and actually enjoy teaching. Working on behavior interventions is something that can unite a staff in a positive and caring way; it bridges those artificial gaps in communication that spring up between professionals in different disciplines.

After all, we are all there for one purpose—to teach children to survive in their world. With ecobehavioral analysis, no one person or factor is to blame for a poor ecological fit; there are no "bad" children, teachers, or other professionals. There are new behaviors and skills to learn, and few of us in the ecology of schools can afford to say, "Don't confuse me with these facts; I know it all."

The ecological management of behavior requires a delicate touch; all interventions should honor the child and the adult. It requires creativity, perception, a strong ethical framework, and a sense of humor. It brings out the best in us. The principles are deceptively simple; the tools are few. But the applications are as elegant as the human mind.

Chapter Twelve Self-Assessment

See Appendix A for acceptable responses.

1. Write a definition of ecological intervention.

2. Replicate Figure 12.1, Choices Available for Interventions.

3. Write examples of each part of Figure 12.1.

    1.

    2.

    3.

    4.

4. Define natural and logical consequences.

continued next page

5. Match the prevention and intervention strategies to the type of classroom:

   a. early childhood   _____ peer tutoring programs

                               _____ remove the weapon, victim, perpetrator

   b. regular classroom   _____ role-playing adaptive behavior

                               _____ cooperative learning activities

   c. resource room   _____ practicing the rules

                               _____ spitting in a cup

                               _____ time out

6. Design an ecological intervention for one student.

7. List five critical elements from each case history.

Jay	Eric	Julie
a.	a.	a.
b.	b.	b.
c.	c.	c.
d.	d.	d.
e.	e.	e.

Changing Teacher Behavior

Upon successful completion of this chapter, the learner should be able to:

1. List at least six examples of poor teaching that might require a self-management program
2. List and briefly describe each of the steps in the self-management process
3. State four rules of thumb to follow when implementing the intervention phase of a self-management program
4. Design a self-management program to strengthen or weaken a behavior (thought or feeling) of the teacher's own choosing

Introduction

In order to change a student's behavior, it is often necessary for the teacher first to modify his or her own behavior. Unfortunately, many teachers are unable to do this and consequently have difficulty modifying the behavior of their students. Over the years I have observed several teachers who, as graduate students, earned an "A" in my behavior management course, but who, as teachers, rated a "D" when it came to applying in their classrooms what they had learned in mine. It's not that they didn't know what to do, or how or when to do it. It was more a matter of not remembering to do it or not being able to because they were too angry or anxious at the time. Here are some examples.

When Mrs. Angst gives Joey a directive, he usually complies, but not before giving her some backtalk. When this happens, the teacher's inclination is to ignore it and concentrate on Joey's compliance. Unfortunately, Mrs. Angst seldom follows her own inclination. Most of the time, she and Joey engage in "verbal fisticuffs":

Joey (J.): "Whatta ya pickin' on me for? I didn't do nothin'!"

Mrs. A.: "Nobody's picking on you, Joey. Stop being paranoid and do as you're told without the backtalk!"

J.: "Paranerd? I ain't no 'paranerd.' (under his breath) You're the 'paranerd.' "

Mrs. A.: "What did you say? Don't be impertinent, young man! Just do as you're told and if you don't watch that mouth of yours, you'll be in detention this afternoon!"

The verbal punches fly back and forth until Joey either shuts up or gets sent to the office for "insubordination." Mrs. Angst knows that Joey's backtalk is reinforced by her attention; even though it's negative, Joey enjoys the attention he gets from her. Unfortunately, it's the only real attention he gets from her or from any of his teachers. Joey also relishes the peer attention he gets during these confrontations. Mrs. Angst knows that she would be better off ignoring Joey's backtalk but she "can't do it." His backtalk makes her so angry that she loses control and, against her better judgment, rushes headlong into a verbal fray she can never win. What Mrs. Angst needs is a self-management program in anger management to help her ignore Joey's backtalk.

Then there is Mr. Cower. He's afraid that some of his students won't like him or might attack him verbally or even physically if he attempts to discipline them. Unlike Mrs. Angst, who is too aggressive, Mr. Cower is too passive and consequently lets his students get away with murder. But they have the same problem: Mr. Cower also knows what he should do but "can't do it." Fortunately, Mr. Cower has tenure. Unfortunately, he also has an ulcer (brought on by job-related stress) and feelings of diminished self-worth. Mr. Cower needs a self-management program to help him become more assertive with his students.

Finally, there is Ms. Rote. She also knows how to use behavior modification but can't seem to remember to use it. She forgets to praise her students in a systematic way. She also forgets to monitor their behavior, with the result that few of her behavior programs are successful. Ms. Rote understands that the problem lies with her application of behavior modification and not with the process itself. She knows she should be more systematic in her use of reinforcement and data collection but feels she "can't do it." Ms. Rote needs a self-management program to help her remember to be more systematic.

These three hypothetical teachers exhibit just a few of the problems that their peers experience in applying behavior management strategies appropriately. Figure 13.1 lists some of the other inappropriate but common teaching behaviors that weaken the efficacy of behavior management in the classroom.

Again, it is not the purpose of this chapter to provide you with self-management programs for each of these problem situations. As in the other chapters, my purpose is to describe self-management strategies in general and leave it to you to choose the most appropriate ones to use in your particular situation.

There are two important points I will make before I go any further. First, the material that follows will not help you become more assertive or less anxious or more controlled or more enthusiastic in all areas of your life. It will merely help you to change your teaching behavior. If you tend to be unassertive or anxious or angry or unenthusiastic by nature (i.e., by trait, not state), and you wish to change, the material in this unit is not likely to help you. If you have an affinity for self-management (some people are not "do-it-yourselfers" and would rather work with a professional therapist) and you wish to make some changes in your life that extend beyond

---

1. Overreacting to student maladaptive behavior (e.g., losing temper, using abusive-provocative language, or getting physical with students).
2. Lecturing students (or "preaching" or talking too much) until they tune you out.
3. Forgetting to praise students when it is appropriate to do so.
4. Not praising with any enthusiasm, so that the praise is perceived by the student as insincere.
5. Praising inconsistently (i.e., not according to schedule) or praising one student (or group of students) more than others.
6. Punishing inconsistently or punishing one student (or group of students) more than others.
7. Taking too long to praise (or punish) a student (i.e., the latency between the student's behavior and the teacher's consequence is too long to be of any value).
8. Attending to student maladaptive behavior when it is more appropriate to ignore it.
9. Being unassertive with students when it is more appropriate to be assertive.
10. Consistently being negative with students (i.e., using "put-downs" and negative comments, pointing out negative behavior, and ignoring positive behavior).
11. Failing to collect data on student behavior when it is desirable to do so.
12. Allowing oneself to be manipulated by students.

Figure 13.1. Examples of maladaptive teaching behaviors.

your teaching, there are several fine textbooks devoted exclusively to self-management (see Mahoney, 1979; Mahoney & Thoresen, 1972; Schmidt, 1976; and Watson & Tharp, 1981). However, if you wish to change some aspect of your teaching behavior, and are willing to go it alone, the material in this chapter should be of some benefit.

Second, you may not always need a formal self-management program to change your teaching behavior. Self-management strategies are only necessary when you find it too difficult to change your behavior by relying solely on willpower.

Self-management is not unlike the rest of the behavior management covered in this text. If you realize that your behavior needs changing, you should follow essentially the same steps previously discussed:

1. Pinpoint the maladaptive and fair-pair target behaviors.
2. Use the task analytical model to make sure that you have all of the necessary prerequisites to engage in the target behavior.
3. Design and implement an intervention.
4. Monitor the behavior (or thoughts or feelings) to be changed, evaluate the efficacy of your intervention, and make changes as needed.

Let's examine each step as it applies to self-management.

Deciding What To Change

One of the most critical steps in the self-management process is recognizing what change is indicated. It's much easier to notice maladaptive behavior in others than in ourselves. Many of us go through our entire teaching careers thinking that everything is fine and that we don't need to improve on anything. For example, I used to think that I was a more than competent lecturer until I heard a tape recording of one of my lectures. It was awful! I had never realized how rapidly I spoke or how disfluent my speech was. I seldom finished a sentence and there were a number of pregnant pauses and several filler words such as "uh" and "um." I never knew how bad I sounded until I had the opportunity to listen to myself on tape. If you are doing something wrong in your teaching, it won't always be obvious to you either. That's why I think it's a good idea for teachers periodically to record their teaching on audiotape or videotape and then listen to or watch themselves to see if anything needs changing. It may turn out to be a painful experience. However, in the long run, it might prove less painful than doing nothing.

Another way to identify inappropriate teaching behavior is to analyze the behavioral data collected during a student intervention. For example, according to the data shown in Figure 13.2, it appears that this teacher's attention is actually reinforcing his student's talk-out behavior. The more he attends to it (T), the more frequently it occurs (S). When he ignores it, it gets weaker. The teacher wouldn't have known this if he hadn't collected data on his behavior as well as his student's.

Once you have identified a teaching behavior that requires changing, apply the "So what?" test (see chapter 3). This test for maladaptive teaching is no different from the one used for maladaptive student behaviors. Simply ask yourself if your behavior is maladaptive. Is your teaching behavior actually or potentially harmful to the physical, social, or academic well-being of your students or yourself? If it is, consider it maladaptive and try changing it. Once you have identified a target behavior, apply the "So what?" test to it also. Here you can be a little selfish. Ask yourself if the target behavior is in your own best interests. If it is, and it does not hurt your students, it passes the "So what?" test. Remember our old friend Mr. Cower? He needs to be more assertive with his students. If, instead of being more assertive, Mr. Cower's target behavior were to become more aggressive, he might think he was acting in his own best interests but his target behavior would probably be harmful to his students and eventually to himself. You just can't go around slapping students or using abusive-

provocative language, even if it does maintain discipline in your classroom. If Mr. Cower's target behavior were to be assertive (rather than aggressive), he would not only be acting in his own best interests but in a way that would be helpful, rather than harmful, to his students. By being assertive he will not only effectively maintain discipline in his classroom; he also will be modeling appropriate behavior for his students rather than the inappropriate (passive) behavior he's been modeling up to now. Ultimately, this will lead to improved physical, social, and academic growth on the part of his students.

More than anything else, a self-management program is dependent upon the teacher's willingness—no, desire—to change. Don't change because you think you ought to; change because you want to! I remember a teacher with very strong religious beliefs who had a student who used profanity in front of her because she knew the teacher would be upset by it. While the teacher was well aware of the student's motives, she was also so strongly opposed to the swearing that she felt she could not, in good conscience, ignore it. Eventually, it was decided that it would be in the best interests of both the student and the teacher for the girl to be removed to another classroom where the new teacher was both willing and able to ignore it. Again, don't try to change your teaching behavior unless you firmly believe that the change is warranted.

As important as it is to describe student behavior so that it passes the stranger test, it is just as important to specify teacher behavior in terms that can be readily understood by anyone and that are not open to interpretation. For example, don't simply say that your target behavior is "to be more assertive with my student." State exactly what behaviors you want to strengthen or weaken. "When I observe my students engaging in behavior I judge to be disruptive, I will immediately intervene by implementing a hierarchy of escalating consequences including the reinforcement of an incompatible response, extinction, punishment (e.g., reprimand, response cost, or time out), and removal from my classroom." If your goal is to ignore student attention-seeking behavior, you might describe it this way: "When I observe my students engaging in behavior I judge to be attention seeking, I will not attend to that behavior in any manner (i.e., I will avoid eye, verbal, or physical contact with the student and avoid responding in any way to students' attention-seeking behavior)."

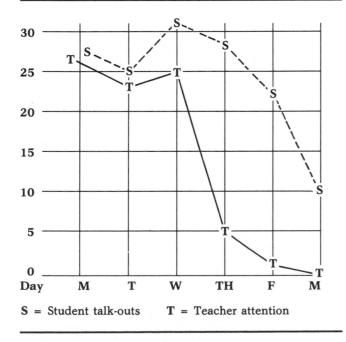

S = Student talk-outs   T = Teacher attention

Figure 13.2. Data regarding student talk-outs and teacher attention.

Measuring Change

Once you have identified and specified a target behavior that passes the stranger and "So what?" tests, you should begin monitoring the behavior to determine a baseline against which to compare your intervention data. One of the problems with collecting data on your own behavior is that it requires you to be aware of it. For example, if you ignore certain students when you shouldn't and are unaware of this behavior when it occurs, it will be impossible for you to collect any data on it. However, it won't be impossible for someone else to monitor it for you. Make arrangements with your aide, if you have one, to monitor your behavior. If an aide is not available, record your teaching on audio- or videotape for a period of time. Many schools have audio- and vidoeotape equipment that is rarely used. Teach one of your students how to use the equipment or arrange the taping situation so that it is self-operating. Focus the camera on the part of the classroom where you expect to be working and turn it on. Then just try to be yourself and behave as you normally do. The machine will go off by itself when it runs out of tape, or you can turn it off when you want to. Whether you use an audio- or videotape recorder, wear a clip-on microphone so that you won't miss any of your verbal interactions with students. Built-in microphones tend to pick up too much background noise, which makes it difficult to distinguish one conversation from another. If you are unable to use any of this equipment, you can ask one or more of your students to monitor your behavior for you, assuming that they are capable of doing this. For example, if you think that you make an inordinate number of negative comments to your students but are not always aware of it when it happens, ask them to record each instance of a negative comment directed at them. Each student should mark down every time you make a negative comment to him or her. At the end of the day, collect the data from each of your students. This will not only tell you how often you make negative comments but to which students you make them. It might also tell you which students are the least reliable at data collection. No system is foolproof. However, don't give up the idea of monitoring your own behavior simply because you can't remember to do it. Look for other ways to accomplish this goal.

When I realized how disfluent my speech was during my lectures, I decided to collect some baseline data. However, I was unable to do this and lecture at the same time. The first thing I did was to tape-record my lectures and listen to them. Because I seldom had the time (or the stomach) to sit and listen to myself for three solid hours, I instead listened to a random 15 minutes here and 10 minutes there. This task soon became so aversive to me that I decided to find a better way. I finally settled on asking my students to collect the data for me. It was unreasonable to expect each student to collect a continuous sample of my disfluent speech for

a 2- or 3-hour stretch. This would obviously keep them from taking notes, commenting, and asking questions. I was able to get around this by requiring each student to take a 1-minute sample of my verbal behavior. I gave one of my students a clipboard with a stopwatch taped to it and an observation and recording (O & R) form. The latter may be seen in Figure 13.3. Students were instructed to start the watch whenever they wanted. It was there to help them determine when their minute of data collection was over. During their 1 minute, they were to mark down each instance of disfluent speech (e.g., ''uh,'' ''um'') in my lecture. When the minute had elapsed, they were to stop the watch, return it to zero, write their initials in the box on the O & R form, and pass it and the clipboard on to the next person. When each student had recorded the data for 1 minute, the clipboard was passed on to me. Once I was back in my office, I quickly analyzed and summarized the data. Each box on the O & R form was the equivalent of 1 minute and each mark in the box was the equivalent of one instance of disfluent speech. By counting the total number of boxes, I was able to determine the total number of instances of disfluent speech. By dividing the total number of minutes into the total number of instances of disfluent speech, I was able to determine my rate of disfluent speech for a given lecture. I then plotted the rate onto a ratio chart like the one shown in Figure 13.4.

Your responses (or lack of responses) should not be the only variable on which you collect data. You should also monitor what happens before you respond (antecedent events) and what happens afterward (consequent events). Both may play an important role in maintaining your current behavior; for this reason, you should know what they are and how often they occur. For example, let's look again at the data on my disfluent speech.

In analyzing my baseline data I found times when I was more disfluent than others. Since the students were instructed to record their data in the boxes in numerical order, it was easy to see at what point in the lecture I was being more or less fluent. In every instance, I started out being fluent but as the lecture progressed (usually after the first 5 or 10 minutes), I started to become disfluent. Further analysis provided two reasons. First, at the beginning of each class I was more aware of the data collection and worked harder at speaking fluently. As the class wore on and I warmed to the subject, I paid less and less attention to the data collection and, consequently, to my fluency. Second, as the class progressed, students were more likely to make comments or ask questions than they were at the outset of the class. I have known for a long time (as do many of my colleagues) that I always feel more in control of the situation when I am lecturing from notes than when I enter into a dialogue with my students. I am

Behaver __Kaplan__

Maladaptive Behavior __DISFLUENT SPEECH__

Counted __"uh," "um..."__

Date __3/27/89__ Begin __6:42 PM__ End __7:30 PM__

Comments: __Covered new material re test construction__

1	2	3	4	5	6	7	8
6:42 Ø TR	zero SK	I BY	☺ LP	none! BR	I NB	I P.W.	III JW
₥ DK	IIII KH	₥ ? MK	J.P.E. ₥	IIII c OL	RS ₥ c	IIII EM	₥ ? I DN
IIII JD	₥ ? SB	IIII SM	III KL	III 7:30 OB			

Rate = # COUNTED / TIME   Rate = 63/21   Rate = 3

Figure 13.3. O & R form recording disfluent speech.

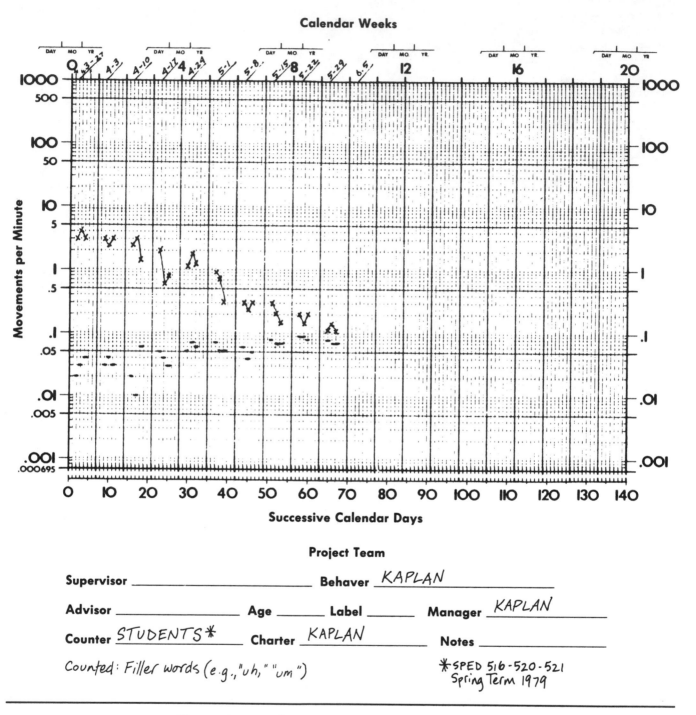

Figure 13.4. Disfluent speech data plotted on ratio chart.

especially susceptible to anxiety when I am asked a question I have difficulty answering or when a student challenges one of my statements and I have to think on my feet for a rebuttal. After this discovery, I began asking my students to mark down each instance of a challenging comment or question coming from the class. They began appearing on my O & R form as "C" and "?". In this way I was able to note the antecedents that might precipitate my disfluent speech. The data in Figure 13.2 show that my instances of disfluent speech increased in frequency after a challenging comment or question from the class. I also noticed, by comparing the data with my comments regarding each lecture, that my rate of disfluent speech seemed to be lower during those class sessions when I was better prepared—that is, when I had a complete set of lecture notes and transparencies and had given the same lecture a number of times before. Whenever I tried to "wing it," my anxiety level went up and this led to more disfluency. This information regarding the antecedent events that appeared to precipitate or elicit my disfluent speech eventually helped me to plan an effective intervention program which is described in the next section.

One final word about monitoring: You must be aware of the possibility of *reactivity*. Reactivity is a phenomenon that generally occurs when we collect data on our own behavior or have someone else do it with our knowledge. We tend to react to this data collection process by changing our behavior. This probably accounts for my deliberate way of speaking at the beginning of my lectures. I was more aware of the data collection procedure at that time than at any other. However, once I forgot about the monitoring I stopped being conscious of my speaking behavior and lost fluency. My advice on the subject of reactivity is to go ahead with your intervention even when it appears that baseline monitoring is having an effect on your behavior. My experience has been that the reactivity will last only as long as the monitoring does. In most cases, once the novelty of monitoring wears off, so does the reactivity.

Effecting Change

Once you have some consistency in your baseline data, you are ready to implement your intervention. Keep in mind that any of the intervention strategies for strengthening or weakening behaviors, thoughts, or feelings that have been discussed in this text for use with students may be effectively employed with teachers in a self-management program. However, there are some rules of thumb that were not previously mentioned.

First, never punish yourself or use another person to punish you for failing to engage in the target behavior or for engaging in the maladaptive behavior. Punishing

yourself can lead to feelings of diminished self-worth, guilt, anger, frustration, and all the other feelings your students experience when you punish them. Having someone else act as the punisher will only make that person an aversive stimulus and eventually will lead to a strained relationship. So don't use your team teacher, foster grandparent, aide, or one of your students to punish your behavior. It will not help you change your own behavior and in most cases will result in your giving up the self-management program. Instead, always reinforce yourself (or have someone else reinforce you) for engaging in the target behavior. Unlike punishment, reinforcing yourself or having someone reinforce you will lead to feelings of increased self-worth, satisfaction, and a motivation to continue your self-management program.

Self-punishment can be harmful to your health.

Second, don't always think of consequent events as the only means of changing your behavior. Remember my earlier comments about the relationship between antecedents and my disfluent speech. I could have ignored these antecedent events and concentrated instead on consequent events in my intervention. For example, I could simply have said that I would reinforce myself for closer and closer approximations of my target behavior, which was zero disfluencies. What I would use as a reinforcer is not important. What is important is that the reinforcer, as a consequent stimulus event (CSE), would be given after my lecture. If this didn't work, I could have introduced the use of reinforcers during my lecture (i.e., after so many minutes of lecturing without going beyond a prespecified number of disfluencies). For example, if 5 minutes passed and I spoke only ten filler words, one or more of my students could have rewarded me with a thumbs-up sign or by holding up a card with the words "Terrific" or "Great!" or "Keep it up!" Again, this reinforcer or

CSE would occur after I responded. However, since my baseline data showed a clear relationship with antecedents such as student questions and comments and my own preparedness to lecture, I decided to intervene by manipulating the antecedent events instead of the CSEs.

First, I made sure that I was adequately prepared for each lecture ahead of time. Whenever I introduced a new lecture or infused an old lecture with new material, I reviewed the lecture notes before class to see if I had a clear understanding of the material. Second, I started practicing diaphragmatic breathing and tried to cue myself to use it in class whenever a student would make a comment or ask a question. I used the DIBs technique (disputing rational beliefs) as a means of self-inquiry in order to identify and dispute any irrational thinking that might be contributing to my anxiety during the lectures. In addition, I placed a sign on the overhead projector with the words "slow down." I also penciled (in bright red) the word "slow" in various places in my lecture notes. This strategy was based on my reasoning that if I had fewer disfluencies during the first 5 to 10 minutes of my lecture, and I spoke in a slow, deliberate fashion during that time, there must be some relationship between the two. Also, because I spoke more slowly and deliberately when I was aware of the data collection going on, I had my students raise the clipboard in front of them high enough for me to see but not so high that it would distract their peers. This served as a reminder (cue) that they were monitoring my speaking behavior, which in turn slowed me down and ultimately resulted in less disfluency. Remember, manipulating antecedents can be more effective in some instances than changing CSEs.

If you forget to reward your students, put up reminders in conspicuous places to help you remember. If you tend to ignore a particular student when you should be attending to him, place him in a conspicuous spot so that you will be more likely to remember to attend to him. If you recognize that your students are manipulating you and you don't want to be manipulated, practice saying cues to yourself (e.g., "Maturity is the ability to withstand present pain for future pleasure.") before responding to them. If you know that your responses are tied to certain antecedent events in the environment, try changing the antecedents and it is more than likely that you will be able to change your responses. Also, whenever it is possible and appropriate, use your students to cue you. I see nothing wrong with a student cueing her teacher to be more attentive to her or to praise her for her desirable behavior. Adults are always prompting children to say "please" and "thank you." If we can't remember to be nice to them, why shouldn't they prompt us to give them social praise when it's appropriate to do so?

When using consequent events to change your behavior, don't always rely on tangible reinforcers. Positive self-talk ("Hey, that was good!" or "I did it!") is inexpensive and easy to give. It can be used immediately after you have engaged in the target behavior. Most important, self-praise helps you to internalize your new behavior by constantly reminding you that the change in your behavior is the prize—not some gift you might buy for yourself. Knowing you can change your behavior is the greatest gift you can ever hope to give yourself. As Mahoney and Thoresen said, self-management means "power to the person" (1972). In addition to self-praise, you might want to use fantasizing as a payoff for a change in your behavior. Fantasize yourself in a week or a month or a year as an extremely effective and successful teacher, all because of your new-found self-management skills. Think of expanding these skills into other aspects of your life where you feel change is warranted.

Make self-talk positive.

Finally, don't focus your self-management project on your behavior if you suspect it is your irrational thinking that needs changing. Figure 13.5 lists a number of irrational beliefs held by teachers I have known over the years. Ask yourself if you subscribe to any of them. If you do, don't take my word for it. Use the DIBs strategy outlined in chapter 9 and see for yourself. Irrational thinking can lead to strong negative emotions that produce maladaptive behavior. If you want to change your behavior, you may first have to change your thinking. Does this sound familiar? Who said that teachers were any different from their students in this respect?

1. I must have the love or approval of all my students, parents of students, and co-workers and it's terrible if I don't.

2. I must prove thoroughly competent as a teacher and it's awful if I don't.

3. When students, parents of students, or co-workers act obnoxiously and unfairly, I must blame and damn them, and see them as bad, wicked, or rotten individuals.

4. When I get seriously frustrated, am treated unfairly, or experience rejection on the job, I must view things as awful, terrible, horrible, and catastrophic.

5. All of my job-related stress is the result of external pressures and events and there is little or nothing I can do about it.

6. When things happen at work that I consider dangerous or fearsome, I must preoccupy myself with these things and make myself anxious about them.

7. It's terrible when my students don't learn and I should consider myself a failure as a teacher.

8. My students should have the same values that I do and it's terrible if they don't.

9. It's awful if my students don't learn what I want them to right away.

10. It's terrible if my students misbehave and I must take it personally.

11. It's just not fair when my classes are overcrowded, when my students are not all bright and polite, when I don't have any or enough planning periods, when I don't have the teaching supplies I need, and when I don't get paid what I think I'm worth.

12. It's better for me not to take my teaching too seriously so that in case something goes wrong, I won't be disappointed.

13. Because of my training in college or the early experiences I've had in teaching, I can't help being as I am today and I'll always be this way.

14. It's terrible when my students experience problems and I must be upset about this.

Figure 13.5. Irrational thinking by teachers.

For example, part of my disfluency problem can be traced to irrational thinking: ''I must have the love and respect of everyone I meet and it's awful if I don't.'' ''I must prove to be competent in everything I do and it's awful if I don't.'' ''All my students must love and respect me and think that I'm a competent teacher and it's awful if they don't.''

This irrational thinking led to the anxiety I experienced in class when I discussed unfamiliar material or had difficulty answering a student's question or found my ideas being criticized. ''Oh, my God. They don't like me. They must think I'm stupid or incompetent or both. What's worse, they'll tell others that I'm stupid and incompetent. Oh, woe is me!'' The anxiety led to disfluency; this, in turn, made me more anxious; this led to more disfluency; and so on. Eventually, if I hadn't done anything about this problem, it probably would have become a self-fulfilling prophecy. I would have become so disfluent that my students would have actually started believing I was incompetent. As it turned out, my self-management program was successful because it didn't just focus my efforts on my behavior but also made an attempt at changing my irrational thinking. I began to carry cards around with me and read from them several times a day. They said things like, ''I'm a worthy person,'' ''Lot's of people like and respect me,'' ''Don't be afraid to look bad,'' ''I'm competent and clever,'' and ''Nobody knows the answer to every question all the time.'' Another card had the names of all the people I could think of who liked and respected me as a professional. I know it sounds bizarre, but after a couple of weeks you actually start believing what you've written on the cards. Use of this technique, along with the changes in antecedent events mentioned earlier, decreased my anxiety states in frequency and intensity. The opinion that my anxiety decreased is based on a subjective assessment of anxiety.

In conclusion, I must simply say that writing this text has been for me the greatest test of self-management. Writing, whether textbooks or a letter to a friend, has always been one of my low-frequency behaviors. I consider it a triumph of self-management that this text ever got written. Willpower had nothing to do with it. So take heart, O ye of little faith. What one can conceive, one can achieve. Power to the person!

Chapter Thirteen Self-Assessment

See Appendix A for acceptable responses.

1. List at least six examples of poor teaching that might require self-management.

    a.

    b.

    c.

    d.

    e.

    f.

2. List and briefly describe each of the steps in the self-management process.

    a.

    b.

    c.

    d.

3. State four rules of thumb to follow when implementing the intervention in a self-management project.

    a.

    b.

    c.

    d.

4. Design a self-management program to strengthen or weaken a behavior, thought, or feeling of your own choosing (see your instructor for feedback).

Part V
Evaluating Change

chapter *14*

Monitoring Behavior

Upon successful completion of this chapter, the learner should be able to:

1. State the differences between the baseline and intervention phases of monitoring
2. Correctly label the aspect of a behavior (i.e., frequency, duration, or intensity)
3. Correctly label the monitoring sample (i.e., continuous and intervention) to use in a given situation
4. Describe how to monitor single behaviors for multiple subjects and multiple behaviors for single subjects
5. Describe how to monitor reciprocal behaviors
6. Describe how to monitor behaviors to get qualitative data
7. Draw a countoon for given behaviors
8. Design an observation and recording (O & R) form for a number of given purposes
9. Correctly state when to use raw score, percentage, rate, and average to summarize data
10. Correctly compute raw score, percentage, rate, and average when given data and told which summarization procedure to use
11. Plot baseline and intervention data on a chart of one's own design
12. Interpret data already plotted on charts

Despite its being last, I consider this chapter the most important in the text. Regardless of which interventions you use to modify your students' behavior, you must hold yourself accountable for their efficacy. If your interventions don't work, you need to find out why and make changes. As a professional educator, you can do nothing less. No teacher should continue to use an intervention that proves to be ineffective at changing student behavior. If you were trying to teach your students to read and your reading method wasn't working, would you continue to use it? Of course not. Why, then, would you continue to use ineffective methods for teaching

social behaviors? This last section of the text will show you how you can become accountable for your teaching. It's not easy but if you really care about your students, it must be mastered.

Monitoring

Collecting data on student behavior is usually referred to as *monitoring*. Monitoring requires that you do two things: observe behavior and record it. We need to observe and record behavior so that we will have a basis for deciding whether or not our behavioral interventions are working. If the behavioral data indicate that our intervention is working, we won't have to change it. If, on the other hand, the data suggest that our intervention is not working, we'll have to try something else.

Baseline and Intervention Phases

There are two phases of data collection: baseline and intervention. Baseline data are collected before any new intervention is attempted. During baseline you continue to consequate the maladaptive behavior in the same manner as before. If you have been ignoring it, continue to ignore it. If you've been punishing it, continue to punish it using the same antecedent stimulus event (ASE). Baseline data are also known as "before" data because this period of data collection takes place before you try out your new intervention. Baseline data are needed to compare with intervention data in order to determine if any change has taken place and if this change is due to variables other than the intervention (e.g., passage of time, external events at home, or student maturation). Baseline data should be collected until there is enough consistency to suggest a pattern or trend.

Intervention data are referred to as "during" data because they are collected during a period of intervention. Intervention data are needed to compare with baseline data in order to determine if any change in the behavior has occurred. Intervention data should be collected until it appears that a change of interventions is indicated or that the present intervention is effective.

229

Many teachers are reluctant to collect baseline data because they are anxious to get on with the new intervention and, hopefully, to change the student's behavior. Others don't believe that any data collection, baseline or intervention, is necessary. Their argument is that they'll know if the student's behavior changes without monitoring it. The following hypothetical case demonstrates the fallacy of both arguments.

Mr. Fix wanted to change little Ajax's swearing in class. He referred the boy to the school psychologist who spent a few days in his classroom collecting baseline data, much to Mr. Fix's chagrin. "Why are you just sitting there writing down what he does? I've already told you what he does. He curses. When are you going to tell me what to do about his cursing?" At the end of the 3 days of baseline monitoring, the school psychologist told Mr. Fix that the data he collected indicated that Ajax's swearing was actually being reinforced by teacher attention. She therefore suggested that Mr. Fix ignore the boy's swearing but continue to monitor it in order to determine whether or not this intervention worked.

Before the school psychologist came on the scene, Mr. Fix thought he would lose his job if he let Ajax get away with swearing. Swearing never bothered him but he was afraid that the rest of his class might pick up the habit and that it would come to the attention of his principal. Now that he had "permission" to ignore Ajax's swearing, he wasn't going to worry about it anymore. In fact, not only didn't he give Ajax any attention when he used profanity; he didn't even bother to monitor his behavior. He thought, "Why bother? If it's my attention that's causing the swearing, it'll go away if I just ignore it. Now that I know it's okay for me to ignore it, I can do it. In no time at all he'll see that swearing won't lead to a payoff and he'll just stop it. Why bother with all that bookkeeping? I'll know when he stops swearing."

Three weeks later, the school psychologist asked Mr. Fix how Ajax was doing. "Swearing? What swearing? Why, Ajax stopped doing that over two weeks ago. Just about the time I started ignoring it." The next day, Mr. Fix was evaluated in his classroom by the principal

and what do you suppose he observed? You guessed it—little Ajax using four-letter words, and I don't mean "Spot" and "Puff." Since Mr. Fix's tolerance for swearing had changed, he had become less aware of it. If he had taken the time to monitor Ajax's swearing during the intervention phase, he would have known by the end of the first week that the intervention wasn't working. Not only had he failed to change Ajax's behavior, but he was evaluated by the principal as a "soft disciplinarian."

The moral of this little tale is simple. If you are going to the trouble of changing a student's behavior, take the time to monitor the change. Without monitoring, you probably won't be able to tell if any change has really occurred. If you don't care whether or not any change has occurred, why bother trying to effect a change in the first place?

Aspects of Behavior

There are two basic aspects of behavior that can be monitored: frequency and duration. *Frequency* refers to the number of times a behavior occurs. *Duration* refers to how long a behavior lasts. Some behaviors lend themselves to frequency monitoring because they occur often, don't last long, and have a readily observable beginning and end. Examples of such behaviors are cursing, telling lies, destroying the property of others, calling out, teasing or criticizing peers, making self-deprecating remarks, smiling, complying with requests, paying compliments, completing assignments, and coming to class on time and prepared.

Frequency data are collected by simply counting the number of times the behavior you are monitoring occurs. For example, if a teacher wanted to monitor the frequency of talk-outs (calling out without raising one's hand) for a particular student, she would simply make a mark on a piece of paper each time the behavior occurred. At the end of the day she would know how many times that behavior had occurred. An example of this may be seen in Figure 14.1.

What the teacher sees...   What *we* see...

What a fool believes, he or she sees.

Behaver _(student)_

Monitor _(teacher)_

Counted _talk-outs (calling out w/o raising hand)_

Date	Frequency	Totals
2-2-89	THH II	7
2-3-89	THH THH	10
2-4-89	THH III	8
2-5-89		
2-6-89		

Figure 14.1. Recording frequency data.

Other behaviors are more appropriate to monitor in terms of duration because they don't occur often, they last a long time, and they don't necessarily have a readily observable beginning and end. Examples of these behaviors include daydreaming, being in (or out of) seat, being on (or off) task, sucking thumb, self-stimming (e.g., rocking in seat or wiggling one's hands), having tantrums, and maintaining eye contact. Another aspect of behavior quite similar to duration is *latency*. This refers to the amount of time that passes between two important acts. For example, you may have a student who is noncompliant (i.e., does not do what you tell her to). One way to monitor the frequency of this behavior is to count the number of times she complies with a request. However, it might also be useful to monitor the latency between the teacher's request and the student's compliance. Some students do what they are told eventually but like to take their time about it. By monitoring the latency of compliance (instead of, or in addition to, the frequency of compliance), you will have more information to use to determine the student's problem as well as the efficacy of your intervention.

Duration data are collected by using a stopwatch to determine the amount of time a particular behavior lasts. For example, to monitor the duration of out-of-seat behavior, start a stopwatch when the student gets out of his seat and stop it when he gets back in it. Then write down the amount of time in seconds, or minutes and seconds, that the student was out of his seat. By resetting the watch each time and recording the duration for each separate out-of-seat behavior, you have duration data as well as frequency data. An example of this is shown in Figure 14.2. This method of collecting duration data is recommended only if you have the time to record each separate duration or wish to monitor the frequency aspect as well.

Behaver _(student)_

Monitor _(teacher)_

Counted _out of seat (bottom not in contact with chair)_

Date	Duration/Frequency								Totals F	Totals D
2-2-89	25"	73"	80"	9"					4	187
2-3-89	84"	50"	39"	72"	19"	21"			6	285
2-4-89	11"	102"	35"	51"	47"				5	246
2-5-89										

Figure 14.2. Combining duration and frequency data.

Another and more practical way to monitor duration of out-of-seat behavior is to stop the watch when the student returns to his seat, but instead of resetting it and starting at zero again, start the watch when the student gets out of his seat again. At the end of the day, record the total (cumulative) time the student was out of his seat. You will not have any data regarding frequency of response, but this may be an easier method for the busy teacher. These data are shown in Figure 14.3.

A less common aspect of behavior that you might wish to monitor is intensity. *Intensity* refers to the quality or force of a behavior as opposed to the quantity (i.e., how many times it occurs). For example, you can measure the intensity of verbal behavior by monitoring the volume (loud or soft) of a person's voice while she is talking. Another group of behaviors often characterized by intensity is the self-injurious act (e.g., biting self).

Data for intensity are collected in the same manner as for frequency. Record each instance of the behavior. However, since you are not only interested in the number of times the behavior occurs but also in how many times it occurs at each level of intensity, you will need to make an adjustment in your monitoring. First, decide what the levels of intensity are going to be and describe them very carefully. For example, suppose that you want to monitor the intensity of a student's tantrum behavior. Let's suppose that at the present time the student's tantrums include loud screaming, lying on the floor, and banging his head. You can't get much worse than this, so call it "severe" and give it an intensity rating of 3. The next lower level of intensity is crying and lying on the floor. This is considered "moderate" and gets a rating of 2. Finally, the lowest level

Behaver _(student)_

Monitor _(teacher)_

Counted _out of seat (bottom not in contact with chair)_

Date	Duration	Date	Duration
2-2-89	240"	2-9-89	432"
2-3-89	117"	2-10-89	290"
2-4-89	205"	2-11-89	
2-5-89	401"	2-12-89	
2-6-89	306"	2-13-89	

Figure 14.3. Recording duration data.

of tantrum is simply crying without lying on the floor. This level is "mild"; it gets an intensity rating of 1. Each of the last two levels of intensity was arbitrarily determined. You just as easily could have identified five levels instead of three. Obviously the fewer levels of intensity you have to work with, the easier it is to record the data. Once you have identified and specified the levels of intensity for the behavior, you are ready to monitor it. When the student has a tantrum, simply decide whether it is mild (1), moderate (2), or severe (3) and make a mark under the appropriate intensity level. At the end of the day, you will know how many tantrums the student had at each level of intensity. By doing a little simple arithmetic (which will be described later), you will also be able to determine the student's average level of intensity for his tantrums. This information is very important. Look at Figure 14.4. This student was averaging five tantrums a day during baseline. Her tantrums consisted of lying on the floor, screaming, and banging her head. During intervention, the data show that her frequency of tantrums was roughly the same per day (i.e., five and six). If we had collected data only on the frequency of daily tantrums, it would appear that the student was not improving, and that the intervention was not effective. However, since we also collected data on the intensity of the student's tantrum behavior, we see that while the total number of tantrums per day didn't change much, there is a big difference in the intensity of her tantrum behavior. The number of severe tantrums involving head-banging and screaming dropped considerably and the student, while still having a large number of tantrums, is now engaging in more moderate behavior, lying on the floor, shaking her head from side to side, and crying, instead of screaming and banging her head.

Behaver _(student)_

Monitor _(teacher)_

Counted _tantrums_

Key: (1) Mild: cries
(2) Moderate: lies on floor, cries, shakes head
(3) Severe: lies on floor, screams, bangs head

Date	Level of Intensity (LOI)			Avg. (LOI)	F
	①	②	③		
2-2-89			ΤΗΤ	3.0	5
2-3-89		IIII	II	2.3	6
2-4-89		ΤΗΤ		2.0	5
2-5-89	III	III		1.5	6
2-6-89					

Figure 14.4. Recording intensity data.

Continuous and Interval Samples

One reason why teachers dislike monitoring student behavior is that it sometimes interferes with their teaching. The best way to monitor behavior is to do it continuously. As long as the student is in plain view, observe and record the frequency, duration, and intensity of his or her behavior. The more data you have, the more reliable they are likely to be. This is why you should always try to use a continuous monitoring sample. However, if you are the only adult in the class or you can't spare your aide for several hours (or even minutes) of monitoring, the only way you will be able to use a continuous sample is if the behavior you are monitoring is one that comes easily to your attention and therefore can be monitored without your having to take time away from your teaching. For example, you will probably have no trouble continuously monitoring behaviors that are loud (shouting or throwing tantrums), that are highly visible (running around the classroom or throwing objects), or that occur only in your presence (calling out instead of raising a hand when you ask the class a question).

However, it is not possible to continuously monitor "quiet" behaviors such as daydreaming, copying work of others, nail biting, thumb sucking, quiet self-stimming (rocking in place or shaking one's head from side to side), making facial grimaces, being on (or off) task, or being in (or out of) seat, especially in a large room with many students. The answer is to monitor these "quiet" behaviors on an interval or time sample basis. Instead of watching the student all day, glance at him several times during the day. You will be able to tell in a 1- or 2-second glance whether or not the student is engaging in a quiet behavior. If you glance at the student 20 times during the course of a school day to determine if he is on or off task, the whole process of observing and recording will take you no more than 1 or 2 minutes: a total of 5 seconds to observe and record the student's behavior multiplied by 20 glances equals approximately 1½ minutes.

Sometimes a continuous sample is not possible and a glance is not enough time to tell you what you want to know about a student's behavior. Remember, an interval can be as brief as a glance in the student's direction or as long as an hour or more. The difference between a continuous sample and an interval sample may be seen in what you do when the student engages in the behavior being monitored. During the continuous sample, monitor the student's behavior all the time she is in your presence. Record every time she engages in the behavior. If you use an interval sample, record the student's behavior only at predetermined times. Although the student may be in your presence all day long and engage in the behavior quite often, you would only record it if the behavior occurred during one of the monitoring intervals. If it did not occur during a monitoring interval, it would not be recorded. You can see by this that the interval method of monitoring is not always as reliable as the continuous method, since a lot depends on the number and length of the intervals as well as when they are scheduled. A teacher who schedules three 2-minute intervals during the morning will probably not get data as reliable as a teacher who uses six 2-minute intervals or even three 5-minute intervals. A rule of thumb to follow is this: The shorter the length of the interval, the greater the number of intervals you should use. This increases reliability. As long as monitoring is conducted correctly, it is better to collect a small amount of data than no data at all. Collect as much as you can without interfering with your teaching.

Figures 14.5–14.7 are examples of the interval sample technique used to monitor the frequency and duration of behaviors. In Figure 14.5 the teacher monitored the frequency of head slapping in a severely retarded student. He took a 1-minute sample of this behavior every hour (i.e., at 9:00, 10:00, 11:00, 1:00, and 2:00) that the student was in his presence. Since he did not have to worry about distracting the student, he simply set a kitchen timer for 60 minutes. When it went off, he reset it for 1 minute and observed the student, marking each instance of head slapping as it occurred. When the 1 minute was up, he reset the timer for 60 minutes and went on with his teaching.

Behaver (student)

Monitor (teacher)

Counted head slapping (self)

Sample interval (1')

Date	Interval					F
	9:00	10:00	11:00	1:00	2:00	
2-2-89	///	ℍℍ	////	//	ℍℍ ///	22
	9:00	10:00	11:00	1:00	2:00	
2-3-89	////	////	ℍℍ /	///	ℍℍ	22
	9:00	10:00	11:00	1:00	2:00	
2-4-89	///	//	ℍℍ	///	////	17
	9:00	10:00	11:00	1:00	2:00	
2-5-89						
	9:00	10:00	11:00	1:00	2:00	
2-6-89						

Figure 14.5. Recording frequency data using an interval sample.

The teacher in Figure 14.6 monitored the frequency of out-of-seat behavior in one of her students. Since she did not have any time at all during the school day when she could monitor the duration of this behavior, she simply glanced at the student's seat every half-hour. An alarm chronograph wristwatch alerted her. If he was in his seat, she wrote a plus on a piece of tape wrapped around her wrist. If the student was out of his seat when she glanced at it, she wrote a zero on the tape.

Figure 14.7 is an example of data collected by a teacher who wanted to monitor the duration of thumb sucking in a third-grade boy who was constantly being teased by his peers for this behavior. Even though he taught this youngster all day, because it was a quiet behavior, he was unable to continuously monitor the thumb sucking without ignoring the instructional needs of his other students. He therefore elected to monitor the behavior only at those times when all of his students (including the target child) were working independently, leaving him free to start and stop a stopwatch while he unobtrusively observed the target child.

Remember that the rule of thumb for deciding whether to use a continuous or an interval monitoring sample is how easily the behavior you are monitoring

2-2-89		2-3-89		2-4-89	
+	0	+	0	0	+
0	0	0	+	0	+
+	0	0	0	0	0
0	+	0	0	0	0
+	0	0	+	+	0
0	0	0	+	0	0
+	+	+	+	0	+

Figure 14.6. Recording on wrist tapes.

comes to your attention. Quiet behaviors often require interval samples so that teachers can collect data without disrupting instruction. On the other hand, behaviors that easily come to the teacher's attention can be monitored continuously because they will not require the teacher to stop what he or she is doing for longer than a second or two to record it. If the teacher wears a wristwatch-type golf counter, he or she can record each occurrence of a behavior without taking any attention away from teaching.

Collecting Data on Single Behaviors for Multiple Subjects

Sometimes a teacher may wish to monitor the behavior of more than one subject at a time. For example, she

may have a class of students who all engage in a great deal of inappropriate talking behavior. Rather than intervening with the entire class, the teacher may wish to focus on the few students who are the greatest offenders. In order to find out who these students are, she has to monitor the behavior of the entire class. Taking baseline data on one student each day would take too much time. She therefore decides to monitor the talking behavior of the entire class in one day. Using an interval sample technique, she monitors the talking behavior of the entire class during a 1-minute sample every half-hour. By looking at a different student every 2 seconds, she is able to record whether he or she is engaged in talking (or listening to someone talking). She records the data on a seating chart attached to a clipboard. Moving from student to student, she records a plus for talking or listening to someone talk or a minus for not talking or not listening to someone talk, in a box representing a student's seat. She uses a small tape recorder with an earplug that emits a recorded beeping sound every 2 seconds. The sound, discernible only to her, tells her when to move from one student to another. Actually, she uses 2 seconds to observe and 2 seconds to record, 2 to observe and 2 to record, and so on. This procedure is illustrated in Figure 14.8.

Collecting Data on Multiple Behaviors for Single Subjects

It is not unusual to want to monitor more than one behavior for a single student. For example, a student may have a number of behavior problems and the teacher may wish to monitor all of them to determine which occurs most frequently or lasts the longest or is the most intense. It may also be that the teacher has decided to modify more than one behavior in a student and needs to monitor the effects of different interventions on multiple behaviors. Whatever the reason, monitoring multiple behaviors is not as difficult as it sounds.

Figure 14.9 shows the data collected by a teacher who monitored three different behaviors in one student. This child made loud noises by clapping her hands together or banging them on the desk; she also asked the same questions over and over again. In addition, she stimulated herself by rocking in her seat and waving her hands in front of her face. The teacher wanted to eliminate all three behaviors simultaneously or at least intervene on all of them at the same time. Using an interval sample, he monitored all of the behaviors for a 5-minute period a minimum of six times during each school day. He did this whenever he thought of it and had the time to do so. Fortunately, he had an aide

Behaver (student)

Monitor (teacher)

Counted thumb sucking (any part inside mouth)

Sample interval

Date	Interval					Duration of Thumb Sucking	Total Time Observed	Percentage
2-2-89	9:30-9:40	480"	2:30-3:00	1215"		3250"	4200"	77
	10:45-11:00	765"						
	1:35-1:45	300"						
	2:10-2:20	490"						
2-3-89	9:25-9:40	369"	2:35-3:00	1010"		2645"	4740"	56
	10:42-11:05	614"						
	1:30-1:40	352"						
	2:12-2:18	300"						

Figure 14.7. Recording duration data using an interval sample.

and a student teacher helping him at this time. Using the recording form shown in Figure 14.9, he simply circled the code for a behavior each time it occurred.

Collecting Data for Reciprocal Behaviors

By "reciprocal" we mean what one person does and what another person or persons do in response. For example, you might wish to find out whether or not a student's clowning behavior is being reinforced by peer attention. This necessitates monitoring both the clowning behavior of the target student and the attending behavior of the peers.

Figure 14.10 shows the data collected by a teacher who wanted to monitor the reciprocal relationship between a student's physically aggressive behavior and the responses of his peers. Specifically, she wanted to see if he was being selective when he punched and slapped classmates or if he was acting impulsively. The impulsive student acts before he thinks, while the selective student decides to act based upon his reflection. Obviously, the former student gets into trouble more readily because he doesn't take the time to consider the consequences. The teacher in this example wanted to find out if the target student was consistently hitting all of his peers, even though many of them were bigger

and tougher and often hit him back harder. Using a continuous sample, she recorded each instance of hitting by the target student, which peer he hit, and the reaction of that peer. Each box on her O & R form represented one separate instance of a "hit" by the target student. By using the code, the teacher was able to record quickly which peer was hit and what his or her response was. At the end of the monitoring period, it became obvious to the teacher that the target student was selective in his attacks, avoiding those peers who had previously responded by hitting him back and seeking out those who did not assert themselves physically. This indicated that the student's hitting behavior was reflective rather than impulsive, which helped the teacher decide upon an appropriate intervention.

Collecting Qualitative Data

Monitoring student behavior can yield qualitative as well as quantitative information. It can tell you when a student engages in a certain behavior as well as how often. It can show you who the student directs his or her behavior at and what happens in response to the behavior. For example, a teacher wanted to monitor the frequency of the hitting behavior of one of his students. He simply counted hits, using a continuous sample, for

Behaver __(CLASS)__

Monitor __(teacher)__

Counted __TALKING W/O PERMISSION (includes listening—__
__i.e., head directed toward speaker)__

Sample __interval (2")__

Time __9:00__

5 −	6 −	15 −	16 +	25 +
4 +	7 +	14 −	17 +	24 −
3 −	8 −	13 −	18 −	23 −
2 −	9 +	12 +	19 −	22 +
1 +	10 +	11 −	20 +	21 +

Figure 14.8. Recording frequency data on single behaviors of multiple subjects.

Behaver __(student)__

Monitor __(teacher)__

Counted __(NY) NOISY (VP) VERBAL PERSEVERATION__
__(SS) SELF-STIMULATION (rocking, hand waving)__

Sample __interval 5'__

Interval	Responses	Totals
9:15–9:20	(NY)(NY)(NY)(NY) NY NY NY NY (VP)(VP) VP VP VP VP VP VP (SS)(SS)(SS)(SS)(SS) SS SS SS	4 2 5
10:35–10:40	NY NY NY NY NY NY NY NY VP VP VP VP VP VP VP VP SS SS SS SS SS SS SS SS	
11:02–11:07	NY NY NY NY NY NY NY NY VP VP VP VP VP VP VP VP SS SS SS SS SS SS SS SS	
1:30–1:35	NY NY NY NY NY NY NY NY VP VP VP VP VP VP VP VP SS SS SS SS SS SS SS SS	

Figure 14.9. Recording frequency data on multiple behaviors of a single subject.

two days. At the end of this period of time, he knew how many hits the student made but had no information regarding who she hit or when she did so. The teacher wanted this information because he reasoned (correctly) that it would help him determine the most appropriate intervention to use. Beginning on day 3 of the baseline phase, he didn't just put a mark down after each hit, but instead wrote the initials of the student who was hit by the target student as well as the time. At the end of two more days of baseline, he could see a pattern emerge. An inordinate number of hits were directed toward the same students and occurred at times during the day when the class was involved in unstructured group activities. With this information, the teacher decided to build more structure into these activities and also to focus on the relationships between the target student and the students she picked on. Some informal questioning of these students brought to light a conflict

that had been going on for a long time. If this teacher had simply collected frequency data or quantitative data on the hitting behavior, he would not have been able to gain any insight into its cause. The qualitative data collected in this example may be seen in Figure 14.11.

Self-Monitoring

Self-monitoring is important for two reasons. First, many teachers feel overwhelmed by the prospect of data collection. In some, it stirs up memories of a dry statistics course. In others it conjures up the image of a cold, calculating scientist in a sterile white lab coat, complete with clipboard and graphs. Many feel that collecting data robs them of their spontaneity, while others view data collection as adding more paperwork to a job already top-heavy in bookkeeping. One answer to the problem may be self-monitoring. Let the students collect data on their own behavior. Would they be honest enough not to cheat and make themselves look good? Read chapter 8 regarding self-monitoring. You'll be surprised. Letting students monitor their own behavior relieves the teacher of much of the burden of data collection.

Behaver _(student)_

Monitor _(teacher)_

Counted _student hits/peer reaction_

Sample _Continuous_   **Date** _2-4-89_

Key: (I) Peer ignores
(VA) Peer verbally asserts
(PA) Peer physically asserts

MJ/I	BR/PA	MJ/I	SL/PA	MJ/VA	ET/PA	MJ/VA	TS/PA
SK/PA	MJ/VA	MJ/I	DL/PA	MJ/VA	MJ/I	PT/PA	MJ/VA
MJ/VA	DK/PA	MJ/I					

Figure 14.10. Recording frequency data on reciprocal relationships.

Second, self-monitoring can make your students more aware of their behavior—when they are "bad" and when they are "good." As I mentioned in chapter 4, awareness of one's behavior is one of the most common prerequisites for engaging in target behaviors.

While the methodology of self-monitoring is discussed in detail in chapter 8, this is a good place to take a look at the countoon. The word "countoon" tells you what's involved in this technique—counting and using a cartoon on which to record the data. Figure 14.12 is an example of a countoon used to record the frequency of hand-raising behavior. The first frame of the cartoon ("What I Do") shows a picture of what the students are supposed to do (i.e., raise their hand when they want to speak). This is usually drawn by the students themselves. The second frame ("How Many") provides the students with a place to record the frequency of their hand-raising behavior. This can easily be converted for monitoring duration or intensity of a behavior. The third frame ("What Happens") is also drawn by the students and shows the consequences of their hand-raising behavior. In this particular example, the student receives one token for each instance of hand raising.

While the countoon is best used to monitor positive (i.e., target) behaviors, it can sometimes be used to monitor maladaptive behavior. Figure 14.13 is an example. This countoon says that for each instance of hitting a peer, the student will be required to wear a heavy mitten on his hand for 5 minutes during free time. This

Behaver _(student)_

Monitor _(teacher)_

Counted _hitting/unprovoked_

Sample _continuous_

Date	Frequency	Totals
2-2-89	⊞ II	7
2-3-89	⊞ IIII	9
2-4-89	MB 8:30 TJ 8:35 TJ 8:36 MB 2:15 TJ 2:16 MB 2:20 MB 2:24	7
2-5-89	MB 8:32 MB 8:33 MB 8:33 TJ 2:12 TJ 2:12 MB 2:13 MB 2:15	7
2-6-89		

Figure 14.11. Recording frequency data of a qualitative nature.

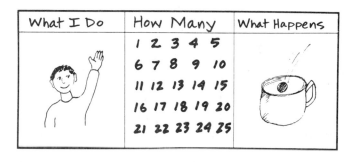

Figure 14.12. Countoon for recording target behaviors.

Figure 14.13. Countoon for recording maladaptive behaviors.

particular student enjoys painting and the mitten makes it difficult for him to paint. Because he has three numbers circled, he's going to have to wear the mitten for 15 minutes. The countoon is usually drawn on a heavy piece of paper that is then laminated so that the data can be erased and the countoon can be reused the next day.

This system can be used one of two ways. Either the teacher tells the student what to mark on the countoon, which would save her the trouble of recording it, or the student is completely on his own to record the data. Again, the teacher must monitor the student's behavior periodically and compare her data with his in order to ensure that the student has been both honest and aware. If the data are left on the student's desk overnight, the countoon serves as a reminder the next morning of what he should or should not do during the new day. He may even wish to set a goal for himself for the new day based upon yesterday's data. This goal can be written or marked on the countoon in the "How Many" frame. As the day progresses, the student has a constant reminder of where he is in relation to that goal. If he doesn't reach it, he can't blame the teacher for biased or inaccurate monitoring. More importantly, if he doesn't think he's going to reach his goal, he can always change it in the middle of the day by simply erasing it and writing a new one. It may be, on the other hand, that he's doing so well that he'll want to raise his goal for the day. This is all possible because he's in control of the data. He's not only informed about what's going on; he's able to react to it.

Observation and Recording Forms

You can be as fancy as you want when it comes to O & R forms. Some people simply use a 3″ × 5″ card or the back of an envelope, while others write on a piece of tape wrapped around their wrists or use a golf counter bought at the local sporting goods shop. Personally, I wouldn't be fulfilled creatively with the back of an envelope, but that doesn't mean that you have to get fancy too. Use whatever you feel comfortable with that is simple to use and easy to read. The figures in this chapter should give you enough ideas to start with.

Summarizing the Data

Once you have collected the data, you need to summarize it. Data may be summarized as raw score, percentage, rate, or average. For those of you who, like me, have a mental block when it comes to math, a little refresher course might be in order.

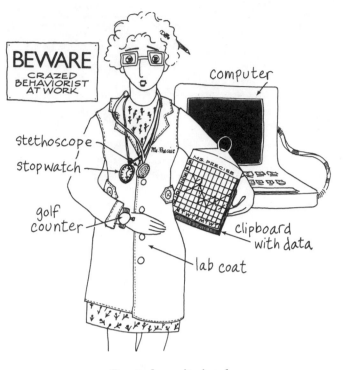

Try to keep it simple.

Raw Score

Raw scores are the total numbers you get before you do anything to them. If you are monitoring the frequency of a student's behavior, raw score is the total number of times the student engaged in that behavior. If you are monitoring the duration of a student's behavior, raw score is the total number of minutes the student engaged in that behavior. Calculating raw score is quite simple. Just count the number of times or minutes the student engaged in the behavior you are monitoring.

Percentage

I am going to assume that you understand what percentage is in the general sense. If not, look it up in a basic arithmetic text before you read any further. When you are monitoring the frequency of a student's behavior and you need to use percentage, simply divide the total number of opportunities the student had to engage in the behavior into the total number of times he actually engaged in it. When you are monitoring the duration of a student's behavior and you need to use percentage, simply divide the total number of minutes you observed the student into the total number of minutes you observed her engaging in that behavior. The percentage that you get will be a decimal such as .85 or .15 (unless you get 100%). These percentages may be read respectively as 85% and 15%.

Rate

Rate may be defined as the average number of times (i.e., frequency of response) a student engages in a particular behavior during a given amount of time (e.g., minutes). It is calculated by dividing the total number of minutes you observed the student into the total number of times she engaged in the behavior. Rate may be expressed as a whole number or as a decimal. Figure 14.14 lists a number of sample rates and how to read each. Pay particular attention to the decimals. Remember that they are rates, not percentages, and are read differently. In my teaching, I have found that rate is often confused with percentage. The difference is that when you calculate rate, you are dividing time (usually minutes) into behavior (frequency of response); when you calculate percentage, you are dividing time (minutes) into time (minutes) or behavior (opportunity to respond) into behavior (frequency of response). An example of using rate to summarize a behavior may be seen in Figure 14.15.

Average

The average may be calculated by dividing the number of values into the sum of those values. An example of this was seen in Figure 14.15. Calculating the average level of intensity of a particular behavior is discussed and outlined in Figure 14.16.

Choosing the Correct Summarization

Before you can decide when to use raw score, percentage, rate, or average to summarize your data, you must understand two important concepts: *free operants* and *controlled operants*.

Free Operants

A free operant is a behavior for which there is no readily observable antecedent or stimulus. It just seems to occur on its own and is often difficult to predict or anticipate. Examples of free operants are unprovoked hits, asking questions, being out of seat, and self-stimulation, such as making animal sounds. Free operants do not appear to be controlled by an obvious environmental stimulus. A student may hit a peer without an obvious provocation. Question-asking behavior does not always have to be preceded by an obvious stimulus from the environment. A student may leave his seat or make animal sounds for no obvious reason. Notice that I keep using the word "obvious." By that I mean not readily observable by the teacher. One student may hit another because of something that student said or did an hour or a day earlier and this is the first chance he had to retaliate, or he might have just remembered the event.

0.01 is read as 1 response per 100 minutes
0.007 is 7 responses per 1,000 minutes
15 is 15 responses per 1 minute
150 is 150 responses per 1 minute
0.15 is 15 responses per 100 minutes or 1½ responses per 10 minutes
0.025 is 25 responses per 1,000 minutes or 2½ per 100 minutes
32 is 32 responses per 1 minute
6 is 6 responses per 1 minute
0.6 is 6 responses per 10 minutes
0.08 is 8 responses per 100 minutes
0.2 is 2 responses per 10 minutes
0.72 is 72 responses per 100 minutes or 7 responses per 10 minutes

Figure 14.14. Reading rates.

Behaver _Joey_

Monitor _Mrs. D._

Counted _says swear words_

Date	Frequency	Time Observed (minutes)	Rate
3-6-89	ℍℍ ℍℍ	60	0.16
3-7-89	ℍℍ ||||	45	0.2
3-8-89	ℍℍ ℍℍ ℍℍ	120	0.125

Figure 14.15. Summarizing frequency data as rate.

At the time he hits his peer, there is no stimulus readily observable to the teacher. Therefore, the teacher must consider the hitting a free operant.

Controlled Operants

A controlled operant is a behavior that is preceded by an antecedent or stimulus that is readily observable by the change agent. Examples of controlled operants are giving answers to questions asked, complying with

Steps: 1. Multiply each frequency by its corresponding intensity.
2. Find the sum of these products.
3. Find the sum of the frequencies.
4. Divide the sum of the frequencies into the sum of the products. Example:

Step	Date	Level of Intensity			Average
		①	②	③	
〜	2-18-89	卌	/	//	
/		5×1=5	1×2=2	2×3=6	
2		5	+2	+6	=13
3		卌	+/	+//	=8
4					¹³/₈ =1.6 (AVG)

Figure 14.16. Computing levels of intensity.

demands given, provoked verbal or physical aggression (e.g., hitting peers after being pushed by them), and saying "Thank you" in response to a compliment given. These are referred to as "controlled" operants because each is controlled by an obvious stimulus from the environment. For example, the number of questions answered is controlled by (i.e., dependent upon) the number of questions asked. The number of times a student complies with a demand is controlled by the number of demands made. The number of provoked aggressive acts a student makes is controlled by the number of provocations she experiences. The number of times a student says "Thank you" in response to a compliment is controlled by the number of compliments he gets.

Now that you know the difference between free and controlled operants, choosing the correct data summarization is a relatively simple matter of remembering the following rules of thumb:

1. If you are monitoring the frequency of free operant behavior for the same amount of time each day, you may summarize the data as raw score. For example, let's say that you monitored the frequency of talk-outs on Monday for 1 hour and recorded 12; on Tuesday you recorded 16, also for 1 hour. You would be accurate if you said that the behavior is getting worse because the total number of talk-outs is increasing. Raw score is computed by adding the number of responses for a given day and entering the total on the appropriate form. You use raw score in this example because you are monitoring the frequency of a free operant behav-

ior (talk-outs) for the same amount of time each day (1 hour).

2. If you are monitoring the frequency of free operant behavior for a different amount of time each day, you must use rate to summarize the data. For example, suppose that you monitored the frequency of talk-outs on Monday for one hour and recorded 10; on Tuesday you monitored the same behavior for 30 minutes and recorded 6. If you summarized these data using raw score, it would appear that the talk-out behavior was decreasing in frequency, because the total talk-outs went down (from 10 to 6). However, if you summarized these data as rate (by dividing the number of minutes into the number of responses), you would see that the behavior was actually increasing in frequency. On Monday the student's rate was 0.16 talk-outs per minute (or 1½ talk-outs per 10 minutes), and on Tuesday, it went up to 0.2 talk-out per minute (or 2 talk-outs per 10 minutes)!

3. If you are monitoring the frequency of controlled operant behavior, regardless of the amount of time observed, you must summarize the data as percentage. Let's say that you were counting "complies with directives given"; on Wednesday you counted five complies and on Thursday you counted eight. If you use raw score, it appears that the student is becoming increasingly compliant. However, if you gave 7 directives on Wednesday and 12 on Thursday, the student's respective percentages would be 71 and 66, which means that the student is actually decreasingly compliant! Percentage is computed by dividing the number of opportunities to respond into the actual number of responses made.

4. If you are monitoring the duration of free operant behavior and the time observed is constant, use raw score. Suppose that you used a stopwatch to monitor the duration of out-of-seat behavior on Monday and Tuesday for a total of 5 hours each day. If the student was out of her seat for a total of 1 hour on Monday and 1½ hours on Tuesday, you could say that her behavior was growing worse. Raw score for duration is computed by adding the number of hours, minutes, and seconds that a student is observed engaging in the behavior being monitored.

5. If you are monitoring the duration of free operant behavior and the time observed varies, use percentage to summarize the data. Let's say that you were monitoring the out-of-seat behavior of a student for 3 hours on Thursday and 5 hours on Friday and his raw score totals were 1 hour and 1½ hours, respectively. Does this mean that he's getting worse? No. You use percentage to summarize your data. He's actually getting better because his percentage of out-of-seat

behavior went from 33% on Thursday (60 minutes divided by 180 minutes) down to 30% on Friday (90 minutes divided by 300 minutes). Percentage of duration is computed by dividing the total time observed into the time observed engaging in the behavior.

6. If you are monitoring the intensity of free operant behavior, use average regardless of the time observed or opportunities given.

Displaying the Data

As with the O & R forms, data display may be sophisticated or primitive. It all depends on how much time you have (or want) to spend on it. The advantage of charting behavioral data instead of simply writing the raw scores, percentages, rates, or averages on a card can be seen in the following experiment. First, scan the data in Figure 14.17. Scan it—don't read it. Next, scan Figure 14.18. Ask yourself which was easier to interpret with regard to trend. In other words, does it take less time to see whether the student is getting better or worse by looking at the data represented by the individual scores (i.e., rates) listed in Figure 14.17 or by a line on the chart shown in Figure 14.18? Obviously, the chart allows faster interpretation of trend. By visualizing trends quickly, we are able to determine in very little time whether or not the intervention is working. This can be a distinct advantage when you have more than one behavioral intervention program in progress. For this reason I recommend the use of charts over tables or matrices as a data display mode. The chart can be as simple as the linear type shown in Figure 14.19 or as sophisticated as the ratio chart in Figure 14.20. The latter is a 6-cycle semilogarithmic chart used by precision teaching exponents to record rate data. The advantage of the semilogarithmic chart is that you can use a simple statistical procedure to predict future performance. Whatever chart you decide to use, you'll be glad you decided to display the data in this manner.

Interpreting the Data

Now that you have collected the data and displayed it on a chart, what does it all mean? The easiest way to interpret the data displayed on a chart is to compare baseline performance with data collected during the intervention phase. This would suggest that the intervention program is working.

For example, in Figure 14.21, the behavior being monitored is audible speech. In this case, the intervention is geared to increase the behavior. Notice that the trend of the data during the baseline phase is consis-

Words Read Correctly (per minute)	
Day	**Rate**
M	50
T	42
W	52
TH	48
F	60
M	65
T	60
W	70
TH	75
F	65

Figure 14.17. Data display on card.

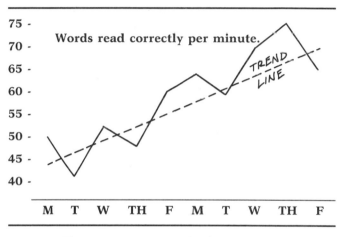

Figure 14.18. Data display on chart.

tent. It shows the behavior at a low level. Now look at the trend during the intervention phase. The trend indicates that the behavior is improving, because the average intensity (i.e., loudness) of the subject's speech is increasing. This means that the intervention is effective.

The news is not as good in Figure 14.22. Here the behavior being monitored is being off task (i.e., eyes directed away from work). Obviously, we want this behavior to decrease. The baseline data suggest a consistently high level of off-task behavior. Unfortunately, so do the data collected during the intervention phase. This suggests that the intervention is not working or has had no effect on the behavior so far.

Figure 14.23 shows a data display for self-stimulation (e.g., rocking in place). The percentages of time spent rocking during baseline are relatively stable, around 75% to 90% of the time observed. However, there is a marked decrease in the behavior beginning at about the third day of the intervention phase. This suggests that the intervention program is working.

Name _____

Objective _____

Movement _____

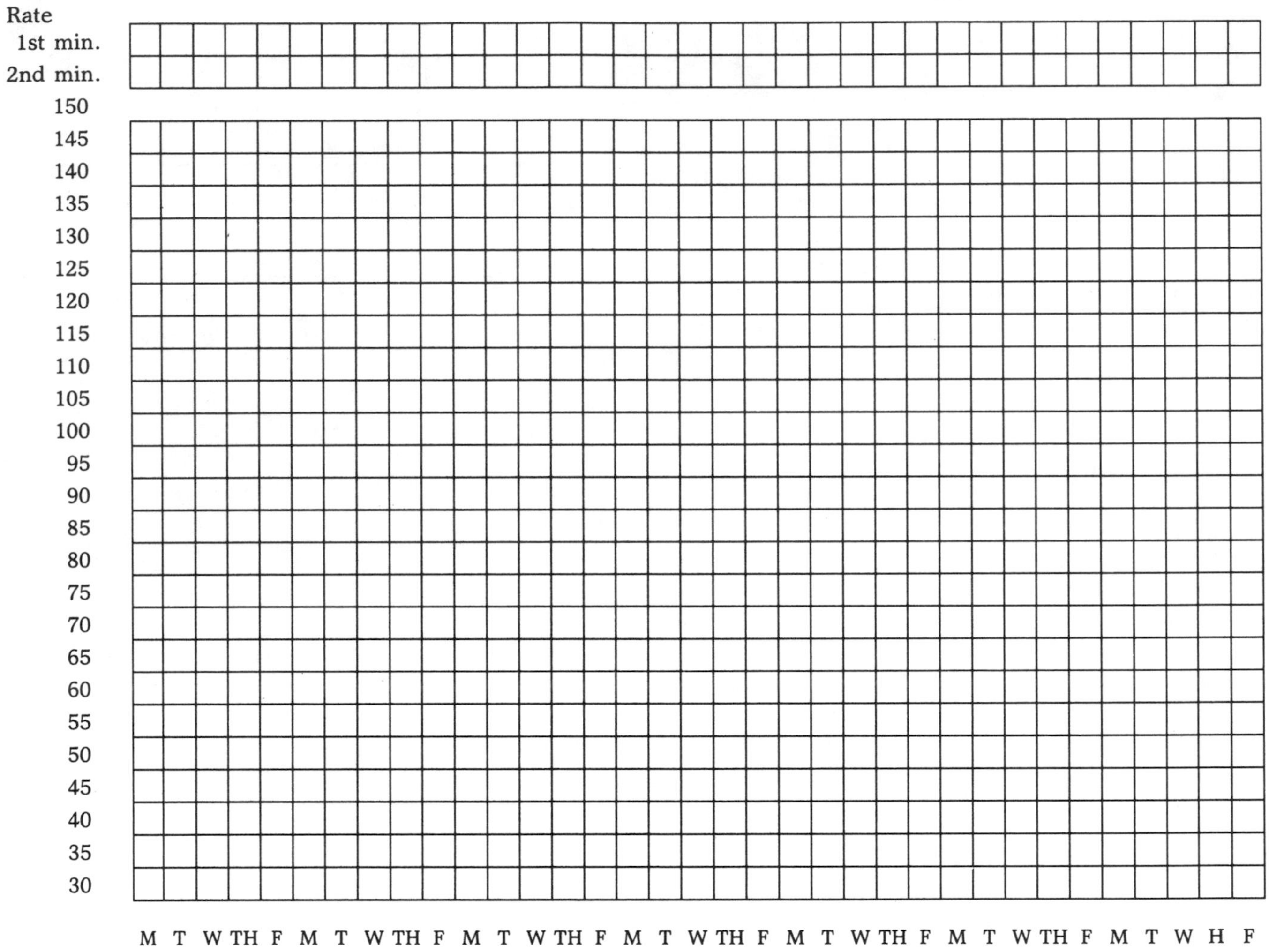

Rate
1st min.
2nd min.

150
145
140
135
130
125
120
115
110
105
100
95
90
85
80
75
70
65
60
55
50
45
40
35
30

M T W TH F M T W TH F M T W TH F M T W TH F M T W TH F M T W TH F M T W H F

Figure 14.19. Linear chart.

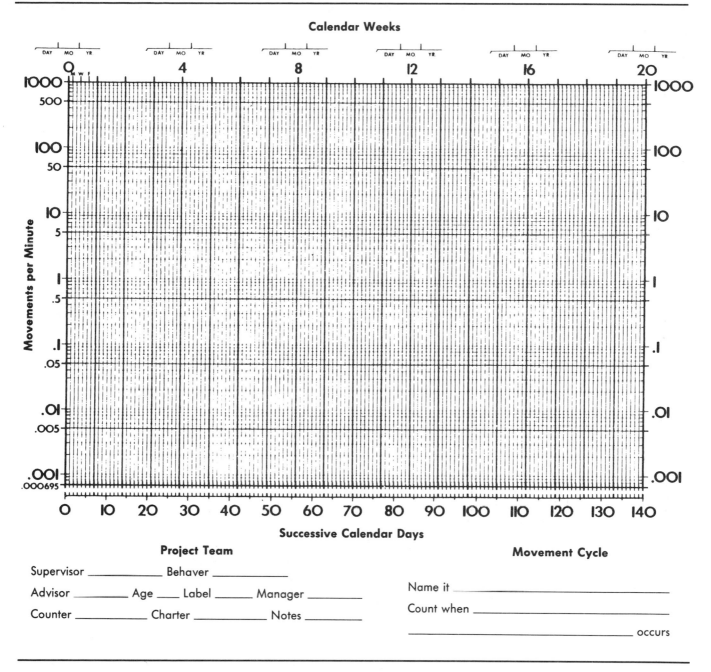

Figure 14.20. Ratio chart.

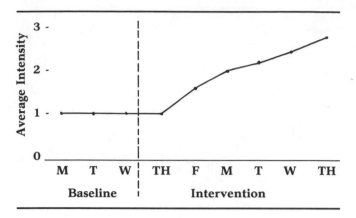

Figure 14.21. Interpreting data regarding audible speech.

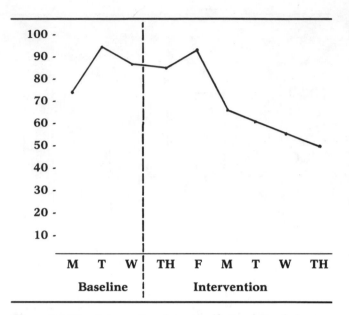

Figure 14.23. Interpreting data on self-stimulating behavior.

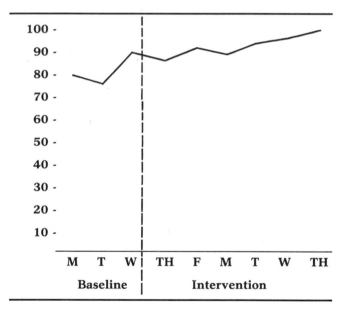

Figure 14.22. Interpreting data on off-task behavior.

Chapter Fourteen Self-Assessment

See Appendix A for acceptable responses.

1. Explain the differences between the baseline and intervention phases of monitoring.

2. Which of the following behaviors should be monitored according to frequency, duration, and intensity? Write "F," "D," and/or "I" on the line next to each.

   _____ a. Daydreams
   _____ b. Makes noise
   _____ c. Hits peers
   _____ d. Sleeps in class
   _____ e. Comes to class prepared
   _____ f. Completes assignments
   _____ g. Stays on task
   _____ h. Interrupts speakers
   _____ i. Is tardy
   _____ j. Has tantrums

3. Write "CS" on the line next to each of the following behaviors if it can be monitored with a continuous sample by a teacher who has 30 students and no aides. Write "IS" if the behavior cannot be monitored by that teacher with a continuous sample and requires an interval sample.

   _____ a. Fist fights
   _____ b. On task/off task
   _____ c. Thumb sucking
   _____ d. Masturbation (rubbing groin area)
   _____ e. Calling out (without raising hand)
   _____ f. Out of seat (i.e., buttocks not in contact with chair)
   _____ g. Successful completion of assignments
   _____ h. Noncompliance
   _____ i. Bowel movements (in pants)
   _____ j. Copying answers (looking at peers' work)

4. Describe how you would monitor the frequency of talking-without-permission behavior for a class of 30 students.

continued next page

5. Describe how you would monitor being out of seat, talking without permission, and hitting for one student in your class.

6. Describe how you would monitor the teasing behavior of one student as well as the responses to teasing in his peers.

7. Describe how you would monitor a student's disruptive behavior (i.e., shouting out at students or teacher) in order to get qualitative data.

8. Draw a countoon for a student who is monitoring a target behavior—for example, being on task (eyes directed at work on desk).

9. Use a separate sheet of paper to design an O & R form to monitor the frequency of a self-injurious behavior, such as head slapping in a single subject using an interval sample.

10. On a separate sheet design an O & R form to monitor the duration of thumb sucking in a single subject using an interval sample.

11. Design an O & R form to monitor the frequency of talking without permission in 25 subjects using an interval sample.

12. Design an O & R form to monitor three different behaviors in a single subject using an interval sample.

continued next page

13. Design an O & R form to monitor the reciprocal behaviors of student hits and peer reactions using a continuous sample.

14. Design an O & R form to monitor the frequency and intensity of a single behavior in a single subject using a continuous sample.

15. For each of the following situations, *underline* the correct summarization procedure.

    a. You are monitoring question-asking behavior and the time you observe changes daily.

        raw score   percentage   rate   average

    b. You are monitoring the duration of in-seat behavior and the time varies from day to day.

        raw score   percentage   rate   average

    c. You are monitoring the frequency of spitting behavior and the time observed remains constant.

        raw score   percentage   rate   average

    d. You are monitoring the intensity of self-injurious behavior (i.e., bites) and the time observed varies daily.

        raw score   percentage   rate   average

    e. You are monitoring the frequency of compliance behavior and the number of directives given varies.

        raw score   percentage   rate   average

    f. You are monitoring the duration of off-task behavior and the time observed is constant.

        raw score   percentage   rate   average

    g. You are monitoring the intensity of tantrum behavior and the time observed remains constant.

        raw score   percentage   rate   average

    h. You are monitoring the frequency of question-answering behavior and the number of questions asked remains constant.

        raw score   percentage   rate   average

continued next page

16. Summarize and interpret the data in each of the following hypothetical cases. Make sure that you answer all questions and show all work somewhere on the page.

Manager: Snow White   **Monitor:** Snow White   **Behaver:** Sleepy   **Behavior:** Yawns

Date	Frequency	Time Observed	Rates
2-18-89	⊬⊬ ⊬⊬ ⊬⊬ ///	50 (minutes)	
2-19-89	⊬⊬ ///	30	
2-20-89	⊬⊬ ⊬⊬ ⊬⊬ ⊬⊬ ////	90	
2-23-89	⊬⊬ ⊬⊬ ⊬⊬	75	
2-24-89	⊬⊬ ////	50	

a. Compute the rates for each date. Write your answers in the column marked "Rates." Show all work on the page.

b. Is Sleepy's yawning behavior getting better or worse? _____

c. Take Sleepy's highest rate and write what it means in your own words. For example: It means that Sleepy is yawning at a rate of _____

Behaver: Frankie   **Manager:** Igor   **Key:** 1 = mild (i.e., throws food)
Monitor: Dr. Stein   **Behavior:** tantrums   2 = moderate (throws people)
3 = severe (ravages countryside)

Date	1	2	3	Average
4-2-90	/	//	⊬⊬	
4-3-90	/	/	///	
4-4-90	//	0	///	
4-5-90	//	//	//	
4-6-90	////	0	/	

continued next page

d. Compute the average intensity for each date and write it in the "Average" column. Show all work on paper.

e. Is Frankie's tantrum behavior getting better or worse according to *intensity*? _____

f. Is Frankie's tantrum behavior getting better or worse according to *frequency*? _____

g. Take Frankie's *lowest* average and write what it means in your own words. For example: It means that _____

Behaver: Baby Ruth   **Manager:** Mr. Goodbar   **Monitor:** Mr. Goodbar

Behavior: thumb sucking   Date 4-5-90   [each box represents a 2' interval]
                                              number in boxes = seconds

21"	25"	32"	18"	72"	112"
24"	37"	19"	120"		

h. Compute the percentage of time Baby Ruth engaged in thumb-sucking behavior for this date. She was observed for a total of 20 minutes. Percentage =

17. Plot the following data:

Baseline (for frequency of talk-outs summarized as raw score)

Day 1, 12; Day 2, 19; Day 3, 15

Intervention (same as for Baseline)

Day 4, 17; Day 5, 11; Day 6, 10; Day 7, 9; Day 8, 5

18. Given the data plotted on the chart for number 17, would you say that the intervention was working? Explain your answer.

Appendix A
Acceptable Responses to Self-Assessments

Important: Your answers need not match mine word for word but should convey the same meaning.

Chapter 1/Acceptable Responses

1. Multiple Choice

   a. R+
   b. R−
   c. extinction
   d. punishment
   e. extinction
   f. R+
   g. punishment
   h. R−
   i. punishment
   j. punishment

   k. extinction
   l. R−
   m. R+
   n. punishment
   o. R+
   p. R−
   q. extinction
   r. R+
   s. R−
   t. punishment

2. Operants and respondents:

   a. Operants: write, read book, walk in hall, talk to peers, eat lunch, look at teacher, run out of classroom, shout out answer, raise hand, wait turn, share materials, line up, play ball, fight, hit peers, cry, tattle, pass notes, have tantrum, come to class, sit down, stand up, say "hello," follow directions, do homework
   b. Respondents: heartbeat, knee-jerk reflex, salivation, yawn, eye blink, body temperature (going up or down), blush

3. Learned and unlearned reinforcers and punishers:

   a. Learned reinforcers: money, tokens, social praise (e.g., "good boy!"), activities (e.g., drawing, listening to music, reading comics), passing grades, smiles, pictures of smiling faces (on assignments), greetings (from favored person), gifts (presents), positive attention
   b. Unlearned reinforcers: food (when hungry), special food treats (e.g., candy, cookies, fruit, juice), warmth (when cold), coolness (when hot), sleep or rest (when tired), physical contact (e.g., touching, holding hand, hugs, pats, rubs), pleasing sounds (e.g., music)

   c. Learned punishers: sarcasm, frown or angry look, reprimand or scolding (e.g., "I don't like that!"), threats (e.g., physical or verbal gesture), failing grades, peer rejection, loss of privilege, fine or penalty, loss of attention
   d. Unlearned punishers: corporal punishment (e.g., paddling or spanking), loud noise, aversive substance (e.g., squirting water in nose or lemon juice in mouth), seclusion or confinement, withholding sustenance (e.g., food, water, light)

4. Reciprocal relationships: Use any example that clearly shows a change in one person's behavior influencing or leading to change in a second person's behavior. Refer to the section on reciprocal relationships and to Figure 1.10 if you have any questions.

Chapter 2/Acceptable Responses

1. Symptom substitution: Symptom substitution is a criticism of behavior modification which says that the latter is not effective because it only treats (i.e., modifies) the individual's symptoms or behaviors and not the underlying cause of the problem. Critics warn that with the underlying cause left untreated, new symptoms or behaviors will eventually surface and have to be dealt with.

2. Any three of the following situations are acceptable responses:

   a. Resensitization is often mistaken for symptom substitution; this occurs when a previously eliminated response ("symptom") reappears as a direct result of a new trauma.
   b. The maladaptive behavior originally eliminated may have been one of a number of similar maladaptive behaviors in a larger behavior (e.g., crying and lying on the floor as part of having a tantrum).
   c. Maladaptive behavior that has been eliminated through behavior modification may reappear in

another situation if the change agent has not programmed for generalization across settings.

d. A change in a person's behavior may bring about change in the environment; this, in turn, can influence the person's behavior.

3. The author believes that symptom substitution can occur, especially in those situations where there are strong emotions (e.g., anger or fear), but that it is not inevitable.

4. To improve maintenance:

a. Always use a schedule of reinforcement (e.g., continuous, fixed, or variable). Behavior that is reinforced on a variable schedule of reinforcement is more likely to maintain over time.

b. Teach the student how to manage his own behavior. The more the student is able to exercise control over his own behavior, the more likely it is that the behavior will maintain.

c. Try to get the student to internalize her behavior (i.e., to engage in the behavior because she wants to). Again, intrinsic control will enhance maintenance.

5. To improve generalization of newly learned behaviors:

a. Teach behaviors that are likely to be reinforced in a variety of settings, such as compliance.

b. Expose the student to a variety of preceding stimuli or cues.

c. Enlist the support and cooperation of as many potential change agents as possible, such as other teachers, peers, or parents.

d. Find out what behaviors your students will need to learn in the new settings and situations they will be going into and teach them.

e. Use fading to gradually change your environment to more closely resemble the new environment your student will be going into.

f. Teach your students self-management skills so that they won't have to rely on others to manage their behavior in other settings and situations.

6. Positive reinforcement can be bribery when the teacher rewards student behavior that is primarily in the teacher's best interest (e.g., not questioning authority). Positive reinforcement should not be considered bribery when the teacher rewards student behavior that is primarily in the student's best interest (e.g., being assertive, staying on task in order to learn, getting along with others).

7. Humanists believe that by giving children more freedom when they are young, they will learn to think for themselves and become more responsible adults. Behaviorists believe that the more outside control children experience when they are young, the more they will master their environment and hence, the more freedom they will have as adults.

8. The author equates freedom with behavioral options. The more choices a person has to behave in any given situation, the more freedom he or she has.

9. Legal implications (you should include all of the following):

a. It may be illegal to operate token systems that use "basics" or "entitlements," such as recess, eating lunch with the peer group, and attending assemblies.

b. It may be illegal to use a token system in special education classes without giving students in the mainstream "equal opportunity" to use the token system.

c. It may be illegal to use behavior modification on a student without following due process.

10. "Yeah, buts":

a. There is an overwhelming amount of research that says behavior modification works. If it didn't work in your particular case, you might not have used it properly; what exactly did you do?

b. Yes, but they also are probably engaging in other, more subtle forms of maladaptive behavior, such as lying, stealing, cheating, or tattling.

c. How much time each day do you spend disciplining your students? With an effective behavior modification program, you would spend less time on discipline and have more time to devote to teaching (and data collection).

d. What kinds of reinforcers are you using? The most effective (praise, positive attention, and free time for favored activities) are also the least expensive.

e. A number of research studies have shown that behavior modification is effective with academic as well as social behaviors.

f. Research does not necessarily support the idea that smaller is better. Competent teachers can be just as effective with 30 students as they are with 20.

g. You have little or no control over what happens in the student's home. However, you do (or should) have control over what happens in your classroom.

h. Yes, if they don't have the opportunity to earn what their peers earn.

Chapter 3/Acceptable Responses

1. Pinpointing:

   a. Is off task: has eyes away from work for more than _____ seconds; has eyes away from work; has head turned away from task; stops writing; has eyes directed at peers instead of work

   b. Is punctual: is in seat when late bell rings; is in room before late bell rings; is in building before late bell rings

   c. Talks out: calls out without raising hand and waiting to be called on; addresses the teacher without permission

   d. Uses leisure time wisely: given free time, engages in task (or behavior) acceptable to teacher

   e. Is considerate of others: does not make disparaging remarks about peers; does not cut in front of peers while waiting in line; helps peers when they ask for it

   f. Lies: makes statements that are obviously untrue; does not state the truth when it is obvious she knows the truth

   g. Steals: takes things that do not belong to him without permission; takes property of others without their consent or knowledge

   h. Talks loudly: talks in a voice audible in all parts of the room; uses a voice that can be heard all over the room

   i. Comes to class prepared: brings pencil, paper, and books to class; brings (whatever is required by teacher) to class

   j. Is out of seat: buttocks are not in contact with seat; no part of body is in contact with seat; stands up (i.e., legs straight); is one step away from seat

   k. Laughs inappropriately: laughs when she sees someone hurt; laughs when she is told something that others consider negative

   l. Is responsible: finishes work without being reminded; successfully runs errands; follows directions as they are given

   m. Accepts criticism: does not cry, display anger, or make denials when work is corrected; when work is corrected, makes necessary changes without dissent or complaint

   n. Is clean: comes to school wearing clean clothes; washes hands before eating without being told; brushes teeth after meals without being reminded

   o. Acts mature: plays with children his own age; engages in behavior indicative of age group

   p. Is withdrawn: does not speak unless spoken to; speaks spontaneously only to one peer; does not initiate contact with peer group

   q. Has tantrums: cries, screams, and curses to get her way; shouts and curses when things don't go her way

   r. Does good work: gets "B" or better on all assignments; has "B" average in all subjects

   s. Has poor self-image: makes self-deprecating remarks often (e.g., "I'm stupid" or "I'm no good at that"); is not willing to try tasks he has performed successfully in past

   t. Is hostile: hits, kicks, and pushes peers without provocation; threatens peers without provocation (e.g., "I'm gonna beat you up!")

2. Fair Pairs:

   a. Is out of seat (i.e., buttocks are not in contact with seat): buttocks are in contact with seat

   b. Does not complete assignments: completes assignments

   c. Calls out without raising hand: raises hand and waits to be called on

   d. Is late to class: is in room before late bell rings

   e. Hits peers when provoked: is assertive when provoked (e.g., says "No" or "Stop it")

   f. Makes disparaging remarks to peers (e.g., "You're stupid"): compliments peers (e.g., "That's a good answer")

   g. Gives up (i.e., stops working) when frustrated: perseveres (i.e., keeps working) or asks for help when frustrated

   h. Is disruptive (directs peers' attention away from task): is on task (i.e., works at task without drawing peers' attention)

   i. Does not speak unless spoken to: initiates conversation with others

   j. Has tantrums (e.g., screams, cries) when request is denied: accepts denial without screaming or crying

   k. Does not follow directives given: complies with directive first time given

   l. Destroys property of others: uses property of others without destroying it

   m. Is truant: attends school on regular basis

   n. Acts passive when teased by peers (e.g., becomes anxious, looks to others for help): acts assertive when teased by peers (e.g., tells them to stop)

o. Gives incorrect responses to questions: answers questions correctly

p. Acts impulsively (e.g., starts responding before teacher has given all directions): waits until teacher gives all directions before responding

q. Eats food with hands: uses utensils to eat food

r. Makes bowel movements in pants: makes bowel movements in toilet

s. Bangs head when upset: tells person how he or she feels when upset

t. Picks nose: uses tissue or handkerchief to blow nose

3. Performance Objectives:

a. Shares belongings with peers: Given an object of his own, the student will, when asked, share the object with a peer. He will do so 80% of the time over a 3-day period.

b. Raises hand without calling out: Given a situation in which it is appropriate for the student to raise her hand and wait to be called on before speaking, she will do so 90% of the time over a 5-day period.

c. Asserts self with peers: When teased, the student will act assertive by telling his peers to stop and stating his feelings. He will do this 100% of the times he is teased over a 3-day period.

d. Is on time to class: The student will be in her seat before the late bell rings 9 out of 10 days.

e. Tells the truth: Given a query from the teacher or peer, the student will answer in a truthful manner 100% of the time over a 2-week period.

f. Accepts criticism: When told that he did something incorrectly, the student will accept this by not crying and by asking how he can correct his mistakes. He will do this 100% of the time over a 2-week period.

g. Gets along with peers: Given all situations where the student is interacting verbally with peers, she will talk to them without making any negative comments (e.g., "You're stupid!") for one week.

h. Uses socially appropriate language: When speaking to others, the student will use language without profanity 90% of the time observed over a 2-week period.

i. Stays in seat: Given situations when it is inappropriate to be out of seat, the student will be in his seat (i.e., buttocks in contact with seat) 90% of the times observed over a 5-day period.

j. Finishes work: The student will finish 100% of assigned work over a 3-day period.

4. The "So what?" test is used to determine whether or not a behavior should be changed and what it should be changed to. This test is used to determine whether or not a behavior should be changed by asking whether or not it is maladaptive (i.e., it presently or potentially interferes with the student's or peers' physical, social, emotional, or academic well-being). If the answer is yes (i.e., it is maladaptive), the behavior passes the "So what?" test and should be changed. The "So what?" test would then be used to determine what the student's behavior should be changed to by asking whether or not the target behavior is a fair pair, is in the student's best interest, and passes the dead man's test.

Chapter 4/Acceptable Responses

1. Essential prerequisites:

a. Complies with all requests first time given:

- Student (S.) knows and understands that she is supposed to comply with a request the first time given.
- S. is aware of when she is and is not complying with a request the first time given.
- S. is capable of controlling her behavior to the extent that she is able to comply with a request the first time given (i.e., if there is no reason beyond her control why she couldn't comply if she was willing to).
- S. knows the consequences of complying with a request the first time given and considers them rewarding.
- S. knows the consequences of not complying with a request the first time given and considers them aversive.
- S. does not consider the consequences of complying with a request the first time given to be less rewarding or more aversive than noncompliance.
- S. knows how to comply with a request the first time given (i.e., she knows how to do what you ask her to do).

b. Stays on task (i.e., completes assignments on time):

- S. knows and understands that he is supposed to complete his assignments on time.
- S. is aware of when he is completing an assignment on time and when he is not.

- S. is capable of controlling his behavior to the extent that he is able to complete an assignment on time (i.e., there is no reason beyond his control why he couldn't complete his assignments on time).
- S. knows the consequences of completing his assignments on time and considers them rewarding.
- S. knows the consequences of not completing his assignments on time and considers them aversive.
- S. does not consider the consequences of completing his assignments on time to be less rewarding or more aversive than not completing his assignments on time.
- S. knows how to complete his assignments on time (i.e., he knows how to do the assignment, how to access help if he needs it, when it is due, etc.).

2. Valid assessments:

   a. Understands rule: When asked what he is supposed to do if he wants to speak in class, S. will answer that he is supposed to raise his hand and wait to be called on. He will respond correctly 3 out of 3 times asked during the course of a school day.
   b. Is aware of behavior: Both the student and the teacher will monitor the student's hand-raising and talking-out behavior over a 3-day period. There will be no less than 80% agreement between data collected.
   c. Knows how to: When asked to demonstrate how he would get the teacher's attention in class, the student will correctly demonstrate the appropriate behavior as judged by the teacher. He will do this 2 out of 2 trials.
   d. Is able to control: The teacher will observe the student over a 5-day period and there will be no instances of impulsivity observed.
   e. Knows the consequences: When asked what the consequences are of raising his hand and waiting to be called on, the student will answer correctly without hesitation.
   f. Considers the consequences rewarding: Given a list of consequences, the student will choose those for the target behavior as most favored 3 out of 3 trials over a 3-day period.
   g. Endorses beliefs: Given a beliefs inventory, the student will not answer "true" to any belief that is incompatible with the target behavior or supports the maladaptive behavior. He will do this 3 out of 3 times over a 3-day period.

3. Steps in the TA model:

   a. Identify and specify the maladaptive behavior.
   b. Identify and specify the target behavior.
   c. Task analyze the target behavior by listing all of the essential prerequisites.
   d. Evaluate the current status of each prerequisite by asking whether or not the student has each; conduct an informal assessment for those prerequisites about which you are in doubt.
   e. Interpret the results of the evaluation by listing all of the prerequisites the student is lacking and writing each in an instructional objective.

Chapter 5/Acceptable Responses

1. Ecobehavioral analysis is the analysis of the environmental factors that support and maintain maladaptive behavior. The assumption of ecobehavioral analysis is that the problem does not reside solely in the student, but is the product of the interaction between the student and the environment.

2. The assumption of ecobehavioral analysis is that the problem does not reside solely in the student, but is the product of the interaction between the student and the environment. The medical model assumes that the student has a physiological, chemical, or metabolic basis for maladaptive behavior; interventions (medication, surgery, etc.) are based on that assumption. The psychodynamic model assumes an emotional basis for maladaptive behavior which resides in the affective area—for example, conflicts with significant others (e.g., parents or other family members). The interventions, such as psychotherapy, are based on that assumption.

3. Factors of the ecology of behavior:

   a. The child's physical, emotional, and cognitive state
   b. The physical setting
   c. Others in the setting, their social and cultural expectations, and their types of activities
   d. The child's family and neighborhood
   e. Community and national norms

4. a. 3
   b. 4
   c. 1
   d. 2

5. Assessments useful in ecobehavioral analysis: Data collection methods and ABC data; running records;

sociograms; Washington Social Code; Flanders' model of teacher behavior; Ecological Niche Breadth Assessment card; Swassing-Barbe check-list; teacher tolerance self-assessment; comfort check; standardized and criterion-referenced tests; interviews with the student

Chapter 6/Acceptable Responses

1. Use positive reinforcement when you wish to strengthen desirable behavior and there is desirable behavior to reinforce.

2. Use negative reinforcement when you wish to strengthen desirable behavior and there is no desirable behavior to reinforce.

3. Using R– effectively:

   a. Always make sure you can do what you say you will do. Don't make any threats you can't carry out.
   b. Always make sure that all avenues of retreat are closed for the student. The only way to avoid or escape from the aversive consequent stimulus event should be by engaging in the desired behavior you wish to strengthen.

4. Using R+ effectively:

   a. Keep the latency between the student's behavior and the reward as brief as possible.
   b. Reinforce behavior according to a schedule of reinforcement (e.g., first continuous, next fixed, then variable).
   c. Reinforce improvement in behavior. Use a shaping program.
   d. Model the desired behavior for your students.
   e. Try to maintain a state of deprivation in the student. Avoid satiating the student with too much of the reinforcer.
   f. Use rewards that are reinforcing to the student, not to you.

5. Examples of reinforcers:

   a. Social: praise (e.g., "That's good. I like the way you did that."); smiles
   b. Token: grades; points earned
   c. Primary: food; hugs
   d. Tangible: pocket comb; colored pencils
   e. Activity: drawing pictures; listening to music

6. Choosing reinforcers:

   a. Observe the student during free time to see what he or she likes to do.
   b. Have the student complete an interest inventory.

7. Schedules of reinforcement:

   a. Continuous
   b. Variable
   c. Continuous
   d. Interval
   e. Ratio
   f. Variable
   g. Fixed
   h. Variable

8. Diagraming schedules:

   a. VI (2:1) without undesirable behavior:

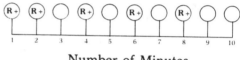

   Number of Minutes

   b. FR (3:1) with undesirable behavior:

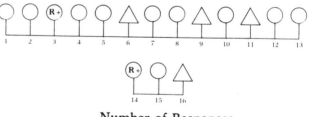

   Number of Responses

   c. FI (2:1) without undesirable behavior:

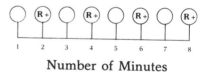

   Number of Minutes

   d. Continuous (ratio) with undesirable behavior:

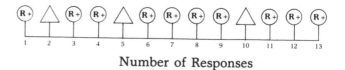

   Number of Responses

9. Shaping program:

Stop: when he stays in his seat for 30 minutes
Start: when he sits down (after being told to)
Reward: peanuts

Successive approximations:

a. When he sits down (after being told to)
b. When he sits in his seat for 2 minutes
c. When he sits in his seat for 4 minutes
d. When he sits in his seat for 6 minutes
e. When he sits in his seat for 8 minutes

Shift criteria for reinforcement when he is able to successfully perform an approximation on a variable schedule of reinforcement. Jump from 2-minute intervals to 3-minute intervals after he is able to stay in his seat for at least 10 minutes at a time. Jump from 3- to 4-minute intervals after he is able to stay in his seat for at least 19 minutes at a time.

10. In shaping, you gradually change the student through differential reinforcement of successive approximations of behavior. In fading, you gradually change the environment or the situation in which the student's behavior occurs.

11. To design a chaining program, first identify the responses in the old behavior chain. Second, write a new behavior chain. Third, model the new behavior chain for the student. Fourth, have the student go through the new chain to demonstrate that she knows what to do. Fifth, reinforce the student whenever she engages in the new behavior; and sixth, if the student reverts back to the old behavior, take her through the new chain right from the beginning again.

12. Questions for a token economy:

a. What are the contingencies for the tokens?
b. What will you use for tokens?
c. What is the ratio between student behavior and tokens dispensed?
d. What will you use for backup reinforcers?
e. Who will dispense the tokens?
f. When will the tokens be dispensed?
g. How will the tokens be dispensed?
h. When and how will the tokens be redeemed?

13. Token economy problems:

a. Student has too many tokens: Build in response cost so that she could lose tokens earned through misbehavior.

b. Student inequities: Pay according to difficulty of work. The higher the level of work (i.e., the more complex the task or the higher the grade level), the more tokens the student may earn.
c. Extortion: Closely monitor tokens earned by your students. Make token reinforcement available to everyone to eliminate a situation where there are "have-nots." Don't let extortion lead to a payoff.
d. Weaning from a token economy: Use a levels system. Require students to purchase entitlements (as opposed to special prizes) with tokens earned.

14. Premack Principle: When a high-frequency behavior is made contingent upon a low-frequency behavior, the low-frequency behavior increases in frequency.

15. Trouble Shooting: Trouble shooting involves asking a number of questions if your reinforcement program is not working. These questions include the following:

a. Does the student have all of the essential prerequisites for the target behavior?
b. Am I using the correct schedules of reinforcement and am I using them correctly?
c. Am I presenting the reinforcers appropriately?
d. Am I using the right reinforcers?
e. Should I be using a shaping program?
f. Am I (or is anyone else) modeling behavior that is incompatible with the target behavior?
g. Are the reinforcers interfering with the target behavior?
h. Am I using the shaping program correctly?
i. Should I have used fading to help the new behaviors generalize?

Chapter 7/Acceptable Responses

1. Extinction and RIBs: Ignore all calling-out behavior and positively reinforce all instances of raising hand and waiting to be called on.

2. Incompatible/competing behaviors:

a. Is out of seat: is in seat
b. Bites self when frustrated: asks for help when frustrated
c. Hits peers when angry: tells peers she's angry
d. Calls out without raising hand: raises hand and waits to be called on

e. Takes things from others without asking: asks others for things without taking

f. Is off task (i.e., looks around room): is on task (i.e., looks at work)

g. Leaves room without permission: requests permission before leaving room

h. Swears for attention: gets attention by asking for it

i. Refuses to comply with request: complies with request

j. Comes to class late: comes to class on time

3. Disadvantages of punishment:

a. It can lead to avoidance or escape behavior (e.g., sneaking, stealing, cheating, lying, running away, and truancy).

b. The punisher may be perceived as a model of aggression (to be emulated).

c. There is a lack of supportive data regarding the long-term efficacy of punishment in weakening behavior.

d. There can be emotional side effects with punishment.

4. When to use punishment:

a. When the maladaptive behavior is so intense or severe that someone might get hurt, including the child

b. When all else fails

5. Punishing effectively:

a. Try to prevent avoidance and escape from the source of the punishment by making it difficult (if not impossible) for the student to cheat, lie, sneak, etc.

b. Minimize the need for future punishment by combining it with RIBs.

c. Never punish in an aggressive manner.

d. Don't hold a grudge against the student you punish.

e. Administer punishment immediately.

f. If response cost is used, give the student the opportunity to earn back what she or he has lost.

g. Try to give a warning before punishing the student.

h. Never threaten a punishment you can't carry out.

i. Try to carry out the punishment in a calm manner without losing your temper.

j. Try to be consistent and always punish the same behavior.

6. Response cost: Tell the student that if he doesn't sit down and stay in his seat (or if he gets out of his seat again), he will lose X number of tokens (assuming he is on a token program). If he continues to misbehave, remove the tokens and tell him why you are doing so and how he can earn them back.

7. Time out: Tell the student she will have to go to time out if she doesn't stop having tantrums (or the next time she has a tantrum). If she continues to misbehave, send her to time out. Tell her how much time she has to spend in time out. If she goes to time out by herself, start the timer. If she fails to go to time out, start a stopwatch and tell her you are going to add time on the watch to her time out. If she is disruptive in time out, add time.

8. Negative practice: Have the student practice hand waving, rocking, or chin touching over and over again until it becomes aversive for him.

9. Reprimands (any eight of the following):

a. Try to reprimand in private (without other students hearing).

b. Use an attention signal (e.g., calling the student's name) as a reprimand if you are not able to reprimand in private.

c. Establish eye contact with the student.

d. Be succinct.

e. Use words the student can understand.

f. Specify the behavior you want the student to stop or start doing.

g. Never be sarcastic.

h. Use if-then statements.

i. Use a normal speaking voice (don't shout).

j. Always finish reprimanding one student before you start on another.

k. Use a nonthreatening, assertive body language.

l. Give the student enough time to comply.

m. If and when the student complies, thank her and praise her for any behavior that is incompatible with the maladaptive behavior.

10. Overcorrection: First, have the student make restitution by apologizing for his insults. Then, have the student verbally give a compliment to at least one peer in the classroom for every hour he is in school over a 5-day period.

11. Hierarchy of escalating consequences: First, try to reinforce all instances of nondisruptive behavior (e.g., talking to peers without making threats or insults) while ignoring any instances of disruptive

behavior. Reinforce peers for ignoring disruptive behavior. If extinction and RIBs fail to weaken this behavior, use a reprimand (e.g., "If you don't stop making threats and insults, I am going to fine you X points for each threat or insult you make"). If the student continues to misbehave, raise the fine. If this doesn't work, send her to time out contingent upon maladaptive behavior. If time out doesn't weaken the behavior, remove her from the classroom.

Chapter 8/Acceptable Responses

1. Reasons for teaching self-management skills (give any three of the following):

    a. Teaching self-management skills can result in the improved generalization and maintenance of behaviors.
    b. Teaching self-management skills can change a student's locus of control (from external to internal).
    c. It is more cost effective to teach students self-management skills since there aren't enough teachers (or counselors) to work with students. At some point, students must assume the responsibility for operating their own interventions.
    d. Training in self-management may be more relevant than many of the other skills or knowledge we teach in school.

2. Components:

    a. Self-assessment (SA): Student evaluates his own behavior and decides whether or not he was doing what he was supposed to and whether or not he deserves to be reinforced.
    b. Self-monitoring (SM): Student keeps a record of her own behavior (i.e., collects daily data and puts on a data display).
    c. Self-reinforcement (SR): Student administers reinforcement to himself when appropriate to do so.

3. Cheating:

    a. Practice random surveillance and give bonuses for honest behavior and fines for cheating.
    b. Suggest to the student that you are going to practice random surveillance (even though you don't have the time).

Chapter 9/Acceptable Responses

1. Characteristics of CBM:

    a. The subjects themselves, rather than external agents such as the classroom teacher, are the primary change agents.
    b. Verbalization—on an overt level, then covert—is the primary component.
    c. Subjects are taught to identify and use a series of steps to solve their problems.
    d. Modeling is used as an instructional procedure.
    e. Most of the CBM literature focuses on helping the individual gain self-control.

2. Cognitions:

    a. Cognitive processes: how we think, the process we use to solve problems
    b. Cognitive structures: beliefs, attitudes
    c. Inner speech: automatic thoughts, self-talk, covert self-instruction

3. Reasons to teach problem solving:

    a. Research suggests that improvement in problem solving can lead to improved classroom behavior.
    b. Children are more likely to choose to use a "solution" to a problem if they thought of it themselves than if an adult supplied it.
    c. Problem solving is a lifetime skill that they can use in or out of school.

4. Problem-solving competencies:

    a. Recognizing a problem: being able to differentiate between instances and not-instances of problems
    b. Problem defining and goal stating: putting the problem into words that will allow the student to determine what changes need to be made
    c. Generating alternative solutions: brainstorming (thinking of) as many solutions to the problem as possible
    d. Evaluating solutions: rating each solution according to its efficacy (i.e., will it help me get what I want without creating new problems for me?) and feasibility (i.e., will I be able to implement the solution?)
    e. Making a plan: taking the best solution from the solutions generated and making a list of things to do to implement it

5. How beliefs are learned: If, every time a child fell down, his parent got upset and communicated to

him that falling down was a terrible thing, the child might grow up believing that every time something "bad" or unpleasant happened to him, it was terrible and he should get upset over it.

6. How beliefs influence behavior: A student believes that people who do things that she doesn't like are bad and deserve to be punished. Somebody calls her a name and this event triggers "You stink!" thinking, which causes her to become angry; her strong negative feelings lead to maladaptive behavior (e.g., hitting the student who called her a name).

7. Assessing beliefs: This can be done by using a teacher-constructed pencil-and-paper assessment. The items should be a direct measure of a student's beliefs and not open to interpretation (e.g., projective test items). The testing should be given more than once to ensure reliability and control for mood and motivation. Several items should be included to measure one belief. The student's performance on the beliefs assessment should be compared with his observable behavior (i.e., what he does and says). Where there are discrepancies, give weight to his behavior. Whenever possible, the student should be allowed to complete the assessment without the teacher present.

8. Modifying beliefs: Have the student complete a DIBs for KIDs form by filling in what happened to her; what she thought about it; how she felt and acted; any evidence to support or dispute her thinking; and, if her thinking was irrational, what she might think instead. Then have her practice saying her new thinking until it becomes internalized.

9. Self-instruction:

   a. The teacher instructs and models the behavior for the student.
   b. The student models the behavior while the teacher provides the instructions.
   c. The student models the behavior while giving himself instructions out loud.
   d. The student models the behavior while giving herself instructions quietly (i.e., whispering).
   e. The student models the behavior while he thinks the instructions.

10. Verbal mediation:

    a. An "essay" consisting of four to six questions (e.g., "What am I doing?" or "What should I

be doing?") is written ahead of time by the teacher and the student.
    b. When the student misbehaves, the teacher requires the student to copy the essay twice at home.
    c. After the first two misbehaviors, the student is required to stay after school to paraphrase the essay.
    d. If the misbehavior continues, the student is required to write the essay from memory.
    e. If this doesn't stop the misbehavior, the student is required to describe orally the situation that typically stimulates the misbehavior and how she will think (i.e., what she will say to herself) when she is tempted to misbehave again.

11. Generalization of CBM skills:

    a. Be a model for your students and use CBM skills in front of them.
    b. Teach each skill to the mastery level so that the students fully understand what to do and how to do it.
    c. Reinforce students when you catch them using CBM skills.
    d. Program for generalization of CBM skills through role-playing and homework assignments.
    e. Discuss the relevance of CBM skills with your students so that they understand why these skills are important.

Chapter 10/Acceptable Responses

1. Rationale for teaching: Students who misbehave in school may do so because of social skills deficits. The benefits of social skills training include (a) the building and maintenance of relationships, (b) the ability to handle the unreasonable behavior of others, and (c) secondary benefits derived from being able to "get along with" people we work with or for.

2. Social skills:
   a. Able to give and receive compliments
   b. Able to greet peers
   c. Able to give and receive warranted criticism
   d. Able to handle unwarranted criticism in an assertive manner
   e. Able to handle manipulation in an assertive manner
   f. Able to acquire things by asking
   g. Able to request help from others

h. Able to give and receive apologies when appropriate
i. Able to provide help to others
j. Able to observe the amenities and courtesies (i.e., being polite)

3. Assessing social skills:

   a. Have an expert such as the student's teacher complete a standardized social skills checklist or use a checklist that comes with a commercially available social skills program.
   b. Use direct observation of behavior in the student's classroom, school building, cafeteria, and school yard; collect frequency data on student's eye contact, how student initiates conversations and asserts self, etc.; compare target student's behavior against data collected for sample from peer group that has the skills in doubt.
   c. Use role playing by having the student demonstrate or model what he or she would do in a given hypothetical situation.

4. Teaching a social skill:

   a. Write an instructional objective first so you will know what behavior is expected of the student and how you will assess his or her performance.
   b. Teach social skills directly through modeling, explanation, and demonstration and provide the student with many opportunities to perform the skill being taught.
   c. Use task analysis to break down complex social skills (e.g., being assertive) into small pieces; do not introduce any new pieces until the student has demonstrated mastery of the old ones.
   d. Help to program for generalization by teaching each social skill in as many different contexts as you would expect the student to use.

Chapter 11/Acceptable Responses

1. Rationale for teaching stress management skills: Children are experiencing more stress in their lives today and seem to be less equipped to manage it than before. There is some evidence that stress and maladjustment are related. If children and youth were taught how to manage the stress in their lives, they might not experience as much maladjustment. Since stress management skills are also self-management skills, students who learn stress management will become more self-reliant.

2. Terms:

   a. *Stressor* is the name we give to those life events that we associate with our stress (e.g., our parents getting divorced or ill, failing a test we wanted to pass, someone making fun of us or a bully threatening to beat us up).
   b. *Stress* is the physiological reaction we experience (in our bodies) when we encounter a stressor.
   c. *Eustress* is good (i.e., exciting, thrilling, joyous) stress that is helpful to us.
   d. *Distress* is bad (i.e., angering, anxiety-causing, frightening, upsetting) stress that is harmful to us.

3. Alarm reaction: Your pupils dilate (to let in more light). The heart beats faster to pump more blood and oxygen to muscles. Muscles tense to serve as armor in case of attack and to get ready, if necessary, to fight or flee. Your blood changes chemically so that clotting time is increased in case you are wounded. Throat and nasal passages stop producing mucus to facilitate passage of oxygen.

4. SUD is an acronym for subjective units of distress. It allows the student to keep track of his stress levels over time. Have him assign values from 1 to 10 to different levels of stress and require him to observe and record these levels for several days or until his self-monitoring is reliable.

5. Somatic-physiological skills (list any of the following):

   a. Before stress: progressive relaxation (PRT), exercise, proper diet, stress inoculation
   b. During stress: diaphragmatic breathing, PRT, stress inoculation
   c. After stress: time management

6. Cognitive-psychological skills (list any of the following):

   a. Before: cognitive restructuring, stress inoculation
   b. During: problem solving, self-instruction
   c. After: thought stopping

7. Social-behavioral skills (list any of the following):

   a. Before: time management
   b. During: self management, assertiveness training

8. Stressors: List any 10 stressors from Figure 11.4.

9. Stress inoculation: This is an integrative approach in that it combines a number of skills such as PRT and cognitive restructuring. The first stage is the conceptual framework stage where students are taught basic concepts of anger and anger management. The second stage involves training in PRT. Cognitive restructuring is taught in stage 3; students try to identify and dispute any irrational beliefs that might be triggering or maintaining their anger. In stage 4, students learn how to write stress scripts (i.e., everything they need to say or do before, during, and after experiencing an anger-provoking stressor). Stage 5 is the inoculation stage. Here students use their stress script in situations where they are exposed to gradually larger and more realistic "doses" of the stressor.

Chapter 12/Acceptable Responses

1. An ecological intervention is one that intervenes with the environmental factors that are evoking or maintaining the student's maladaptive behavior.

2.

	Pleasing +	Displeasing −
Give +	+ Reward Anticipated Behavioral Effect: ↑ a	− Punishment Anticipated Behavioral Effect: ↓ b
Take −	c − Cost Reinforcement Anticipated Behavioral Effect: ↓	d + Negative Reinforcement Anticipated Behavioral Effect: ↑

3. Examples from Figure 12.1:

   a. Reward: a favored activity; free time; a treat to eat or drink; a hug, smile, or praise
   b. Punishment: a frown; scolding; a spanking; sarcasm
   c. Cost Reinforcement: minutes of recess lost due to off-task behavior; a toy that hits being put on a shelf
   d. Negative Reinforcement: going out for recess when work is finished; walking without holding teacher's hand when able to walk quietly

4. Natural consequences are those consequences that come from the natural environment with no planning or design by another (e.g., if you touch a hot stove, you will get burned). Logical consequences are designed or planned by another, but the connection between the behavior and the consequence is easily made by the child (e.g., if you don't do your work, you can't earn free time with us; if you hit Tim, he will hit you back).

5. Prevention and intervention strategies: All of the choices could be applicable across settings; the intervention phase of each would include a design to teach the adaptive behavior needed to perform (see response 6).

6. The design of the ecological intervention should include:

   a. Pertinent environmental factors
   b. Assessment information on the student's ability to perform in the environment
   c. A plan for teacher behavior
   d. A data collection system
   e. Criteria for success
   f. A plan for fading the intervention
   g. A plan for generalizing

7. Jay: ADD; off task 95% of the time; peers reject him; low academic achievement; high potential for learning; speech therapy; kinesthetic learner; good auditory skills; low impulse control; bonus: age: 9-4; grade: 4

   Eric: Learning disabled; low academic skills; disruptive; runs away; wets and soils pants; tantrums; screamer; poor hygiene; low nurturance; punitive home environment; visual perception deficit; kinesthetic learner; bonus: age: 8-7, grade: 3

   Julie: Learning disabled; previous physical abuse; current neglect; monitored and removed by CSD; foster placement; poor tool skills; low academic achievement; out of seat to teacher 72%; bonus: age: 9-7; grade: 3

Chapter 13/Acceptable Responses

1. Poor teaching: List any six from Figure 13.1.

2. The self-management process:

   a. Pinpoint the maladaptive and fair-pair target behaviors (i.e., identify and specify the teaching behavior you want to change, apply the stranger and "So what?" tests, identify and specify the fair-pair target behavior, and apply the stranger and "So what?" tests).

b. Make sure you have all of the essential prerequisites for the target behavior by using the task analytical model to assess each of them.

c. Design and implement an intervention.

d. Monitor the behavior (and/or thoughts or feelings) to be changed, evaluate the efficacy of your intervention, and make changes as necessary.

3. Rules of thumb:

a. Never punish your behavior.

b. Try modifying antecedents as well as consequences in your intervention program.

c. Use covert reinforcers (e.g., fantasy) as well as overt (i.e., tangible) reinforcers.

d. When necessary, focus your intervention on your thinking.

4. Designing a self-management program: See your instructor for feedback or refer to the text.

Chapter 14/Acceptable Responses

1. Baseline vs. intervention: Baseline data are collected *before* any intervention (or new intervention) is attempted. Intervention data are collected *during* the time that a new intervention is being attempted.

2. Monitoring frequency, duration, and intensity of behaviors:

a. F or D (daydreams do not tend to differ with regard to intensity or force)

b. F, D, or I

c. F or I (you wouldn't collect data on duration here because someone could get seriously hurt while you were looking at your stopwatch)

d. F or D (like daydreams, sleep does not tend to differ with regard to intensity)

e. F (duration or intensity of response cannot be measured)

f. F (while intensity cannot be measured, you might want to monitor the length or duration of the latency—the amount of time it took the student to complete the assignment)

g. F or D (intensity cannot be measured)

h. F (you would probably be more interested in how many times the student interrupted than

in how long each interruption lasted or how forceful it was)

i. F (duration could be measured if you wanted to know how late a student was; intensity is not a factor here)

j. F, D, or I

3. Continuous or interval sampling:

a. CS (would easily come to your attention)

b. IS (would not easily come to your attention; continuous monitoring would interfere with your teaching)

c. IS (same as b)

d. IS (same as b)

e. CS (same as a)

f. IS (assume that looking for daylight between the child's buttocks and chair would interfere with your teaching)

g. CS (assuming that you grade the assignments, this behavior would easily come to your attention)

h. CS (again, assuming that you give the commands, this behavior would easily come to your attention)

i. CS (need I say more?)

j. IS (too quiet; you'd have to watch this behavior intermittently)

4. Monitoring single behaviors with multiple students: I would make a seating chart with each student's name or initials in or by the box representing his or her seat. I would take an interval sample every 30 minutes and look at one student at a time in a predetermined order, recording in his or her box whether or not he or she was talking.

5. Monitoring multiple behaviors with single students: I would use a code for each behavior (e.g., "OS" for out of seat, "T" for talking without permission, and "H" for hitting) and, assuming that each behavior came easily to my attention, I would write down the code letter each time the behavior occurred.

6. Monitoring reciprocal behaviors: I would use an O & R form with boxes on it. Each box would represent an instance of teasing by the target student. Assuming that the behavior came easily to my attention, each time it occurred I would write down a code letter or letters in the box for each response (e.g., "PA" for physically aggressive response, "VA" for verbally aggressive response, "I" for ignoring response, "A" for assertive response, and "T" for tells teacher).

7. Monitoring for qualitative data: I would use an O & R form with boxes on it. Each box would represent an instance of disruptive behavior by the target student. Each time the student shouted at a peer or at me, I would write down the initials of the person he shouted at, what precipitated the shouting, and/or what the consequences of the shouting were.

8. Countoon: See your instructor for feedback or refer to the examples in the chapter.

9.–14. Observation & recording forms: See your instructor for feedback or refer to the examples in the chapter.

15. Summarization:

   a. rate
   b. percentage
   c. raw score
   d. average
   e. percentage
   f. raw score
   g. average
   h. percentage

16. Computing and interpreting data:

   a.

Date	Rates
2·18	$50\overline{)18}$ = .36
2·19	$30\overline{)8}$ = .26
2·20	$90\overline{)24}$ = .26
2·23	$75\overline{)15}$ = .20
2·24	$50\overline{)9}$ = .18

   b. Sleepy's yawning behavior is getting *better*.
   c. Sleepy is yawning at a rate of *36 yawns per 100 minutes or 3½ yawns per 10 minutes.*
   d.

Date	1	2	3	Average
4·2	$1\times1=1$	$2\times2=4$	$5\times3=15$	$8\overline{)20}$=2.5
4·3	$1\times1=1$	$1\times2=2$	$3\times3=9$	$5\overline{)12}$=2.4
4·4	$2\times1=2$	$0\times2=0$	$3\times3=9$	$5\overline{)11}$=2.2
4·5	$2\times1=2$	$2\times2=4$	$2\times3=6$	$6\overline{)12}$=2.0
4·6	$4\times1=4$	$0\times2=0$	$1\times3=3$	$5\overline{)7}$=1.4

   e. Frankie's tantrum behavior is getting *better* according to *intensity*.
   f. Frankie's tantrum behavior is getting *better* according to *frequency*.
   g. Frankie's average level of intensity on April 6 is mild to moderate (1.4).
   h. Percentage of thumb-sucking behavior =

$$21+25+32+18+72+112+24+37+19+120 = 480"$$

$$60\overline{)480}" = 8' \quad 20\overline{)8'} = .40$$

17.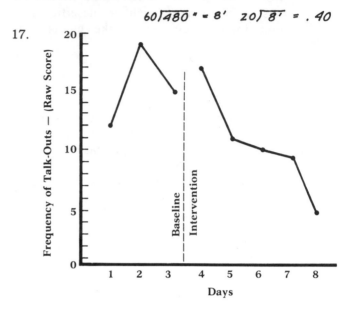

18. The intervention is working because the frequency of talk-outs is decreasing given the downward trend of the data.

Appendix B
Legal Rights Checklist

Note: The following is presented as a sample or example of a legal rights checklist that might be used in the public schools. Many of the items originated from material in *Legal Challenges to Behavior Modification* (Martin, 1975). It is suggested that: (1) the checklist be used only in cases where changes in student behavior are substantial enough to necessitate changes in his or her individualized education program (IEP), (2) a copy of the checklist be kept on record in the student's file, and (3) the party completing the checklist do so under the guidance of an administrator such as the building principal.

Student _____ Age _____ Grade _____

School _____ Teacher _____

Maladaptive Behavior _____

Target Behavior _____

Party Completing Checklist _____ Date _____

Directions: Make all necessary comments directly after each of the following items.

1. Maladaptive Behavior
   a. The student's maladaptive behavior is presently or potentially interfering with his or her (and/or his or her peers') physical, emotional, social, and/or academic growth:

   b. The maladaptive behavior is actually occurring (or the target behavior is failing to occur) regularly enough to justify intervention:

   c. The school initiating the intervention and in which the intervention will take place has a legitimate interest in the behavior that it is attempting to modify:

2. Target Behavior
    a. The target behavior is in the best interests of the student and will benefit him or her more than it will benefit the school and/or the persons initiating the intervention:

    b. The target behavior is written as an objective complete with measurable criteria for acceptable performance. The latter should have been established through appropriate procedures (e.g., an analysis of ecological baseline data):

    c. The target behavior reflects a positive change (i.e., a strengthening of an adaptive behavior) rather than a negative change (i.e., weakening of a maladaptive behavior):

    d. The student's problem could not be solved by changing someone else's behavior instead of his or hers:

    e. The intervention does not involve changing a behavior that is actually constitutionally permissible:

    f. It has been determined through a diagnostic procedure that the student has all of the essential prerequisites for the target behavior:

3. Intervention
    a. The intervention does not call for one group of students to be treated significantly differently from another group to the extent that the distinction may be considered illegal:

    b. The intervention does not call for the student to lose a constitutionally protected right or privilege:

c. That which the student is legally entitled to will not be used as a reward for desirable behavior:

d. There are efficacy data available on the use of the strategy or strategies employed in the intervention with subjects similar to the student to warrant its use with the student:

e. The intervention is available to all students who might benefit from it in addition to the target student:

f. No student who might benefit from the intervention will be denied access to it because he or she has been assigned to a "control" group:

g. Should it become necessary to employ aversive strategies in the intervention, this will not occur until less drastic alternatives have been tried first and it has been demonstrated that (a) the less drastic measures were not effective and (b) the aversive strategies are effective.

h. The student will not be needlessly isolated from others during the intervention unless his or her behavior becomes disruptive to the learning environment:

i. Should it become necessary to use time out as part of the intervention, safeguards will be in place to assure that it can only be used for a few minutes:

4. Monitoring and Evaluation: The student's progress will be reviewed continuously or at least at reasonably short enough intervals so that a change in the intervention may be implemented quickly if no progress is evident:

5. Due Process
   a. A meeting has been held to discuss the intervention with the student and his or her parents:

   b. All concerned parties have consented to participate in the intervention:

Appendix C

Sample Assessment Workups Using the Task Analytical Model[1]

Diagnostic Evaluation 1

Maladaptive Behavior
Upon being let off her school bus in the afternoon, D. immediately crosses the road in front of her house without first looking to see if there are any cars approaching from either direction (i.e., up or down the road). This behavior is life-threatening, and thus maladaptive, because she is running the risk of being hit, and possibly killed, by a car driven by a motorist who fails to see or heed the flashing red lights on the school bus.

Target Behavior
Immediately after getting off the school bus, D. will check for oncoming cars (i.e., look up and down the road). She will do this before proceeding to cross the road 100% of the time.

Student _____ Evaluator _____ Date _____

Target Pinpoint ___ See Target Behavior _____

Prerequisites	Current Status	Assessments	Results
1. D. knows she must check for approaching cars before crossing the road.	Yes—She is able to tell me this in her own words.		
2. D. knows why this behavior is important.	Yes—When asked "Why?" answers "So I won't be killed."		
3. D. is aware of her behavior (i.e., knows when she looks/does not look for cars before crossing the road).	No.	D. and I will observe and separately record her pre-crossing behavior for 5 consecutive days, noting if she looks or does not look for cars before crossing the road. Should be 100% agreement.	Only 60% agreement. NO PASS

[1]The material in this Appendix represents work performed by graduate students in the author's behavior management course. The subjects of these workups are real people. It should be understood that the author's students were not required to list more than eight prerequisites for the target behavior in the assignment. Special thanks for this material are due to LaDona Stram, Alodie Didier, Debbie Brosten, and Susan Foster.

Prerequisites	Current Status	Assessments	Results
4. D. is capable of checking for cars.	Yes—She has done this before after being prompted or when she knows I'm observing.		
5. D. knows she may be hit by a car and injured or killed if she does not look for cars before crossing.	✗ Yes—This seems obvious but let's find out for sure.	When asked, "What might happen to you if you don't look for cars before crossing a road?" D.'s answer will imply one of the following: being hit, injured, or killed by a car.	D.: "You could get killed." PASS
6. D. wants to avoid this consequence.	✗ Yes.	When asked how she feels about being injured or killed, D. will imply by her answer that she wishes to avoid it.	D. answered: "Not very good. . . . because I wouldn't see my family or parents any more." PASS
7. D. knows she will avoid being injured or killed by engaging in the target behavior.	✗ Yes.	When asked, "What might happen to you if you look for cars before crossing a road?" D. should indicate by her answer avoidance of injury or death.	D. said: "You can get across safely." PASS
8. D. thinks it is better to avoid being hit than to be hit.	✗ Yes.	Ask D. which she would prefer, being hit or not being hit by a car. Her answer should imply not being hit.	D. answered: "Are you crazy! Nobody wants to be hit by a car." PASS
9. D. knows *how* to check for oncoming cars (i.e., stops, does not proceed to cross, and looks up and down the road).	Yes—She has done this when prompted or when she sees I'm watching her.		
10. D. knows *when* to engage in the target behavior (i.e., immediately after getting off the bus and before proceeding to cross the road).	Yes—She has done this cor- rectly while knowing she was being observed.		
11. D. does not hold a belief that is incompatible with engaging in the target behavior.	✗ Yes.	Given a pen-and-paper inventory about her beliefs, D. will not have any beliefs that are incom- patible with looking for cars before crossing the road.	D. did not agree with any incompatible beliefs. PASS

Prerequisites	Current Status	Assessments	Results
12. D. is able to remember the target behavior (i.e., without prompting spontaneously engages in it).	✓ Yes.	Observe D.'s behavior immediately after getting off the bus for 5 consecutive days. There should be at least one incidence of spontaneously eliciting the target behavior (i.e., she will look up and down the road for cars without being given any cues).	On 5/6 D. correctly looked for cars without prompting. PASS
13. D. is able to control impulsivity (i.e., can control any competing impulses to engage in nontarget behaviors, such as running across the road to say "Hi!" to a friend, long enough to check for cars before crossing).	No—She consistently follows non-target-oriented impulses.		

Name _D._   Date _May 2, 1989_

Directions: Read each of the following sentences. If you agree
with what a sentence says circle (I agree). If
you do not agree with what a sentence says circle
(I disagree). Be honest and answer the way you really
feel not the way you think you should feel.

1. If someone tells me they like me I feel good.
    (I agree)   I disagree

2. If I got hit by a car I could get hurt.
    (I agree)   I disagree.

3. When the red lights are flashing on my school bus cars on the
    road always stop.
    I agree   (I disagree)

4. It is best to believe what an adult says.
    (I agree)   I disagree

5. When my bus driver lets me off the bus it is always safe to
    cross to the other side of the road.
    I agree   (I disagree)

6. If I got hit by a car I could die.
    (I agree)   I disagree

7. It is better to believe what another person says than to find
    out for myself.
    (I agree)   I disagree

8. Sometimes a child needs to look out for herself.
    (I agree)   I disagree

_____ Page 2

9. I like koala bears.
    (I agree)   I disagree

10. It is possible to get hurt crossing a street.
    (I agree)   I disagree

11. The driver of a car can always see a person who is crossing a
    road.
    I agree   (I disagree)

12. I always look up and down a road before crossing.
    (I agree)   I disagree

13. Everyone who drives a car knows that the flashing red lights on
    a school bus mean stop.
    I agree   (I disagree)

14. I enjoy sailing on a sunny day.
    (I agree)   I disagree

15. If my bus driver tells me it is O.K. to go I don't need to look
    up and down the road for cars.
    I agree   (I disagree)

16. It is fun answering all these questions.
    (I agree)   I disagree

17. Even if my bus driver tells me it is O.K. to cross, I must
    check the road for cars before crossing.
    (I agree)   I disagree

18. Sometimes the driver of a car cannot see a child crossing a road.
    (I agree)   I disagree

_____ Page 3

19. There is no reason to look for cars before crossing a road.
    I agree   (I disagree)

20. Flying in an airplane can be really fun.
    (I agree)   I disagree

21. Some car drivers do not stop when the red lights of a school
    bus are flashing.
    (I agree)   I disagree

22. Sometimes a bus driver cannot see that a car is coming down the
    road.
    (I agree)   I disagree

23. No matter what anyone tells me I must always check to see if
    cars are coming before I cross a road.
    (I agree)   I disagree

24. I am happy that this is the last question!
    I agree   (I disagree)

Comments:
_D_ beliefs are very compatible w/ target behavior
PASS

Name _D._

Directions: Each day please (circle) which of the following you did
when you got off the school bus, before you crossed the
road. Be honest. This is just a record of what you do
and you will not get into trouble no matter what you
circle. Here is the code:

means you looked for cars before
you crossed the road

means you did not look for cars
before you crossed the road

Date _May 5_ Today I:		
Date _May 4_ Today I:	(eyes open)	
Date _May 5_ Today I:	(eyes open)	
Date _May 6_ Today I:		
Date _May 7_ Today I:		

Name **D.**   Date **May 4, 1989**

Directions: Answer the following questions using your own words.

1. What might happen if you don't look for cars before crossing a road?

   you could get killed.

   Why? because a car would run over you

2. How do you feel about what you said above happening to you?

   terrible!

   Why? because I wouldn't see my family or parents any more

3. What might happen if you do look for cars before crossing a road?

   you can get across safely

   Why? because you looked for cars

4. How do you feel about what you said above happening to you?

   good

   Why? because I don't want to get killed

5. Which would you prefer happened to you? (1. or 3.) Use your own words. Are you crasy! Nobody wants to be hit by a car

---

Summary

The results of this diagnosis indicate that D. does indeed have the necessary prerequisites for engaging in the target behavior with two exceptions: *awareness of behavior* and *control of impulsivity*. As the attainment of these prerequisites is crucial to the consideration of any intervention strategy for the target behavior, the following performance objectives are given:

1. D. and an observer will keep separate records of her pre-road-crossing behavior for 5 consecutive days, noting if she looks or does not look for cars before crossing the road. Their records will agree 100%.

2. Upon being presented with a pleasing distractor (e.g., a friend waving to her from across the road as D. gets off her school bus), D. will control her impulse to immediately cross the road, checking first for oncoming cars. She will do this for 5 consecutive days.

Name **D.**   Observer_____

Behavior __looks for cars(i.e. up and down the road) before proceeding__
__to cross to the opposite side__

Time observed __one opportunity daily @ approximately 3:20 p.m.__

Length of observation period __5 consecutive days (5-3 thru 5-7-89)__

Code L=looked for cars   NL=did not look for cars

Date	My observation	D's observation	Do they agree?
5/3	NL	NL	yes
5/4	NL	L	no
5/5	NL (looked after crossing)	L	no
5/6	L	L	Yes
5/7	NL	NL	yes

Percent agreement: 60%

Comments: on 5/6 D. looked for cars before crossing (the target behavior) — consider self-management as a possible intervention strategy.

Diagnostic Evaluation 2

Maladaptive Behavior
E. is a student in my classroom. The majority of the time E. does not follow teacher directions. Instead she engages in maladaptive behaviors such as ignoring the direction, verbally refusing to do her work, talking out without permission, or engaging in off-task behaviors such as drawing, wandering around the room, or playing with papers or pins on her bulletin board.

Target Behavior
The target behavior is for E. to follow teacher directions the first time given within 1 minute.

Student _____ E. _____ **Evaluator** _____ D. _____ **Date** _____

Target Pinpoint ___ E. will follow teacher directions the first time given within 1 minute of being given the ___ instruction.

Prerequisites	Current Status	Assessments	Results
1. E. knows that she is supposed to follow teacher directions the first time given within 1 minute.	Yes—When asked, E. has answered that she needs to follow teacher directions when they are given.		
2. E. knows and understands the reasons behind the rule.	No.	Asked why it is important to follow directions, E. will respond with at least two of the following: to complete work in the allotted time, to complete work without disturbing others, to earn points.	At first she said, "I don't know." Then she added, "To get points." NO PASS
3. E. values following teacher directions as much as I do.	No.	Given the following list of behaviors, E. and I will each rate which ones are important (100% agreement is needed): listening to teacher, being in seat, completing work, talking out, walking around, raising hand.	E. thought listening to the teacher and walking around were important. NO PASS
4. E. is aware when she is following directions and when she isn't.	No—When I take points away from E. for not following directions, she will often argue that she was following directions.		

Prerequisites	Current Status	Assessments	Results
5. E. is capable of hearing the directions given.	Yes—Auditory testing shows her hearing to be within normal ranges.		
6. E. knows the consequences for not following directions.	Yes—When asked what happens when you don't follow directions, E. has responded correctly.		
7. E. considers those consequences aversive.	✓ Yes.	E. will list things that she finds aversive at school. Her list will include consequences that have been used in the past.	E. listed being on Level 1, being sent out of the room, missing recess, and being left out of the group. PASS
8. E. knows the consequences for following directions.	Yes—When asked, E. has answered correctly.		
9. E. finds these consequences rewarding.	Yes—I have noticed E. beam when she's been praised for following directions. She also gets really excited when she earns points, stickers, and/or free time.		

Summary

E. passed the assessments for prerequisite 7 in addition to having prerequisites 1, 5, 6, 8, and 9. She does not have prerequisites 2, 3, or 4. In order for E. to be able to accomplish the target behavior, she probably first needs to work on understanding why it is important to follow teacher directions, valuing the behavior as much as I do, and becoming aware of when she is engaging in the targeted behavior. Therefore, E. needs to work on the following objectives:

1. Given the question, "Why do you need to follow teacher directions?" E. will respond with at least two of the following answers: to complete work in the allotted time, to complete work without disturbing others, and to earn points.

2. Given the following list of behaviors, E. and I will each rate the important ones with 100% agreement: listening to teacher, being in seat, completing work, talking out, walking around, and raising her hand.

3. E. will demonstrate that she is aware of when she is following teacher directions by keeping a written record of her responses to following directions for 3 days. Her responses and mine will meet with at least 80% agreement.

Diagnostic Evaluation 3

Maladaptive Behavior

My subject is a black female, age 13. N. has been a resident for the past 9 months at a residential treatment facility for emotionally disturbed children. For the first 3½ months of her placement, N. resided in the Intensive Care Unit, a coeducational, secure unit. At the present time, N. resides in one of the open units, which each houses a maximum of 13 girls.

My present position is that of a Childcare Specialist at this facility. Presently I am employed part-time and work in all three units, both open and secure. I have known and worked with N. in both the secure and open settings since her placement.

N. does not verbally identify her feelings (i.e., anger, sadness, fear) when asked to do so. At the present time, N. expresses feelings only in a nonverbal manner (i.e., with facial and body expression, by withdrawal, by refusal to talk). This nonverbal communication is maladaptive in that it requires others to make guesses regarding what she is feeling.

Target Behavior

N. will identify her feelings verbally when asked to do so at an appropriate time, 100% of the time. When N. is experiencing strong emotion, exhibited by an angry face, crossed arms, threatening body stance, etc., I will ask, "What's bothering you?" N. will respond with, "I'm angry," instead of my having to assume that she is angry.

Student _____ *N.* _____ Evaluator _____ *L.* _____ Date _____

Target Pinpoint _____ See Target Behavior _____

Prerequisites	Current Status	Assessments	Results
1. N. knows and understands that we expect her to express her feelings in a verbal manner.	Yes—When asked how we expect her to handle situations when she is upset (mad, sad, scared), N. replies, "Talk about it."		
2. N. knows and understands why we expect her to express her feelings in a verbal manner.	Yes—When asked, N. can express in her own words why we want her to express her feelings verbally— that is, so others can "know why I'm acting the way I am."		

Prerequisites	Current Status	Assessments	Results
3. N. values the verbal expression of her feelings as much as I do. That is, she agrees with me that the verbal expression of her feelings will be better for her than her present maladaptive behavior.	No—When N. does appropriately express her feelings (verbally), it is difficult to tell whether she is doing it to avoid what she thinks might happen if she doesn't, or if it is because she values it.	N. was read (due to poor reading skills) four hypothetical situations that describe the target behavior (verbal expression of feelings) and the maladaptive behavior (nonverbal expression of feelings). I will ask her which person she would most like to be. I will compare N.'s results to mine. They should be comparable 100% of the time. (List of hypothetical cases follows.)	N. chose no. 1. I chose either no. 2 or no. 4. NO PASS
4. N. is aware of her present manner of expressing her feelings.	Yes—After an incident of inappropriate expression of feelings, N. can describe how she let others know how she was feeling.		
5. N. knows when she is exhibiting the maladaptive behavior.	Yes—When asked after an incident whether she handled it well or not, N. makes the correct response.		
6. N. is capable of expressing her feelings in a verbal manner, instead of her present nonverbal expression of her feelings.	Yes—I have observed her expressing her feelings verbally on occasions. At times, when pushed or threatened with something she dislikes, N. will verbally express her feelings.		

Prerequisites	Current Status	Assessments	Results
7. N. knows the consequences of expressing her feelings in a non-verbal manner and considers them aversive.	Yes—N. can tell you what happens in her own words, to both herself and others, when she expresses her feelings nonverbally. Also, N. will at times express herself verbally to avoid something she considers aversive.		
8. N. knows the consequences for expressing her feelings verbally and considers them rewarding.	No—N. has not experienced enough success with appropriate verbal expression to know what the results are.		
9. N. does not consider expressing her feelings nonverbally more rewarding than expressing them in a verbal manner.	No—N. does get a lot of attention for expressing her feelings in a nonverbal manner and may find this rewarding.	N. will be read a series of problems and possible solutions. The list of solutions includes examples of both the target behavior and the maladaptive behavior. N. will be asked to identify which of the options she would prefer. I will do the same. We should agree 90% of the time. (List follows.)	N.'s results agree with mine approximately 40% of the time. N.'s response usually involved some type of withdrawal or aggressive response rather than a statement of her feelings. NO PASS
10. N. knows how to express her feelings in a verbal manner.	Yes—Often after an incident occurred, N. was able to tell me how else she might have showed me what she was feeling, and responded with an example of a verbal form of expression.		

Hypothetical Cases

These hypothetical cases were read to N. due to her poor reading skills. I did this because I wanted to know that N. was responding to what I wanted her to. I explained to N. that I was going to read her some examples of how people might handle different situations. If she could choose, which person would she like to be?

Example 1 (Chosen by N.):

Mary just got a letter from her mother. In this letter, her mother told her that her grandmother is in the hospital and is very sick. Mary and her grandmother have always had a very close relationship. When Mary read this letter she felt very sad and scared that her grandmother might die. Nobody else had read the letter, and Mary went to her room without saying a word. When called for dinner, Mary was still upset and said, "Go away!"

Example 2 (Acceptable):

Tom had a favorite pet dog he had raised since he was a puppy. One day his neighbor called and told him that they were very sorry, but they found Tom's dog dead. Someone must have hit it with a car. Tom was very sad about this. The next day at school it was hard for him to do much work. When the teacher asked him why he was not working, Tom told his teacher that he was very sad because his dog got hit and killed by a car.

Example 3:

During recess today, the girls were choosing teams to play basketball. Ann wanted to play too, but when she went over to get on a team, the others laughed at her and said she wasn't good enough to play. Ann felt both angry and sad about this. She returned to her desk in her classroom and sat down. For the rest of the afternoon, Ann didn't talk to anyone even when they talked to her because she was still so upset.

Example 4 (Acceptable):

Amy and Sue share a bedroom. Sue is very messy, and Amy gets in trouble as well when they have a messy room. Amy has been working for a special privilege and does not get it because she got into an argument about cleaning their room. Amy tells Sue that she is feeling angry with Sue over not keeping their room clean and causing her to lose her privilege.

Problems and Solutions

——————— = *N.'s Response*
— — — — — — = *My Response*

For any one of the problems I will tell you about, there are many ways you could handle them. I will read you both the problems and some of the ways you could solve them. I want you to tell me which one you think that you would pick. You can pick more than one if you want to.

1. If all your friends were invited to a party and you weren't:
   a. get mad and not talk to anyone
   b. go to the party anyway
   c. ask if you were forgotten
   d. tell someone that you feel left out
   e. cry

2. If you were sent to your room as a punishment for something you didn't do:
   a. go to your room and pout
   b. not say anything, but not go to your room
   c. assertively state your feelings
   d. run away
   e. write down how you feel when you are treated unfairly

3. If your sister ran away from home and you didn't know where she was:
   a. go looking for her
   b. make up stories about where she is
   c. run away too
   d. <u>tell your parents you are scared</u>
   e. pretend she hasn't gone away

4. If another kid called you a fatso:
   a. hit her
   b. <u>ask him why he said that</u>
   c. <u>call her a name back</u>
   d. cry
   e. <u>assertively tell him you don't like name calling</u>
   f. not say a word

5. You have problems at home and your caseworker tells you that you can't live at home anymore:
   a. run away
   b. <u>tell everyone that you want to stay at home</u>
   c. <u>say there aren't any problems</u>
   d. <u>tell your family and caseworker how scared and sad this makes you</u>
   e. <u>say you hate your caseworker and blame it on him or her</u>

6. Your father gets a new job and you have to move to a new city and start at a new school:
   a. <u>tell your friends how much you'll miss them</u>
   b. blame your father
   c. refuse to move
   d. <u>cry a lot</u>
   e. be mean to your friends so that you won't miss them

7. You go to your locker and find that it has been broken into and your radio is missing:
   a. <u>report the theft to the office</u>
   b. accuse everyone hoping someone confesses
   c. cry all day in your classes
   d. <u>take a radio you think might be yours</u>
   e. <u>ask if anyone knows who took it, stating that stealing makes you angry</u>

8. Someone gives you a surprise party:
   a. blush and smile, but do not say thank you
   b. <u>thank everyone and have a good time</u>
   c. get embarrassed and act angry
   d. claim it's not your birthday
   e. be obnoxious, loud, silly, but thankful

9. Your best friend picks a new best friend:
   a. <u>send your ex-best friend mean notes</u>
   b. <u>tell stories about your ex-friend</u>
   c. <u>become best friends to both of them</u>
   d. not say or do anything—just accept it
   e. <u>tell your ex-best friend you were hurt and feel left out</u>

10. You have a crush on a boy and he ignores you:
    a. don't tell anyone about your crush
    b. <u>follow him around</u>
    c. tell him you like him
    d. <u>tell your mother how you feel and ask for her advice</u>
    e. buy him things

Summary

It was necessary to conduct assessments on only 2 out of the 10 prerequisite behaviors. The remainder I was able to determine based both on my observation of N. and discussions and interactions we have had in the past. It was clear that another 1 out of the 10 prerequisite behaviors (no. 7) was also lacking. When the behaviors were assessed, I determined that N. was lacking the prerequisites in both cases that I had earlier found questionable. N. is lacking prerequisites 3, 7, and 9. Therefore, N. needs to work on the following objectives:

1. Prerequisite 3: Given a pencil-and-paper values assessment (this may be read orally and recorded), N. will identify that she values the verbal expression of her feelings by identifying these solutions rather than nonverbal expression of feelings at least 75% of the time. This assessment will occur in a 3-week time period following the completion of this initial assessment.

2. Prerequisite 7: N. will demonstrate that she knows the consequences of expressing her feelings verbally by telling me when she had an opportunity to do so, how she handled the situation, and how it ended up. This will occur as appropriate situations arise. It may be necessary for me to initiate this in the beginning.

3. Prerequisite 9: Given a pencil-and-paper assessment similar to the initial assessment, N. will identify which out of a number of options regarding the expression of feelings she might choose. N.'s choices will agree with mine 90% of the time. This assignment is to be completed approximately 3 weeks after the completion of the initial assessment.

Diagnostic Evaluation 4

Maladaptive Behavior

The subject, D., is a student I see ½ hour each day for group reading instruction that supplements the classroom reading program. I see him in the reading room, which is separate from the classroom.

Periodically during the last 3 weeks, D. has not been arriving to reading class on time. He arrives 10 to 15 minutes late, which I consider maladaptive because:

1. If the prepared reading lesson does not begin on time, the other members of the group also do not receive the full benefit of the lesson and the learning environment is disrupted.

2. If the lesson has started when D. arrives late, he has missed instruction time, and since he needs extra reading instruction, it is not in his best interest to lose out on it.

Thus, not arriving on time could be maladaptive to D. and his group peers in terms of their academic well-being.

The pinpoint of the maladaptive behavior is: "Does not arrive on time for reading instruction in the reading room."

Target Behavior

D. arrives on time for reading instruction.

Student _____ D _____ Evaluator _____ A _____ Date _____

Target Pinpoint ___ D. will be in the reading room when reading class begins at 10:35 A.M. 90% of the time. ___

Prerequisites	Current Status	Assessments	Results
1. D. knows when he is to be in reading class.	Yes—He's been coming at the same time since Nov. 1980.		
2. D. knows why he is supposed to attend reading class on time.	✓ Yes—D. answered assessment questions to my satisfaction.	a. When asked to answer verbally why it is important for him to be in the reading room when class begins, D. will answer to the teacher's satisfaction 100% of the time. b. when asked to answer "yes" or "no" to the following questions, D. will answer to the teacher's satisfaction 100% of the time. i. Is it important for you to be in the reading room on time so that everyone can start the lesson on time? (yes) ii. Is it important for you to be in the room on time for reading class so that you do not miss out on new skills being taught? (yes)	D. was unable to verbalize (a) so I assessed using (b). D. answered "yes" to each question. PASS

Prerequisites	Current Status	Assessments	Results
3. D. is able to get himself to reading class (no internal or external conditions are preventing him).	Yes—He did so prior to the onset of maladaptive behavior; I checked his records again and checked with his classroom teacher and no new conditions were preventing him.		
4. D. is aware that he is not coming to class on time.	✗ Yes—D. was able to answer what he was doing and where he should be to my satisfaction.	When asked to describe verbally what he is doing (not in class) and where he is to be (in class), D. will do so to the teacher's satisfaction 100% of the time.	A.: "What are you doing?" D.: "I'm playing on the playground." A.: "Where are you supposed to be now?" D.: "With you, upstairs." PASS
5. D. knows the consequences for not arriving to class on time.	✗ Yes—D. answered assessment questions to my satisfaction.	When asked to answer "yes" or "no" to the following questions, D. will answer to the teacher's satisfaction 100% of the time. a. When you come late to class do you have to have the reading lesson during lunch recess? (yes) b. When you come late to class do you have to take the assignment home to finish it because you did not have time to finish in class? (yes)	D. answered "yes" to both questions. PASS
6. D. considers the consequences aversive.	✗ No—D. did not include homework as an aversive consequence.	When asked to name all the things he doesn't like about school, D. will do so and include the consequences of being late to class 100% of the time.	D. named: a. "people yelling at me" b. "missing recess" c. "sitting by myself" d. "my Mom being called" (on phone) e. "staying after school" NO PASS—did not include finishing assignments at home.

Prerequisites	Current Status	Assessments	Results
7. D. knows the consequences for arriving on time for class.	✓ Yes—D. answered assessment questions to my satisfaction.	When asked to answer "yes" or "no" to the following questions, D. will do so to the teacher's satisfaction 100% of the time. a. When you come to class on time do you learn new things about how words are made and understood? (yes) b. When you come to class on time do you have your answers on assignments checked right away? (yes) c. When you come to class on time do you get to play a reading game if you finish your assignment early? (yes)	D. answered "yes" to all the questions. PASS
8. D. considers consequences rewarding.	✓ Yes—D. included playing reading game as something he likes to do.	When asked to name all the things he likes to do at school, D. will do so and include one or more of the consequences listed in prerequisite 7.	D. named: a. field trips b. "working with the Rubik's Cube" c. "playing that Snake Game (reading game) d. recess e. "painting at the art station" f. "reading in that new book you gave me" PASS

Summary

The results of this diagnosis show that D. is lacking only one of the required prerequisites (prerequisite 6) for arriving to class on time. He lacked this prerequisite because he does not consider aversive all of the consequences associated with the maladaptive behavior.

Performance objective for prerequisite 6: When asked to name all the things he does not like about school, D. will do so and include the consequences of being late to class 100% of the time.

Appendix D
Interest Inventory

Note: While the following material would probably be suitable for use with students of any age, read it carefully beforehand and make any changes in content and/or vocabulary you deem necessary.

Student _____ Age _____ Grade _____

School _____ Teacher _____

Interviewer _____ Date _____

1. What do you like to do in your spare time? _____

   What do you usually do right after school? _____

   In the evening? _____

   On the weekend? _____

   With whom do you like to (play, hang out, spend time)? _____

   _____

2. How many brothers and sisters do you have? _____

   How old are they? _____

   Do you (play, hang out, spend time with) them? _____

3. What kind of work do your parents do? _____

   Are there any (jobs, chores) you are expected to do at home? _____

   Which do you prefer? _____

4. Do you belong to any (clubs, groups, organizations)? _____

   Why do you belong? _____

5. Do you take lessons in anything (e.g., swimming, piano, gymnastics, horseback riding)? _____

   _____

   How long have you taken these lessons? _____

   What are your hobbies? _____

6. Do you (receive an allowance, earn any money)? _____

   For doing what? _____

   What do you usually spend your money on? _____

   If you had money of your own, what would you spend it on? _____

   _____

7. How often do you go to the movies? _____

   With whom do you usually go? _____

   Which are the two best movies you ever saw? _____

   Which of these movies do you like the best? Comedy, Melodrama, Western, Romance, Musical, Adventure, Fantasy, Cartoon, Science Fiction, Murder, Horror, Other?

   _____

   Who is your favorite actor? Actress? _____

   Why? _____

8. What are your favorite television programs? _____

   How much time do you spend watching television? _____

9. What are your favorite radio stations? _____

   How much time do you spend listening to the radio? _____

10. Do you or your family have a pet? _____

11. What subjects do you like best at school? _____

    Least? _____

12. Do you enjoy reading? _____

    Do you like to have someone read to you? _____

    How much time do you spend just reading? _____

    Do your parents encourage you to read at home? _____

    What are some books you read lately? _____

    Do you have a library card? _____

    How often do you use it? _____

    Do you get books from the school library? _____

How many books of your own do you have? _____

What are some books you would like to own? _____

How many books are in your home? _____

What kind of reading do you like best? Adventure, Science, Animal Stories, Fantasy, Science Fiction, Plays, History, Novels, Poetry, Mysteries, Biographies, Fairy Tales, Other?

_____

What newspapers do you read? _____

Which part do you read first? _____

Do you get any magazines at your house? _____

Do you read them? _____

What is your favorite magazine? _____

13. What would you like to do when you (grow up, finish or graduate from school)? _____

_____

14. If you had free time right now to do anything you wanted, what would you most like to be doing?

Name five things. _____

_____

Appendix E

Commercially Available Programs and Materials

Note: The following is a partial listing of commercial programs that teach many of the skills discussed in chapters 8 through 11. In most instances, I have included a sentence or two to give you some idea of what they cover and what level of student they were designed for. Addresses of publishing companies follow. If you are particularly interested in cognitive restructuring programs and materials, I suggest that you send for the Institute of Rational Emotive Therapy catalog.

Anderson, J. (1981). *Thinking, changing, rearranging: Improving self esteem in young people.* Eugene, OR: Timberline Press.
A program in cognitive restructuring for use with students "from about 10 upward." Consists of a paperback book for student use with reading and writing activities.

Bedford, S. (1974). *Instant replay.* New York: Institute for Rational Living.
A cognitive restructuring story book for elementary-age students. Can be used as a supplement to other materials.

Biofeedback, biodots and stress. (Available from Biodot International, Inc., P.O. Box 46229, Indianapolis, IN 46229, 317-637-5776.)
Temperature-sensitive dots which, when placed on the skin, serve as simple biofeedback measures and allow children (and adults) to monitor their stress levels. Comes with teacher's "manual" and lesson on stress. Most appropriate for elementary-age students.

Camp, B. W., & Bash, M. A. (1981). *Think aloud: Increasing cognitive skill, a problem-solving program for children.* Champaign, IL: Research Press.
Combines training in verbal mediation, self-instruction, and problem solving for elementary students. Available in a small-group program (designed for use with 6- to 8-year-olds) and three classroom programs for grades 1–2, 3–4, and 5–6. Heavily researched and field tested on hyperactive and aggressive students.

Cautela, J. R., & Groden, J. (1978). *Relaxation: A comprehensive manual for adults, children, and children with special needs.* Champaign, IL: Research Press.

Includes descriptions of relaxation techniques for varied populations as well as procedures for teaching these techniques.

Garcia, E. J., & Pellegrini, N. (1974). *Homer the homely hound dog.* New York: Institute for Rational Living. Another cognitive restructuring storybook for elementary-age students. Best used as a supplement to other materials.

Gerald, M., & Eyman, W. (1981). *Thinking straight and talking sense.* New York: Institute for Rational Living. A comprehensive program in cognitive restructuring for students "above the fifth grade." Includes activities, exercises, stories, and information for students, all in a student workbook format. Notes for teachers are included in the workbook.

Goldstein, A. P. (1988). *The prepare curriculum.* Champaign, IL: Research Press.
A comprehensive social skills program in textbook form. It includes methods and samples of materials for training in problem solving, interpersonal skills, anger control, moral reasoning, and stress management, among others. It also includes material on classroom management and transfer and maintenance. Designed for adolescents and younger children who are deficient in prosocial skills.

Goldstein, A. P., & Glick, B. (1987). *Aggression replacement training: A comprehensive intervention for aggressive youth.* Champaign, IL: Research Press.
A textbook on aggression replacement training (ART), a comprehensive research-based program for juvenile offenders. It includes methods and samples of materials for behavioral (structured learning), affective (anger management), and cognitive (moral education) components.

Goldstein, A. P., Sprafkin, R. P., Gershaw, N. J., & Klein, P. (1980). *Skillstreaming the adolescent: A structured learning approach to teaching prosocial skills.* Champaign, IL: Research Press.
A comprehensive social skills curriculum for secondary-level students. Based on the Structured Learn-

ing approach, which involves modeling, role playing, performance feedback, and transfer training. Covers 50 prosocial skills. For students who display aggression, immaturity, or withdrawal.

Hazel, J. S., Schumaker, J. B., Sherman, J., & Sheldon-Wildgen, J. (1982). *Asset: A social skills program for adolescents*. Champaign, IL: Research Press.
Group instruction. Videotaped material providing models of appropriate and inappropriate social interaction skills are available, as are lesson plans, training procedures, and skill sheets. Covers skills such as giving and accepting negative feedback, resisting peer pressure, problem solving, and negotiation.

Jackson, N. F., Jackson, D. A., & Monroe, C. (1983). *Getting along with others: Teaching social effectiveness to children*. Champaign, IL: Research Press.
For students from elementary and middle school as well as mildly retarded people between the ages of 18 and 35. Comes with program guide and skills lessons and activities for the 17 core social skills taught. Color videotapes are available.

Knaus, W. (1974). *Rational emotive education: A manual for elementary school teachers*. New York: Institute for Rational Living.
A comprehensive program in cognitive restructuring. Uses the format of a teacher's manual with descriptions of several student activities for working on specific types of irrational thinking, such as mistake making, catastrophizing, and stereotyping.

Kranzler, G. (1974). *Emotional education exercises: A rational emotive approach*. (Write to the author at Counseling Department, College of Education, University of Oregon, Eugene, OR 97403).
A comprehensive program in cognitive restructuring for secondary-level students. Includes methods and examples of materials in a spiral notebook format that serves as a teacher's manual.

Mannix, D. S. (1986). *I can behave: A classroom self-management curriculum for elementary students*. Austin, TX: PRO-ED.
An illustrated storybook comprised of 10 stories and 125 full-page drawings. Each story focuses on a specific classroom problem such as not taking turns or talking too loud. Storybook comes with manual and lesson plans. Field tested.

McGinnis, E., & Goldstein, A. P. (1984). *Skillstreaming the elementary school child: A guide for teaching prosocial skills*. Champaign, IL: Research Press.
A comprehensive social skills curriculum for elementary-age students. Covers 60 specific prosocial skills including asking for help and apologizing.

Merrifield, C., & Merrifield, R. (1979). *Call me RET-man and have a ball*. New York: Institute for Rational Living.
An introduction to RET in comic book form. For secondary-level students and adults. Supplemental material.

Platt, J. J., & Spivack, G. (1976). *Workbook for training in interpersonal problem solving thinking*. Philadelphia Department of Mental Health Sciences, Hahnemann Medical College and Hospital.
Heavily researched and field-tested program in problem-solving skills. Write to the authors in Pennsylvania.

Sheinker, J., & Sheinker, A. (1988). *Metacognitive approach to social skills training: A program for grades 4 through 12*. Rockville, MD: Aspen Publishing.
Focuses on self-management. Appears to work best with students who display no overt antisocial behavior. Teacher acts as a facilitator (rather than teacher) for each 40-minute lesson. Multimodal—incorporates art and music into lessons.

Waksman, S. A., & Messmer, C. L. (1986). *The Waksman social skills curriculum: An assertive behavior program for adolescents*. Austin, TX: PRO-ED.
For children and adolescents. Focuses on teaching assertive skills. Can be taught in 20-minute lessons. Comes with teacher's manual and worksheets for students.

Walker, H. M., McConnell, S., Holmes, S., Todis, B., Walker, J., & Golden, N. (1983). *The Walker social skills curriculum: The ACCEPTS program*. Austin, TX: PRO-ED.
Designed for use with students in grades 1 through 6. Uses a direct-instruction approach. Comes with videotape, teaching scripts (for 28 skills), and behavior management procedures.

Walker, H. M., Todis, B., Holmes, D., & Horton, G. (1985). *The Walker social skills curriculum: The ACCESS program*. Austin, TX: PRO-ED.
Similar to the ACCEPTS program but geared toward the middle and high school student. Covers skills in three basic areas: relating to peers, to adults, and to yourself.

Waters, V. (1979). *Color us rational*. New York: Institute for Rational Living.
RET coloring book for elementary-age students. Supplemental material.

Waters, V. (1980). *Rational stories for children*. New York: Institute for Rational Living.
Another cognitive restructuring storybook for elementary-age students. Supplemental material.

Weissberg, R. P., Gesten, E. L., & Liebenstein, N. L. (1980). *The Rochester social problem-solving program*. (Available from Center for Community Study, 575 Mt. Hope Ave., Rochester, NY 14620.)
No information available.

Wells, R. H. (1986). *Personal power: succeeding in school (Vol. I)*. Austin, TX: PRO-ED.
Consists of three volumes: (1) succeeding in school, (2) succeeding with others, and (3) succeeding with self. Text consists of 90 lesson plans (20–30 minutes each). For secondary-level students.

Aspen Publishing, Inc.
1600 Research Blvd.
Rockville, MD 20850

Institute for Rational Emotive Therapy
(formerly Institute for Rational Living)
45 E. 65th St.
New York, NY 10021-6593

PRO-ED, Inc.
8700 Shoal Creek Blvd.
Austin, TX 78758

Research Press
2612 Mattis Ave.
Champaign, IL 61820

Timberline Press
Box 70071
Eugene, OR 97401

In order for you to get the best feelings from these exercises, there are some rules you must follow. First, you must do exactly what I say, even if it seems kind of silly. Second, you must try hard to do what I say. Third, you must pay attention to your body. Throughout these exercises, pay attention to how your muscles feel when they are tight and when they are loose and relaxed. And, fourth, you must practice. The more you practice, the more relaxed you can get. Does anyone have any questions?

Are you ready to begin? Okay. First, get as comfortable as you can in your chair. Sit back, get both feet on the floor, and just let your arms hang loose. That's fine. Now close your eyes and don't open them until I say to. Remember to follow my instructions very carefully, try hard, and pay attention to your body. Here we go.

Hands and Arms

Pretend you have a whole lemon in your left hand. Now squeeze it hard. Try to squeeze all the juice out. Feel the tightness in your hand and arm as you squeeze. Now drop the lemon. Notice how your muscles feel when they are relaxed. Take another lemon and squeeze it. Try to squeeze this one harder than you did the first one. That's right. Real hard. Now drop your lemon and relax. See how much better your hand and arm feel when they are relaxed. Once again, take a lemon in your left hand and squeeze all the juice out. Don't leave a single drop. Squeeze hard. Good. Now relax and let the lemon fall from your hand. (Repeat the process for the right hand and arm.)

Arms and Shoulders

Pretend you are a furry, lazy cat. You want to stretch. Stretch your arms out in front of you. Raise them up high over your head. Way back. Feel the pull in your shoulders. Stretch higher. Now just let your arms drop back to your side. Okay, kittens, let's stretch again. Stretch your arms out in front of you. Raise them over your head. Pull them back, way back. Pull hard. Now let them drop quickly. Good. Notice how your shoulders feel more relaxed. This time let's have a great big stretch. Try to touch the ceiling. Stretch your arms way out in front of you. Raise them way up high over your head. Push them way, way back. Notice the tension and pull in your arms and shoulders. Hold tight, now. Great. Let them drop very quickly and feel how good it is to be relaxed. It feels good and warm and lazy.

Shoulder and Neck

Now pretend you are a turtle. You're sitting out on a rock by a nice, peaceful pond, just relaxing in the warm sun. It feels nice and warm and safe here. Oh-oh! You sense danger. Pull your head into your house. Try to pull your shoulders up to your ears and push your head down into your shoulders. Hold in tight. It isn't easy to be a turtle in a shell. The danger is past now. You can come out into the warm sunshine, and, once again, you can relax and feel the warm sunshine. Watch out now! More danger, hurry, pull your head back into your house and hold it tight. You have to be closed in tight to protect yourself. Okay, you can relax now. Bring your head out and let your shoulders relax. Notice how much better it feels to be relaxed than to be all tight. One more time, now. Danger! Pull your head in. Push your shoulders way up to your ears and hold tight. Don't let even a tiny piece of your head show outside your shell. Hold it. Feel the tenseness in your neck and shoulders. Okay. You can come out now. It's safe again. Relax and feel comfortable in your safety. There's no more danger. Nothing to worry about. Nothing to be afraid of. You feel good.

Jaw

You have a giant jawbreaker bubble gum in your mouth. It's very hard to chew. Bite down on it. Hard! Let your neck muscles help you. Now relax. Just let your jaw hang loose. Notice how good it feels just to let your jaw drop. Okay, let's tackle that jawbreaker again now. Bite down. Hard! Try to squeeze it out between your teeth. That's good. You're really tearing that gum up. Now relax again. Just let your jaw drop off your face. It feels so good just to let go and not have to fight that bubble gum. Okay, one more time. We're really going to tear it up this time. Bite down. Hard as you can. Harder. Oh, you're really working hard. Good. Now relax. Try to relax your whole body. You've beaten the bubble gum. Let yourself go as loose as you can.

Face and Nose

Here comes a pesky old fly. He has landed on your nose. Try to get him off without using your hands. That's right, wrinkle up your nose. Make as many wrinkles in your nose as you can. Scrunch your nose up real hard. Good. You've chased him away. Now you can relax your nose. Oops, here he comes back again. Right back in the middle of your nose. Wrinkle up your nose again. Shoo him off. Wrinkle it up hard. Hold it just as tight as you can. Okay, he flew away. You can relax your face. Notice that when you scrunch up your nose that your cheeks and your mouth and your forehead and your eyes all help you, and they get tight, too. So when you relax your nose, your whole face relaxes too, and that feels good. Oh-oh. This time that old fly has come back, but this time he's on your forehead. Make lots of wrinkles. Try to catch him between all those wrinkles. Hold it tight, now. Okay, you can let go. He's gone for good. Now you can just relax. Let your face go smooth, no wrinkles anywhere. Your face feels nice and smooth and relaxed.

Stomach

Hey! Here comes a cute baby elephant. But he's not watching where he's going. He doesn't see you lying there in the grass, and he's about to step on your stomach. Don't move. You don't have time to get out of the way. Just get ready for him. Make your stomach very hard. Tighten up your stomach muscles real tight. Hold it. It looks like he is going the other way. You can relax now. Let your stomach go soft. Let it be as relaxed as you can. That feels so much better. Oops, he's coming this way again. Get ready. Tighten up your stomach. Real hard. If he steps on you when your stomach is hard, it won't hurt. Make your stomach into a rock. Okay, he's moving away again. You can relax now. Kind of settle down, get comfortable, and relax. Notice the difference between a tight stomach and a relaxed one. That's how we want it to feel—nice and loose and relaxed. You won't believe this, but this time he's really coming your way and no turning around. He's headed straight for you. Tighten up. Tighten hard. Here he comes. This is really it. You've got to hold on tight. He's stepping on you. He's stepped over you. Now he's gone for good. You can relax completely. You're safe. Everything is okay and you can feel nice and relaxed.

This time imagine that you want to squeeze through a narrow fence and the boards have splinters on them. You'll have to make yourself very skinny if you're going to make it through. Suck your stomach in. Try to squeeze it up against your backbone. Try to be as skinny as you can. You've got to get through. Now relax. You don't have to be skinny now. Just relax and feel your stomach being warm and loose. Okay, let's try to get through that fence now. Squeeze up your stomach. Make it touch your backbone. Get it real small and tight. Get as skinny as you can. Hold tight, now. You've got to squeeze through. You got through that skinny little fence and no splinters. You can relax now. Settle back and let your stomach come back out where it belongs. You can feel really good now. You've done fine.

Legs and Feet

Now pretend that you are standing barefoot in a big, fat mud puddle. Squish your toes down deep into the mud. Try to get your feet down to the bottom of the mud puddle. You'll probably need your legs to help you push. Push down, spread your toes apart, and feel the mud squish up between your toes. Now step out of the mud puddle. Relax your feet. Let your toes go loose and feel how nice that is. It feels good to be relaxed. Back into the mud puddle. Squish your toes down. Let your leg muscles help push your feet down. Push your feet. Hard. Try to squeeze that mud puddle dry. Okay. Come back out now. Relax your feet, relax your legs, relax your toes. It feels so good to be relaxed. No tenseness anywhere. You feel kind of warm and tingly.

Conclusion

Stay as relaxed as you can. Let your whole body go limp and feel all your muscles relaxed. In a few minutes I will ask you to open your eyes, and that will be the end of this session. As you go through the day, remember how good it feels to be relaxed. Sometimes you have to make yourself tighter before you can be relaxed, just as we did in these exercises. Practice these exercises every day to get more and more relaxed. A good time to practice is at night, after you have gone to bed and the lights are out and you won't be disturbed. It will help you get to sleep. Then, when you are a really good relaxer, you can help yourself relax here at school. Just remember the elephant, or the jawbreaker, or the mud puddle, and you can do our exercises and nobody will know. Today is a good day, and you are ready to go back to class feeling very relaxed. You've worked hard in here, and it feels good to work hard. Very slowly, now, open your eyes and wiggle your muscles around a little. Very good. You've done a good job. You're going to be a super relaxer.

From "Relaxation Training for Children" by A. S. Koeppen, 1974, Oct., *Elementary School Guidance and Counseling, 9,* pp. 16–20. Published by American School Counselor Association, a division of American Association for Counseling and Development, 5999 Stevenson Avenue, Alexandria, VA 22304.

Glossary

Alarm reaction: The first stage in Selye's *General Adaptation Syndrome* (1976). It is sometimes referred to as the "fight or flight response."

Antecedent stimulus event (ASE): Any environmental stimulus that elicits a response. Examples in the classroom are cues, prompts, questions, or commands from the teacher and negative or positive attention from the peer group (e.g., insults, compliments, greetings).

Arrangement: In a schedule of reinforcement, the number of consecutive correct or desirable responses the student has to make before being reinforced.

Aversion therapy: A type of behavior therapy in which an unwanted behavior (e.g., smoking or alcoholism) is weakened by pairing it with an aversive stimulus (e.g., a nausea-inducing drug).

Baseline: That phase in a behavior change program when there is no change in what the teacher does to modify the student's behavior. This does not necessarily mean that the teacher does nothing to modify the behavior. It means that she or he continues to do the same thing he or she has been doing (which could be nothing). Data collected during the baseline phase will be compared with data collected during the intervention phase to see if there is any change in the student's behavior. Also known as the *before phase*.

Behavior, maladaptive: Any behavior a student engages in which is considered currently or potentially harmful to the student's or another person's social, emotional, physical, or academic well-being. Any behavior considered to be maladaptive passes the "So what?" test and should be modified.

Behavior management: A term loosely used to describe any direct attempt to modify a student's behavior. It is often used synonymously with *behavior modification*.

Behavior modification: A model of behavior change based on the laboratory findings of B.F. Skinner. It involves the systematic application of antecedents and consequences for the purpose of strengthening, maintaining, or weakening operant behavior.

Behavior, target: The behavior required of the student at the successful termination of the intervention. This change in the student's behavior has to be in his or her best interest in order to pass the "So what?" test.
Note. In much of the research literature, the term *target behavior* is used to denote maladaptive behavior (i.e., the behavior you wish to change).

Behavior therapy: A form of behavior modification that includes techniques such as aversion therapy and systematic desensitization. It is used primarily by psychologists and psychiatrists in clinical settings or in private practice. Refer to Wolpe (1969).

Behavioral setting: A physical setting. A specific time and place with a particular set of activities and inhabitants.

Chaining: A technique used to strengthen new behaviors in students. It involves identifying a set (i.e., chain) of stimulus-response links and having the student perform them from the beginning of the chain over and over again.

Change agent: In a behavior modification program, the person responsible for changing the behavior of another (e.g., teacher, peer, parent).

Cognitions: The mental activities engaged in by human beings. They include (but are not limited to) cognitive events (i.e., one's stream of consciousness), cognitive structures (e.g., beliefs or attitudes), cognitive processes (i.e., the mental machinations or system one uses to solve problems), and inner speech (i.e., our "self-talk").

Cognitive behavior modification (CBM): An offshoot of behavior modification, CBM is the label given to a number of strategies designed to indirectly modify one's behavior by first modifying one's cognitions. Examples of such strategies include self-instruction and verbal mediation (to change our self-talk), problem solving (to change cognitive processes), and cognitive restructuring (to change our beliefs or attitudes). Refer to Meichenbaum (1977) and Harris et al. (1985).

Cognitive restructuring: A type of CBM strategy that is used to modify a person's beliefs or attitudes. The term is often used synonymously with *rational emotive therapy* (see Ellis & Harper, 1961). It involves identifying negative beliefs that trigger strong negative emotions, then attempting to dispute them and replace them with positive beliefs that produce less intense (and more productive) emotions.

Consequent stimulus event (CSE): The effect produced by the operant on the environment. It is the result after a behavior occurs that serves to strengthen or weaken the operant.

Contingency: The conditions under which a CSE occurs. For example, the teacher who tells the class that only students who finish their work may go to the movie in the assembly is using work completion as a contingency or *condition* for the CSE (seeing the movie in the assembly).

Contingency contracting: A comprehensive behavior modification program (in some instances, it is called *contingency management* and is used synonymously with behavior modification) popularized by the work of Lloyd Homme and based on the earlier research of David Premack. It involves the use of contracts between teachers and students with the latter contracting or agreeing to perform low-frequency behaviors (e.g., completing assignments) in return for engaging in high-frequency behaviors (e.g., free time at a favored activity) as a reward. Refer to Homme et al. (1969).

Countoon: An observation and recording form used by the student to monitor his or her own behavior. It is usually in the form of a card taped to the student's desk and includes three components: (1) a cartoon drawing of what the student does (usually the target behavior), (2) a number chart on which the student counts each instance of the behavior being monitored, and (3) a cartoon drawing of what happens if the student reaches a prespecified number (i.e., the CSE).

Data, duration: Information regarding a person's behavior that shows how long the behavior lasts. It is usually collected on behaviors that last a long time (e.g., daydreaming) or occur so fast or frequently that they don't have a readily observable beginning and end (e.g., waving one's hand back and forth in self-stimulating behavior).

Data, frequency: Information regarding a person's behavior that shows how often the behavior occurs. It is usually collected on behaviors that don't last long and do occur frequently, and which have a readily observable beginning and end (e.g., hitting peers, telling lies, or noncompliance).

Data, intensity: Information regarding a person's behavior that shows how forceful the behavior is. It is usually collected on behaviors ranging in force from soft to hard, quiet to loud, restrained to wild. Examples are having temper tantrums, speaking loudly, and injuring oneself (e.g., self-biting).

Dead man's test: The test applied to a target behavior to make sure it is a *fair pair*. If a dead man can't engage in the target behavior, it's a fair pair. If a dead man can engage in the target behavior, it's not a fair pair.

Deprivation: A state of need in the student that must exist for reinforcement to occur.

Deviant behavior: Also known as *maladaptive behavior* or *dysfunctional behavior*.

Disputing irrational beliefs (DIBs): One of the techniques used in cognitive restructuring, it requires the student (with or without the teacher's help) to evaluate the validity of his or her belief. This can be done by asking one or more questions about the belief (e.g., "Does it help keep me alive?" "Does it make me feel better?" "Is it based on reality?").

Distress: Physiological responses (e.g., tense muscles, sweating, shaking, changes in voice, raised pulse) that are associated with negative emotions such as anger and anxiety.

Ecobehavioral analysis: Applied behavioral analysis that incorporates an environmental perspective on behavior. The basic assumption is that maladaptive behavior is the result of a "poor fit" between the child and the environment. Therefore, the goal of the analysis is to identify the student and environmental characteristics that contribute to the poor fit and the resultant maladaptive behavior.

Ecobehavioral niche: The role an organism fulfills in one of the various ecosystems available to it.

Ecosystem: The total environment in which an organism exists; physical, social, emotional, and cognitive factors are included in the ecosystem. See also *environment*.

Efficacy: A technical word used in the research literature, synonymous with *effectiveness*. When you ask what the efficacy of an intervention is, you want to know how effective it was.

Environment: The complex matrix of physical, social, and cultural conditions that affect the growth and development of an organism. See also *ecosystem*.

Eustress: Physiological responses associated with positive emotions such as joy.

Extinction: The weakening of an operant by withholding a known reinforcer contingent upon the emission of the operant. For example, a known reinforcer for hand-raising behavior is teacher attention. A teacher usually calls on a student who raises his or her hand. Calling on the student tends to reinforce hand-raising behavior. In extinction, the teacher may forget to call on the student whose hand is raised, with the result that hand-raising behavior is weakened. In *planned extinction*, the teacher deliberately withholds the known reinforcer in order to weaken the behavior.

Fading: The process of gradually changing the environmental (i.e., antecedent or consequent) events surrounding a student's response. For example, token reinforcement or a certain stimulus or cue might be faded out to get the student to perform without it. This differs from shaping primarily in that the latter requires a gradual change of the student's response.

Fair pair: When the strengthening of a target behavior directly leads to the weakening of a maladaptive behavior, the two behaviors may be referred to as a *fair pair*. Examples are strengthening in-seat behavior to weaken out-of-seat behavior and strengthening on-task behavior to weaken off-task behavior. Change agents are encouraged to use fair pairs when attempting to modify student behavior.

General adaptation syndrome (G.A.S.): The three-stage model of stress first described by Hans Selye (1976). It includes: (1) the alarm reaction (the fight or flight response, which doesn't last very long), (2) the stage of resistance (which may last years and is characterized by physical evidence of stress, such as gastrointestinal or sleep disorders), and (3) the stage of exhaustion (when the body breaks down and disease may appear).

Generalization: In behavior modification, the transfer of learning from one environment or situation to another. For example, we may say that generalization has occurred if a student's newly acquired hand-raising behavior in one class is also demonstrated in other classes whether or not the same ASEs and CSEs are occurring in all of the classes.

Hierarchy of escalating consequences: The technique of using several consequences to weaken a student's behavior. Consequences are presented from least severe (i.e., punishing) to most severe.

Individualized education program (IEP): Plan of instruction required by law (PL 94-142: Education of All Handicapped Children Act of 1975) for every student certified as handicapped and eligible for special education.

Internalization: In behavior modification, the state in which a person engages in a behavior without the use of extrinsic antecedents (e.g., reminders) or consequences (e.g., rewards). In other words, the person engages in the behavior because he or she believes it is appropriate to do so. This requires a change in attitude as well as of behavior.

Intervention: The phase in a behavior change program when the teacher implements an intervention that is different from the one that was used during baseline. Data collected during the intervention phase will be compared with baseline data to see if there is any change in the student's behavior. This is also called the *during phase*.

Latency: The total time that elapses between the response and the CSE (or between the ASE and the response).

Levels system: A system whereby students in a token economy are "promoted" from one level to the next based upon their improved behavior. Since each level is another step away from the token system, it is often used to wean students away from a token economy.

Locus of control: The degree to which an individual perceives the events in his or her life to be under his or her own control. Refer to Rotter (1966).

Maintenance: In behavior modification, the length of time the behavior change lasts once it has been attained.

Modeling: The process of providing a person with a visual, verbal, or manual representation of the behavior you want her or him to engage in. This is also known as *imitation learning* (Bandura, 1969).

Monitoring: Observing and recording behavior.

Negative practice: A form of punishment in which the person is required to engage in the maladaptive behavior over and over until it becomes so aversive that he or she will not want to engage in it again: for example, making a student spit into a jar over and over as a punishment for spitting in the classroom.

Operant: Any voluntary behavior that produces an effect on the environment. Examples are walking, talking, reading, and writing.

Operant conditioning: A form of learning popularized by B. F. Skinner, it forms the basis of behavior modification.

Operants, controlled: Behaviors that are controlled by (or dependent on) the behaviors of others. Examples are "answers questions" (controlled by questions asked), "hits when provoked" (controlled by provocations), and "complies with commands" (controlled by commands given).

Operants, free: Behaviors that do not appear to be controlled by (or dependent upon) any observable behavior of another person. Examples are "asks questions," "hits" (without provocation), and "gets out of seat."

Overcorrection: A form of punishment in which the person is required to (1) make restitution by restoring the situation to its former state and (2) practice an exaggerated form of behavior that is incompatible with the behavior you want to weaken. For example, if the student insulted a peer, he or she would make restitution by apologizing to the peer and then paying a compliment to every student in the class.

Performance objectives: Statements that describe the student's behavior after a successful intervention. They not only describe what the student will do but under what conditions and how well she or he will perform. By attention to the performance objective the teacher will know when the student no longer needs instruction or intervention.

Pinpoint: The name given to the brief statement that describes the student's maladaptive or target behavior. To be considered a pinpoint, the statement must pass the stranger test. Examples of pinpoints are "is in seat before the late bell rings," "does not complete assignments," "hits peers without provocation," and "speaks in a voice audible to everyone in the room."

Pinpointing: The act of writing a pinpoint.

Poor fit: Used to describe a maladaptive behavioral response to a particular behavior setting or ecosystem. It implies a reciprocal relationship between the environment and the maladaptive behavior it evokes without placing blame solely on the behavior.

Precision teaching: A behavioral approach to instruction pioneered by Ogden Lindsley, precision teaching involves: (1) pinpointing the academic or social behavior to be modified, (2) preparing and implementing the instructional plan, (3) evaluating student progress through direct and continuous measurement, (4) plotting the test data on ratio (logarithmic) charts, (5) estimating and interpreting the learning trend (i.e., how fast the student is learning), and (6) making instructional decisions based on these trends. Refer to Kunzelmann et al. (1970).

Premack Principle: Based on research conducted by David Premack, who found that when high-frequency behavior is made contingent upon low-frequency behavior, the low-frequency behavior tends to increase in frequency. Also known as "Grandma's Rule": Children who eat their vegetables get their dessert.

Prerequisites: According to the task analytical model, these are all of the "person" variables, such as skills, knowledge, attitudes, and temperament, necessary for a student to engage in a given target behavior.

Problem solving: A type of CBM strategy in which students are taught how to solve intra- and interpersonal problems.

Progressive relaxation training (PRT): The name usually given to the tense-release system of deep-muscle relaxation developed by Edmund Jacobson. It may be used by itself as a somatic-physiological stress management skill or integrated with other skills as in stress inoculation.

Punishers: These are CSEs that serve to weaken the operants they follow. Punishers may range in severity from a reprimand (e.g., "Stop that!") to corporal punishment such as paddling. Whether or not a CSE is a punisher depends entirely on the effect it has on the operant it follows. It makes no difference whether or not the person presenting the CSE thinks it is a punisher. If it weakens the operant it follows, it is a punisher. If it strengthens the operant it follows, it is actually a reinforcer.

Punishers, learned: Aversive CSEs that have to be paired with other aversive CSEs before they can effectively weaken the operants they follow. Examples include failing grades, abusive-provocative language (e.g., teasing, threats, sarcasm), and rejection.

Punishers, unlearned: Aversive CSEs that can effectively weaken the operants they follow without first having to be paired with other aversive CSEs. In other words, they can weaken an operant on their own. An example would be anything that causes physical pain.

Punishment: The act of weakening an operant by following it with the presentation of an aversive CSE. For example, if a student talking without permission is told to stop by the teacher, and this serves to weaken the talking behavior, we can say that punishment of talking behavior has occurred.

Punishment, corporal: A form of punishment in which physical pain or discomfort is administered. Examples are paddling a student to weaken smoking on school property or spraying water into the nostrils of an autistic child to weaken self-injurious behavior.

Rational emotive therapy (RET): Pioneered by the work of Albert Ellis, this is a form of cognitive therapy in which students are taught that it is not what happens to them that makes them upset and causes them to behave in a counterproductive manner, but rather what they *think* about what happens to them. A form of RET called *rational emotive education* is used with children and youth. See Knaus (1974).

Reactivity: The change in a person's behavior brought about solely by monitoring his or her own behavior. This occurs during the baseline phase when the individual is not using any (new) intervention. It is usually attributed to increased awareness in the individual as a result of self-monitoring.

Reinforcement: The act of strengthening an operant by following it with the presentation of a CSE the person likes, wants, or values or by removing a CSE the person considers aversive. The two kinds of reinforcement are *positive* and *negative*.

Reinforcement, differential: Reinforcing a behavior one wants to strengthen and not reinforcing a behavior one does not want to strengthen. This is a very important component of a *shaping* program.

Reinforcement, extrinsic: Strengthening an operant with external CSEs. In other words, reinforcement such as a token or verbal praise comes from the environment. A student who engages in a low-frequency behavior, such as doing a difficult homework assignment, will probably need extrinsic reinforcement to stay on task.

Reinforcement, intrinsic: Strengthening an operant with internal CSEs. In other words, reinforcement comes from engaging in the behavior. A student who engages in a high-frequency behavior such as comic book reading is usually getting intrinsic reinforcement, without needing tokens or verbal praise for this behavior. The student does it because of the pleasure he or she derives from it.

Reinforcement, negative: The strengthening of an operant by following it with the removal of an aversive CSE contingent upon the occurrence of the operant. For example, if a student doesn't like schoolwork and also doesn't like detention, the teacher can negatively reinforce (strengthen) the student's schoolwork behavior either by threatening detention if he or she doesn't do the work or by actually keeping the student in detention until the work is done.

Reinforcement, noncontingent: Presenting a reward to the student without making it contingent upon some positive behavior: for example, letting a student leave class early whether or not she or he has completed the work.

Reinforcement, positive: The strengthening of an operant by following it with the presentation of a CSE the person likes, wants, or values. For example, if a student likes praise but doesn't like schoolwork, the latter may be strengthened by praising the student for each completed assignment. If the student does more schoolwork, we may say that positive reinforcement has occurred. If the student does not do more schoolwork, all we can say is that we presented a CSE that had no effect on the desired behavior.

Reinforcement, shifting criteria for: The conditions under which you will move from one successive approximation to another in a shaping program. Typically, one waits until the student can perform an approximation on a variable schedule of reinforcement before moving to the next approximation.

Reinforcers: CSEs that serve to strengthen the operants they follow. Examples are listening to a person speaking, laughing at someone's joke, and complimenting a person's behavior or appearance.

Reinforcers, activity: CSEs that allow the student to engage in a favored activity contingent upon performing the desired operant. Examples are doing work from another class, taking over as teacher, reading comic books or magazines, listening to music, and working on arts and crafts projects.

Reinforcers, learned: CSEs that have to be paired with other CSEs before they can strengthen the operants they follow. Examples are smiles, verbal praise, passing grades, and money. Also known as *secondary reinforcers.*

Reinforcers, social: CSEs that meet a person's psychosocial needs. Examples are smiles, eye contact, handshakes, pats on the back, compliments, and other verbal praise.

Reinforcers, tangible: CSEs that are physical objects (e.g., toys, coloring books, pocket combs, and crayons).

Reinforcers, unlearned: CSEs that do not have to be paired with other CSEs to strengthen the operants they follow. Examples include anything that provides physical comfort or pleasure (e.g., being held) or helps the individual meet a biological need (e.g., being fed). Also known as *primary reinforcers.*

Reinforcing incompatible behaviors (RIBs): A behavior modification technique used to weaken a maladaptive behavior by strengthening a fair-pair target behavior in its place: for example, strengthening in-seat behavior in order to weaken out-of-seat behavior.

Replicate: A technical word for repeating something, as in "to replicate an intervention."

Reprimand: A form of punishment usually administered verbally, such as "Stop that!" Facial expressions and posture can also function as a reprimand.

Respondent: Refers to behaviors controlled by the autonomic nervous system, such as the heartbeat, salivating, and the eye-blink reflex.

Respondent conditioning: A form of learning pioneered by the Russian psychologist Pavlov. Also known as *classical conditioning.*

Response cost: An aversive technique used to weaken behavior. It involves the removal of something the individual prizes (e.g., tokens earned) contingent upon maladaptive behavior.

Sample, continuous: A method of data collection in which the behavior is monitored as long as it occurs and the teacher is present to record it. It is the most reliable method of data collection because it yields the greatest amount of data.

Sample, interval: A method of data collection in which the person's behavior is monitored only at pre-specified times. It is not as reliable as a continuous sample and should be used only when the teacher cannot teach and monitor the student's behavior at the same time. Examples of behaviors that typically require interval sampling are quiet behaviors such as daydreaming, being off task, or being out of seat.

Satiation: This occurs when a known reinforcer loses its reinforcing properties due to overuse. For example, a child who formerly complied with directives when given peanuts may become satiated on them and may no longer be willing to comply with directives when given peanuts.

Schedule of reinforcement: This tells the change agent *when* to reinforce the student. There are three basic schedules: continuous, fixed, and variable.

Schedules, continuous: Schedules of reinforcement used when you want to condition a response that is new to the student. The student is reinforced for every correct response or is reinforced continuously over time.

Schedules, fixed: Schedules of reinforcement used when moving from a continuous schedule to a variable schedule of reinforcement. The student is reinforced for a certain number of *consecutive* desired responses or units of time engaged in the desired behavior. Examples of fixed schedules of reinforcement are reinforcing the student for every two consecutive correct responses or for every consecutive 4 minutes on task.

Schedules, interval: Schedules of reinforcement based on the *amount of time* the student engages in the behavior. For example, a student on a fixed-interval schedule of 2:1 would be reinforced once every consecutive 2 minutes of being on task. A student on a variable-interval schedule of 3:1 would be reinforced on the average of every 3 minutes of in-seat behavior.

Schedules, ratio: Schedules of reinforcement based on the *number of responses* a student makes. For example, a student on a fixed-ratio schedule of 4:1 would be reinforced once for every four consecutive directives complied with. A student on a variable-ratio schedule of 2:1 would be reinforced on the average of every two instances of raising a hand to get the teacher's attention.

Schedules, variable: Schedules of reinforcement used to maintain a new response learned by a student. The student is reinforced for an unpredictable number of desirable responses or over an unpredictable amount of time. For example, a variable-ratio (VR) schedule with a 5:1 arrangement would mean that the student was being reinforced on the average of every fifth desirable response. A variable-interval (VI) schedule with a 2:1 arrangement would mean that the student was reinforced for engaging in desirable behavior on the average of every 2 minutes.

Self-instructional training (SIT): A CBM strategy used to help students control their impulsivity and learn new (and complex) tasks. It involves several steps, beginning with the teacher modeling and verbalizing the target behavior for the student and ending with the student modeling the target behavior while thinking through the steps. See Meichenbaum (1977).

Self-management: A set of skills used by students (or teachers) to manage their own behavior. These include: (1) self-assessment, in which students evaluate their own behavior and decide whether or not they are behaving appropriately; (2) self-reinforcement, in which students determine how much they should be reinforced for their behavior and dispense the reinforcer; and (3) self-monitoring, in which students collect daily data on their behavior and evaluate the efficacy of the intervention. Also known as *behavioral self-control, self-directed behavior,* and *self-regulated behavior.* See Workman (1982).

Self-stimulating behavior: Behavior typically seen in the severely handicapped (e.g., rocking, hand waving, self-touching).

Shaping: The process of gradually changing a person's behavior by reinforcing progressively closer approximations of the target behavior. This differs from fading primarily in that the latter requires changing the environmental (i.e., antecedent and consequent) events surrounding a student's behavior; in shaping, changes are made in the behavior. For example, a student who is seldom in seat more than 2 minutes at a time might be reinforced for progressively closer approximations of the target behavior (e.g., "stays in seat for 15 minutes at a time"). First, the student would be reinforced for being in seat for 2 minutes, then 3 minutes, then 4, 5, and so on until the target behavior is performed.

"So what?" test: An informal test applied to the maladaptive and target behaviors to determine whether or not the behavior change is necessary and appropriate. A negative or undesirable behavior would pass the "So what?" test if it met the criteria for being maladaptive. A positive or desirable behavior would pass the "So what?" test if it could be shown that the change in the student's behavior (i.e., the target behavior) would result in weakening the maladaptive behavior and would be in the student's best interest.

Social skills training: The term used to describe instruction in a number of interpersonal skills (e.g., being assertive, sharing, and giving and receiving criticism) that many students with behavior disorders seem to be lacking. The trend now is to make social skills training a regular part of the curriculum in classes on behavior disorders along with reading, writing, and arithmetic.

Stranger test: An informal test applied to maladaptive and target behaviors to determine whether or not they have been stated as pinpoints. If a stranger can derive the same meaning from such statements as the person who made them, they are said to pass the stranger test and may be considered pinpoints. For example, "is hostile" would not pass the stranger test because a stranger might have a different interpretation of "hostile" than the person making the statement. However, "kicks peers when teased" would pass the stranger test because it is highly unlikely that a stranger would derive a different meaning from this than the person making the statement.

Stress: The physiological changes experienced in the presence of stressors from the environment (or from thinking about them). For a more technical definition, see Selye (1976).

Stress inoculation: An integrative stress management strategy used to cope with anger or anxiety. It includes several stages: (1) conceptual framework or teaching basic concepts regarding stress (anger or anxiety) and stress management, (2) training in PRT, (3) identifying and disputing irrational beliefs, (4) writing stress scripts, and (5) using stress scripts in graduated stress situations. See Meichenbaum (1985).

Stress management: Includes a wide range of skills used to help the individual cope with the stressors and stress in his or her life. To be effective, it should be holistic. In other words, stress management should be preventive as well as restorative and should have benefits that are psychological and behavioral as well as physical.

Stressors: Those events in our lives that tend to produce stress. Examples of stressors in children and youth include parental divorce or illness in family, failing in school, being rejected by peers, moving to a new community, and entering a new school.

Subjective units of distress (SUD): A subjective way of monitoring stress in the individual. Students are taught to monitor their own stress by periodically gauging their stress level on a scale of 1 (calm) to 10 (distressed). It is one of the ways to evaluate the efficacy of stress management programs.

Successive approximations: The steps in the shaping process that tell the change agent when to reinforce the student. Each step describes behavior that is a closer approximation of the target behavior. For example, if the target behavior is to complete 100% of the assignments and the student currently has only completed 10%, successive approximations might be 20%, 40%, 60%, and 80%. While each of these steps is not the target behavior, it is a closer approximation of the target behavior than the preceding one.

Symptom substitution: A criticism of behavior modification based on the idea that behavioral interventions won't work because they only treat the symptoms (i.e., behavior) and don't get at the underlying cause of the problem. The weakened symptom is thought to be replaced by another, different, symptom.

Task analysis: The breaking down of a task into its smaller parts. See Howell et al. (1979).

Task analytical model: Based on the concept of task analysis, the TA model provides a set of guidelines for assessing learning problems for both academic and social behaviors. See Howell et al. (1979); Howell & Kaplan (1980).

Time out: Technically, time out (TO) refers to a strategy that involves the removal of all reinforcement for all behavior for a period of time (ideally, not to exceed 1 minute per year in the student's age). Practically speaking, TO has been used as a form of punishment in which students are isolated from their peers for an undetermined amount of time (e.g., "Go to the office!").

Token economy: A comprehensive behavior modification program popularized by the work of Nathan Azrin and Teodoro Ayllon in a state mental hospital. It involves the use of secondary reinforcers such as tokens (i.e., points, chips, stars, or play money) contingent upon prespecified target behaviors. The tokens are turned in at a later time for backup reinforcers such as food, favored activities, or other tangible items. The advantage of the token economy is that because the tokens act as substitutes for the backup reinforcers, they may be given at times when it would be inappropriate to give a backup reinforcer. Also, because the tokens are generalized reinforcers, like money, they can be given again and again without the likelihood of satiation.

Verbal mediation: A type of CBM that involves self-talk, in which students ask themselves a series of questions. These include: (1) "What am I doing?"; (2) "Why shouldn't I do it?"; (3) 'What should I be doing instead?"; and (4) "Why should I be doing it?" Initially, students respond to these questions in writing. The goal of the program is to get them to automatically *think* through these questions on their own. See Blackwood (1970).

References

Allen, J. (1980). Jogging can modify disruptive behaviors. *Teaching Exceptional Children, 12,* 66–70.

Argulewicz, E., Elliott, S., & Spencer, D. (1982). Application of cognitive-behavior modification for improving classroom attention. *School Psychology Review, 11,* 90–95.

Ayllon, T., & Azrin, N. H. (1968). *The token economy.* New York: Appleton-Century-Crofts.

Azrin, N., & Lindsley, O. (1956). The reinforcement of cooperation between children. *Journal of Abnormal and Social Psychology, 52,* 100–102.

Bandura, A. (1969). *Principles of behavior modification.* New York: Holt, Rinehart & Winston.

Bandura, A., Ross, D., & Ross, S. A. (1963). Imitation of film-mediated aggressive models. *Journal of Abnormal and Social Psychology, 66,* 3–11.

Becker, W. C., & Engelmann, S. (1973). *Summary analyses of five-year data on achievement and teaching progress with 14,000 children in 20 projects.* (Tech. Report No. 73.) Eugene, OR: University of Oregon Follow-Through Project.

Becker, W. C., Engelmann, S., & Thomas, D. R. (1971). *Teaching: A course in applied psychology.* Chicago: Science Research Associates.

Bem, S. (1967). Verbal self-control: The establishment of effective self-instruction. *Journal of Experimental Psychology, 74,* 485–491.

Bijou, S. W., & Baer, D. M. (1961). *Child development. Volume 1: A systematic and empirical theory.* New York: Appleton-Century-Crofts.

Birnbrauer, J., & Lawler, J. (1964). Token reinforcement for learning. *Mental Retardation, 2,* 275–279.

Blackwood, R. (1970). The operant conditioning of verbally mediated self-control in the classroom. *Journal of School Psychology, 8,* 251–258.

Bolstad, O., & Johnson, S. (1972). Self-regulation in the modification of disruptive classroom behavior. *Journal of Applied Behavior Analysis, 5,* 443–454.

Bornstein, M. R., Bellack, A. S., & Hersen, M. (1977). Social-skills training for unassertive children: A multiple-baseline analysis. *Journal of Applied Behavior Analysis, 10,* 183–195.

Bornstein, P., & Knapp, M. (1981). Self-control desensitization with a multi-phobic boy: A multiple baseline design. *Journal of Behavior Therapy & Experimental Psychiatry, 12,* 281–285.

Bornstein, P., & Quevillon, R. (1976). The effects of a self-instructional package on overactive preschool boys. *Journal of Applied Behavior Analysis, 9,* 179–188.

Bowers, D. S., Clement, P. W., Fantuzzo, J. W., & Sorensen, D. A. (1985). Effects of teacher-administered and self-administered reinforcers on learning disabled children. *Behavior Therapy, 16,* 357–369.

Bradley, R., & Gaa, J. (1977). Domain specific aspects of locus of control: Implications for modifying locus of control orientation. *Journal of School Psychology, 15,* 18–24.

Camp, B. (1980). Two psychoeducational treatment programs for young boys. In C. Whalen & B. Henler (Eds.), *Hyperactive children: The social ecology of identification and treatment.* New York: Academic Press.

Camp, B. W., & Bash, M. S. (1981). *Think aloud: Primary Level.* Champaign, IL: Research Press.

Camp, B., Blom, G., Herbert, F., & Van Doorwick, W. (1976). *Think aloud: A program for developing self-control in young aggressive boys.* Unpublished manuscript, University of Colorado School of Medicine, Boulder.

Chandler, L. A. (1985). *Assessing stress in children.* New York: Praeger.

Christensen, C. (1974). *Development and field testing of an interpersonal coping skills program.* Toronto, Canada: Ontario Institute for Studies in Education.

Clark, L., Gresham, F. M., & Elliott, S. N. (1985). Development and validation of a social skills assessment measure: The TROSS-C. *Journal of Psychoeducational Assessment, 4,* 347–358.

Clonce v. Richardson, 379 F. Supp. 338 (W.D. Mo. 1974).

Cohen, H. L., & Filipczak, J. (1971). *A new learning environment.* San Francisco: Jossey-Bass.

Crandall, V. C., Katkovsky, W., & Crandall, V. J. (1965). Children's beliefs in their own control of reinforcement in intellectual-academic achievement situations. *Child Development, 36,* 91–109.

De Voge, C. (1977). A behavioral approach to RET with children. In A. Ellis & R. Grieger (Eds.), *Handbook of rational-emotive therapy.* New York: Springer Publishing.

Dewey, J. (1938). *Experience and education.* New York: Macmillan.

Di Giuseppe, R. A. (1977). The use of behavior modification to establish rational self-statements in children. In A. Ellis & R. Grieger (Eds.), *Handbook of rational-emotive therapy.* New York: Springer Publishing.

Dixon, R., & Engelmann, S. (1979). *Corrective spelling through morphographics: Teacher's presentation book.* Chicago: Science Research.

Drummond, D. (1974). *Self-instructional training: An approach to disruptive classroom behavior.* Unpublished doctoral dissertation, University of Oregon, Eugene.

Dunlap, L. (1942). Technique of negative practice. *American Journal of Psychology, 55,* 270–273.

D'Zurilla, T. J., & Goldfried, M. R. (1971). Problem solving and behavior modification. *Journal of Abnormal Psychology, 78,* 107–126.

Eisen, P. (1979). Children under stress. *Australian and New Zealand Journal of Psychiatry, 13,* 193–207.

Elkind, D. (1981). *The hurried child: Growing up too fast, too soon.* Reading, MA: Addison-Wesley.

Ellis, A. (1962). *Reason and emotion in psychotherapy.* New York: Lyle Stuart Press.

303

Ellis, A., & Harper, R. A. (1961). *A new guide to rational living.* N. Hollywood, CA: Wilshire.

Engelmann, S., & Brunner, E. C. (1973). *Distar Reading I.* Chicago: Science Research Associates.

Erickson, E. (1963). *Childhood and society* (2nd ed.). New York: Norton.

Erickson, E. (1964). *Insight and responsibility.* New York: Norton.

Evans, R. I. (1968). *B. F. Skinner: The man and his ideas.* New York: E. P. Dutton.

Feindler, E. L., & Fremouw, W. J. (1983). Stress inoculation training for adolescent anger problems. In D. Meichenbaum & M. E. Jaremko (Eds.), *Stress reduction and prevention.* New York: Plenum.

Felner, R. D., Stolberg, A., & Cowan, E. L. (1975). Crisis events and school mental health referral patterns of young children. *Journal of Consulting and Clinical Psychology, 43,* 305–311.

Finch, A., Wilkinson, M., Nelson, W., & Montgomery, L. (1975). Modification of an impulsive cognitive tempo in emotionally disturbed boys. *Journal of Abnormal Child Psychology, 3,* 45–52.

Fishe, D. W., & Cox, J. A. (1960). The consistency of rating by peers. *Journal of Applied Psychology, 44,* 11–17.

Flanders, N. A. (1964). *Interaction analysis in the classroom: A manual for observers.* Ann Arbor: University of Michigan School of Education.

Fleming, C. (1983). Evaluation of an anger management program with aggressive children in residential treatment. *Dissertation Abstracts International, 43* (12-B), 41–43.

Fox, R., Luszhi, M. B., & Schmuck, R. (1966). *Diagnosing classroom learning environments.* Chicago: Science Research Associates.

Fuller, P. (1949). Operant conditioning of a vegetative human organism. *American Journal of Psychology, 62,* 587–590.

Gagne, R. (1965). *The conditions of learning.* New York: Holt, Rinehart & Winston.

Garrison, S. R., & Stolberg, A. L. (1983). Modification of anger in children by affective imagery training. *Journal of Abnormal Child Psychology, 11,* 115–130.

Gersten, J. C., Langer, T. S., Eisenberg, J. G., & Orzek, L. (1974). Child behavior and life events. In B. S. Dohrenwend & B. P. Dohrenwend (Eds.), *Stressful life events: Their nature and effects.* New York: Wiley.

Gewirtz, J. L., & Baer, D. M. (1958). Deprivation and satiation or social reinforcers as drive conditioners. *Journal of Abnormal Psychology, 57,* 165–172.

Gilligan, C. (1987). *In a different voice.* Boston: Harvard University Press.

Glass, C. (1974). *Response acquisition and cognitive self-statement modification approaches to dating behavior training.* Unpublished doctoral dissertation, Indiana University, Bloomington.

Glynn, E. (1970). Classroom applications of self-determined reinforcement. *Journal of Applied Behavior Analysis, 3,* 123–132.

Glynn, E., Thomas, J., & Shee, S. (1973). Behavioral self-control of on-task behavior in an elementary school classroom. *Journal of Applied Behavior Analysis, 6,* 105–113.

Goldfried, M. (1973). Reduction of generalized anxiety through a variant of systematic desensitization. In M. Goldfried & M. Merbaum (Eds.), *Behavior change through self-control.* New York: Holt, Rinehart & Winston.

Goss v. Lopez, 419 U.S. 565 (1975).

Gottman, J., Gonso, J., & Rasmussen, B. (1974). *Social interaction, social competence and friendship in children.* Unpublished manuscript, Indiana University, Bloomington.

Gresham, F. M. (1981). Social skills training with handicapped children: A review. *Review of Educational Research, 51,* 139–176.

Gresham, F. M. (1985). Utility of cognitive-behavioral procedures for social skills training with children: A critical review. *Journal of Abnormal Child Psychology, 13,* 411–423.

Gump, P. V. (1977). Ecological psychologists: Critics or contributors to behavioral analysis. In A. Rogers-Warren & S. F. Warren (Eds.), *Ecological perspectives in behavioral analysis.* Baltimore: University Park Press.

Hall, R. V., Panyan, M., Rabon, D., & Broden, M. (1968). Instructing beginning teachers in reinforcement procedures which improve classroom control. *Journal of Applied Behavior Analysis, 1,* 315–322.

Harris, A., & Kapche, R. (1978). Behavior modification in schools: Ethical issues and suggested guidelines. *Journal of School Psychology, 16,* 25–33.

Harris, K. R., Wong, B. Y. L., and Keogy, B. K. (Eds.) (1985). Cognitive-behavior modification with children: A critical review of the state-of-the-art [Special issue]. *Journal of Abnormal Child Psychology, 13*(3), 329–476.

Hart, B. M., & Risley, T. R. (1968). Establishing use of descriptive adjectives in the spontaneous speech of disadvantaged preschool children. *Journal of Applied Behavior Analysis, 1,* 109–120.

Hartig, M., & Kanfer, F. (1973). The role of verbal self-instructions in children's resistance to temptation. *Journal of Personality and Social Psychology, 25,* 259–267.

Hewett, F. (1964). Teaching reading to an autistic boy through operant conditioning. *Reading Teacher, 17,* 613–618.

Hinshaw, S. (1984). Self-control in hyperactive boys in anger-inducing situations: Effects of cognitive-behavioral training and of methylphenidate. *Journal of Abnormal Child Psychology, 12,* 55–77.

Hollander, E. P. (1964). Validity of peer nomination in predicting a distant performance criterion. *Journal of Applied Psychology, 49,* 434–438.

Holman, J. (1977). The moral risk and high cost of ecological concern in applied behavioral analysis. In A. Rogers-Warren & S. F. Warren (Eds.), *Ecological perspectives in behavior analysis.* Baltimore: University Park Press.

Homme, L. E., with Csanyi, A. P., Gonzales, M. A., & Rechs, J. R. (1969). *How to use contingency contracting in the classroom.* Champaign, IL: Research Press.

Howell, K. W., & Kaplan, J. S. (1980). *Diagnosing basic skills: A handbook for deciding what to teach.* Columbus, OH: Charles Merrill.

Howell, K. W., Kaplan, J. S., & O'Connell, C. Y. (1979). *Evaluating exceptional children: A task analysis approach.* Columbus, OH: Charles Merrill.

Hren, C., Mueller, K., Spates, C. R., Ulrich, C., & Ulrich, R. E. (1974). The learning village elementary school. In R. E. Ulrich, T. Stachnik, & J. Mabry (Eds.), *Control of human behavior: Vol. 3. Behavior modification in education*. Glenview, IL: Scott, Foresman.

Humphrey, L., & Karoly, P. (1978). Self-management in the classroom. Self-imposed response cost versus self-reward. *Behavior Therapy, 9,* 592–601.

Hundert, J., & Bastone, D. (1978). A practical procedure to maintain pupils' accurate self-rating in a classroom token program. *Behavior Modification, 2,* 93–112.

Jacobson, E. (1929). *Progressive relaxation*. Chicago: University of Chicago Press.

Johnson, J. H., & McCutcheon, S. (1980). Assessing life stress in older children and adolescents: Preliminary findings with the Life Events Checklist. In I. G. Sarason & C. D. Spielberger (Eds.), *Stress and anxiety.* (Vol. 7). New York: Hemisphere.

Jones, M. C. (1924). The elimination of children's fears. *Journal of Experimental Psychology, 7,* 382–390.

Kaplan, J. S., & Kent, S. (1986). *PRE-MOD II: A computer-assisted program in behavioral analysis*. Austin, TX: PRO-ED.

Karnes, M., Teska, J., & Hodgins, A. (1970). The effects of four programs of classroom intervention on the intellectual and language development of 4-year-old disadvantaged children. *American Journal of Orthopsychiatry, 40,* 58–76.

Kassinove, H., Crisci, R., & Tiegerman, S. (1977). Developmental trends in rational thinking: Implications for rational-emotive school mental health programs. *Journal of Community Psychology, 5,* 266–274.

Kazdin, A. (1973). Covert modeling, model similarity and reduction of avoidance behavior. *Journal of Abnormal Psychology, 81,* 87–95.

Kendall, P., & Braswell, L. (1982). Cognitive-behavioral self-control therapy for children: A components analysis. *Journal of Consulting & Clinical Psychology, 50,* 672–689.

Kennedy, R. (1982). Cognitive-behavioral approaches to the modification of aggressive behavior in children. *School Psychology Review, 11,* 47–55.

Kettlewell, P. W., & Kausch, D. F. (1983). The generalization of the effects of a cognitive-behavioral treatment program for aggressive children. *Journal of Abnormal Child Psychology, 11,* 101–114.

Knaus, W. (1974). *Rational-emotive education: A manual for elementary school teachers*. New York: Institute for Rational Living.

Knaus, W., & Block, J. (1976). *Rational-emotive education with economically disadvantaged inner-city high school students: A demonstration study*. Unpublished manuscript.

Knaus, W. J., & McKeever, C. (1977). Rational-emotive education with learning disabled children. *Journal of Learning Disabilities, 10,* 10–14.

Kobasa, S. C., Maddi, S. R., & Pucetti, M. C. (1982). Personality and exercise as buffers in the stress-illness relationship. *Journal of Behavioral Medicine, 11,* 101–114.

Kunzelmann, H. P. (Ed.), Cohen, M. A., Hulten, W. J., Martin, G. L., & Mingo, A. R. (1970). *Precision teaching: An initial training sequence*. Seattle, WA: Special Child Publications.

Lazarus, A. (1959). The elimination of children's phobias by deconditioning. *South Africa Medical Proceedings, 5,* 161–165.

Leon, J. A., & Pepe, H. J. (1983, September). Self-instructional training: Cognitive behavior modification for remediating arithmetic deficits. *Exceptional Children,* 54–60.

Lindsley, O. R. (1964). Direct measurement and prosthesis of retarded children. *Journal of Education, 147,* 62–81.

Litrownik, A., Freitas, J., & Franzini, L. (1978). Self-regulation in mentally retarded children: Assessment and training of self-monitoring skills. *American Journal of Mental Deficiency, 82,* 499–506.

Lovaas, O. I., Schaeffer, B., & Simmons, J. Q. (1965). Building social behavior in autistic children by use of electric shock. *Journal of Experimental Research in Personality, 1,* 99–109.

Lovitt, T. C., & Curtiss, K. A. (1969). Academic response rate as a function of teacher- and self-imposed contingencies. *Journal of Applied Behavior Analysis, 2,* 49–53.

Luria, A. R. (1961). *The role of speech in the regulation of normal and abnormal behaviors*. New York: Liveright.

Maag, J. (1988). *Treatment of adolescent depression with stress inoculation*. Unpublished doctoral dissertation, Arizona State University, Tempe.

Mager, R. F. (1962). *Preparing instructional objectives*. Belmont, CA: Fearon Publishers.

Mahoney, M. J. (1979). *Self-change: Strategies for solving personal problems*. New York: Norton.

Mahoney, M., & Mahoney, K. (1976). Self-control techniques with the mentally retarded. *Exceptional Children, 42,* 338–339.

Mahoney, M. J., & Thoresen, C. E. (1972). Behavioral self-control: Power to the person. *Educational Researcher, 1,* 5–7.

Marholin, D., & Steinman, W. (1977). Stimulus control in the classroom as a function of the behavior reinforced. *Journal of Applied Behavior Analysis, 10,* 465–478.

Martin, R. (1975). *Legal challenges to behavior modification*. Champaign, IL: Research Press.

Matson, J. L., & Ollendick, T. H. (1988). *Enhancing children's social skills: Assessment and training*. New York: Pergamon.

Matson, J. L., Rotatori, A. F., & Helsel, W. J. (1983). Development of a rating scale to measure social skills in children: The Matson Evaluation of Social Skills with Youngsters (MESSY). *Behaviour Research and Therapy, 21,* 335–340.

Maultsby, M. C. (1984). *Rational behavior therapy*. Englewood Cliffs, NJ: Prentice-Hall.

Meichenbaum, D. (1977). *Cognitive behavior modification: An integrative approach*. New York: Plenum Press.

Meichenbaum, D. (1985). *Stress inoculation training*. New York: Pergamon.

Meichenbaum, D., Gilmore, B., & Fedoravicius, A. (1971). Group insight vs. group desensitization in treating speech anxiety. *Journal of Consulting and Clinical Psychology, 36,* 410–421.

Meichenbaum, D., & Goodman, J. (1971). Training impulsive children to talk to themselves: A means of developing self control. *Journal of Abnormal Psychology, 77,* 115–126.

Mikulas, W. L. (1978). *Behavior Modification*. New York: Harper & Row.

Miller, S. R., Osborne, S. S., & Burt, E. (1987). The use of mediation essays in modifying inappropriate behavior of three behaviorally disordered youth. *Teaching: Behaviorally Disordered Youth, 18–27.*

Moletzky, B. (1974). Behavior recording as treatment: A brief note. *Behavior Therapy, 5,* 107–111.

Monohan, J., & O'Leary, D. (1971). Effects of self-instruction on rule breaking behavior. *Psychological Reports, 79,* 1059–1066.

Moreno, J. L. (1953). *Who shall survive? Foundations of sociometry. Group psychology and sociograms* (2nd edition). New York: Random House.

Mowrer, O. H., & Mowrer, W. M. (1938). Enuresis—A method for its study and treatment. *American Journal of Orthopsychiatry, 8,* 436–459.

Neill, A. S. (1960). *Summerhill: A radical approach to child rearing.* New York: Hart.

Neill, A. S. (1966). *Freedom not license.* New York: Hart.

Novaco, R. (1975). *Anger control: The development and evaluation of an experimental treatment.* Lexington, MA: Heath & Co.

Nowicki, S., & Strickland, B. (1973). A locus of control scale for children. *Journal of Consulting and Clinical Psychology, 40,* 148–154.

O'Connor, R. D. (1969). Modification of social withdrawal through symbolic modeling. *Journal of Applied Behavior Analysis, 2,* 15–22.

O'Leary, K. D. (1968). The effects of self-instruction on immoral behavior. *Journal of Experimental Child Psychology, 6,* 297–301.

O'Leary, K. D. (1972). Behavior modification in the classroom: A rejoinder to Winett and Winkler. *Journal of Applied Behavior Analysis, 5,* 505–511.

O'Leary, K. D., Becker, W. C., Evans, M. B., & Sandargas, R. A. (1969). A token reinforcement program in a public school: A replication and systematic analysis. *Journal of Applied Behavior Analysis, 2,* 2–13.

Palkes, H., Stewart, M., & Freedman, J. (1972). Improvement in maze performance on hyperactive boys as a function of verbal training procedures. *Journal of Special Education, 5,* 337–342.

Patterson, G. R. (1965). An application of conditioning techniques to the control of a hyperactive child. In L. P. Ullmann & K. Krasner (Eds.), *Case studies in behavior modification.* New York: Holt, Rinehart & Winston.

Patterson, G. R. (1969). Behavioral intervention procedures in the classroom and in the home. In A. E. Bergin & S. L. Garfield (Eds.), *Handbook of psychotherapy and behavior change.* New York: Wiley.

Pavlov, I. P. (1897). *Lectures on the work of the principal digestive glands.* St. Petersburg.

Pawlicki, R. (1976). Effects of self-directed modification training on a measure of locus of control. *Psychological Reports, 39,* 319–322.

Pearl, R. (1985). Cognitive-behavioral interventions for increasing motivation. *Journal of Abnormal Child Psychology, 13,* 443–454.

Pennsylvania Association for Retarded Children v. Commonwealth of Pennsylvania, 334 F. Supp. 1257 (E.D. Penna. 1971).

Phillips, E. L., Phillips, E. A., Fixsen, D., & Wolf, M. (1971). Achievement Place: Modification of behavior of predelinquent boys within a token economy. *Journal of Applied Behavior Analysis, 4,* 45–61.

Premack, D. (1959). Toward empirical behavior laws: 1. Positive reinforcement. *Psychological Review, 66,* 219–233.

Prieto, A. G., & Rutherford, R. (1977). An ecological assessment technique for behavior disordered and learning disabled children. *Behavioral Disorders, 2,* 169–175.

Rachman, S. (1963). Spontaneous remission and latent learning. *Behavior Research and Therapy, 1,* 133–137.

Reese, E. P. (1966). *The analysis of human operation behavior.* Dubuque, IA: William C. Brown.

Renne, C. M., & Creer, T. L. (1976). Training children with asthma to use inhalation therapy equipment. *Journal of Applied Behavior Analysis, 9,* 1–11.

Reynolds, H. H. (1966). Efficacy of sociometric ratings in predicting leadership success. *Psychological Reports, 19,* 35–40.

Reynolds, H. J., & Risley, T. R. (1968). The role of social and material reinforcers in increasing talking of a disadvantaged preschool child. *Journal of Applied Behavior Analysis, 1,* 253–262.

Rhodes, W. C., & Paul, J. L. (1978). *Emotionally disturbed and deviant children: New views and approaches.* Englewood Cliffs, NJ: Prentice-Hall.

Rice, F. P. (1975). *The adolescent.* Boston: Allyn & Bacon.

Rogers, C. R. (1969). *Freedom to learn.* Columbus, OH: Merrill.

Rogers-Warren, A. K. (1984). Ecobehavioral analysis. *Education and treatment of children, 7*(4), 283–303.

Rotter, J. B. (1966). Generalized expectancies for internal versus external control of reinforcement. *Psychological Monographs, 80* (Whole No. 609).

Roush, D. (1984). Rational-emotive therapy and youth: Some new techniques for counselors. *Personnel and Guidance Journal, 62,* 414–417.

Rueda, R., Rutherford, R. B., & Howell, K. W. (1980). Review of self-control research with behaviorally disordered and mentally retarded children. In R. B. Rutherford, A. G. Prieto, & J. E. McGlothlin (Eds.), *Severe behavior disorders of children and youth.* Reston, VA: Council for Children with Behavior Disorders.

Sandler, I. N., & Block, M. (1979). Life stress and maladaptation of children. *American Journal of Community Psychology, 7,* 425–440.

Sarason, I. (1973). Test anxiety and cognitive modeling. *Journal of Personality and Social Psychology, 28,* 58–61.

Schlesser, R., & Thackwray, D. (1984). Impulsivity: A clinical developmental perspective. *School Psychology Review, 11,* 42–46.

Schlicter, K. J., & Horan, J. J. (1981). Effects of stress inoculation on the anger and aggression management skills of institutionalized juvenile delinquents. *Cognitive Therapy and Research, 5,* 359–365.

Schmidt, J. A. (1976). *Help yourself: A guide to self-change.* Champaign, IL: Research Press.

Schneider, M. (1974, Fall). Turtle technique in the classroom. *Teaching Exceptional Children*, 22–24.

Schwitzgebel, R. (1964). *Streetcorner research: An experimental approach to the juvenile delinquent.* Cambridge, MA: Harvard University Press.

Sebald, H. (1981). *Adolescence: A social psychological analysis* (rev. ed.). Englewood Cliffs, NJ: Prentice-Hall.

Selye, H. (1976). *The stress of life.* New York: McGraw-Hill.

Sheehan, J. (1951). The modification of stuttering through non-reinforcement. *Journal of Abnormal and Social Psychology, 46*, 51–63.

Shinn, R. (1972). *Culture and school: Socio-cultural significances.* San Francisco: Intext Educational Publishers.

Shipman, W. M. (1984). Emotional and behavioral effects of long-distance running on children. In M. L. Sachs & G. W. Buffone (Eds.), *Running as therapy: An integrated approach.* Lincoln: University of Nebraska Press.

Shmurak, S. (1974). *Design and evaluation of three dating behavior training programs utilizing response acquisition and cognitive self-statement modification techniques.* Unpublished doctoral dissertation, Indiana University, Bloomington.

Simon, S. B., Howe, L. W., & Kirschenbaum, H. (1972). *Values clarification: A handbook of practical strategies for teachers and students.* New York: Hart.

Skinner, B. F. (1938). *The behavior of organisms: An experimental analysis.* New York: Appleton-Century.

Skinner, B. F. (1971). *Beyond freedom and dignity.* New York: Knopf.

Smith, R. M., Neisworth, J. T., & Greer, J. G. (1978). *Evaluating educational environments.* Columbus, OH: Merrill.

Spivack, G., & Shure, M. (1974). *Social adjustment of young children: A cognitive approach to solving real-life problems.* San Francisco: Josscy-Bass.

Staats, A. W., Staats, C. K., Schutz, R. E., & Wolf, M. (1962). The conditioning of textual responses utilizing "extrinsic reinforcers." *Journal of the Experimental Analysis of Behavior, 5*, 33–40.

Swap, S. M. (1974). Disturbing classroom behaviors: A developmental and ecological view. *Exceptional Children, 41*, 163–172.

Swap, S. M., Prieto, A. G., & Harth, R. (1982). Ecological perspectives on the emotionally disturbed child. In R. L. McDowell, G. W. Adamson, & F. H. Wood (Eds.), *Teaching emotionally disturbed children.* Boston: Little, Brown.

Tasseigne, M. W. (1975). A study of peer and adult influence on moral beliefs of adolescents. *Adolescence, 10*, 227–230.

Thorndike, E. L. (1921). *The psychology of learning.* New York: Teachers College, Columbia University.

Thurman, S. K. (1977). Congruence of behavioral ecologies. A model for special education programming. *Journal of Special Education, 2*, 329–333.

Tuersky, A., & Kahneman, D. (1973). Availability: A heuristic for judging frequency and probability. *Cognitive Psychology, 5*, 207–232.

Ulmann, L. P., & Krasner, L. (1969). *A psychological approach to abnormal behavior.* Englewood Cliffs, NJ: Prentice-Hall.

Ulrich, R. (1967). Behavior control and public concern. *Psychological Record, 17*, 67–78.

Vygotsky, L. (1962). *Thought and language.* New York: Wiley.

Walker, H. (1979). *The acting-out child.* Boston: Allyn & Bacon.

Walker, H., & Buckley, N. (1972). Programming generalization and maintenance of treatment effects across time and across settings. *Journal of Applied Behavior Analysis, 5*, 209–224.

Watson, D. L., & Tharp, R. G. (1981). *Self-directed behavior: Self-modification for personal adjustment.* Monterey, CA: Brooks/Cole.

Watson, J. B. (1913). Psychology as a behaviorist views it. *Psychological Review, 20*, 158–177.

Watson, J., & Raynor, R. (1920). Conditioned emotional reactions. *Journal of Experimental Psychology, 3*, 1–14.

Webster's new world dictionary of the American language: College edition. (1958). New York: World.

White, B. L. (1975). *The first three years of life.* Englewood Cliffs, NJ: Prentice-Hall.

Williams, C. (1959). The elimination of tantrum behavior by extinction procedures. *Journal of Abnormal and Social Psychology, 59*, 269.

Williamson, D. A., Moody, S. C., Granberry, S. W., Lethermond, V. R., & Blouin, D. C. (1983). Criterion-related validity of a role-play social skills test for children. *Behavior Therapy, 14*, 466–481.

Wilson, R. (1984). A review of self-control treatments for aggressive behavior. *Behavioral Disorders, 9*, 131–140.

Winett, R. A., & Winkler, R. C. (1972). Current behavior modification in the classroom: Be still, be quiet, be docile. *Journal of Applied Behavior Analysis, 5*, 499–504.

Winkler, D. R. (1975). Educational achievement and school peer group composition. *Journal of Human Resources, 10*, 189–204.

Winn, M. (1983). *Children without childhood.* New York: Pantheon Books.

Wolpe, J. (1958). *Psychotherapy by reciprocal inhibition.* Palo Alto, CA: Stanford University Press.

Wolpe, J. (1969). *The practice of behavior therapy.* New York: Pergamon Press.

Wong, B. Y. L. (1985). Issues in cognitive-behavioral interventions in academic skill areas. *Journal of Abnormal Child Psychology, 13*, 425–442.

Wood, R., & Flynn, J. (1978). A sclf-evaluation token system vs. an external token system alone in a residential setting with predelinquent youth. *Journal of Applied Behavior Analysis, 11*, 503–512.

Workman, E. (1982). *Teaching behavioral self-control to students.* Austin, TX: PRO-ED.

Workman, E., & Hector, M. (1978). Behavior self control in classroom settings: A review of the literature. *Journal of School Psychology, 16*, 227–236.

Workman, E., Helton, G., & Watson, P. (1982). Self-monitoring effects in a four year old child: An ecological behavior analysis. *Journal of School Psychology, 20*.

Wyatt v. Stickney, 344 F. Supp. 373 (M.D. Ala. 1972).

Zakay, D., Bar-El, Z., & Kreitler, S. (1984). Cognitive orientation and changing the impulsivity of children. *British Journal of Educational Psychology, 54*, 40–50.

Zimmerman, E. H., Zimmerman, J., & Russell, C. D. (1969). Differential effects of token reinforcement on instruction-following behavior in retarded students instructed as a group. *Journal of Applied Behavior Analysis, 2*, 101–111.

Author Index

Subject Index